Capitalism, Institutions, and Economic Development

Based on a timely reassessment of the classic arguments of Weber, Schumpeter, Hayek, Popper, and Parsons, this book reconceptualizes actually existing capitalism. It proposes capitalism as a procedural solution to the problems of spontaneously coordinating public institutions that enable durable market-based wealth generation and social order. Few countries have achieved this. A novel contribution of the book is that it identifies a practical sequence of economic and institutional shortcuts to real capitalism.

The book challenges current orthodoxies about varieties of capitalism and relativist recipes for economic growth, and it criticizes culturalist and incrementalist viewpoints in institutional economics. It calls on the social sciences to help in constructing dynamic open societies of the twenty-first century by reclaiming older ideas of 'social economics'. Better and faster solutions will emphasize crisis-induced change, rational leadership, ideological persuasion, institutional engineering, rules-based market freedom, and the universalistic formal-procedural impersonality of optimal regulatory systems.

As well as being aimed at academics in the social sciences, this book is intended for experts and practitioners in the field of international development, and higher-level students in political economy, economic sociology, and development studies.

Dr Michael G. Heller is a political scientist specializing in development issues. He has held research and teaching positions at universities in Mexico (Colegio de México), the United Kingdom (School of Oriental and African Studies), Argentina (Universidad de Cuyo), and Australia (University of Technology Sydney).

Routledge frontiers of political economy

Capitalism, Institutions, and Economic Development

Michael G. Heller

Routledge
Taylor & Francis Group

LONDON AND NEW YORK

First published 2009
by Routledge
2 Park Square, Milton Park, Abingdon, Oxon OX14 4RN

Simultaneously published in the USA and Canada
by Routledge
270 Madison Ave, New York, NY 10016

Routledge is an imprint of the Taylor & Francis Group, an informa business

Typeset in Times by Wearset Ltd, Boldon, Tyne and Wear
Printed and bound in Great Britain by TJI Digital, Padstow, Cornwall

British Library Cataloguing in Publication Data
A catalogue record for this book is available from the British Library

Library of Congress Cataloging in Publication Data
Heller, Michael G.
Capitalism, institutions, and economic development/Michael G. Heller.
p. cm.
Includes bibliographical references and index.
1. Capitalism. 2. Economic development. 3. Economics–Sociological
aspects.
I. Title.
HB501.H439 2009
330.12′2–dc22   2009004076

ISBN10: 0-415-48259-3 (hbk)
ISBN10: 0-203-87340-8 (ebk)

ISBN13: 978-0-415-48259-2 (hbk)
ISBN13: 978-0-203-87340-3 (ebk)

To my father –
Frank Heller

Contents

8   Making the change   274

Preface

The goal of this book is to provide a new framework for understanding institutional change and economic policy during contemporary capitalist transitions. It questions conventional explanations of capitalism, and it aims to demystify the process by which countries can become capitalist. I argue the following: (1) capitalism is a replicable *institutional* system and a feasible policy objective; (2) *impersonally* regulated market expansion is the capitalist method of creating and sustaining national prosperity.

It is important to ask what capitalism is, why it is worth having, and how it can be obtained. Questions such as these were familiar to earlier generations of social scientists who sought enlightenment without embarrassment in the study of universal solutions, intended rationality, and optimal institutional designs. In recent years, a postmodern preoccupation with varieties of capitalism and relativist recipes for development has been both cause and consequence of growing but unjustifiable uncertainty. There is great reluctance to identify systemic technical characteristics of the evolving modern institutional order of economic regulation in a composite and practical manner, and to view it favourably in spite of the difficulties of predicting and preventing all of its imperfections. The social sciences may as well continue to call this system 'capitalism' rather than employ any other more or less unsatisfactory label such as 'liberalism' or 'modernity'. But the commonplace description of capitalism only as a method of economic action with private ownership, free enterprise, and profit making is no longer adequate.

How can we recognize real capitalism today? Do we know which are the indispensable conditions of its existence? In what order, if any, should these conditions make their appearance? Why has capitalism not developed in the majority of societies? Although much of this knowledge does exist already, either it is ignored or its multiple strands are not yet consolidated in a single framework. This book provides the elements of such a theory. It does so mainly by weaving together several thick threads of argumentation that criss-cross the writings of Max Weber and Joseph Schumpeter. This is social science on a grand scale. If it is to be to given a name then it should be one that Weber and Schumpeter themselves used, namely 'social economics' or 'sociological economics'.

My principal objective has been to reinterpret, reorganize, and freely adapt Weber's ideas on the origins and features of capitalism, and also Schumpeter's ideas on the evolution of modern capitalist economies, and to try to produce, on those firm foundations, a credible theorization of telescoped capitalist institutional change in the developing areas of the world. The recombination of Weber's central theme relating to the formal impersonality of modern state institutions with Schumpeter's central theme relating to the discontinuous disequilibrium of socioeconomic change captures the challenges of the contemporary world fairly well. In order to broaden the policy applications of Weberian and Schumpeterian insights, I have developed a set of complementary hypotheses about the potential for motivated and reasoned government strategy during crisis-induced sequences of capitalist transition.

The role of crises is a core theme of the book. Crises signal a disproportionality between changes in the economic domain and absent or inappropriate change in the government domain, and they provide the incentive for radical institutional change. There are, very broadly, two overlapping forms – capitalist crises and development crises. From a Schumpeterian perspective, capitalist crises are part of the normal functioning of innovation cycles. The design and effective utilization of optimal regulatory architecture by governments inevitably tends to lag behind profit-driven innovations in the products and processes of leading branches of the economy. Rational regulation is difficult even when it is not compromised by interest-group politics. Depending on the speed, complexity, magnitude, and multiplier effect of industrial, financial, and managerial innovations, the consequences of a delayed or unsuccessful institutional response can be devastating. In contrast, the kinds of development crises experienced in Latin America and Asia in the 1980s and the 1990s should be easier to avoid. Statist as well as deregulatory models of economic governance may be logical and coherent in their own terms, and can produce positive growth outcomes for a period of time. However, policymakers who lead state activism on one hand, or neoliberalism on the other, are often blinded to predictable consequences of prolonging the economic model and enjoying its benefits while giving insufficient attention to the corresponding regulatory imperative or regulatory effect.

A major contributing cause of most disproportionality crises is accumulated government discrimination in favour of interested groups, typically resulting in such problems as easy credit, socialized risk or moral hazard, and privileged contracting. In effect, by a variety of means government grants too many individuals, firms, or sectors a systemic 'escape clause', sheltering them at least partially from the objective market mechanism. Weber warned of losses in society's adaptive efficiency when the ultimate penalty of 'extinction' for non-compliance with structural laws of the market is absent in economic life. Schumpeter regarded crisis as the opportunity to establish market and regulatory discipline – dead wood can be cleared away, rationalization can occur, and recovery prepares the ground for future waves of economic and institutional innovation. Furthermore, Weber's writings on capitalism are particularly important for what they reveal about the nature of the impersonal form of state regulation – the primary and perhaps sole economic function of the true modern state – which promotes market freedom while suppressing patterns of political economy that would lead to negatively destructive crises. An implication of the analysis, therefore, is that today's upheavals in the capitalist economies share some of the characteristics and dynamics of classic development crises in countries transiting to capitalism. This simply amounts to recognizing that the two dozen or so 'capitalist' countries are themselves in continuing transition, or that 'capitalism' is a moving target, which, as its position changes, must be reconceptualized.

The focus of this book is on cognitive and volitional factors – knowledge, rationality, ideas, interests, and responses to survival imperatives – that enable successful capitalist transitions. Key among them is the potential force of ideology, which is a product of social-scientific knowledge. Capitalism has forever been at an ideological disadvantage not so much because of its historical record but rather because of the way that it has been explained by intellectuals and social scientists. An impersonal institutional order is inherently difficult to comprehend, describe, and legitimize. Perhaps the most contentious claim is that if capitalism were understood in the terms employed in this book, it would look more appealing as an ideology. Ideas are a vital element of the argument because logic and evidence suggest that ideas can trump interests and culture in the causal chain of capitalist transitions. In my view, far too much attention is paid to culture and interests, although I hope to have fairly described the considerable influence they do have.

Leura, New South Wales
2009

1 Institutional capitalism

A common fallacy of our time is that because the institutions of the more advanced countries evolved over many generations so too must the developing countries follow their own evolutionary path and slowly create institutions that match their special needs and values. Any effort to shortcut the evolutionary process, goes the argument, will be a recipe for disaster. The error of this view lies in the conviction that there are no universal truths about institutions, that a society only sets itself such institutional tasks as it can solve through original experimentation and learning, and that the task only presents itself when the social conditions for its solution already exist. The argument advanced in this book is that if an institutional solution has been tried and tested, knowledge of it can be used to advantage by other societies. With appropriate knowledge, motives, resources, opportunities and leadership, it is possible to compress the evolutionary process by imitating the successful institutional systems. Contemporary societies in transition to capitalism have no need to rediscover by a long and costly route of trial and error the institutions that enable durable prosperity and dynamic social order.

The term 'capitalism' is used unusually in this book to describe a particular kind of institutional system found in the more advanced societies, one which has arisen as a solution to the problem of coordinating the institutional subsystems of market regulation, law, public administration, and political representation. This is a general solution manifested in rules about institutional procedures, rules about the functions of key institutional subsystems, and rules about the formulation and enforcement of rules. It is quite different from the everyday temporal and conjunctural solutions that must continually be found to resolve problems of context, such as new regulations for new markets or new methods for managing a public service. Rather it encompasses overarching principles that enable modern society to coordinate its institutional forces in such a way that the everyday tasks can be accomplished most effectively without threatening the survival and further evolution of the system.

I will examine the institutional nature of capitalism, and priorities of institutional change in a capitalist direction, themes which have a long history in the social sciences. I draw on the scholarship of Weber, Schumpeter, Hayek, Popper, and Parsons, among others. In contrast to many present-day social scientists, these writers expressed considerable intellectual confidence in capitalism and had a keen sense of the *policy* dimensions of capitalist transitions. In exploring and adapting their work I have aimed for a composite and favourable analysis of capitalism's institutional architecture and the methods of its construction. Two insights emerge, which can be the building blocks of ideas that communicate the nature of capitalist transition to the agents of change.

1   There is only one form of capitalism. Organizations of the state are the institutional centre of capitalism. Capitalism is characterized, above all, by the enforceable *impersonality* of state procedures. This means, for the most part, that state organizations operate predictably 'without regard to persons'. Within reason, the capitalist state does not systematically discriminate among individuals and groups to achieve economic or political outcomes. In these terms, few countries can today be called 'capitalist'. Even those that can be so classified still break many of capitalism's institutional rules.
2   Effective shortcuts to capitalism follow a *disequilibrium* sequence. In most cases, the sequence will be markets to law, law to bureaucracy, and bureaucracy to democracy. Crises pattern the sequence and provide opportunities and incentives for change. It is usually unavoidable that transitional countries will need to embrace volatility and pursue discontinuous paths of economic and institutional change when constructing impersonal institutions.

Technological frontiers have advanced to the point where it is now easier than ever before to foment economic revolutions. Arguably, the technical, scientific, financial, and managerial resources needed for capitalist transition are available in the world on a demand-and-supply basis. As long as there is relatively free trade of goods and services, and relatively free competition in ideas, the vectors of capitalist transition should be mobile. But if the obstacles to development are in principle surmountable and capitalist transition is feasible, what currently prevents it from occurring in more countries?

One central argument in the following pages is that the demand for institutional change is determined in large part by the supply of knowledge in the form of ideas or ideologies. Societies are normally able to choose their own destiny. Yet since they can only choose from among known alternatives, the prospects of emulating capitalism depend on available knowledge of capitalism. Capitalism was not *designed*, so there is no blueprint to follow. Nevertheless, now that capitalism does exist its unique characteristics and outcomes can be *defined*. It should be possible to identify not only the institutions of capitalism but also the means of obtaining them. There is no logical reason why social scientists – and development practitioners and political leaders – should not explain capitalism persuasively in public-policy terms. This chapter makes a start towards that objective by defining capitalism institutionally and explaining the procedurally impersonal nature of the essential formal institutional subsystems of the state.

One capitalism, not many

This section sets the scene for a new conceptualization of capitalism by briefly describing more conventional viewpoints. First, considerable attention has been given in recent years to the supposed functional equivalencies of so-called 'varieties of capitalism'. Commonalities among 'types' of capitalism are easy enough to discern if one adopts the dictionary definition of capitalism. The *Oxford English Reference Dictionary* describes capitalism as 'an economic system in which the production and distribution of goods depend on invested private capital and profit-making', or 'the dominance of private owners of capital and production for profit'. Using that explanation, it is possible to fit non-socialist state-coordinated economies, many mixed economies, and liberal market economies, all of very different size and sophistication, into one general category. The view that capitalism has evolved in such diverse forms can be found in writings that categorize types of capitalism according to whether they are state-guided, dominated by particular groups and organizations, or competitive and entrepreneurial. The valid general point is that there are different forms of economic organization or economic governance among many nations that allow private ownership of property. Depending on the context and circumstance of its application, each of these models might prove to be more or less encouraging of economic growth (Baumol *et al.* 2007).

In practical terms the 'capitalist diversity' approach has much in common with a second line of enquiry that eschews all mention of capitalism and seek instead to identify the relative merits of different 'recipes' for economic growth (Rodrik 2007). Recipe studies examine workable combinations of sectoral and multilevel policy 'ingredients' in a national or global economy, and their applicability or sequencing according to the condition and history of the economy in question. It is typically argued that *all* the policies for economic growth and institutional change must *always* be context-specific. Recipe studies deal with much the same basic and indispensable debates about economic governance found in the 'varieties of capitalism' literature.

Each approach has its merits, but neither will easily accommodate a single vision of an ideal institutional system that is universally functional for enabling economic growth and improvements in social policy and governance. To give an idea of how large is the gap between these two approaches and the one adopted in the present book, it may help to borrow the culinary metaphor used recently by the World Bank-sponsored Commission on Growth and Development (2008) to qualify its support for the policy 'recipe' approach – 'There are many different recipes for pasta. The precise ingredients and timing are different for each. But if you leave out the salt or boil it too long, the results are distinctly inferior' (ibid.: 5). The Commission may be saying that although it is helpful to experiment with workable permutations of economic and social policy in different national contexts and at different times in history, it is also important to remember that a few general rules apply in all recipes. My aim is to move the analysis a few steps back, and to examine more fundamental relations of cause and effect.

If pasta making is the metaphor, you cannot grade the quality of varieties of genuine and counterfeit pasta until you know how the cereal is grown and how the grain is turned to flour dough. The essence of capitalism resides not in the potential policy models or their many applications and effects, but rather in some more basic qualities of the institutional actions that give rise to them.

Capitalism is often equated simply with market growth. Dynamic market enclaves in an economic territory are sometimes labelled 'capitalist' even when the legal, administrative, or political institutions are underdeveloped. States that have engineered rapid national economic growth for two or three decades are routinely called 'capitalist' before they have built modern institutions. Even in sociology the economic view of capitalism seems to be dominant. Many sociologists conceive of social institutions, such as the legal system and parliament, as merely contingent supports for the capitalist economic system. Peter Berger's (1987: 206) opinion that 'capitalism is an economic system and nothing else' could not be more blunt. Randall Collins (1999: 204) similarly describes capitalism as the 'quantitative dominance of market dynamics such that all other structures are reduced to minor roles'. On these grounds, Collins claims to have detected 'Asian routes to capitalism' and even a 'Buddhist capitalism' in early modern China and Japan.

I identify 'market freedom' as the primary *economic* characteristic of capitalism. Capitalist economies cultivate market freedoms above all else. The key to understanding capitalism, however, lies on the institutional side. Market freedom, which is the necessary condition of long-run economic growth, operates only in a territorial structure of legal, administrative, and political subsystems of the state. Market freedoms cannot be effective or durable without certain institutional supports. Capitalism only exists in societies where state institutions perform jointly to maintain market freedom, rule of law, definite limitations on the functions and powers of the state bureaucracy, and free political representation. On this definition, 'capitalist' is not yet the right descriptor for societies like Brazil, India, or China. As a rule of thumb, in today's advanced capitalist economies the allocation of resources is mostly by the price mechanism, and individuals have equal rights and opportunities to buy and sell, to profit from private enterprise, and to enter new markets. Yet the reasons for the long-run success of this economy are institutional. It is not the size of an economy or even the extensiveness of market transactions that denotes capitalism, but rather an impartially regulated open-market economy, judicial independence and the enforcement of general laws, impersonal public administration, and a system of free political representation. These are demanding criteria. A country can qualify for membership of the Organization for Economic Cooperation and Development (OECD) – the 'club of capitalist nations' – with somewhat less.

'Capitalism' has become a fungible and misused concept. If defined too narrowly as an economic system of capital ownership and profit making, capitalism is bound to be misunderstood in the societies where people's lives could be improved by a transition to capitalism. It might seem strange to make these claims in a book that draws on the ideas of Max Weber. He employed many descriptors – among them, 'booty', 'pariah', 'political', 'robber', 'mercantile', 'fiscal', 'adventurer', 'imperialist', and 'non-ethical' – to capture the uneven historical permutations of emerging capitalism, the inconsistencies of evolving norms in transitional societies, and disproportionalities between capitalism's nascent institutional and economic systems. Weber denoted these types as obstacles to overcome in the staggered unfolding of secular, bourgeois, rational, or modern capitalism. A valid reason for the distinctions was that capitalism has never conformed perfectly to the ideal type. 'Robber capitalism' and 'modern routinised capitalism ... are ultimately different but everywhere intertwined' (Weber 1978: 1118). With hindsight, however, it is clear that Weber's descriptors were weaknesses in the analytical architecture. One dramatic example in *The Protestant Ethic* reads as follows: 'capitalism existed in China, India, Babylon, in the classic world, and in the Middle Ages' (Weber 1992: 52). That conceptual slippage has blurred Weber's theory of capitalism. Arguably, his varieties of capitalism left a legacy of confusion that has bedevilled the analysis of capitalism ever since. 'The essential point', as Talcott Parsons (1949: 631) said, 'is that modern capitalism is one socioeconomic system, not two.'

It should be pointed out, furthermore, that capitalism is a territorial institutional system, not a world system. Despite the pressures of globalization that have waxed and waned for over five centuries, capitalism remains the national exception rather than the global rule. There is no circumstance in the world today where the institutionally bounded market society would not coincide territorially with the political community, a politically guaranteed legal order, and the nationalization of all legal norms regulating the relations between the people of that territory. The determinants of capitalism's evolution lie in the institutions that structure and regulate market society within a political territory. Weber's concept of 'separate political community' is congruent with the 'nation state'. It denotes the existence of: (1) a territory; (2) the capacity to use force to maintain domination over the territory; and (3) an institutional system that regulates social and economic action within the territory (Weber 1978: 54–6, 901–4). A political community is a neutral organizational category that says nothing about the normative content of state action. It may be a robber state, or a constitutional state.

Contemporary capitalism does, of course, have global dimensions. The citizens of most precapitalist countries are linked into the centres of advanced capitalism as producers, wholesalers, retailers, and consumers of tradable goods and services, including media communications. Multinational enterprises and international organizations already influence the allocation of resources in precapitalist countries, and may be vectors for the spread of markets and commercial ethics. Politicians, bureaucrats, judges, entrepreneurs, scholars, and intellectuals in the developing societies assimilate sophisticated and globally mobile ideas about capitalism. They are also enmeshed in cross-national political and economic networks, or in associations that articulate global interests. All of these forces transcend political communities.

But a capitalist world system could exist only if formal authorities of law, administration, and political representation were centralized globally and took precedence over national state institutions. Enforceable international regulations governing political or economic action have not yet developed to the point where they can significantly influence the global experience of capitalism. Until they do, capitalism will remain a market order whose integrated institutional structures evolve within territorially bounded political units. The present study uses the social system as the unit of analysis and focuses on changes in independently subsisting political communities where vectors of capitalism are tolerated or rejected. On the other hand, it is nowadays unimaginable that one nation state could thrive as a viable *economic* community without being integrated in the world economy. The *market* system has been globally extensive for centuries.

It is also worth considering whether capitalism has a *purpose*. In a well-known polemic, Friedrich Hayek argued that capitalism has no 'end' or purpose. A society with a 'prescribed common end' will stifle dissent, suppress liberty, and thereby eliminate the possibility of spontaneous change, which Hayek believed was the only true condition of progress. The argument is an important one and will be explored in this book. At this point, that debate can be circumvented in favour of a 'policy ends' hypothesis about capitalist transition. Various instrumental objectives commonly associated with national development can equally be treated as policy justifications for deliberate capitalist transition. Universal end goals of socioeconomic development, especially continuous increases in a society's standard of living, have historically been most closely associated with capitalism rather than with precapitalism or any alternative form of social order. An argument that I will put forward later is that although the practical essence of capitalism really lies in the institutional or procedural 'means' for obtaining these ends, a clear ideological vision of the ends can provide a motive for creating the means.

In this book I discuss not only 'economic ends', but also behavioural, procedural, and social-order effects of capitalism, such as a sense of security and predictability about the processes of legal, administrative, and political life, which are 'institutional ends'. The effects of the procedural and social-order gains relate broadly to institutional performance. We see this equally in the efficient provision of services such as infrastructure, health, and education, and in the relative safety afforded by effective rule of law, all of which impact on the prospects for economic growth.

It may be reasonable to say that capitalism's *material* end is economic growth. The policies that generate *sustained* growth will foster patterns of ownership and organization, and methods of exchange, profit making, and capital accumulation that characterize capitalist economies. In fact, growth is both a means *and* end of capitalist development, since wealth creation is the precondition for the pursuit of social objectives in mass society. In the words of Nobel Laureate, Amartya Sen (1999: 14): 'The usefulness of wealth lies in the things that it allows us to do – the substantive freedoms it helps us to achieve.' The Indonesian economist, R. M. Sundrum, similarly said:

> The advantage of economic growth is not that wealth increases happiness, but that it increases the range of human choice.... The case for economic

growth is that it gives man greater control over his environment, and thereby increases his freedom.

(in Arndt 1987: 177)

Hayek wrote: 'Strictly speaking, no final ends are economic, and the so-called economic goals which we pursue are at most intermediate goals which tell us how to serve others for ends which are ultimately non-economic' (Hayek 1982: vol. 3, 168). In addition, since opportunity for socioeconomic mobility is one of the surest ways of legitimizing a social order, economic growth has a doubly important function. 'Without growth', points out Gellner (1994: 203), 'mobility is a risky zero-sum game, in which anyone's gain is balanced by someone's loss. Nothing much is gained in the aggregate, and instability is the price.'

Finally, it must be emphasized that the achievement of economic growth is not just a matter of suppressing the *symptoms* of bad institutions. For growth to be durable through time, it is necessary to make changes to the *system* of institutions in a country. It is often remarked that the primary constraint on economic growth in developing societies is 'rent seeking'. Rent-seeking analysis, which criticizes the welfare losses from non-market politicization of economic life, is a powerful explanation of blocked development. If governments selectively control entry into markets, they create the political incentives for populations of rent seekers to obtain government-granted rights or permissions to enter into production and trade. The pursuit of political influence by economic actors 'in contexts where institutional structures create opportunities for private gain that do not involve increased production' is a major source of inefficiency, which generates 'social waste rather than social surplus' (Brennan and Buchanan 2000: 134; Buchanan 1980: 4). Rent seeking is a competitive but usually unproductive struggle for scarce resources, since government restrictions on economic activity mean that competition for rents must be added to the costs of competition in product markets (Krueger 1980). Rent seeking generates vested interests in its own perpetuation. By de-legitimizing markets in the eyes of the public, rent seeking probably also has negative ideological consequences.

> The existence of rent-seeking surely affects people's perceptions of the economic system. If income distribution is viewed as the outcome of a lottery where wealthy individuals are successful (or lucky) rent-seekers, whereas the poor are those precluded from or unsuccessful in rent-seeking, the market mechanism is bound to be suspect.... People perceive that because of competitive rent-seeking the market mechanism does not function in a way compatible with socially approved goals. A political consensus therefore emerges to intervene further in the market, rent-seeking increases, and further intervention results. While it is beyond the competence of an economist to evaluate the political impact of rent-seeking, the suspicion of the market mechanism so frequently voiced in some developing countries may result from it.

(Krueger 1980: 69–70)

Having specified what an inadequate institutional environment looks like in rent-seeking terms – as well as the greed and predation of political rulers who create the incentives for rent seeking – it may then seem reasonable to conclude that economic growth would occur naturally if this constraint on growth were removed (Jones 2000). In the past, development economists unwisely recommended a quite different strategy for achieving economic growth – massive injections of capital targeted at specific sectors and enterprises, guided by elaborate blueprints, planned and implemented by coercive states. For many years it was also common to encounter the claim in studies of the political economy of developing countries that state and private economic activities arising because of advantages gained through politically generated economic rents can be the effective foundations for capitalist development. Nothing could be further from the truth.

But economists who find rent-seeking theory helpful for the analysis of market dysfunctions in developing countries would generally also concede that rent seeking cannot be eliminated without better institutions. Rent seeking is not the underlying *cause* of dysfunctional institutions and bad economic policy; it is only one among other *symptoms*. Without a theory to explain the institutions that enable economic growth we cannot know why rent seeking ever disappears. The removal of obstacles to growth really means *building* better institutions. They cannot be built until knowledge exists of the more optimal institutional architecture. 'Capitalism' may not be the most satisfactory descriptor for the optimal institutional system that constrains rent seeking and related forms of state dysfunction. However, it needs to be acknowledged that the factors propelling economic growth have over time constituted a definite historical category of institutional system, which, because it exists, requires a name. As a preliminary hypothesis, I conceptualize 'capitalism' as a policy orientation whose purpose is to remove the obstacles to durable economic growth. Once it is appropriately defined, capitalism can be confidently proposed as a system of institutional means that performs comparatively well in the pursuit of *all* of the conventional developmental ends.

Impersonal order

If we are to understand capitalism we must look for institutional commonalities among societies where capitalism proved to be sustainable in the long run. Throughout the book I will focus on impersonality as the generic variable of effective capitalist institutions. As a way of introducing the topic, this section reviews some noteworthy attempts to analyse the broader process of depersonalization in modern society and economy.

Commentary on the growing impersonality of social and economic orders was already evident in the writings of eighteenth-century philosophers and economists. In particular, Adam Smith's famous metaphor of the 'invisible hand' – which was employed slightly differently in several of his writings, including *The Wealth of Nations* (Smith 2000) – suggested, among other things, that there is an impersonal force in market exchange. Yet, as Rothschild (2001) argues, it was an ambiguous metaphor. Smith well understood the political realities of markets, the interventionist instincts of governments, the inclination of governments to single out private interests for protection, and the desire of merchants and manufacturers to look for monopoly positions and to make transactions in close proximity to others whom they think they can personally trust. He was committed also to individual enlightenment and moral responsibility. Yet in his effort to persuade public officials to abstain from systematic intervention in the economy, Smith may have thought it both useful and ironic to appeal to the official's natural 'love of system' (Rothschild 2001: 137). The joke, if that is what it was, about an unseen hand of the market, with the implication of a providential order lying beyond human invention, planted one of the most enduring and also controversial ideas in social science.

From our present vantage point, the importance of Smith's metaphor lies in the juxtaposition of three facts about modern economic life. The first is that nations become rich by encouraging economic freedoms and the division of labour. The second is that the initial emergence of liberal economic orders was in some respects a 'blind' process by which economic actors learnt to orientate their behaviour towards ever more impersonal market forces. In pursuing their visible self-interest in markets, individuals serve a common social good that can remain invisible to them. Third, competitive markets evolve in two ways: (1) *organically* as a self-organizing system shaped by inherent laws of motion, and (2) *instrumentally* as a mechanism subject to human interests and controls. While policymakers should be reminded that their economic designs are based on limited knowledge and limited foresight, the market is a mechanism of nature that coordinates human actions to social ends. We need not choose between theories of voluntarist or spontaneous market organization. It is enough simply to know that the reasons for the efficiency of markets are both abstract and concrete. Markets operate 'behind men's backs', but can only do so well by staying within a visible framework of constructed rules or institutions.

In the eighteenth century a broader preoccupation related to social consequences, good and bad, of the profit orientation of commercial society. Economic agents cooperated and conspired in ventures, but were, in another sense, anonymous buyers and sellers subject to the disciplining and impersonal forces of demand and supply. Smith's contemporary, Adam Ferguson, also recognized that wealth creation was the consequence of that 'mighty engine', the division of labour. But he was wary of its corrosive effect on civil society. The 'separation of professions' in the commercial state 'breaks the bonds of society'. Man becomes 'a detached and solitary being'. He is 'set in competition with his fellow-creatures, and deals with them as he does with his cattle and soil, for the sake of the profits they bring' (Ferguson 1996: 24, 206).

Such concerns would go to the heart of Karl Marx's studies of the 'objectifying' effects of the industrial division of labour. From the vantage point of modern state-regulated market societies, Marx's theses on the oppressive and exploitative nature of capitalist production look wrong. Yet, in the nineteenth century a profoundly transformative labour process was underway. Thanks to the industrial revolution many people, or their offspring, would soon enjoy much higher standards of living. However, the short-run choices they faced – as in some developing countries today, where many people abandon rural communities and migrate to towns and factories – were disruptive and had an 'alienating' effect on sectors of the population (Jay and Jay 1986). As Marx described it, capitalist forces of industrial production, wage labour, and money-based commodity exchange caused producers to become separated – abstractly – from the products of their labour, from other producers, and from nature itself. Commerce, said Marx, dissolved the natural bonds of society, creating 'isolated individuals' who were deprived of the personal interactions that sustained common values. Dehumanized capital, 'personified' by the exploitative capitalist, eventually appropriates all of the 'personality' of capitalist society (Marx 1973).

Contemporary studies of the labour process largely discredit Marx's view. It is certainly true that changes in the work environment, and mass employment in large organizations, do impact on people's psychological perceptions of their personal status, worth, or power in the workplace (Heller *et al.* 1998). But, it is not the division of labour itself that causes alienation, social atomization, estrangement, or the exploitation of man by man. A further general point is that capitalism could not have survived as long as it has if organizations of society had been sapped of all their personality. Organizations could not function if their constitutive individuals did not establish some lasting relationships of varying intensity, internally as well as externally. Like markets, organizations are a social framework within which can be cultivated honesty, empathy, dependability, obligation, shame about transgressing obligations, and trust, reliability, discipline, and reciprocity. Good organizational leadership often depends on whether managers can develop a rapport with their subordinates. Levels of creativity, efficiency, and job satisfaction in the workplace are frequently higher when there is a sense of solidarity among employees.

Two of the great nineteenth-century sociological theories of human evolution sought to explain why social and economic relations were growing ever more impersonal. Ferdinand Tönnies's (2001) thesis of the *Gemeinschaft* (small-scale community) and the *Gesellschaft* (large-scale society) preceded Durkheim's (1984) quite similar contrast between the 'mechanical solidarity' of traditional society and the 'organic solidarity' of modern society. In the homogeneous traditional community, life is conditioned by common local identity, personal relationships, ascribed status, and conformity with community practice. In contrast, modernization, rationalization, urbanization, industrialization, and expansion of markets produce heterogeneous and impersonal relations between people. Economic relationships increasingly take the form of arm's-length contractual arrangements and specialized participation in the division of labour. Individualism starts to take precedence over community as a force of social and economic change.

For a long time, the reactions of social scientists to these manifestations of modernization were cautionary or critical. Tönnies complained about the 'transitory and superficial' nature of *Gesellschaft*, and Durkheim warned of the anomie that might result if modern society did not substitute new behavioural norms for the old communitarian restraints. Idealizations of community past and fears that markets corrode present communities persist in many forms today (Marglin 2008). However, the weight of historical evidence suggests that these concerns rest on weak foundations (McCloskey 2006). Some types of community are lost as people's needs and desires change, while others no longer serve their original function. New communities are formed while others are maintained. The dismantling of old community and the building of new community can improve relationships in the impersonal society.

> Men still form real groups and enter into real social contacts of all kinds, and try to satisfy their emotional social needs as well as they can.... Personal relationships of a new kind can arise where they can be freely entered into, instead of being determined by the accidents of birth.
>
> (Popper 1962: vol. 1, 175)

The sociologist, James Coleman, has explained the process by which societies built relatively impersonal organizations to substitute more or less effectively for many roles that were previously performed by communities. Following Weber, Coleman (1990a; 1993) traces the evolution of the 'purposively constructed social organization' to the Middle Ages and to the legal invention of the corporate actor as a fictitious juristic person. Law of limited liability later reinforced the status of such organizations as social units distinct from individuals and the family unit. Among the earliest corporate bodies with 'legal personality' were churches and boroughs in medieval England, which were economic entities in their own right and existed separately from the royal household. From the eighteenth century onwards organizations designed for particular purposes, such as administration and education, became the leading forces of social, economic, and political change in Europe and North America. Organizations of political representation would eventually become more powerful than individual heads of state. Economic organizations similarly transformed the physical and social environment by spearheading industrialization.

Weberian bureaucratic, legal, and economic rationalization, argues Coleman (1993: 14), 'is now upon us in full force'. Modern organizations establish control relations between *positions* and *offices* as opposed to control relations between *persons*. Social control in primordial society depended on informal relationships that 'enforced obligations', 'guaranteed trustworthiness', and 'suppressed free riding' (Coleman 1990a: 651). Norms, reputation mechanisms, and status were 'imposed by family, community, and religious bodies'. The constructed organization, in contrast, 'uses rules, laws, supervision, formal incentives, and sanctions by designated agents' of the state to achieve similar ends (Coleman 1993: 9–10). In Coleman's terminology, this is a transition from a self-sustaining 'natural' order of 'simple social relations' resting on reciprocal ties, to an order of 'complex social relations' that are, in effect, 'constructed by an outsider'. The important relationships in modern society are regulated by a 'third party' – the state – which supplies the 'interdependent incentives' for their continuation. Organizations create 'a well-defined boundary' separating the new institutional structure from the informal community.

Douglass North (1990) has revisited the economic dimension of this historical process in his analysis of the passage from small-scale personalized exchange to impersonal exchange with arm's-length economic transactions, and finally to impersonal exchange with 'third-party enforcement' of 'rules of the game' by modern states. The movement to state-regulated impersonal exchange is a universal transition that many societies are still far from completing. As I will show in a later chapter, recent theorizations of these changes were foreseen in considerable detail by Max Weber (1978), who identified a complex continuum of irregular overlapping transitions in the development of modern economic regulations, taking shape as an uneven historical progression from unthinking custom to informally enforced convention and, finally, to impersonal formal law. Weber identified the nature of impersonal exchange in the market in terms of appropriation and state enforcement of property rights. But he also explained the corresponding depersonalization of the state *itself*, a secular trend that is largely neglected by present-day institutional economics, economic sociology, and political science.

Underlying all favourable conceptualizations of the impersonal society is the idea that norms of modern social order are internalized by individuals and institutionalized in the state. In *The Social System*, Talcott Parsons (1991) describes traditional societies as 'particularistic'. People's obligations are to members of the group or the community. In modern liberal society, role expectations no longer relate only to the brotherhood or the social network. Rather, a 'universally valid moral precept becomes important, such as the obligation to fulfil contractual agreements' or to select people by their 'technical competence' (ibid.: 62). State institutions play the crucial role in emancipating market exchange from particularism and preventing economic policy issues – such as measures to extend exchange relationships or to protect property rights – from becoming political problems (ibid.: 123–7). Older and newer normative orders continue to coexist as societies modernize. Moreover, when human beings *design* institutions their value judgements, constrained cognitive powers, and competing interests all come into play. No legal construction, for example, can ever be completely objective. Ultimately, however, the state does enforce the impersonal social order. Ernest Gellner (1988) compares agrarian societies where the means of coercion were in the hands of rulers, warriors, and clerics, with modern societies where coercion is vested in a single agency, the state. The state's role is to enforce formal rules. By upholding impersonal rules as formal law, society avoids transferring to government and the market the personal or parochial loyalty and arbitrary violence of tribalism. Friedrich Hayek similarly observed that the conflict between arbitrary and universal justice is resolved by impersonal state law.

The rise of the ideal of impersonal justice based on formal rules has been achieved in a continuous struggle against those feelings of personal loyalty which provide the basis of the tribal society but which in the Great Society must not be allowed to influence the use of the coercive powers of government.

(Hayek 1982: vol. 2, 143)

In broader terms, Hayek (1982: vol. 3, 162) indicated the superiority of 'a society in which no longer the known needs of known people but only abstract rules and impersonal signals guide action towards strangers'. This idea serves to introduce what is perhaps the most impassioned contemporary depiction of impersonal society. In *The Open Society and Its Enemies* (1962: vol. 1), Karl Popper describes 'the transition from the closed to the open society as one of the deepest revolutions through which mankind has passed' (ibid.: 175). The open society is a 'depersonalized society' (ibid.: 174). In many everyday activities, such as market exchange, there is neither the compulsion nor the need to form personal relationships. Normative rules of the open society, administered as formal law, are built, modified, and enforced by human beings. The origins of the open society lie in the growth of trade and commerce (ibid.: 177). The market erodes parochial domination and status distinctions, allows access to new ideas, encourages individualism, and creates pressure for the creation of legal frameworks that apply universally to rulers and the ruled, to insiders and outsiders. In the open society, social status is decided competitively. People are free to enter new relationships.

The closed society, in contrast, is a 'natural' state characterized by personalized institutions that exhibit 'unvarying regularity' like the 'laws of gravity' or the 'succession of the seasons'. Social relations and customs appear to be 'unalterable', beyond human control, and 'as inevitable as the rising of the sun' (ibid.: 57–8). The closed society is collectivist. Mobility is limited. In tribal society bound together by organic factors such as kinship and taboo, status is determined by 'concrete physical relationships' between persons (ibid.: 173). These are ideal types, since Popper also recognized that institutions cannot be completely impersonal. As he said, 'the uncertainty of the personal element' in institutions is never eliminated. It is not possible to create 'foolproof institutions whose functioning does not very largely depend upon persons' (Popper 1991: 66).

Popper argues that the institutions of the open society must be created with the objective of balancing the power of political leaders and organizing the state for long-term economic policy (1962: vol. 2, 131–3). The challenge lies in 'designing institutions for preventing even bad rulers from doing too much damage'. Political 'detachment' is needed in order to limit the 'discretionary' powers of rulers. 'Impartiality' and 'equality before the law' are rational and objective goals of institutional construction in the open society (ibid.: 234–8). Popper outlines two forms of economic intervention (ibid.: 131–3). The optimal type is 'institutional or indirect', which is the method of 'designing a legal framework of protective institutions'. The suboptimal form, which is the cause of uncertainty and obfuscation in society, is 'personal or direct'. Discretionary state powers have an inherent tendency to multiply unexpectedly, as every intervention requires future adjustments. The advantage of the indirect or institutional approach is that it can 'make allowances for unforeseen and undesired consequences'. Whereas discretionary economic interventions can seem to be arbitrary and transitory, 'the legal framework can be known and understood by the individual citizen [because] its functioning is predictable'.

We return to these themes when examining Weber's studies of capitalist institutions. In some respects, Popper's theory of the 'open society' has a Weberian flavour. However, the visions presented by Popper and by the other writers reviewed in this section remain incomplete. Capitalism, I argue, is characterized most precisely not by the impersonality of society in general or by impersonal economic exchange in the market, but rather by *institutional* impersonality. The next task is to identify the constitutive elements of the impersonal institutions.

The institutional system

Relevant capitalist institutions will be defined here as *organizations* of state that formally enact and enforce rules governing individual and group interactions in a market society. This Weberian conceptualization of 'institutions' is surprisingly uncommon now in the social sciences. It differs from definitions of institutions that include informal rules, norms, customs, or culture, as well as formal organizations. Precisely what Weber meant by 'institution' is a matter of debate (Swedberg 1998: 39, 224). Arguably, however, his clearest meanings are to be found in passages dealing with the 'compulsory organizations' of the state, i.e. a political community, where regulatory and administrative norms are *formally* prescribed, coordinated, and enforced within a territory (Weber 1978: 48–53, 1380). State organizations 'impose' *objective* criteria of action upon officials and citizens irrespective of their particular interests, desires, and status. Institutions encompass a formal order in which 'rationally established rules and an enforcement apparatus codetermine individual action'. Membership of state institutions includes persons of ultimate authority, leaders in policy making positions, and administrative staff who join in the activity of the organization. The state institution establishes the normative rules that in principle are binding on its own agencies as well as on citizens. The function of an institution is to monitor and enforce the rules of conduct deemed to be legitimate and effective within the interrelated state-regulated spheres of a social order.

A distinction should be drawn between universalistic formal procedural norms operative in an organized institutional environment and the more dispersed sets of social norms based on common values. An institution's procedural norms do not necessarily reflect the society's informal norms. Parsons made a useful distinction between norms and values. 'Norms', he said, can be thought of as 'patterns of desirable behaviour which *implement* values in a variety of contexts'. Often they are the means of establishing 'consensus at the procedural level'. Norms underlie the 'institutionalization of procedures' (Parsons 1999: 261–2). My focus in this book is on the impersonal procedural norm of the formally organized institutions of the state in capitalist society. For the purpose of analysing capitalist transitions, the values implemented by the procedural norm will be defined as culture-neutral. In other words, they have universal characteristics.

In three respects, the approach taken here need not conflict with a view of institutions as rules – including informal rules – that regulate or legitimize behavioural expectations with or without compulsory codification and enforcement machinery. In the first place, formal rules evolved originally from some of a society's informal customs and conventions. Second, informal patterns of motivation or conformity, such as morals, do continue to condition action to a greater or lesser degree in the context of institutional roles and positions. 'Institutionalized procedures', as defined here, are simply the legal and formal procedural norms viewed as binding rights or obligations in the organized structure of the political community. The legal system is the formal institutionalization of norms, in particular the procedural norms. Third, precapitalist institutional fields of transitional societies are especially likely to incorporate *proto*-institutional ethics or normative systems, which are more or less binding upon human behaviour in the absence of compulsory enforcement machinery. Markets, in addition, combine formal and informal regulatory sanctions at every level of their modern development. It is clear, nevertheless, that informal governance of markets becomes less determinative of economic outcomes as modernization proceeds.

At this point it is possible to introduce a general conceptual schema of the capitalist social order, comprising four universal spheres of institutional action:

1   A proto-institutional ethic of honesty in *market exchange* that begets an informal regulatory order and facilitates the expansion of trade, whose historical origins date from a post-communitarian tolerance of voluntary economic association and market competition. Over time, the ethic fuses with an evolving legal system.
2   A formal, universally accessible, and calculable *legal system* that enshrines political and economic rights of opportunity and fair dealing, guaranteeing, in particular, continuous calculability of the enforcement of property and contract rights by the state's administrative and legal staff, mainly on behalf of plaintiffs.
3   A coordinated *state administration* of services oriented to formal normative procedures that ensure more or less consistent and objective means-end decision making throughout the public organizations, with a minimum of case-by-case discretional powers. Its norms are non-discriminatory, i.e. they are impartial.
4   Democratic institutions guaranteeing free *political representation*, i.e. the existence of formal procedures for the competitive selection of policies and leaders. As the peak coordination mechanism, parliament (broadly defined) is the final source of authority for policy initiatives in all state institutional domains.

These institutional spheres are indispensable conditions of capitalism's evolution for two interrelated reasons. First, the economic pattern of advanced capitalism could not be sustained in the absence of proportional and continuous developments of ethical and formal market regulation, legal rights, public administration, and free political representation. These four spheres or domains are *subsystems* of the whole. Second, without the countervailing powers and functions of all institutional spheres, it would not be possible for *one* sphere to operate effectively as a pillar of capitalist society. Capitalism requires the ongoing and systematic *interaction* of these four spheres. In practical ways, the institutional spheres are reciprocally functional in maintaining the formal procedural impersonality of the capitalist institutions.

This proposal for theorizing capitalism in terms of four institutional spheres of action suggests, of course, ideal-type institutions. Real institutional systems never attain the perfection of the ideal. The approximate ideal of institutional capitalism at its current levels of development is close to the pattern of contemporary institutional life in most of the OECD countries. Nevertheless, as I argue in this book, humankind is capable of intentionally rational institutional construction. The ideal type is not beyond the realms of possibility in design terms. Constructions take shape in the mind as devices for approximating historical reality, and they sometimes do appear in reality. Theoretical constructions can shape human consciousness, and can help decision makers to systematically select from among alternative actions. An ideal type with 'logical or teleological consistency' can have 'power over man' (Weber 1947: 324).

How, in practice, does one conceptualize the ideal type with 'teleological consistency'? Answer: By translating the ideal type into logical *policy-relevant* categories. Although we have not yet examined either its components or its dynamics, it is possible to say that the social system of capitalism refers to a structured interaction of institutions, which has a purpose in so far as these institutions are required for capitalism's existence and survival. A 'system' is a complex of interconnected parts or devices that function together as a whole, for a purpose, and within specified boundaries. Talcott Parsons (1991: 19) defined the social system as one society that contains 'all the structural and functional fundamentals of an independently subsisting system'. Here, the whole *system* will refer to the empirically self-subsisting capitalist society. The *boundary* mechanism is the territorial political community. The *parts* are the state's institutional subsystems. In the contemporary world, the capitalist institutional system manifests empirically in a single society, not as a global system.

Once capitalism is conceptualized as an institutional system or social order, it is logical also to identify the fields of market regulation, law, administration, or political representation as institutional *subsystems*. As capitalism advances, its institutional spheres become more clearly demarcated as formal subsystems, with specifiable functions in reproducing the capitalist social order. In an earlier version of this argument Parsons and Smelser (1956: 16–19) outlined key features of a social system, in which each 'subsystem' of the overall 'system of action' is conditioned by four 'functional imperatives'. By adapting this schema, it is possible to visualize capitalist subsystems in terms of four functions:

1 Reproduce an institutionalized normative system and manage its inherent tensions.
2 Attain instrumental institutional goals in organizational policy contexts.
3 Increase control over outcomes by adapting goals to changing policy environments.
4 Integrate a social system by harmonizing the relations between its subsystems.

Subsequent chapters will indicate ways in which this schema of subsystem functions can be used to analyse and organize the *instrumental* depersonalization of developing states. System imperatives like these turn out to be relevant to all proposals for *emulating* capitalist institutions. The more that policy considerations enter into the argument, the more helpful it becomes to substitute institutional 'sphere' or 'domain', implying passive or incorporeal vehicles of human action, with the harder organizational notion of 'subsystem', implying praxis. These terms are semantically distinct in so far as institutional *subsystem* has teleological connotations suggesting instrumental and purposeful means-oriented action towards a stipulated end. Institutional *sphere*, on the other hand, might seem to be more compatible with the nomenclature of abstract evolution, which comes about without intent or design.

Institutional domains

This section outlines capitalism's four institutional spheres of action. The descriptions draw on key insights in Weber's *Economy and Society* (1978). It can be noted that the institutional explanation of capitalism proposed is separate from but not incompatible with Weber's discussion of the 'economic presuppositions' of capitalism in his *General Economic History* (1981: 275–8), where he refers to modern capitalism as a mode of organizing the 'provision of everyday wants' characterized by rational calculability. Capitalism's *economic* presuppositions are: (1) capital–profit accounting; (2) generalized market freedom; (3) mechanization; (4) calculable adjudication and administration of law; (5) free labour markets; and (6) the commercialization of economic life.

Weber did not conceive of capitalism as an institutional 'system'. Nor did he theorize the systematic interactions between market ethics, law, administration, and representation. In these and other ways my approach is different, since it aims to take Weber's institutional analysis a step further. I argue that Weber laid the foundations for a complete theory of subsystem interactions in modern capitalism. He singled out the performative role of each institutional sphere, indicated the approximate causal weight that each sphere exerts upon others, and explained how procedural norms cultivate an impersonal social order within each of the institutional spheres. Standardized and calculable procedural impersonality with respect to the rules of state regulation is a common thread throughout Weber's studies of modern institutions. Weber's theories tell us that capitalism's system encompasses not only the procedural norms of modern economic behaviour, but also the procedural norms of legal, administrative, and political subsystems. His writings provide many of the elements needed for an integrated theorization of impersonal institutional exchange *and* impersonal economic exchange, which is generally missing from contemporary theories of institutions.

The *ethical* condition of capitalism is an informal consensus arising among market actors as a direct result of the expansion of markets and the need for agreements on the justice of market competition. In the traditional community, profiting from transactions with members of one's own community is frowned upon, while exchanges with outsiders, if permitted at all, are often conducted with complete ruthlessness. The norms that emerge as a society modernizes have the effect of eliminating ethics that subordinate economic exchange to social approbation by status, kinship, or ritual. They also eliminate prohibitions on usury, limitations on goods that may be exchanged, and other rulership traditions that constitute obstacles to free economic exchange. The predatory ethic that permits relations with outsiders to be acceptably conducted in a hostile, unpredictable environment of distrust and cheating diminishes as the market encroaches on more areas of human interaction. Parties to exchange see the benefits of trade. But, sustainable trading demands that some of the moral principles of the communal economy be extended to the external economy.

A post-communitarian ethic of honesty in competitive market exchange is usually evident today wherever arm's-length transactions are frequently repeated without resort to legal arbitration. The guiding principle of extensive market orders is that the pursuit of material gain be kept within regulated bounds of fair dealing. Most partners to exchange recognize their mutual interest in honesty. For reasons of self-interest, technical efficiency, and social virtue they subject themselves willingly to informal ethical restraints. 'Fair dealing' is moral, but it is also the most efficient way of earning money.

The market breaks down fraternal and exclusionary norms. It becomes 'the most impersonal relationship of practical life into which humans can enter' (Weber 1978: 636). The depersonalization of markets is only to be expected. There is little room for charity in commercial relationships. The absence of charitable virtues in economic life largely explains the hostility shown towards markets among many individuals who are not primary economic actors. As Weber points out, however, even unjust economic relations like slavery are still 'ethically' regulated in their own particular ways. The market community is special in the sense that its coercive nature stems not from personal relationships of brotherhood or authority, but only the abstract inevitability of having to adapt to structural imperatives of market competition and the threat of economic failure.

> Formally, the market community does not recognize direct coercion on the basis of personal authority. It produces in its stead, a special kind of coer-

cive situation which, as a general principle, applies without any discrimination.... The sanctions consist in the loss or decrease of economic power and, under certain conditions, in the very loss of one's economic existence.

(ibid.: 731)

The *legal* condition of capitalism relates to the necessary 'continuity' of economic relationships. In precapitalist societies, continuity in, for example, income sharing or orderly taxation depends on strict taboos or social conventions enforced by the political authority in the absence of a separation of powers. It is always difficult to create conditions for the sustainability of profit making. An economic ethic, no matter how strong it is, cannot provide a guarantee of continuity. Repeated and extensive acquisition and exchange in complex markets requires that the legal system be the 'arbiter of last resort'. Weber understood that in premodern England formally enacted legal norms were not determinant factors of the *original* capitalist evolution (Swedberg 1998: 105–7). But that was the exception to the rule. Since then and everywhere, *continuous* market exchange, production of goods, and financing of enterprises has always been easier when there existed a legal system that is formally calculable. Traditional ambiguity or arbitrariness in the administration of rights has been eliminated wherever markets are highly developed. Laws protect business enterprise from being compelled to undertake an exchange, and guarantee the legitimacy of the methods by which exchange occurs. Economic transactions in an advanced trading system require at least a perception that the legal security of property and contractual claims does not need to be repeatedly tested.

The economic movement to capitalism is a transition to validly enforced rules of the game, the creation of a fully fledged system of property and contract rights, and formally regulated free competition. Weber's key insight about the legal foundations of capitalism was that in modern economies one looks for 'the complete appropriation of all material means of production by owners and the *complete absence of all formal appropriation of opportunities for profit in the market*' (1978: 161). By standardizing consensual understandings with third-party mechanisms for the enforcement of norms, the legal machinery of modern society evolves in such a way that it becomes the impersonal means of last resort for resolving conflicts of interest and discouraging malfeasance in the marketplace, and for protecting the zone of economic competition from monopolistic closure. Once economic rights are secured by precedent in a binding system of formal codes and procedures that operate independently of political parties, of economic enterprises, and of state agencies, it is no longer possible for such rights to be arbitrarily attached to an individual, group, or class.

The *administrative* condition of capitalism is that the state's sphere of action be delimited and impersonal. Conduct of official business will be continuous, consistent, and relatively calculable. The state's instrumental operations will be oriented to definite and easily understood formal procedures for formulating and implementing public policy. Public agencies increase their effectiveness the more that officials act with a minimum regard to their personal relations, feelings, or popularity, and with a maximum regard to their assigned duties, defined powers, and technical competence. The powers of modern officialdom can never rest solely on the accumulation of political or material assets, or on the personality of individual officials. Of greater importance are demonstrable qualifications, aptitudes, and accumulated knowledge assets for leadership and administration. Above all, routine public authority by state agencies is based on the principle of 'equality before the law'. The creed of modern public administration is the application of general decision criteria rather than decisions made 'case by case'.

The capacity of the state to eliminate organizational incentives for the pursuit of private or group interests within public agencies lies initially in its ability to reduce the personal discretion that officials exercise in their dealings with each other and with social and economic groups. Eventually, modernizing states must find a good balance between the risks and the efficiency of delegating discretion in public administration. The priority, however, is for the state to adopt policy paths that involve the least amount of delegated discretion, and to raise the level of discretion and the scope of state activity *only* in proportion to increases in institutional capacity. For the state to sustain its responsiveness and flexibility it concentrates on core public services and essential power objectives. Weber proposed minimizing the transitional state's economic functions. By limiting its direct interventions the state increases its control and adaptive efficiency, and reduces opportunities for collusion and evasion of control. States that do not achieve substantial procedural impersonality are those that have extended too far beyond the primary functions of legal regulation, natural monopoly infrastructure, and monetary and fiscal policy.

The *political* condition of capitalism is 'free representation' with voluntary association and the competitive selection of leaders and policies. Free representation is most developed in the modern parliament (or equivalent peak collegial mechanism), where representatives exercise authority over those who elected them and retain their decision-making autonomy only as long they can continue to prove their electoral worth. Key features of the modern political system are the calculability of operating procedures, legally regulated mechanisms for political compromise, and committee work with representation by experts. As in all of capitalism's institutional spheres, *procedural impersonality* is the prerequisite for effective free representation. Modern parliament, like modern law and bureaucracy, displays 'the general tendency to impersonality' and 'the obligation to conform to abstract norms' (Weber 1978: 294). Rather like competitive economic enterprises in the market, political parties exercise their domination within the law. Political battlefields, like markets, need formal rules.

Whether capitalism and democracy belong together is a question that continues to divide scholars, not least because it is difficult to establish the significance of authoritarian periods that preceded capitalism in modern societies. Democracy is plainly not the *first* condition of capitalism. On the other hand, it is logically inconceivable that extensive markets, complex legal systems, and the impersonal bureaucracies of advanced capitalism could continue to evolve in the absence of a countervailing system of free political representation. Weber's explicit interest in the relationship between democracy and capitalism is evident in three areas. First, he pointed out the commensurability between market freedom and free political representation in terms of their shared reliance on competition, leadership, and the formal regulation of action. The systematically competitive selection of leaders and policies in an impersonal framework of rule of law produces political decisions that favour the maintenance of capitalism. Second, Weber argued that parliament is the essential counterweight to state bureaucracy. Without supervision by parliament, the administrative agencies would stifle capitalism. In the absence of democratic controls and a formal separation of powers, state agencies and officials would pursue their self-interest and would fall in with non-state interests. Third, parliament becomes the organ of state empowered to negotiate, define, coordinate, and monitor the procedural norms that regulate all state subsystems of policy and enforcement, including law.

Interactive subsystems

As already noted, in a capitalist system, the four subsystems – proto-institutional ethical regulation, and the formally impersonal institutions of law, public administration, and free political representation – are operationally *interactive*. If these institutions were not reciprocally conditioned on a more or less equal basis, capitalism would not exist. The question is: to what extent, and in what manner, do these subsystems interact? In some important respects the executive powers of government, which in democracies normally reside centrally in the offices of the elected presidency or ministerial cabinet, have a coordinating role. Despite the formal checks and balances and the separation of powers, all of which deliberately fragment state authority, the executive has authority to supervise the public bureaucracy and, to a lesser extent, the judicial system. In the exercise of their policy functions, political leaders can also – in practice and by example – exert influence over the evolution of ethics in society. All of these are multi-path relationships. Even when the executive has ultimate authority at one point in time, the action of the executive is itself in some degree a product of the actions of other parts.

The point to bear in mind in the present context is that in the advanced institutional system there is a kind of 'invisible hand' at work when three conditions are met – parliamentary competition, absence of monopoly due to the division of powers, and impersonal procedural interaction among the institutional subsystems. This more or less invisible mechanism for spontaneous coordination takes its clearest form in the shared formal rules of *rival* institutional spheres.

Because the institutional subsystems of capitalism are not bound together by a concrete common 'purpose', their integration largely depends on *how* they interact. There must be continuous and fluid dialogue between institutional subsystems. Each subsystem has a distinctive function, as well as a separate organizational structure. Appearances suggest that the system is segmented and pluralistic. Yet, if one subsystem could not connect with the other subsystems, the system could not exist. A disproportionate interpenetration between two subsystems, or excessive influence of one subsystem upon another, would also interfere with the evolution of the system as a whole. So how does this system operate? The prerequisite for institutional integration is the *activated* impersonal procedural norm, which provides needed incentives for reciprocity between functionally distinct and competing subsystems. A capitalist institutional system evolves blindly – guided by the invisible hand of impersonal norms – only if the *procedures* that shape state organizational behaviour are sufficiently predictable. Actors in each domain depend on the conduct of actors in all the other domains to perform their own roles and satisfy their own interests.

Therefore, a major motivation for efficient institutional behaviour will be a utilitarian interest in the procedural value of *predictable* and *easy* processes among subsystems. The analogy with the predictably regulated market environment for business firms is not perfect, but neither is it wholly misplaced. The everyday procedural practicality of state activity depends on whether common norms of behaviour and known rules of action will prevail. The expectation is that actors in each sphere share a general interest and face similar organizational sanctions, even if they do not share exactly the same interests, values, or ideologies. So, a common goal in the institutional and economic spheres is to achieve relative certainty about organizational or regulatory procedures, which facilitates action by permitting more or less accurate expectations about how others will act and react.

It follows, then, that it must be a part of every subsystem's function to promote and monitor the procedural norms of each of the other subsystems. When an innovation (such as a new property right or a welfare reform) emerges in one domain, the manner in which the other domains react and adapt to it will be critical to its success. The four institutional spheres are well matched in this regard. Many innovations can be tried and tested by *all* the subsystems. If a new property right is to be fully adopted it must prove itself to be economically efficient, enforceable in law, administratively feasible, and politically legitimate. When they evaluate the merits of this innovation, the competing interests in each subsystem can at least ascertain that opinion making and decision making by all the involved parties was oriented to general rather than particularistic criteria. As the sociologist Jeffrey Alexander (1995: 114) has written, 'impersonal worlds' are always 'the first criterion for universality'. He goes on to say: 'The more individuals share conceptions of their impersonal worlds, the more individual practice can be subject to extra-personal control, the more it submits itself to universal criteria of evaluation.'

A positive feature of the mode of institutional interaction in advanced societies is the framework of checks and balances that regulates against monopolistic closure in markets as well as organizations. In capitalist society, any effort to structure social or economic relationships for the perpetual benefit or exclusion of one group can be countered by legitimate and institutionalized rights of usurpatory action (competition in the market, legal redress, administrative accountability, or political agitation). Even within a single institutional subsystem, exclusionary practice can still be counterbalanced by opportunities and rights to marshal the resources of a competing subsystem against the threat. Examples of these 'checks' could include: political action to eliminate bureaucratic corruption; legal actions to resolve disputes between producers and consumers; legal action against government policy; and political and administrative action to counter prejudices in the legal system.

Unique to modern capitalism, therefore, is a process by which formal institutions interact systematically and together evolve spontaneously in the absence of a *single* coordinating mechanism. This could not happen unless organizational behaviour in institutional subsystems conforms, in most instances, to impersonal procedural norms. It is easier to calculate action or outcomes in a social order where behaviour is oriented to universal rules governing institutional action rather than to the commands of particular persons or the preferences of particular groups. In reality, of course, people continue to form desirable, valuable and enduring personal attachments in the family, the workplace, in voluntary associations, and neighbourhoods. Old and new forms of community support individuals and soften the strains of life in an increasingly impersonal regulatory environment. But, interpersonal relations no longer matter most for aggregate welfare in society. In Weber's words, the more that economic enterprises *and* apparatuses of the state act legitimately 'without regard for persons', the more likely it is their actions will conform to 'calculable rules' rather than to 'love, hatred, and purely personal, irrational, and emotional elements which escape calculation' (Weber 1978: 975). In these ways, the reciprocal conditioning of institutional domains acquires the exceptional *continuity* that is highly valued in capitalist societies.

Depersonalization is not widely accepted by scholars as a necessary institutional condition of capitalism, and capitalism is not normally conceptualized as a form of institutional interactivity. Instead, debate often focuses on *bilateral* reciprocity between institutional domains, such as whether market freedom and democracy belong together, or the extent to which market economies require formal law. These simple pairings generally give an incorrect impression of the critical interrelationships between institutional spheres. They do not take into account multiplier effects of the interrelationships within an overarching institutional system.

To give just one example, much has been made of Max Weber's observation in a footnote that 'capitalism and bureaucracy have found each other and belong intimately together' (ibid.: 1465). Advocates of state-coordinated or activist economic policy may seize on Weber's theoretical pairing of bureaucracy with capitalism with relish (Evans 1995: 29). But they would be wrong to do so. The passages corresponding to the footnote leave no doubt that Weber was discussing the primacy of the *legal* underpinnings of effective bureaucratic action. 'Modern capitalist development', said Weber, depends on 'progress toward the bureaucratic state, adjudicating and administering according to rationally established law and regulation'. Capitalist enterprise requires 'a legal and administrative system, whose functioning can be rationally predicted, at least in principle, by virtue of its fixed general norms' (Weber 1978: 1394–5).

These passages are consistent with Weber's emphasis on *impersonal* rather than *discretionary* state regulation. He always gave very short thrift to direct state economic intervention. Only in 'irrationally constructed states' has the 'discretion' of public officials

> permitted the development, and often the exuberant prosperity, of the capitalism of traders and government purveyors and of all the pre-rational types known for four thousand years, especially the capitalism of the adventurer and the booty-seeker, who lived from politics, war, and administration.
>
> (ibid.: 1395)

When the strongest pairing in society is between markets and bureaucracies, the booty seeker is most likely to benefit. Booty seekers – whose acquisitive methods depend on political privilege, deception, crime, or risk taking that endangers others – do not disappear in modern capitalism. They are discovered in corporations, in well-endowed pressure groups, in government, and even in local neighbourhood associations. The comparative advantage of a capitalist institutional system is that the subsystems of law, administration, and representation are countervailing powers. Because of it, the activities of booty seekers are routinely exposed and expunged from politics and the economy.

Precapitalist countries usually already display some of the institutional preconditions for capitalist transition. But even those with large and globally competitive economies have not constructed the institutional *system of subsystems* that sustains advanced capitalism. Even fewer have undertaken the reforms that revolutionize procedural interactions within the state and between the state and economic actors. In precapitalist countries the four institutional spheres of capitalism may already coexist to some degree. Separately these spheres may at times even be active sites for promoting markets, procedural justice, clean administration, or pluralistic political representation. However, precapitalist societies lack more or less equal intensity and purpose of action among these institutional spheres. One or another sphere is disproportionately evolved. Political liberalization has spread faster than market liberalization, or bureaucracy has grown much faster than markets, law, or democracy. By examining these kinds of interactions it is possible to discover which of the institutional segments lag behind and by how much.

In other words, by focusing on the interactional procedural norms of the state it is possible to identify what is *lacking* in the development of one or more institutional spheres of precapitalist societies. The analyst can know what subsystem relationships should look like when they are 'in balance'. Impersonal procedural norms strengthen the formal advantages of citizens to make claims against power holders by universalizing rights and role expectations that rest on transparent rules rather than on particularistic relationships. A depersonalized regulatory order legitimizes the political and economic competition that sustains economic growth *and* social order. As I will argue in later chapters, the process of capital-ist transition necessarily involves disequilibrium and conflict. Nevertheless, it is possible to minimize the turbulence and to emerge from it in a better condition if societies begin the journey with a clear idea of the attainable 'steady-state' insti-tutional balance described in this and the previous section.

The precapitalist state

If capitalism is impersonal, it follows that the precapitalist social order is person-alist or interpersonal. Some provisos apply when adopting a binary distinction between precapitalism and capitalism, and when we claim that modernization, i.e. a transition from precapitalism to capitalism, can occur in the right con-ditions. Analysis of the passage from 'tradition to modernity' will be banal or naive if it suggests a very simple linear change or a process that is in almost every respect identical in different societies. In many practical ways the trans-itions to capitalism are neither inevitable nor uniform. There is no *exact* point of transition between traditional and modern orders, which *coexist* within a single society for generations. Weberian scholars regard modernizing societies as 'in transition' or 'partial development' (Bendix 1964; Eisenstadt 1973). Advanced societies, which can be called 'capitalist', also remain in evolution. It may be useful to view capitalism as a moving target that regularly needs to be reconcep-tualized in order to account for the changes occurring in its organism. In addi-tion, since politics and institutions can decay, and policy errors are often made, it is possible for crises to erupt and for reversals to occur.

Intermediate developments between precapitalism and capitalism are, of course, desirable in their own right, and this book explores a transformational sequence in pursuit of the end goal. Arguably, however, it is neither necessary nor helpful to identify and specify a set of fine distinctions along the continuum to modern society. A feasible quantitative classification might apply measures of per capita income. A qualitative classification could apply measures of state effectiveness, for example by using worldwide surveys of 'quality of govern-ance'. At the lower end of either scale would normally be found the poorest countries, and industrializing countries would lie somewhere in the middle. Membership of the OECD might be a convenient though far from perfect classi-fier for 'capitalism'. But none of this explains much. The method adopted in this book is to conceptualize capitalist, precapitalist, and transitional countries according to the *commensurability* between national institutions and particular economic policies, the phase reached in the policy *sequence* of capitalist trans-ition, or the types of *crises* that countries experience (Chapters 6 and 7). At this point in the discussion no such distinctions are needed because the initial objec-tive is to specify fundamental categories – 'what is before' and 'what comes afterwards' – rather than the unpredictable and ill-definable intermediate states.

Totalizing concepts such as 'capitalism' or 'modernization' attempt to capture the predominant features of societies at similar stages of development for the purpose of analysis and comparison. They also give a name to the primary means-end *policy* dilemma faced by development practitioners. These categories speak of historical choices, not of historical imperatives. Fear about the 'homogenization' of societies during capitalist modernization has placed many scholars in an untenable position. They seek to question the universality of genuinely neutral operational systems that clearly work tolerably well in the more advanced societies. Yet in a post-socialist world they have failed to suggest practical 'system' alternatives for the governance of developing societies. Observing a global convergence towards the formal institutional arrangements that had previously been found only in Western countries, Alexander (1995) argues that the onus is on intellectuals to interpret what is truly 'universal' in the new age. They should begin, he says, by accepting that 'structures like democracy, law, and market are functional requisites if certain social competencies are to be achieved' (ibid.: 46). If societies choose to modernize, they must acquire knowledge of the institutional and economic structures that will enable such change.

I argue that the precapitalist state is *interpersonal* and the capitalist state is *impersonal*. This is a simple device for comparing systems by reducing their characteristic condition of existence to a procedural or normative variable. The objective, following the method suggested by Dogan and Pelassy (1984: 164), is to introduce a useful contrast between two types, 'each of which is broad enough to cover a wide array of systems and forms'. The interpersonal–impersonal dichotomy directs attention to dominant and opposing orientations of a whole institutional order within a given territory, and the effects of that order on economic and political decision making. It allows a rudimentary differentiation between the policy-making conditions of developed and underdeveloped societies. By abstracting from the complex realities of multiple normative and procedural tendencies, it becomes possible to explore the *central* institutional dynamic that is most likely to condition the policy process in a society.

Many societies in Asia and Latin America, and some in Africa, long ago established the formal organizational *façade* of the 'depersonalized' state. The cogs of these deceptive states are in perpetual motion. They create legal decrees, new public agencies, electoral contests, and they modify bureaucratic structures. Below the surface, however, real decision making is systematically ad hoc, conducted through informal channels and according to individual or group loyalties rather than a general public authority. Influence on policy is exercised by personal connections and the social networks of political and economic interest groups. Even in the more advanced precapitalist societies, dyadic exchanges of favour, patronage, and loyalty may still be systemic. Empirical studies of neopatrimonialism indicate that clientelist power brokerage in societies of low and medium development remains the principal motive force of public policy (Crouch 1979; Purcell and Purcell 1980; Clapham 1990; Van de Walle 2001). Political divisions inside the state reflect struggles for personal authority, status, or rents, rather than functional specialization and genuine policy debate. Clientelism and patronage are typical motive forces that keep the cogs of state in motion.

The concepts Weber used to define 'patrimonialism' generally remain accurate for describing the characteristics of contemporary precapitalist societies. Patrimonial political domination is normatively opposed to the impersonal division of powers in the modern legal-administrative state with formal checks and balances. Leadership may revolve on dispensation of status or economic benefices in return for political support. Citizens expect rulers not to exceed their powers and to remain within traditional bounds of legitimate rulership. Yet rulers wield great personal power and can exploit their authority almost as though it were a private economic asset. Public and private spheres are not clearly demarcated in public decision making. Public office is often indirectly or directly the source of private power and wealth. Elite structures are concentric circles of declining power wielded through patron–client affiliations in economic and political life. On the inner and outer rims, individuals are at constant risk of losing influence if they fall from favour for purely personal reasons. Justifications for authority are arbitrary, and policy is unpredictable. Interpersonal states operate a form of closure and exclusion that depends on concrete social relations between individuals as opposed to abstract relationships mediated by impersonal institutions. Social mobility depends in many ways on informal microlevel connectivity.

In comparison with capitalist states, precapitalist or patrimonial states are less meritocratic and more informal, discretionary, arbitrary, unpredictable, and interpersonal. Although Weber's descriptions were historical, their relevance to the present is plain to see. In law, the citizen encounters 'informal judgements rendered in terms of concrete ethical or other practical valuations' according to the judge's discretion (Weber 1978: 976). 'A feature of the patrimonial state in the sphere of law making' is 'completely arbitrary decision-making ... serving as a substitute for a regime of rational rules' (ibid.: 1041). Its 'anticapitalist effect' is felt in the 'instability of all legal guarantees' (ibid.: 1095–6). Relations between officials and citizens rest on 'concrete consociation and compromises of individual power-holders', and on the 'concrete arrangements between them' (ibid.: 643). Political-bureaucratic power 'derives from the treatment of the office as a personal right and not ... from impersonal interests' (ibid.: 1029). In the most backward precapitalist states, 'practically everything depends explicitly upon personal considerations: upon the attitude toward the concrete applicant and his concrete request and upon purely personal connections, favours, promises and privileges' (ibid.: 1041). Citizens transact their public business with 'the ad hoc official whose powers are defined by a concrete purpose and whose selection is based on personal trust, not on technical qualification' (ibid.: 1030).

The formally regulated freedoms for political or legal disputation that are given by procedural checks and balances in capitalist society are weak or nonexistent in precapitalist society. Typically, interpersonal economic policy making in the contemporary precapitalist state will be attuned to the needs of rent seekers. Rent seekers appropriate public dispensations for the pursuit of private gain, including permits for production and trade, or fees and taxes that benefit some groups and not others. Competition for rents is a process of expending resources to secure government-granted political rights to enter into production or exchange. In short, the main difference between interpersonal precapitalism and impersonal capitalism lies in the dominant state procedural norm.

Face-to-face and discretionary procedures become less determinative of economic or political outcomes as a society advances towards capitalism. This book emphasizes the personalistic patterning at the interstices of economic and political life as a defining characteristic of developing societies. Capitalist transition is, in large part, a movement at the level of the state from interpersonal relations to impersonal procedures.

Informality or formality?

This section examines some debates about the relative merits of formal and informal economic governance, and the influential claim that cultural context influences the effectiveness of formal institutions. The issues will be treated theoretically under various headings in later chapters, but are introduced here in order to indicate their relevance to the preceding conceptual discussion of pre-capitalism and capitalism.

Relative 'trust' in cultural or informal norms as opposed to formal institutions is a theme that has received increasing attention from sociologists and economists in recent years. The *Oxford English Reference Dictionary* defines trust as 'a firm belief in the reliability of a person or thing'. Mark Granovetter, whose writings on the interpersonal embeddedness of economic life laid the foundations for new economic sociology, makes the broad claim that 'the production of trust in economic life' depends *mainly* on 'concrete personal relations' and on 'networks of social relations' rather than on 'impersonal institutional arrangements' (Granovetter 1985). I disagree, but it is not difficult to see why this view has arisen. Weber (1978: 346) said about organizations in general, be they public or private, that their members are quite likely to pay more attention 'expressly or silently' to the 'personal characteristics' of applicants for membership than to their impersonal qualifications. He also pointed out that market competition is itself a form of 'social relationship, above all that of competition, between the individual participants who must mutually orient their action to each other' (ibid.: 43).

Since market exchange generally involves 'bargaining, negotiation, remonstration or mutual adjustment' between buyers and sellers, it is hardly surprising that many of them will 'get to know each other well' (Hirschman 1992: 123). Some markets are more 'personal' than others. Wholesale markets or markets for production inputs often foster networked relationships. Spot markets and consumer markets where large numbers of buyers meet small numbers of sellers for short periods of time tend to be more anonymous. Consumer markets, on the other hand, can be 'socialized' in so far as they depend on reputations. It is clear that markets are not just *disembodied* machinery for adjusting supply to demand. Good business relationships must be maintained. Trust can be socially constructed by repeat buying and selling, and also by regular credit arrangements. The practice of socializing or networking with business partners and business rivals might help to discourage malfeasance. The fact that interpersonal relations can just as often be social structures that support thievery does not, of itself, invalidate the claim that longstanding personal contact between business people generates trust and facilitates the 'mobilization of resources for collective action' (Granovetter 1992: 6). For these and other reasons, it may be correct to call the market a 'social construction'. Few people would deny that business relations are often mixed up with social relations.

Yet economic sociologists who emphasize the personalistic nature of many economic transactions have often been strangely reluctant to concede that all sustainedly successful economies rely, in the final analysis, on a very solid framework of impersonal regulatory institutions. A market order that is generalized throughout mass society crosses a threshold of interactivity between formal institutions that takes precedence over interpersonal and informal relations. The decisive issue is the background operability of impersonal norms of third-party regulation, which encourages a corresponding self-regulation among the parties to exchange. Personal connectivity may be rational and desirable. But a research focus on the microlevel networks that regulate transactions has often meant a corresponding neglect of macrolevel procedural norms that are unique and indispensable to the institutional order of modern economies.

The broad issue is the *mix* of informal social capital as a source of trust, and trust in formal mechanisms for the codification, monitoring, and enforcement of behavioural norms. Dasgupta (2005a) suggests five ways of establishing trust and credibility in economic and non-economic transactions. The first is 'mutual affection' in families and households. The second is a disposition towards sociability and reciprocity, which Dasgupta suggests may be an evolutionary selection of norms. Ethics of honesty are cultivated by upbringing and socialization, and sanctioned by informal enforcement within a group. They are also internalized by individuals who feel shame about violating customs. A third mechanism is the coercive 'external enforcer' of agreements, which in modern society is the state. The state enforces laws that offer certain guaranteed rights to all those who engage in economic exchange. A condition for this arrangement is that the state must itself be *trusted* to enforce the law. A fourth mechanism comprises the informal incentives that individuals have to establish good reputations. Reputation has a utility function in business, but is also a social good in its own right. The fifth mechanism is 'mutual enforcement in long-term relationships', namely the informal sanctions imposed by a group on those who violate norms or break agreements.

Whether an interpersonal network is good for development will depend on how it is used. Dasgupta paints a vivid picture of the precapitalist landscape, and questions the underlying causality. Personalistic relations can be a solution to the problem, but may also be its cause.

> In countries where the law does not function well, where officials regard the public sphere to be their private domain, where impersonal markets are often absent, communitarian relationships are what keep people alive, if not well; hence their attraction for many contemporary development economists. But we need to bear counterfactuals in mind. It could be that communitarian relationships prevent impersonal transactions from taking place.

Moreover, personal obligations inherited from the past can prevent public officials from acting dispassionately.

(ibid.: 28)

In poor countries where a formal legal system is not extensive or not trustworthy, informal trust without the prospect of third-party enforcement may be the only option. In economic development, however, the objective should be to extend the market mechanism. Ideally, market exchange will be impersonal. But since communitarian institutions arise from interpersonal networks, they can crowd out markets. As Dasgupta says, 'where networks and markets are substitutes, they are antagonistic' (ibid.: 20). Networks may block the development of markets. If networks personalize transactions they are likely to be exclusionary rather than inclusionary. Indeed networks can be unequal, exploitative, or violent, especially when rule of law is absent. The 'dark side' of communitarian institutions and social capital, says Dasgupta, is 'their capacity to permit one group to exploit another within long-term relationships' (2005b: 3). Powerful members of a network may monopolize the benefits of cooperation, as often occurs when patron–client relationships are pervasive and longstanding. For an economist, Dasgupta is unusually adamant about the importance of this issue. 'Determining the right interplay between interpersonal networks and the impersonal public institutions remains', he says, '*the central problem of the social sciences*' (Dasgupta 2005a: 28).

James Coleman (1990a) reached much the same conclusion. As urban-industrial *Gesellschaft* society erodes social capital, purposefully constructed private or public organizations expand to the point of taking over roles previously assigned to interpersonal social relations in primordial society. Developing societies are worse off if personalism is allowed to congeal within the formal institutions. Informal normative systems that predominate in traditional societies with weak states and underdeveloped markets rely more heavily on coercion than on incentives and rewards. Power is more unequal and more easily manipulated in primordial communities. Their traditional methods of reaching consensus discourage creativity and innovation. The destruction of many primordial social controls was therefore an essential step in the construction of modern societies. Where formal organizations predominate, the mechanisms of social control are increasingly 'detached from persons' (Coleman 1993). As primordial social capital disappears it leaves a vacuum. A function of government is to facilitate the emergence of new corporate mechanisms that can 'fill the voids' of key social functions previously performed by face-to-face contact.

A major question that a theory of institutions should answer is how and under what conditions a formal institutional structure comes into being, buttressed by formal laws or rules rather than by an informal structure supported by norms. This is part of a broader agenda ... that of developing theory for the constructed social organization that is coming to replace the primordial or spontaneous social organization that was the foundation of societies of the past ... [Now] societies are undergoing a major change from the form of organization that generates norms and within which institutional structures grow around the norms, to a form of organization more fully based on purposive design.

(Coleman 1990b: 337)

The historical facts are clear enough. In complex modern economies, the background boundary structure of state-enforced economic rights and regulations has taken over the main functions previously performed by informal behavioural codes. It is extremely costly to build trust and regulate transactions among many diffuse interests engaged simultaneously in multiple, distant, and often unrepeated exchanges. Because of the division of labour, increasing specialization of productive activity, and arm's-length exchange within and between market societies, it is unlikely that informal norms can be either legitimate or reliable as a primary mode of regulating economic life. State agencies are more effective in this role as long as citizens perceive them as able and willing to impartially sanction the violation of norms when necessary. Formal institutions that define and protect economic rights *en masse* – without systematic case-by-case variation in the implementation of those rights – reduce uncertainty and lower transaction costs.

Douglass North (1990) has analysed the adaptive efficiency of institutional structures in the more advanced societies, focusing particularly on the continuity of property rights as a determinant of relative economic performance. In this respect, he follows a tradition of scholarship dealing with the institutional foundations of modern economic order that dates back to Weber and beyond. Social order and economic exchange in *pre*modern society depends on a dense social network of ties and obligations. Personalized exchange regulated by ethical rules, reciprocity, and informal consensus about the justice of economic arrangements is a 'way of life' (North 1981: 182). In modernizing societies, however, the older forms of economic regulation become gradually less important. Impersonal exchange in advanced competitive markets is coercively but impartially regulated by the state (North 1990: 35, 58–9). This has meant, in effect, that formal political bodies and judicial systems are guided by codified laws and constitutions in monitoring and enforcing property and contract rights. Capitalist evolution has been a 'lengthy and uneven' transition 'from unwritten traditions and customs to written laws' (ibid.: 46).

The shackling of arbitrary behaviour of rulers and the development of impersonal rules that successfully bound both the state and voluntary organizations were a key part of this institutional transformation.

(North 1990: 129)

As these statements indicate, North believes that countries must somehow create the formal institutions that regulate impersonal exchange. The questions that follow have to do with culture. Is culture an obstacle to the development of the right institutions? Can culture dissuade reformers and citizens from placing their trust in formal institutions as a solution to development problems? On these issues, North parts company with Weber. His central argument is that society cannot build the effective formal institutions *until* its culture is 'hospitable' to such change. Before this can happen there must *first* be a change in the 'culturally derived norms of behaviour' (ibid.: 140). The emergence of a regulatory state *first* 'entails the development of effective informal norms of behaviour that will undergird the formal rules' (North 2005: 120). Formal rules are an *addendum* to the informal rules. They achieve little unless they are consolidated informally. The formal rules only enable cultural constraints to become more effective in society.

Although it is not apparent how new and more 'effective' norms might be 'developed', North is clearly not saying that a period of market expansion and the rapid development of market ethics could give rise to political pressures for regulation and the invention or systematic enforcement of relevant laws. Instead, his discussion suggests intergenerational evolution over centuries and across a wide spectrum of deep-seated social or moral norms. He is obviously sceptical about the ability of reformers to build institutions in the present. However much they may wish to construct a modern state, policymakers are hostages to their cultural heritage, which resists rapid change. Institutional change is therefore *necessarily* slow and incremental. Societies get locked in to inefficient institutional structures. Above all, North emphasizes the 'tenacious survival ability' of informal constraints, which provide 'the comfortable feeling of knowing what we are doing and where we are going' (1990: 83). Cultural traits persist despite changes in the formal rules. If anything, the 'informal constraints' are likely to 'modify, supplement, or extend formal rules' rather than the reverse (ibid.: 87). Dysfunctional rules and organizations are stable because habits, customs, and conventions are costly to change.

Francis Fukuyama (1995; 2004; 2008) similarly views culture as the one variable that has overriding importance in determining development outcomes and the effectiveness of formal institutions, while simultaneously acknowledging the vital functions and superior performance of formal institutions in the advanced societies. He argues that the efforts of reformers in developing societies to subject political and economic processes to rule of law by passing laws, mandating new political procedures, or designing administrative structures will fail if the underlying 'informal matrix of norms, beliefs, values, traditions, and habits' remains unchanged (Fukuyama 2008: 199). In a region like Latin America, formal institutions rooted in law 'matter much less than people think' because they cannot be made to work until there exists 'a different kind of political culture' (ibid.: 195–6). Political culture, according to Fukuyama, is the reason why formal institutions do not work as they theoretically should, and why one institution works well in one country but badly in another. Moreover, the underlying structural divisions in society, which create problems of injustice and poverty, interact with political culture and determine short-run political action. All of this explains why institutional design priorities, such as rule of law, are not put into practice.

Fukuyama is especially keen to emphasize that more or less equally success-ful systems of political representation take variegated institutional forms. There is no *single* formal institutional framework for democracy. The Weberian theory of democracy tends to support that argument, but with some important caveats. The essential proviso in Weber's writing is that parliamentary 'free political rep-resentation' subject to impersonal norms of conduct, competitive selection of leaders, and formal divisions of power is a distinctive and universally valid pro-cedural system encompassing subsystems that may differ in operational and architectural detail within and among societies. Indeed, in an adaptive social system the formal institutions should differ in detail, even if their guiding pro-cedural principles and purposes remain *precisely congruent*. In not dissimilar ways, systems of common law and civil law might in theory work tolerably well as means to similar ends in diverse societies *as long as* they perform imperson-ally and predictably in resolving conflicts and safeguarding economic rights. In this limited sense, it may be useful to argue that 'context' will determine the optimality of the institutional structure, if by that we mean only that one type of institution has – for whatever reason – succeeded in one society but failed in another.

Disagreements do arise, however, about what elements to include within the category of 'culture' or 'informality', especially when these elements are blamed for the dysfunction of a formal institution or for the failure to implant a new institutional form. Does culture really explain why an institutional form succeeds in one society but fails in another? Or, can a better explanation be found in culture-neutral cognitive and volitional factors of resistance to that institution? When we examine what social scientists actually mean when they say that 'culture' impedes the effectiveness of formal institutions in developing coun-tries, it often turns out that they are referring to variables such as patronage, cli-entelism, privilege, cronyism, a post-election practice of 'winner-takes-all', disregard of law and due process, disrespect of rules, autocratic manipulation of power, strongman politics, and so on. Yet if all the items on that list are, in fact, problems shared in common by many or all developing societies in different parts of the world, they can hardly be termed 'cultural' – unless it is being sug-gested that *underdevelopment* is a cultural condition. Were we to try to measure the 'distinctiveness' of a 'political culture' by how a country ranks in compara-tive indices of 'corruption and governance', as Fukuyama (2008: 213) seems to suggest we can, then *all* countries at the bottom levels of such indices – be they in Africa, Southeast Asia, or Latin America – should, *ipso facto*, share the culture. Then, 'culture' would be meaningless as a concept for distinguishing between populations or between social systems.

Looking ahead

It would be wrong (not to mention patronizing) to presume as a general rule that people acquiesce in corruption, clientelism, privilege, or patronage because they are culturally conditioned to do so, or because it is comfortable for them to continue doing what they have always done. A social scientist who has firsthand knowledge of developing countries could rationally calculate that, *if* offered a clear and informed choice between a continuation of traditional politics and the certain introduction of a transparent and impartial institutional system, the vast majority of people in those countries would sensibly opt for the latter in spite of the lobbying of interest groups that see greater benefits in the status quo. Furthermore, irrespective of culture, people are highly responsive to incentives. If impartial institutions change the incentives, behaviour will change in some significant degree. After a certain point in the evolution of societies, the formal institutions are more likely to be able to modify the informal norms in key areas of economic regulation. State institutions can shape informal norms and control socialization by applying measures that will change the *environment* of social action almost overnight. They may do so, among other methods, by exposing populations to market forces and enforcing laws.

In addition, an advantage some latecomer countries have is that foundational norms for effectively regulating markets are already codified in their legal systems or can be copied from the codes of advanced legal systems and improved on. The remaining problem is one of *enforcement* rather than culture. If enough senior functionaries in the peak leadership organizations of the state in a developing country are willing to focus time and resources on *implementing* a few basic procedural norms above all else, as can happen when political regimes change and technocrats come to power following economic crises, the problems of 'culture', while not disappearing, become much less significant.

It is doubtful that the nebulous informal norms of partially modernized societies are strong enough or sufficiently homogeneous to prevent the enactment of a radical and intelligent reform launched at the apex of the formal power structure. By comparison with a few concrete formal institutions and their concrete purposes, the functions of the multiple, random, abstract, and often competing informal norms found within a single society are elusive, inconstant, and difficult to pin down. All too often, the attribution of development outcomes to 'whole culture' is a handy device used to explain a big difference between societies that the analyst's experience of life does not equip them to comprehend by other means. The assumed problem of culture in transitions to capitalism dramatically diminishes if the *defining* characteristic of effective formal institutions is their *perpetual procedural quality*, and if the relevant procedures are, in principle, culture-neutral or simply 'modern'. By the same token, clientelism, patronage, rent seeking, communitarian politics, and related phenomena, which are *also* culture-neutral, are among the symptoms rather than the causes of institutional dysfunction.

It is fashionable now to say that 'context' should determine policy choice. One reason given is that the effort to fit advanced institutional forms into developing countries is bound to fail if the social dynamics of those countries are unlike the ones that prevail where the institutions have been successful. The current orthodoxy is to dismiss standardized prescriptions for formal institutional construction. One of my objectives in this book is to show why there is no requirement to change the society before changing its institutions. Nor is it necessary for reformers to compromise the root functions of a successful institutional form, or to go out of their way to avoid a mismatch with the prevailing social system (indeed the 'mismatch' is the precondition for the change). Institutional dysfunction in developing countries can, in fact, generally be reduced to *one* missing standardization within the existing edifices. The façade of a formal institution may have a modern appearance even when the interior areas are squatted by predators, patronage mongers, and rent seekers. Without standardized wiring and plumbing the edifice cannot be made habitable for a better class of occupant, and cannot reach its full potential. Human capital formation, ethics, and written laws are part of the solution. But the conduit for change is procedural. A deliberate effort to activate the impersonal procedural norm is crucial for recruiting better people and inducing them to make better decisions. It is also vital for creating interactivity and complementarity between the indispensable institutional subsystems. This norm may have had a cultural anchorage in the past. Strictly speaking, however, it is neutral and procedural.

The institutional subsystems of transitional countries are characteristically over-reliant on informal norms, which do not provide the level of generalized trust that a modern polity and economy demand. This chapter has offered some initial justification for the view that a predominance of interpersonal and personalistic norms in decision-making processes is the highest common factor in institutional underdevelopment. The success of capitalist transition depends on the regularity of action stemming from the impersonal procedural principle that increasingly governs political and legal decisions and the making of economic policy. No matter how diverse in culture, economic structure, or geography, all countries eventually face this challenge. In societies transiting to capitalism the purpose of institutional change is to consciously diminish the influence of traditional sectors by building and growing the modern sectors. Although this is not an easy project, it is less difficult and considerably faster than changing society's culture. Common-sense responses to the political and economic system spread awareness among people that strongly built and impartial formal institutions would eliminate their forced reliance on patronage and clientelism. The process is more likely to occur with a sense of urgency when the informal norms no longer feel 'comfortable' (if they ever did). I will argue that, at such moments, common sense can combine with ideology and effective leadership to bring about meaningful change.

2   The modern state

Today, the homo politicus, as well as the homo oeconomicus, performs his duty best when he acts without regard to the person in question, *sine ira et studio*, without hate and without love, without personal predilection and therefore without grace, but sheerly in accordance with the impersonal duty imposed by his calling, and not as a result of any concrete personal relationship.

(Weber 1978: 600)

I propose Max Weber's theories as a foundation for a new approach to the study of capitalism and capitalist transition. Weber was born to a German merchant family in 1864. He died in 1920 before completing the writings assembled in *Economy and Society* (first published in German in 1922), his greatest work. Weber studied law, and he taught political economy at universities in Germany and Austria. Among his collaborators and friends were leading figures of twentieth-century economics and sociology, including Schumpeter, von Mises, Sombart, and Simmel. Weber left his characteristic mark on major intellectual controversies of the period. He was active in German politics, and wrote widely on sociology, economics, politics, law, philosophy, comparative history, and culture. The themes of his scholarship and his opinions on economic policy reflect his engagement in debates on the side of the German Historical School as well as on the side of its main rival, the Austrian School. Today, however, Weber is best known as one of the founders of modern sociology. His economic sociology offered perhaps the most rigorous twentieth-century counterweight to Marxian political economy. More broadly, and in the best sense of the term, Weber was a social scientist. His systematic development of methods and theoretical concepts for the social sciences dealing with social and economic action, rationality, bureaucracy, organization, and power is unmatched by any scholar before or since. Of most relevance in the present context is Weber's central interest in the nature of 'capitalism'.

My argument grows out of Weber's emphasis on the impersonal procedural norms of state institutions in capitalist societies. In addition, I present Weber's theories of capitalism as explanations of the logic of a development strategy favouring (1) the construction of a parametric state with classical liberal economic functions, (2) market expansion as the driving force for legal reforms, (3) the short-run precedence of legal change over administrative and political change, and (4) the short-run precedence of political leadership over political participation. Weber clearly demonstrated, on technical grounds, why bureaucracy must be rationalized and why politics must be democratic in modern capitalism. In the absence of free political representation bureaucracy's power escapes supervision and feeds on economic irrationalities. On the other hand, Weber's theories can show why market-led and law-led transitional sequences to capitalism are usually more appropriate in developing societies than bureaucracy-led and democracy-led sequences.

In this and the following chapter I will single out Weberian ideas that seem most relevant to the understanding of contemporary transitions to capitalism. Some steps in the analysis build on Weber's concepts or suggest alternative concepts that fit better with current realities. His best-known essay, *The Protestant Ethic and the Spirit of Capitalism* (1992), which often misleads people about Weber's view of the nature and origins of capitalism, is only briefly discussed. Weber himself said that this essay treats 'only one side of the causal chain' of capitalism (ibid.: 27). I concentrate on *Economy and Society* (1978), which can be read as a brilliant though somewhat inscrutable manual for the practitioners of capitalist transitions. My objective is to distil the practical inferences from Weber's extraordinary vision of ideal state action, a chain of reasoning made up of many elements that are often only loosely held together under seemingly disparate thematic headings, and to reassemble the elements that most tellingly reveal the present-day potential for constructed capitalism.

Weberian theory

As noted, two main Weberian arguments are advanced in this book. The first deals with the creation of impersonal state procedures, and the second treats the issue of policy sequencing during capitalist transitions. Both themes are largely absent in the academic literature on Weber. This might be because Weberian theorists have not been interested in using Weber's writing to explore policy strategies for capitalist transition. On the other hand, it is fair to say that there are significant differences between my interpretations and those of other writers. Although arguments about capitalism set out in the following pages can be understood without prior knowledge of esoteric controversies in Weberian theoretical literature, I will err on the side of caution. This section provides an outline of the most relevant debates, and explains my own approach.

The first area of potential disagreement concerns Weber's systematic and cross-thematic discussion of 'impersonality'. I take this to be his most significant contribution to the study of capitalism. It receives little if any attention in the main books on Weberian theory to have appeared in the last decade – Swedberg (1998), Turner (2000), and Camic *et al.* (2005). This is surprising when one considers that throughout *Economy and Society* Weber emphasizes the overriding significance of factors of impersonality at critical points in his analysis of markets, law, administration, and representation, and that he employs this concept, along with the concept of 'rationality', to denote the *highest* levels of development of economies and institutions. Although Swedberg (1998: 44, 111) discusses impersonality and depersonalization in passing, he treats them as problematic trends running counter to morals, ethics, and charity. In secondary literature it has also long been usual to equate Weber's concept of impersonality negatively with a constrictive 'iron cage' of social relationships in the modern world (Sayer 1991). One of my aims in this book is to demonstrate beyond reasonable doubt – on the evidence of the existing translations of his work – that Weber regarded depersonalization as a civilizing force; one that is potentially recognizable by citizens, rulers, and market actors alike, and which underlies the evolution of capitalist ethics and laws. Institutional depersonalization seems to be a normative force that can free societies from unjust economic and political relationships.

The second example of conflict with conventional interpretations of Weber relates to my effort to identify the Weberian 'sequence' of capitalist transition – markets to law, law to bureaucracy, and bureaucracy to democracy. The only equivalent effort I am aware of to tease out a developmental sequence from Weber's writings on capitalism is by Randall Collins (1986: 19–44). He claims to find a 'causal chain' of 'institutional preconditions for capitalism' that 'fell into place for the first time' in Europe during the Middle Ages. However, this 'institutional complex' is not well defined – it is not sufficiently precise. It consists, according to Collins, of the 'destruction of the obstacles to the free movement or economic transfer of labour, land, and goods' and the 'creation of the institutional supports for large-scale markets' such as 'property, law, and finance', 'economic ethics', a 'bureaucratic state', and 'citizenship rights' (ibid.: 26–31). Some of the 'institutions' that Collins describes are, in fact, indistinguishable from the *economic* presuppositions of capitalism (for example, he speaks of private enterprise and its methods of accounting as 'institutional').

Moreover, if there is any clear direction in Collins's causal chain of capitalism it seems to work in reverse. He writes of 'a combination of the bureaucratic state with political citizenship, *resulting in* a calculable legal system; as well as a methodical, nondualistic economic ethic' (ibid.: 47). This neglects the possibility that the legal system and the *preceding* economic ethic may be preconditions of the particular *type* of bureaucracy that Weber linked to capitalism. The causal process, i.e. the nature and cause of reciprocal effects between institutions, is nowhere clearly identified. The normative-procedural dimensions of intra-institutional and inter-institutional processes are, likewise, altogether missing from Collins's analysis. Finally, although he rightly stresses Weber's emphasis on 'the pattern of relations among the various factors' of capitalist transition, Collins asserts, misleadingly in my view, that the 'series of combinations of conditions had to occur together' (ibid.: 34–5). My attempt to define the Weberian categories of institution was summarized in Chapter 1. In this and later chapters I will suggest a new way of conceptualizing the dynamic elements of the unfolding causal sequence.

On the other hand, my own interpretation as well as that of Collins could fall foul of a strong and well-founded current in Weberian theory that rejects all explanations suggesting a predominance of 'universal laws' or 'causal chains'. Roth argues that Weber's 'developmental scheme' explores 'logical states or conditions' and 'left the actual historical sequences open' (Roth 1978: xxxv–lv). Roth goes on to say, 'in the absence of a reductionist one-factor scheme and of historical "one-way streets", the relationship of economy, society and polity became for Weber a multi-faceted set of problems'. Kalberg (1994: 144–5) expands on this theme, arguing that Weber rejected a strongly causal 'world formula' of modernization. A theory of causal chains, says Kalberg, risks obscuring Weber's distinctions between 'facilitating' and 'necessary' causal forces. It may get in the way of explaining how 'configurations of forces *interact* in a dynamic fashion' to influence development outcomes, and might ignore the 'conjunctural' and 'contextual' factors that prevent the crystallization of causal forces (ibid.: 143–92).

These are useful warnings in the present context, though they are probably unduly restrictive. There are alternative ways of reading Weber in relation to themes such as 'universality' and 'sequencing'. The greatest difficulty may lie only in how the theoretical principles are applied. For example, the lists of 'necessary' forces suggested by Kalberg (ibid.: *passim*) are no more persuasive than the ones proposed by Collins. Kalberg includes under this category conditions that can be *outcomes* of capitalism or characteristics that are not *unique* to capitalism, such as technology and science, social classes, rational rulership, money, profit making, and markets. On my reckoning, all of these can be present in precapitalist societies for long periods of time. At best they only *facilitate* capitalist transition. Kalberg neglects other factors that are *necessary* for capitalism.

As can be surmised from this brief review of the secondary literature, conflicting views on matters of fundamental importance to perceptions of capitalism give reason to look again at Weber. Some of Weber's true meaning may be lost in the translation of his work. Nevertheless, the assembly of words in the English-language books that bear his name, which I will refer to in the following pages, conjure up a vision of capitalism that is unique, neglected, and helpful in explaining contemporary capitalist transitions.

Because this book focuses on contemporary capitalist transitions, my approach aims for *policy* relevance. The institutional conditions of capitalism are sufficiently small in number to be understood by policymakers. If the institutional conditions of transition are not kept to a manageable minimum, developing countries will be discouraged from trying to emulate them. In addition, the development sequence that I detect in Weber's writings requires an explanation of necessary and logical interactions between institutionally specific spheres. Weber does not depict a macrolevel developmental scheme of linear proportions. History has not worked in this way. Yet as the following chapters aim to show, it is possible to identify logical relationships between institutions that have equivalent reciprocal functions, e.g. between market expansion and the need for ethics, between market ethics and the need for impersonal law, between law and the need for impersonal bureaucracy, and between bureaucracy and the need for impersonal democracy. Taking suitable care, it is possible to combine these partial insights in a proposal for universal policy sequences.

None of the causal interrelationships are simple. Nevertheless, theory and history combine in Weber's writings to suggest important policy lessons for the present. Intentionally or not, Weber revealed his own preferences about the relative priorities among conditions of capitalism. Ideally, changes in all four spheres would occur together and 'act jointly' to produce capitalist outcomes. In reality, the surrounding social environment generally imposes too many constraints on the agents of change for action to occur simultaneously on all fronts. So it is advisable to think about breaking the process up into stages that reflect the relative strengths and priorities of discrete causal forces. These can justifiably be called 'universal' prescriptions if their logic is persuasive enough and sufficiently *neutral* to apply more or less *uniformly* in almost all the contemporary contexts of capitalist transition.

Weber usually avoided explicit prescriptions for policies that 'ought' to be pursued, emphasizing instead that the analysis of economic or political life is one thing, but value judgements another. Nevertheless, a normative-constructivist approach to institutional change clearly can be reconciled with his theories and studies of European states during the original capitalist transitions. Although Weber dealt mainly with capitalism's evolution over the long span of history, his analysis of state functions offers a practical and remarkably contemporary viewpoint, which is compatible with the idea that concerted action during compressed policy sequences will produce capitalist outcomes. Developing-country officials today could implement changes that are observed or inferred in Weber's theories. They could simulate the sequences of the original European transitions during discrete policy regimes of limited duration, and build the institutions more rapidly.

Parametric state

This chapter examines the state-centred dynamics of capitalist transition. *Long*-run capitalist evolution is the subject of theorizing about incrementally adaptive institutions responding to spontaneous and dispersed societal pressures that are rarely strong enough to cause significant departures from societal equilibrium. *Short*-run capitalist transition, on the other hand, is regarded here as a discontinuous disequilibrium process, where means to the end necessarily depend on utilizing technical instruments of the state. Either path can arrive at capitalism in the end. Yet, it is incumbent upon social science to examine how capitalist society can be constructed in the present.

In this regard the role of the state is indispensable. It is the only association in society with the legitimate authority to sanction and enforce institutional reforms. Although aspiring capitalist states often take on roles that they are not at all well equipped for and would be performed much better by markets or by civil society, it is difficult to imagine how a fully system-wide capitalist transition could be pursued without the interventions of a strong developmental state. The vision presented in Chapter 1 was of capitalism as a procedural system of institutional subsystems. It should in theory be possible to emulate and construct each of the subsystems during one policy regime, and to weave reformed sub-systems together within the time-span of one generation.

Two factors that must be examined are the policy priorities of the state during capitalist transitions and the qualities of a developmental state. The state establishes the policy priorities. Good policies have to be sustainable policies, and will always reflect volitional and cognitive strengths of policymakers. However, there is an incommensurability or tension between the 'priorities' and the 'strengths'. A strong developmental state would ideally undertake several tasks of institutional reform simultaneously rather than one at a time. Once the transition to capitalism is underway, the state has enough to do defending the emerging impersonal regulatory order against counter-pressures from interest groups. A strong developmental state is undeviating in maintaining its essential minimum functions, and in resisting pressures to indulge particularistic demands of politics, profit, and welfare. The policy priorities, on the other hand, need to be sequenced only because state strength is, in practice, very rare in developing societies. If the developing states were 'strong' at the outset, policy sequencing would be unnecessary. Therefore, the policy sequence examined in this book can be viewed, in effect, as a mechanism for building state strength.

In order to explain the sources of state strength we must first distinguish the transitional state from the modern state. What are core characteristics and roles of a modern state? Must the priorities and qualities of a 'transitional state' be different? What is the nature of the capitalist state, and what do precapitalist states have to 'do' to become capitalist? These questions return us to the simple typology of precapitalist and capitalist societies discussed in Chapter 1. How does a precapitalist society move to a condition that is closer to the evolved capitalism found in some advanced societies? The Weberian perspective developed in this chapter suggests that transitional states should aim, from the outset, for *parametric* competencies. A contemporary conceptualization of the transitional state, one which is compatible with Weber's writing, regards the state as either parametric or *pervasive* depending on the *intensities* of its actions and the *proximities* of contact among economic actors and institutional actors.

I borrow these terms from Gordon White (1984), who wrote about a transition from 'pervasive' to 'parametric' methods of regulating industrial development in third-world socialist countries. Early stages of industrialization seemed to justify

> an overall planning framework, selective regulation of external economic ties, decisive action to influence the generation of savings and allocation of productive investments, direct management of key nascent industrial sectors, [and] systematic political mobilization of support for economic programmes and redistribution.
>
> (ibid.: 116)

Constraints on the efficiency of pervasive states were eventually recognized in the 1980s. Economic power partially devolved to non-state actors, as states retreated to more parametric functions. Decision making decentralized to local administrative and production units. There was a move away from administrative, political, or moral incentives, and towards material and economic incentives. Increasingly, the price mechanism guided economic allocations.

An equivalent distinction exists at the other end of the spectrum in developed market economies where policymakers have devised regulatory strategies for privatization and market liberalization (Kay and Vickers 1988). 'Structural regulation', which resembles parametric state action, is concerned with the initial structure of markets and comprehensive codes of conduct. A parametric regime minimizes state intervention and reduces the need for direct interaction between state regulators and businesses. Structural regulation aims to remove incentives and opportunities for undesirable behaviour. In contrast, 'conduct regulation', which more resembles pervasive state action, involves the piecemeal supervision of businesses, the issuing and enforcement of directives, a layered framework of detailed rules for market conduct, and bureaucratic procedures designed to monitor business behaviour. Frequent and close contact between firms and state officials facilitates interest-group pressure, which structural regulation is designed to minimize.

These are broad ideal types, and, in reality, the necessary regulation may fall between the two. This might be the case, for example, when structural-parametric regulation requires that public regulators should have access to market data collected by private companies in order for the regulator to make decisions about appropriate behavioural codes. This may require some intrusive supervision and monitoring, and complete transparency on the part of companies. The caveat, however, is that public regulators do not set and monitor performance targets with respect, for example, to a firm's growth, product types, or export achievements as a condition of subsidies or shelter from competition. Nor is government regulation used to create incentives for private firms to contribute to state-defined sociopolitical restructuring or distributional outcomes such as easy credit for property purchases. Rather, structural-parametric regulation is designed to ensure that market operations meet universal rule criteria relating to public safety, security against generalized risks, promotion of competition and honesty, and prevention of fraud. The parametric state focuses its limited resources on non-discriminatory regulation.

The term 'parametric', as employed here, draws on the non-mathematical meaning of 'parameter', defined as 'a constant element or factor serving as a limit or boundary' (*Oxford English Reference Dictionary*). It follows then, that the parametric state is formally delimited. The state operates at the boundaries of the social system. It regulates economic, social, and political life at arm's length. As will be seen, the legal system is the primary mechanism of boundary maintenance. A pervasive state, in contrast, is an activist or *dirigiste* state. The ideal Weberian developmental state is a parametric state, whose emergence is both the cause and consequence of institutional reforms that cultivate impersonal procedural norms in the economy and in state organizations. Unlike the pervasive state, the parametric state aims to avoid taking discretionary action to achieve distributive outcomes in social or political life, or – what is often the same thing – to achieve particular production and consumption outcomes in economic life. In economic policy, for example, pervasive states are routinely discriminatory towards firms and sectors, whereas the parametric state focuses on non-discretionary regulatory policy. A pervasive state may attempt to administer an economy by central planning and political mobilization, promotion and protection of selected production units, or the mobilization of private savings and investments. Parametric states leave most market decisions to enterprises. Resource allocation is mainly by means of the price mechanism. The ideal state's role is to design and enforce universal rules for the safe and proper structure *and* conduct of competitive economic action. By and large, it does not create incentives for industry and finance to mix business activity with the promotion of social or political goals that benefit specific groups of the population rather than the whole population.

Ideal characteristics of the parametric state relate to its procedures, which should be formal, impersonal, calculable, predictable, unambiguous, and continuous. Because it is relatively unfettered by direct concrete pressure from substantive interests, state policy *at the boundary* can be more adaptive and flexible. At the boundary, the state is more likely to be responsive both to society and the external world. The impersonal procedural norm is the constant element that establishes the parameters of an ideal state's scope of action. In a long historical perspective, the creation of state parameters was a vital step in the emergence of modern states. Weber showed why the precapitalist state, where roles and positions are a function of 'personal' and 'discretionary' rather than 'impersonal interests', is typically characterized by competition among public offices for private incomes or status-related compensations that can be derived from public administration – 'each office has some substantive purpose and task, but its *boundaries* are frequently indeterminate' (Weber 1978: 1029). The indeterminacy of state boundaries is a result of arbitrary demands made by officials for compensation. Yet, the indeterminacy of claims made upon the state by groups within it creates 'a strong incentive for the gradual *delimitation* of administrative jurisdictions'. The process of delimitation acquires greater force under pressure from the demands of broad-based non-state groups that have an interest in the type of public administration that is formal, impersonal, and calculable.

State and economy

Weber offered a general outline of the minimalist roles of the parametric state. Aside from a duty to defend its territory against attack by outside powers, the primary functions of the modern state are *enactment, administration, and enforcement of laws*. Secondary functions are *monetary and fiscal policy*, and management of *natural monopoly services*. This is not the description of the ideal state that is commonly sought after. There is a tendency, Weber observed, for people to value the 'prestige of the state' so highly that they hold out 'the ideal of an expansive state' as an ultimate political end. However, 'there are certain things which the state cannot do' (1949: 46–7). The state is often valued for its own sake when in reality it is only an instrument for the pursuit of values or interests. Weber said that states are better at *facilitating* than *creating* outcomes. Their greatest strength is the capacity to 'eliminate obstacles' rather than to find solutions:

> In the sphere of value-judgements … it is possible to defend quite meaningfully the view that the power of the state should be increased in order to strengthen its power to eliminate obstacles, while maintaining that the state itself has no intrinsic value, that it is a purely technical instrument for the realization of other values from which alone it derives its value, and that it can retain this value only as long as it does not seek to transcend this merely auxiliary status.
>
> (Weber 1949: 47)

The state is uniquely able to facilitate capitalist transitions because, to quote Weber's famous phrase, it is the only entity able to claim 'the monopoly of the legitimate use of physical force within a given territory' (1947: 78). In fact, the modern state rarely has to resort to violence. It is generally more successful when it employs 'legal compulsion' to achieve its ends (Weber 1978: 64–5). There is no doubt, on the other hand, that a state is by far the most powerful instrument for pursuing *any* goal, regardless of whether the goal benefits the nation. Political organizations that rule through the implicit threat of force can have as their objective the defence of all sorts of economic groups and values that are not compatible with capitalism (ibid.: 901–2). The state can attempt many things. The important questions are whether it can succeed, and whether the attempt was wise. For example, once there exists an 'all-embracing economic community of nations', a nation's interest may not coincide with all of the various national interests (Weber 1994: 16). In an era of globalization, in other words, not all state expressions of interests will be good for the nation. Because the state has so much power, it is important to understand how it may be used instrumentally to serve economic interests. Weber (1978: 193–4) discusses six ways in which a state's impact on the economic system has consequences for the constellations of interests. They can be summarized as follows:

1   States favour national interests as providers of goods and services;
2   States support substantive interests when regulating foreign trade;
3   States regulate economic activity within their territory;
4   Dominant attitudes towards different types of economic activity, such as profit making, reflect the sociopolitical make-up of the state;
5   Within the state, authorities compete for power and largesse on behalf of their own departments;
6   The way a state finances itself shapes the economy and the state itself.

State action can benefit economic interests even when – in terms of criteria that accord with the ideal type – it should not do so. Although Weber was often reticent about declaring his own policy preferences, there is no doubt that he strongly opposed statist economic policy, which in his day was most closely associated with the sustentation of the 'robber capitalists' of the European *rentier* economies and of the political classes that benefit in *rentier* economies. Weber was, at heart, an economic liberal, whose analyses of the economic history of mercantilism recall Adam Smith, and whose monetary theory and critique of economic planning recall Ludwig von Mises. In his political writings, Weber (1994) attacked activist strategies, whether socialist, corporatist, populist, or communitarian. He advised transitional countries against 'taking the economy into social control'. He warned against all programs that 'promote the "ethical" equalization of life-chances as the economic practice and outlook of the masses rather than the economic selection of those who are commercially most effective'. He sought the eradication of bureaucratic centralism. He advocated 'working to spread the old, fundamental, individualist notion of inalienable human rights'. He also anticipated the 'powerful influx of Western ideas', which would help to break down anti-capitalist conservatism in the transitional societies (ibid.: 59–74).

An early lecture written in 1895 and titled 'Nation State and Economic Policy' was Weber's (1994) most openly political pronouncement on state policy. It was, to his later regret, 'brutally' nationalistic (Swedberg 1998: 183). In fact, the lecture can be read as a subtle rejection of popular nationalistic opinion about state functions. Economic nationalism, argued Weber, need not take the form of direct interventions in the economy. Aspiring capitalist groups would be better off *without* the protection of the state. They can become powerful by their 'emancipatory' economic struggles, and then develop the political maturity to 'assume the direction of the state', or to persuade it to broadly serve their interests. Every nation's destiny lies in the power of the state, and the policies that express its power. The fact that the state is the bearer of ultimate power also means it can potentially decide matters of economic policy on its own initiative, such as 'the questions of whether, and how far, the state should intervene in economic life, or whether and when it is better for it to free the economic forces of the nation from their fetters and to tear down the barriers in the way of their autonomous development' (Weber 1994: 17). All that he subsequently wrote on the matter suggests that Weber thought it better for the state to 'free' economic forces. The interesting question is *how* this should happen. As we will see, Weber's opinion seems to have been that a transitional state – equivalent, say, to Germany or Russia in the early 1900s – should begin in a manner commensurate with its eventual existence as a capitalist state. The state should get its boundaries and procedures right from the outset.

Formality of state

Weber wrote extensively about the long evolution of the modern state, and its emergence under pressure from commercial and political interests. His analysis of the characteristics of effective state systems is a useful starting point for understanding the contemporary potential for transitional states to emulate modern states in the short run. It helps that Weber achieved his vision of the ideal state in large part by explaining precapitalist states that do not function well. By comparing modern and premodern states it is possible to discover what the reform priorities of modernizing societies should be. In this section I look for relevant lessons in Weber's description of the 'primary formal characteristics of the modern state'. First:

> [The state] possesses an administrative and legal order subject to change by legislation, to which the organized activities of the administrative staff, which are also controlled by regulations, are oriented. This system of order claims binding authority, not only over the members of the state [and] the citizens ... but also to a very large extent over all action taking place in the area of its jurisdiction. It is thus a compulsory organization with a territorial basis.
>
> (Weber 1978: 56)

As discussed in Chapter 1, the modern Weberian state comprises three formal institutional spheres – law, administration, and representation. These terms refer to a legal subsystem (including judges who preside over a court and make or interpret laws), an administrative subsystem (bureaucratic agencies of the state, which participate in policy design but mainly implement policies, and which can also be the enforcers of laws), and a representative political subsystem (the peak collegial mechanisms for selecting political leaders and for debating and approving public policy). The fluid interactivity of law, administration, and political representation in capitalist societies indicates that effective state action necessarily involves overlapping domain jurisdictions. Each sphere has a function of supervision, implementation, enforcement, or legitimation in relation to each of the other spheres. A few broad examples will suffice: Law regulates the economy, but also public administration and politics. Politics defines the operational modes of law and administration. Political or legal initiatives need to be properly interpreted, applied, and enforced by state administrative agencies. For these reasons, all domains of state action must share a common procedural norm. Since the formal and impersonal procedures of the state are vitally important to capitalism, law has a special role to play in regulating the procedural norms of other state spheres. The only way that bureaucracy and political representation *become* modern is by adopting modern *legal* procedural norms.

Legal standing is the *first* principle of the modern state. Thus, the legal characteristic of the capitalist state is that there is a 'fusion' of law-making and law-finding organizations 'into the one compulsory association of the state, now claiming to be the sole source of all legitimate law' (ibid.: 653, 666). Regardless of whether a modern society practises common law or civil law, it is still the elected political representatives in parliament, or the equivalent peak collegial body, who pass legislation and regulate the appointment of senior legal officers.

Courts make or find laws through legal adjudication in response to the demands of plaintiffs. Official bodies or public agencies carry and administer law. Legal scholars point out that 'law is the product of "government" in the broadest sense' (Friedman 2002: 177). However, it can also be said that laws determine the character of government. In Weber's words, 'the limitations on the power of the state by law and vested rights create those restraints upon its freedom of action to which it must adjust itself' (Weber 1978: 644). Governments pursue political objectives, and their laws are the outcome of tumultuous political struggles. Nevertheless, modern polities must have legal standing in order to legitimate their rule.

The separation between public and private law is also relevant to understanding the modern state. Weber emphasizes the difference between *public* law, i.e. legal norms or instructions of the state regulating its own actions and its own duties with respect to the manner in which it pursues its goals, and *private* law 'issuing from the state', which regulates how non-state actors can conduct themselves in relation to each other (ibid.: 641). Laws emanating from the state are regarded as legitimate by all those who lead their lives outside the state. The modern state itself is defined in terms of

> factually and legally regulated relationships, partly unique and partly recurrent in character, all bound together by an idea, namely the belief in the actual or normative validity of rules and of the authority relationships of some human beings towards others.
>
> (Weber 1949: 99)

The situation was quite different in the patrimonial state, 'when all law, all jurisdictions, and particularly all powers of exercising authority were personal privilege, such as, especially, the prerogatives of the head of the state' (Weber 1978: 643). Premodern states lack the functional 'separation of the private and the official sphere'. Aside from ill-defined cultural constraints upon the scope of state action, the precapitalist exercise of official power remains 'entirely discretionary' (ibid.: 1028–9). Officials compete for the favour of their superiors, and to establish independent centres of power or to finance their own retinues of clients. Whereas the modern state operates through the abstract routines of impersonal regulation, in the patrimonial state concrete and interpersonal relationships are decisive in the determination of policy.

> [The] entire system of public norms of the patrimonial state ... lacks the objective norms of the bureaucratic state and its 'matter-of-factness' which is oriented toward impersonal purposes. The office and the exercise of public authority serve the ruler and the official on which the office was bestowed, they do not serve impersonal purposes.
>
> (ibid.: 1031)

Weber argued that those who have most to fear from a formal institutional order are demagogues and authoritarians whose power and influence depends on their ability to provision individuals and groups discretionally with substantive goods, services, and privileges. If they are not formally constrained these rulers can channel benefits, garner loyalty, and elicit actions by arbitrary and particularistic means (ibid.: 811–13). A goal of modernizing societies, then, is to establish 'the dominance of a spirit of *formalistic impersonality*', which effectively 'diminishes the dependency of the individual upon the grace and power of the authorities' (ibid.: 225–6, 812). Formal 'equality of treatment' has appealed to economic and political interest groups that see benefit for themselves in organizational continuity, institutionalized rights, and a calculable legal-administrative order. Even if regulations are enacted expressly for the purpose of pursuing utilitarian interests within the state or with the support of the state, the very formalism of regulatory procedures reduces state dysfunction by standardizing all of the behavioural possibilities (ibid.: 226). Formalism is a prerequisite for impersonal rule.

> the bureaucratization of the state and of law in general ... [presupposes] the conceptual separation of the 'state', as an abstract bearer of sovereign prerogatives and the creator of legal norms, from all personal authority of individuals ... [It] was left to the complete depersonalization of administrative management by bureaucracy and the rational systematization of law to realize the separation of the public and the private sphere fully and in principle.
>
> (ibid.: 998)

In short, the formalism of the state relates both to the fusion of legal-administrative bodies and the separation of public from private legal orders. Today, the depersonalization of state organizations is manifested most visibly in state procedural policies, which in practice are constructible rule mechanisms for decision making and for recruitment processes. These are examined in the next section.

Ideal procedural norms

In the premodern state, administrative power is obtained through outright purchase, privilege, patronage, personal connections, personal characteristics, social status, or the rendering of political services. The modern impersonal state, in contrast, formalizes three procedural rules for the acquisition and management of power:

1   Impersonal procedures are followed when deciding who will be employed by the state, and what functions and responsibilities they will have;
2   Impersonal rules of conduct regulate the internal governance of state agencies;
3   Impersonal procedures govern the state's relations with non-state groups.

The 'disciplined mechanism' of the modern state results from the 'purely impersonal character of the office' (Weber 1978: 968). Recruitment criteria include formal qualifications that demonstrate technical expertise or competence acquired through training, examination, and specialization – 'only persons who qualify under general rules are employed' (ibid.: 956). The formality of the recruitment process with its stress on technical knowledge has a 'levelling', i.e. equalitarian, effect within state administrations (ibid.: 225). The official is not able to claim a right to own the office or to derive private income from it. In the modern state, there is a definite separation between the official's public and private life. The incentive system comprises salaries and promotions, which, in effect, are 'mechanical' and therefore calculable procedures (ibid.: 963).

Modern bureaucracy is a form of 'domination through knowledge', and, as such, it is a source of 'extraordinary power' (ibid.: 225). Yet, if the right to hold office by virtue of educational qualifications were to become just another source of group closure within bureaucracies, the flexibility and efficiency of the state would be diminished. So, it is essential that officials learn a sense of duty, and can see the advantages – in terms of formal benefits such as promotion – of impersonal norms of conduct. A key to this process is 'formal equality of treatment' for all officials (ibid.: 225). In procedural terms, officials are demarcated from one another by their assigned duties, administrative powers, specialization, and objective expertise. 'Regular disciplinary procedures' and the elimination of 'arbitrary disposition' in relationships between the different ranks of administration function to formalize the 'right to the office' (ibid.: 1000).

The state's internal rules of conduct are stable. Officials work within an unambiguous structure of 'general rules' (ibid.: 958). Friction and emotion in the conduct of official business is minimized (ibid.: 225). Primary relationships are with 'the office' and its 'impersonal and functional purposes' (ibid.: 959). Supervision systems, grievance procedures, and the process of maintaining formal records sustain the impersonal order, and reinforce the official's *interest* in a sense of duty. Within the state, authority is constrained by rules about means of compulsion that can be employed to achieve goals. Hierarchical powers of command are well developed, so those who control the machinery of the state can be confident of dominating by virtue of their legal authority. Each official is only 'a small cog in a ceaselessly moving mechanism', which they can neither start nor stop. The official will snap back into gear after a disturbance to this mechanism regardless of extraneous economic or ideological factors (ibid.: 988). There develops 'an attitude set on habitual virtuosity in the mastery of single yet methodically integrated functions' (ibid.). If it has these characteristics, the bureaucracy is, in technical terms, 'the most rational known means of exercising authority over human beings' (ibid.: 223).

In its *external relations* with economic and political interests, the modern state acts in a similar manner. It maintains its 'horror of privilege', its 'demand for equality before the law', and its 'principled rejection of doing business "from case to case"' (ibid.: 983). The legally regulated form of modern bureaucracy is not 'administration in the sense of free decision from case to case', which gives rise to privilege as distinct from 'general norms' (ibid.: 654). A hallmark of the modern state is 'bureaucratic impartiality', the 'abstract validity of one objective law for all' (ibid.: 1041).

The principal force for institutional change in the transition from precapitalist to modern administration is the emerging market order. 'Today', said Weber, 'it is primarily the capitalist market economy which demands that the official business of public administration be discharged precisely, unambiguously, continuously, and with as much speed as possible' (ibid.: 974). Economic development generates 'an urgent need for stable, strict, intensive, and calculable administration' (ibid.: 224). The state's 'political and procedural predictability [is] indispensable for capitalist development' (ibid.: 1095). It is evident, therefore, that capitalism's need for an impersonal state is one and the same thing as the need for a *calculable* state. It can also be observed that the procedural norms of the parametric state are congruent with the formal procedural norms that apply to the regulation of modern economies (ibid.: 162). Calculable and formal state administration is a requirement for effective profit making in capitalist societies. Market freedom would not be possible without a legal order that guarantees contract and property rights.

Weber's description of state administration as 'machinery' is sometimes misinterpreted to mean that formal state routines are inflexible. Yet state machinery could not operate without *creativity* on the part of the officials. Public work is not very different from work in a private office. In one the worker is separated from the means of production and in the other from the means of administration. Whether in government or private enterprise, however, some artistry is expected of even the lowest employee.

> Independent decision-making and imaginative organizational capabilities in matters of detail are usually also demanded of the bureaucrat, and very often expected even in larger matters. The idea that the bureaucrat is absorbed in subaltern routine and that only the 'director' performs the interesting, intellectually demanding tasks is a preconceived notion of the literati and only possible in a country that has no insight into the manner in which its affairs and the work of its officialdom are conducted.
>
> (ibid.: 1404)

Nor is the modern state rule-bound by 'red tape' (ibid.: 223). Rules for compliance with a bureaucratic order are 'intellectually analyzable rules', which are established for specific purposes (ibid.: 244). They are 'not sacred' and unchanging rules (ibid.: 1117). In fact, the more underdeveloped the state is, the more likely that the citizenry and the bureaucrat will be wrapped up in red tape. A modern state may perform well with just a few good rules. In a modern state, says Weber, the only absolutely universal norm of conduct is that the 'creative administration' conforms to objective criteria and does not constitute 'free, arbitrary action and discretion' or 'personally motivated favour and valuation' (ibid.: 979).

In some respects, the 'moving spirit' of modern administrators is unlike that of politicians, entrepreneurs, or lawyers (ibid.: 1403). Officials must 'remain outside the realm of the struggle for power', which is the 'lifeblood of the politician [and] the entrepreneur'. Officials seek office 'for the sake of salary and rank' rather than for the powers it will confer (ibid.: 1411). The official can express opinions on the rights and wrongs of a decision, but will not resign as might a politician who disagrees with his colleagues, and will not go to court as might an entrepreneur who is refused a government authorization (ibid.: 1404). The motive of the civil servant also differs from the lawyer who 'has been taught to fight for, and effectively represent, a given cause' (ibid.: 1427). Unlike politicians, state administrators must treat individuals and groups in society as *bearers* of rights that were created by politicians and legal professionals. Their task is to administer these rights and assist in the enforcement of law (ibid.: 644–7). The roles of the vast majority of the civil servants in a modern state are limited to 'technical affairs' of policy interpretation as opposed to policy design (ibid.: 1419).

The 'institutional order' of the modern state, says Weber, is an uneven 'product of evolution' (ibid.: 905). In developing countries today the shell or façade of the bureaucratic state, with its organizational hierarchies and departments, and with its legal-administrative functions, already exists. What it lacks is the kind of formal procedural impersonality that Weber described. The precapitalist state is not unambiguous, stable, calculable, or speedy in its responses to changes in the environment, or impartial in its relations with non-state groups. If Weber's portrayal of the modern state is accepted, then it is clear that one of the core design and construction tasks facing precapitalist states today is the systematic enforcement of the impersonal procedural norm in public administration. Only when it acquires a 'rational character with rules, means-ends calculus, and matter-of-factness predominating', Weber suggests, will a state administration be able to achieve the kinds of 'revolutionary results' that in the past have 'destroyed' precapitalist structures (ibid.: 1002).

Legal regulatory function

Enforcement of the impersonal procedural norm should have the automatic effect of limiting the tasks the state could undertake according to its own rules. Impersonal norms delimit the functions of the state because state roles that involve case-by-case discretion by public officials or preferential treatment towards sectors of society could not be maintained without jeopardizing the procedural commitment to formality, impartiality, and relative predictability of state action. Discretionary industrial or welfare policies conflict with non-discretionary legal and administrative regulations. Basic state functions, according to Weber, are the maintenance of order, defence, law making, monetary and fiscal policy, and services that private groups cannot or do not provide. The terms Weber employed when describing the character of modern systems of law or administration – e.g. 'calculable', 'matter-of-fact', and 'unambiguous' – refer to how a state organization should operate when it performs a limited number of functions. Modern bureaucracy develops through the 'intensive and qualitative expansion of the administrative tasks' rather than 'their extensive and quantitative increase' (ibid.: 971).

Levels of bureaucratization have been influenced in different societies by many factors, including the requirement for standing armies to defend land frontiers, the need to manage scarce natural resources, and the sheer 'complexity of civilization' (ibid.: 969–73). The varying intensity of administration displayed by states reflects the tasks deemed necessary 'by the state apparatus for continuous management and discharge in its own establishment' (ibid.: 972). Less justifiable reasons for bureaucratization have included 'the manifold tasks of social welfare policies which are either saddled upon the modern state by interest groups or which the state usurps for reasons of power or for ideological motives' (ibid.: 972–3).

In Weber's view, service functions of the state, such as economic and welfare policies and the provision of infrastructure, are *secondary* functions. In contrast, a state's *primary* legal-regulatory function is to promote and then defend universal 'interests' and universal 'rights'. In theory, modern market economies could do without state legal guaranties if customs, conventions, and the private interests of market participants were all strongly and systematically supportive of contractual obligations and property rights. In reality, this is not possible – 'an economic system, especially of the modern type, could certainly not exist without a legal order with very special features which could not develop except in the frame of a public legal order' (ibid.: 336). Market interests recognize this too.

> Among those groups who favour formal justice we must include all those political and economic interest groups to whom the stability and predictability of the legal procedure are of very great importance, i.e. particularly rational, economic, and political organizations intended to have a permanent character. Above all, those in possession of economic power look upon a formal rational administration of justice as a guarantee of 'freedom'.
>
> (ibid.: 813)

Legality, as noted earlier, legitimates the state's domination over economic life. Weber recognized three principles for the legitimation of domination (ibid.: 215–16, 954). The first is personal authority wielded by an individual who displays skilled leadership, heroism, and charisma. The second is personal authority grounded in tradition, which demands obedience to a person whose position is sanctioned by age-old customs of leadership. The third – modern – form is authority by virtue of formal legal authority in the context of an 'established impersonal order', where 'obedience' is 'given to the *norms* rather than to the *person*'. In all three cases the form of authority implies the existence of 'an interest (based on ulterior motives or genuine acceptance) in obedience' (ibid.: 212).

But customs, material advantages, or ideals are not sufficient for maintaining state rule. A belief in the *legitimacy* of domination is also required. Weber argued that in modern society the only valid forms of legitimacy are binding and impersonal norms, which are 'consciously made' and correctly formalized in law (ibid.: 37, 954). A condition of legal-administrative legitimacy is that positions within the state uphold 'impersonal interests', which 'endeavour to provide legal guarantees for the ruled', as opposed to 'personal rights', which uphold traditional discretionary privileges and demands for 'compensation' (ibid.: 1029). An institutional framework for social or economic action can be deemed legitimate if people have faith in its dependability and rightness, i.e. because institutional behaviour conforms to valid moral criteria of provisioning *as well as* to legal regulation.

A practical problem of legitimation that is always apparent in economic life relates to 'privileges'. In most situations, privileges are negative and in conflict with capitalism. Negative privileges include, in particular, the political or economic privileges granted by patrimonial rulers to clients in return for loyalty, services, or remittances. Also included are economic monopolies or exclusionary advantages upheld by the state for 'legally privileged groups' (ibid.: 342). Weber referred to this situation, which many modern economists call 'rent seeking', as one that arises if an 'economic or social monopoly is guaranteed, or, conversely, when privileged status groups or monopolized groups are completely or partly exempt' (ibid.: 349–50). Thus:

> It is quite possible that a private individual by skillfully taking advantage of the given circumstances and of personal relations, obtains a *privileged* position which offers him nearly unlimited acquisitive opportunities. But a capitalist economic system is obviously greatly handicapped by these factors.
>
> (ibid.: 1095)

Economic entrepreneurs, in the aggregate and in the long run, have fought against negative privileges since the earliest days of capitalism. They have done so purely out of recognition that such privilege would not guarantee their present and future interests.

> [They] had to demand an unambiguous and clear legal system, that would be free of irrational administrative arbitrariness as well as of irrational disturbance by concrete *privileges*, that would also offer firm guarantees of the legally binding character of contracts, and that, in consequence of all these features, would function in a calculable way.
>
> (ibid.: 847)

On the other hand, Weber sometimes used the term 'privilege' differently, as a right that is compatible with capitalism. It is important to understand the meaning of this second usage in order not to confuse it with the first. During the original transitions to capitalism there first emerged rights that may be regarded in purely legal terms as 'privileges'. Positive privileges permit economic autonomy or a universal freedom and increase the probability of an individual having power of control over objects and persons that are relevant to an action, such as an economic transaction (ibid.: 667–8). Once these rights acquire legal certainty as enforceable state regulations they become a 'legally guaranteed expectation' or an administrative 'reflex' ensuring their durability. Positive privileges constitute two core liberties associated with competitive economic action.

> Privileges are of two main kinds: The *first* is constituted by the so-called freedoms, i.e. situations of simple protection against certain types of interference by third parties, especially state officials, within the sphere of legally permitted conduct; instances are freedom of movement, freedom of conscience, or freedom of disposition over property. The *second* type of privilege is that which grants to an individual autonomy to regulate his relations with others by his own transactions. Freedom of contract, for example, exists exactly to the extent to which such autonomy is recognized by the legal order.
>
> (ibid.: 668)

Rules about freedom and autonomy, especially the universalistic rights of property and contract, are ideal-type *parametric* rules of the modern liberal state. They maximize freedoms within the boundaries of legally permitted conduct, and they minimize the red tape and meddling associated with bureaucratic regulation. At the same time they aim for universal objectives that even the most rule-bound pervasive state order would also claim for itself, notably economic development and a peaceful social order.

Yet, the rules of freedom and autonomy identified by Weber in these passages are distinctive in one vital respect. In contrast to the discriminatory or discretionary activist state that uses its legal-administrative powers directly to *prescribe* or *prohibit* selected economic and political activities, the non-discriminatory state – in a perfectly ideal form – uses its powers only to *permit* autonomy and freedom across a spectrum of political and economic activity subject to general rights upheld equally for all people by the state. In this way, it eliminates undesirable forms of economic and political action. In effect, Weber presented a normative distinction between *positive* and *negative* privileges, which may be described as follows.

1   Positive privileges include the property and contract rights that permit universal economic freedoms subject to the rule of law. Formal rules of economic freedom are expressly created to ensure that economic outcomes can largely be decided peacefully and by competition and compromise among economic actors without direct interventions by the state.
2   Negative privileges, on the other hand, constitute prescriptions or prohibitions that relate to particularistic economic claims, and which limit economic autonomy or economic freedom. If the latter are subject to the rule of law, it will be a law that is created only for the purpose of granting particularistic privileges that are, in effect, exclusionary. In this case state intervention directly regulates not only the procedural *means* of economic activity, but also its *ends*.

This idea is further developed when Weber contrasts two ideal procedural types of state regulative action in the economic sphere (ibid.: 74–5). The first (pervasive) type is *ends-oriented*: 'economic policy which seeks to regulate both the ends and the procedures of economic activity'. Here, the state acts in much the same way as a guild, trade union, or business cartel does. It restricts economic activity to the advantage of its members and allies. The second (parametric) type is *means oriented*: 'enforcement of a formal order which would leave the economic activity of individual households and enterprises entirely free and confine its regulation to the formal function of settling disputes connected with the fulfilment of free contractual obligations'. In the latter case the state does not employ its legal powers to intervene discretionally in economic life by directing or incentivizing enterprises to enter or exit an area of production or commerce. Whereas ends-oriented regulation might include some economic freedom and autonomy, the enforcement of a formal order would in theory be the *means* preferred by the 'laissez-faire state', which Weber says corresponds more closely to the 'modern property system'.

The distinction I make between *parametric* and *pervasive* states resembles Weber's distinction between 'means-oriented' or 'ends-oriented' states. There is a clear difference between (1) parametric orders that enforce impersonal rules and promote the formal equalities of opportunity provided by market freedom, and (2) pervasive orders that enforce substantive rules and protect some enterprises from the consequences of market freedom. As noted, an equivalent difference is that between *structural* regulation and *conduct* regulation in the context of privatization or market liberalization. Structural regulation is arm's-length state action concerned with general rules of market organization and ex ante codes of conduct that aim to remove the *incentives* for undesirable behaviour. The stress is on procedural rather than substantive regulation, and credible threats of legal enforcement. Examples include merger or antitrust legislation designed to reduce the likelihood of uncompetitive conduct. Conduct regulation involves state directives to address the *behaviour* of enterprises, for example, treating prices, wages, tariffs, production and productivity targets, supervision of enterprises, detailed conduct rules, and state monitoring of enterprise performance. Conduct regulation is more likely to require regular personal contact between private firms and public officials. In underdeveloped polities that lack rigorous legal oversight or a formal separation of powers, conduct regulation is especially susceptible to interest-group closure.

Service function

Legal regulation is the primary function of the modern state. The secondary functions of the state are mainly technical economic services relating to monetary policy, fiscal policy, and infrastructure provision. Weber argued that the modern state should not overburden itself with economic actions that fall outside the regulatory sphere. Had he been writing today, he would no doubt have excluded most if not all public utility services from his list of basic state functions. Weber (1978: 224, 973) named the post, railway, telegraph, telephone, public roads, and waterways, as 'technical pacemakers of bureaucratization' that 'can only be administered publicly'. Only agencies of state administrations had the capacity, in Weber's day, for precise and speedy delivery of mass services over large distances. Today these services are no longer viewed as natural monopolies of the state, and have been wholly or partially privatized in many countries. Indeed, Weber did not believe that the choice between public or private ownership depends on the nature of the good or the service being supplied. In general terms, 'the effectiveness of market freedom increases with the degree to which sources of utility, particularly the means of transport and production are appropriated' as 'property rights' (ibid.: 112–13). Weber spoke out strongly against state ownership of enterprises, which produces a type of bureaucratization that retards capitalism (ibid.: *passim*). Yet even if some branches of production do lie in the hands of the state, they still 'cannot do without prices' (ibid.: 111).

Monetary and fiscal policy, on the other hand, *are* a natural monopoly of the state. As formally rational activities, they have a unique affinity with administration and law. Monetary policies change the quantity of money in circulation, the interest rate, and the rate of exchange. A 'monetary system with the highest possible degree of formal rationality' is one condition for the 'maximum rationality of profit making in a capitalist economy' (ibid.: 161–2). Monetary policy is less easily manipulated for particularistic ends than industrial policy. On this issue, Weber acknowledged the influence of Ludwig von Mises. He also anticipated Hayek's later criticism of 'discretion in monetary policy' on the grounds that 'monetary policy and its effects should be as predictable as possible' (Hayek 1960: 334; Weber 1978: 78). Given the risk of leaving monetary policy to the discretion of officials and politicians, a broadly *rule-based* approach to monetary targets is preferable. The modern state assumes two natural monopolies in monetary policy: regulation of the monetary system, and the issuing of money (Weber 1978: 166–74). In an ideal-type laissez-faire state, said Weber, monetary policy would be 'the most important function in the realm of economic policy' (ibid.: 160).

To give but a few examples: Weber was sceptical about the short-term political or sectoral economic gains from manipulating exchange rates as means of managing consumption and production (ibid.: 178–9). He warned of states falling under the influence of business groups that want leverage over monetary policy. A common target is exchange-rate policy due to its impact on the price and availability of foreign loans and imports. Weber also opposed 'deliberate regulation of business credit', which is typically a method of 'substantive regulation' for 'influencing the direction of the production of goods' in a 'planned economy' (ibid.: 181). The printing of new money should similarly be avoided because it causes inflation, which is 'a particular way of increasing the purchasing power of certain interests' (ibid.: 183, 187). Administrative money creation dictated by the 'mood of the bureaucracies' alters the 'substantive validity' of money in ways that may only serve negatively privileged profit making and clientelist wage concessions. It does, in any case, cause 'tremendous unsettlement of the market economy' (ibid.: 193).

Weber's interest in fiscal policy revolved around two issues: methods of public financing that are more or less favourable to capitalism's development, and the impact of this financing on the nature of economic activity. Since the state is 'the largest receiver and the largest maker of payments', its choices about taxation, spending, and monetary policy determine the health of an economy (ibid.: 167). How the state obtains the means to pay for the activity and staff of public administration is the source of 'the most direct connection' between the state and the economy (ibid.: 194). Weber examined this connection by comparing sources of state financing. An early method in many parts of the world was the 'farming out' of tax collection to private individuals in return for a benefit, a share in the revenue, or a payment from the political authority. Tax farming deeply influenced the distribution of power and wealth in societies. Weber regarded it as a primitive form of entrepreneurship, which eventually disappeared along with the similar practice of leasing political offices to the highest bidder. Tax farming 'tends to check the development of capitalism by creating vested interests in the maintenance of existing sources of fees and contributions', and does not 'encourage the orientation of profit making activity in the market' (ibid.: 199). Other sources of intermittent or permanent state financing in traditional societies include compulsory payments, and informal or non-monetary contributions. Intermittent and informal payments are still common practice today in precapitalist societies as a means of currying the favour of politicians and officials in return for protections.

State-owned economic enterprises have also been important sources of government revenue. Weber considered this an undesirable source of public financing. Wherever a state 'satisfies its wants by public enterprises or by production for the market, private capitalism tends to be eliminated' (ibid.: 351). Weber argued instead for a permanent form of financing by means of 'money contributions without economic production' (ibid.: 196–7). By this he meant a system of universal taxes as proportion of income, wealth, or transaction turnover; duties on specific consumption items or transactions; and fees for government services. The only precondition for universal taxation is 'a developed money economy' (ibid.: 964). This is the method best suited to the modern state and capitalism. In Weber's words: 'A state based exclusively on money contributions, conducting the collection of the taxes (but no other economic activity) through its own staff … provides an optimal environment for a rational market-oriented capitalism' (ibid.: 199). Problems arise, however, if 'capitalist enterprise becomes subject to extensive regulation by the state' (ibid.). By smothering the profit incentive, such measures could dry up the state's financing, which has come to rely on taxing capital, profit, and income created in the private-market economy. In such circumstances, a state might be forced to return to older forms of financing, i.e. ones that are particularistic rather than universal.

Clearly inimical to capitalism is the financing of state administration 'by means of burdens which are associated with privileges', as, for example, when 'cartels with monopolistic rights' have 'a corresponding obligation to make money contributions' to the state (ibid.: 197). Privileges also exist when a state grants tax exemptions, or when it requires contributions from individuals or groups on the basis of property, incomes, or occupations. Neither approach is compatible with a universalistic rules-based approach to state economic action. Privileged modes of state financing have often 'contributed to the closure of social and economic opportunities, to the stabilization of status groups, and thus to the elimination of private capital formation' (ibid.: 351). Many developing-country states even today obtain a significant portion of their finances from control of the means of production, by granting market privileges to monopolistic enterprises that effectively repress the market mechanism and divert investment into unproductive rent seeking (ibid.: 199–200).

Weber repeatedly stresses the importance of being able to calculate and predict the actions of the state in modern society. In the fiscal sphere, it is the 'the calculability of the tax load' that is important for profit-making enterprises (ibid.: 200). The tax should not be so burdensome as to divert resources from market investment (ibid.). Adam Smith (2000: 887–90) made the same argument about 'certainty' and convenience in taxation, and the need to keep taxation within bounds in order to encourage economic activities that create employment and discourage smuggling or evasion. One final consideration, however, is whether tax farming is really incompatible with capitalism. A state-regulated form of tax farming might today be beneficial in societies where, because of corruption, evasion, and inadequate procedures, the state is unable to collect taxes effectively. Many public services previously undertaken directly by the state are now successfully subcontracted to private enterprise. There appears to be no obvious 'Weberian' reason why a hard-pressed state should not outsource the collection of contributions to public revenue to the private sector, but only as long as the 'rights' of the contractor are not precapitalist benefices.

Representational function

After legal regulation and natural-monopoly servicing, the third task of the modern state is to establish a permanent representational system for the effective selection of political leaders. The topic of democracy will crop up in later chapters whenever we discuss the 'Weberian sequences' of capitalist transition, and so it is important to provide an outline of how Weber viewed the essential characteristics and purposes of the modern form of parliamentary representation. The reasons Weber gave for the technical superiority of parliamentary democracy appear, in their fundamentals, to be just as relevant today as they were at the turn of the twentieth century. Weber could not conceive of either modern law or modern administration in the absence of a formal separation of powers in which parliament has become the principal countervailing institutional force.

Weber said nothing to suggest democracy must have *causal* precedence in the transition to capitalism. He also makes it very clear that parliament can only operate well in a society that has already established requisite rule of law. Although he recognized the legitimizing function of democracy and dismissed as patronizing any doubts about the ordinary voter's ability to understand how political debates affect their own interests, Weber was sceptical about the value of grassroots or directly participatory democracy in mass society. He did not, for example, support democracy on ethical grounds. It may be true that democracy is a social good in its own right because of its intrinsic fairness and the 'procedural utility' derived from positive values attributed to participation, feelings of connectedness and control, and the processes of self-determination and co-determination (Frey 2008). But subjective feelings about the moral worth or pleasure of democracy were only of passing interest to Weber. The utility of democracy lies not in the expression of the will of the electorate itself but rather in the instrumental effect of this *technical method* on the selection and training of effective leaders who then 'exercise authority over the electors' (Weber 1978: 293–4).

Real democracy requires decisive and unemotional leadership by a relatively small number of elected representatives with clearly defined responsibilities (ibid.: 1459–60). Power is delegated to party representatives in parliament and to technical experts who are accountable to parliament within a framework of formal checks and balances: 'The voters exert influence *only* to the extent that programs and candidates are adapted and selected according to their chances of receiving electoral support' (ibid.: 1396). 'Direct democracy', in which everyone is considered qualified to pass opinion and decide the management of affairs, may operate sufficiently well at the personal level in a community or in a small organization, but is 'technically inadequate' for mass society (ibid.: 289–92, 948–52). Although the 'battle cry' for *direct* democracy is heard from the poor in their fight against the rich and powerful, it lacks the formal checks and balances provided when political parties compete in parliament, and it tends to be captured by the very people who are wealthy and powerful enough to dedicate themselves to political activity.

> [The] term 'democratization' can be misleading. The demos itself, in the sense of a shapeless mass, never 'governs' larger associations, but rather is governed. What changes is only the way in which the executive leaders are selected and the measure of influence which the demos, or better, which social circles from its midst are able to exert upon the content and the direction of administrative activities by means of 'public opinion'. 'Democratization', in the sense here intended, does not necessarily mean an increasingly active share of the subjects in government. This may be the result of democratization, but it is not necessarily the case.
>
> (ibid.: 984–5)

The name Weber gave to the organizational nature of modern democracy was 'free representation' (ibid.: 292–7). Obligatory and organized free political representation evolves in societies once they attain a size and level of complexity requiring that a minority of members represent the majority of citizens in society. In modern politics, the representatives exercise authority over the community or organizations that elect them. The representative 'is not bound by instruction but is in a position to make his own decisions' and is 'obligated only to express his own genuine conviction' (ibid.: 293). Free representatives are not simply the 'agents' for promoting the interests of others. In premodern societies, on the other hand, the role of 'representative' is usually appropriated by the chief or the ruling group. Another transitional or oligarchic form of representation is one in which representatives are elected or rotated but are still only 'agents' under 'instruction' from the elite, lacking the autonomy to make choices or pass judgement on behalf of citizens. Free representation is most highly developed in the modern parliament, which is the representative body of party organizations: 'It is the parties which present candidates and programs to the politically passive citizens' (ibid.: 294). The term 'parliament' is, in this respect, generic. It can refer to a variety of systems, including ministerial or presidential systems, in which single or multi-chamber bodies of elected representatives are granted public decision-making powers.

Democracy is 'technically superior' in exactly the same way that all the institutional subsystems of capitalism are superior, namely that each is characterized by procedural impersonality, calculable rules, and safeguards against permanent appropriations of monopolistic power. Weber traces the legal orientation of democracy back to the evolution of citizenship, which gave rise to 'legal consciousness' of formal equality among all individuals. Citizenship was conterminous with cities, mass markets, mass publics, mass demands, free labour, universal taxation, militarism, and an emerging alliance between the state, capital, and citizenry in medieval Europe (Weber 1981: 315–17). In turn, the development of citizenship would eventually lead to universal suffrage, which effectively resolved the growing need of the elite to secure the cooperation of the masses. In the modern state, citizens are all formally equal in elections for the selection of leaders. Equal voting rights are impersonal, and 'citizenship' suggests a person's impersonal status *vis-à-vis* the state, i.e. the absence of dependence on interpersonal relations of patronage or privilege as the source of status.

> Equal voting rights means in the first instance simply this: ...the individual ...is not, as he is everywhere else, considered in terms of the particular professional and family position he occupies, nor in relation to differences of material and social situation, but purely and simply as a citizen. This expresses the political unity of the nation rather than the dividing lines separating the various spheres of life.
>
> (Weber 1994: 103)

The rationality of parliamentary procedures is uppermost in Weber's analysis. With its written rules and predictable operating procedures, parliament shares the formalism of modern law and administration. Especially important is the fact that 'modern parliamentary representation ... shares with legal authority the general tendency to impersonality, the obligation to conform to abstract norms, political or ethical' (Weber 1978: 294). If the political struggle is not channelled through legally constituted representative bodies, political decision making will be dominated by the unregulated, emotional forces of popular justice and demagoguery. Modern society requires 'orderly responsible political leadership by parliamentary leaders' (Weber 1994: 125). That, in turn, depends on clear rules – 'the "rules of war" on the electoral battlefield can be regulated by law' (Weber 1978: 1396). Procedural norms that are institutionalized in parliament act as a disciplining force upon all of its members.

Modern parliaments have much in common with modern markets. The politician and the entrepreneur are moved by a similar spirit. The 'struggle for personal power, and the resulting personal responsibility, is the lifeblood of the politician as well as of the entrepreneur' (ibid.: 1404). Weber was pragmatic about the motives and methods of political parties, which operate much like any bureaucratic or market organization. Within parties one finds interest groups, exclusionary closure, patronage, demagogy, and deception. Parties are compelled to seek finance and influence by any available and permitted means, and so they must run along 'economic' lines. In addition, their internal structure of control is typically authoritarian and secretive. Only a 'hard core' within the party defines the political programme The methods engaged by parties to attain power and maintain solidarity can be ruthless. Political parties can just be vote-getting machines and vehicles for patronage. Demagogues may administer the parties, and networks of cliques may dominate them. It goes without saying, however, that parliaments should be strong enough in procedural terms to resist informal patronage dispensed by or on behalf of party 'bigshots'. Weber argued that there is no place for the 'guild instinct' in parliament, which would prevent the emergence of new people and new ideas (ibid.: 1414). The conflict between parties should be about policies rather than efforts to divide up spheres of influence among organs of the state (ibid.: 1422). 'Genuine parliamentary representation', he emphasized, is characterized by a 'voluntaristic play of interests' through parties that are 'inherently voluntary organizations' with a voluntary following (ibid.: 299, 1395–6).

Of course, politicians are just as likely to 'live off' politics as to 'live for' politics. Leaders are no more likely to be selfless, idealist, or ethical than the bureaucrats who compete for promotion and privileges: 'Here as there, personal interests are usually at stake' (ibid.: 1415–16). Yet the important point is that despite the monopolistic tendencies of political parties and the interested motives of politicians, a well-run parliament forces the parties to *compromise* over policy. The abstract compulsion to compromise is where the parallels between market freedom and free representation are most evident.

> Compromise is ... the dominant form in which conflicts of economic interest are settled ... Naturally, compromise also prevails in parliamentary politics, in inter-party relations, in the form of electoral compromise or

compromises on legislative proposals ... [The] possibility of compromise is one of the chief merits of the parliamentary system.

(Weber 1994: 102)

Weber's explanation of the superiority of modern parliament over alternative systems of representation underscores the competitive process for selecting and training effective political leaders, which, again, is not dissimilar to the routines of selection in the competitive market. In both situations, the successful individuals will be cool-headed, quick-witted, and adaptively efficient, because they cannot escape the consequences of their choices. A wrong decision meets with public exposure and signifies personal failure. Politicians face the threat of deselection or electoral defeat. A strength of parliamentary democracy is that 'the voter makes the leaders of the party which appointed the officials responsible for their performance' (Weber 1978: 1457). Modern parliament, like the modern market, is a place of voluntary association with formal checks and balances that penalize the misuse of power. Political leaders are under pressure to show they can be trusted. Naturally, the motives for seeking power in parliament may be selfish or idealistic. But in a democracy, 'universal human frailties at least do not prevent the selection of capable leaders' (ibid.: 1416).

The politician and, above all, the party leader who is rising to public power is exposed to public scrutiny through the criticism of opponents and competitors and can be certain that, in the struggle against him, the motives and means of his ascendancy will be ruthlessly publicized.

(ibid.: 1450)

In short, parliament is the procedural *mechanism* for recruiting effective leaders. When parliament is a strong institution – a place of genuine contestation and with powers to supervise other organs of state – then capable and talented politicians with highly developed 'power instincts' and proven 'qualities of political leadership' will be attracted to work in it (ibid.: 1409). In order to secure the top positions politicians must cultivate their supporters within parliament. This requires special training and skills. The procedures of parliament ensure that their reputations and qualifications for the job are continually tested (ibid.: 1414–15). Politicians must also acquire support outside parliament among individuals, communities, associations, and in the party apparatus. The 'essence of politics' in a democracy 'is *struggle*, the recruitment of allies and of a *voluntary* following' (ibid.: 1414).

Weber singled out the function of the parliamentary commission of inquiry as evidence of the virtues of modern parliamentary systems. It might seem to be an 'unspectacular right', but the parliamentary inquiry is really a 'basic precondition' of the adequacy of parliament's 'share in government' (ibid.: 1419). Politicians have to 'prove their mettle' to their colleagues as well as to unelected public officials by acquiring knowledge of policy facts. 'Steady and strenuous' work in parliamentary commissions of inquiry, supported by parliament's legal right to obtain access to the necessary facts – always under public and media scrutiny, and always in direct contact with other government agencies which report to these commissions – gives the parliamentary member 'intensive training' for effective and responsible leadership. Parliamentary commissions weed out the demagogues and the dilettantes. They produce 'skilled professional parliamentarians' (ibid.: 1427–8). This is the best institutional structure for 'the political education of leaders and led' (ibid.: 1420). Weber's precise and straightforward conceptualization of the ideal impersonally regulated parliament draws our attention to the defects of the many contemporary varieties of façade democracy. In the precapitalist countries we find that parliaments are not impersonally regulated or genuinely competitive, and they do not train effective leaders.

Dysfunctions of state closure

The next stage in the analysis requires that we move away from the ideally operating legal-administrative and political spheres, and focus instead on the ease with which negative interests can capture the policy process, especially in the executive and administrative branches of government. The main point to make is that Weberian theory suggests a logical correlation between increases in state functions and the underdevelopment of impersonal procedural norms. The more discretionary tasks the state assumes, the less likely it is that the quality of its performance will improve. Furthermore, if institutions remain underdeveloped a further expansion of state roles will increase the likelihood of abuse and misuse of state power. It would not be stretching the argument too far to say that the principal cause of state dysfunction in transitional societies is the tendency of states to extend themselves far beyond their parametric functions of law and monetary or fiscal policy, without performing these basic functions as a priority.

These problems tend to manifest themselves in certain internal and external behavioural characteristics of state agencies with respect to the way in which they conduct economic interventions. In this section, I adapt Weber's discussion of exclusionary group 'closure' with the purpose of specifying the modes of monopolistic closure – within or involving the state – that are most likely to impede the process of capitalist transition (Weber 1978: 43–6, 341–8). A preliminary distinction is as follows:

1 '*External* closure' occurs between state agencies and private economic groups when business pursues profit-making opportunities through political connections.
2 '*Internal* closure' occurs within the state when public officials collude and compete among themselves in pursuit of narrow substantive interests.

Assuming the state in question is a 'transitional' state, i.e. one that has gone some way towards capitalism, then a characteristic of both types of closure is that private interests, or a private-interest government, effectively hijack the public interest and the state itself. It will also be assumed, for the purpose of the argument, that the state has evolved to the point of staking a *legitimate* legal claim for political authority by 'virtue of mandate or permission' and the protection of equal rights (ibid.: 904, 908). In the long-run evolution of this state it was perhaps the case that no group ever *intended* that the state should become an association of predators, patronage mongers, or demagogues, or that it would rule only on behalf of a narrow elite. Rather, state dysfunction occurs because private interests have been able to capture and exploit the existing agencies of the state for their own benefit. These agencies might not have been created expressly to service private interests, yet this is the eventual outcome. Even though profit making may already be the dominant mode of economic action, the manner of regulating enterprises allows some economic groups routinely to obtain profit-making privileges through the state rather than competing for genuine profit advantages in the market. State *dysfunction* can then mean two things. It can mean that state policy making does not operate in a manner that is favourable to capitalist transition, or it can mean that a state does not live up to the agreed normative expectations of society or of the state itself.

We then ask: what type of profit making correlates with the dysfunctional state? This is important, because the types of profit making prevalent in a society at any moment are a reflection of the nature of the political authority and the mode of regulating economic action. We have seen that Weber viewed economic life as structured to a substantial extent by how the state regulates economic activity and how the state finances itself. When confronted with a situation of state dysfunction, the analyst must ask whether the state's economic policies focus on regulation of the ends of economic activity, the means and the ends, or only the means. I have noted that only *means*-oriented state regulation, which confines the state mainly to enforcing an impersonal legal order of economic rights, is really compatible with capitalism. The universalistic legal-administrative preconditions of maximum formal rationality in *capitalist* profit making that are relevant to the present discussion are as follows:

1   'Complete appropriation of all material means of production by owners and the complete absence of all formal appropriation of opportunities for profit in the market; that is, market freedom'.
2   'Complete absence of substantive regulation of consumption, production, and prices, or of other forms of regulation which limit freedom of contract or specify conditions of exchange. This may be called substantive freedom of contract.'
3   'Complete calculability of the functioning of public administration and the legal order and a reliable purely formal guarantee of all contracts by the political authority. This is a formally rational administration and law.'

(Weber 1978: 161–2)

As these strenuous definitions suggest, capitalist profit making requires voluntary, continuous, standardized, and free exchange among enterprises bound together by the market and by their mutual adherence to existing state laws governing economic action. Modern conditions of profit making in a capitalist order contrast starkly with the characteristic modes of profit making in precapitalist societies, which Weber regarded as 'politically oriented' or purely '*capitalistic*' opportunities for profit, which are economically 'irrational' (ibid.: *passim*). Capitalis*tic* economic action signifies an orientation to profits and capital accounting in a market economy that can, however, be thoroughly monopolistic and lacking impersonal transactional rules (ibid.: 113). Weber seems to have intended the term '*capitalistic*' to mean a transitional form of profit making in the movement towards modern capitalism.

The following forms of profit making are most likely to depend on *internal* or *external* interest-group closure, and on a state's willingness to supply monopolistic privileges to groups:

1   'Orientation to opportunities for predatory profit from political organizations or persons connected with politics'.
2   'Orientation to the profit opportunities in continuous business activity which arise by virtue of domination by force or a position of power guaranteed by the political authority'.
3   'Orientation to profit opportunities in unusual transactions with political bodies'

(ibid.: 164–5)

I will employ the term *political profit making* to describe opportunities for economic advantage that arise from or depend on political decisions. In practice, these are always materially motivated forms of interest-group closure centred on the state. The objective of the actors is to curb open economic competition by restricting profit opportunity to some groups or individuals and by singling out for themselves the most attractive sectors for making profits. This situation can continue even after the state has achieved complete control over the legal and administrative infrastructures of a territory, which, though they may be formalized, are not yet procedurally impersonal. Typically, political profit making occurs when sustained money making in the market depends on political connections or on discretionary support provided to the enterprise by the state. Monopolistic privileges exclude outsiders who are not similarly favoured. If a voluntary arrangement by agreement with public officials for the appropriation of economic advantages by private groups is carried out with state protections and state subsidies – with the effect of excluding others from exploiting a profit opportunity – it is, in effect, an imposition on competitors. Monopolists have then used *the state* to abolish the market freedom of others.

I will employ a closely related term, *regulatory closure*, to describe the competitive process of monopolizing the market advantages created by political authorities. This involves conflict and compromise between individuals and organizations with the intention of excluding or restricting others from enjoying similar access to economic opportunities. Alliances and rivalries between business interests or between state administrative and political interests focus on influencing the agencies of economic governance. Only at a later stage might the state's authority be invoked to gain formal control over these advantages, and to neutralize the resistance of groups that remain disadvantaged. Thus, unlike market freedom, regulatory closure is not oriented to a legal order. Rather it consists of unofficially sanctioned market and political competition. Property rights remain insecure. However, the ultimate objective of actors may be the formal appropriation of market opportunities and economic rights granted by political authority for the exclusion of competitors. The appropriations might include: political allocations of market rights, public subsidies, goods, or services, substantive bureaucratic restrictions on the exchange of utilities or on market freedom, and preferential limits on rights of control and disposal of property.

Organizations and social or economic relationships of *all* types exhibit 'closure' tendencies. Weber's main concern was the state-centred dynamic of monopolization rather than the market-based form of monopolization. The difference is that monopolization strategies in the market are temporary if they are not sustained by the state, and therefore need not destroy market freedom. The monopolization of economic privileges that become rights granted by the state, on the other hand, can indefinitely suppress market competition. Because the power wielded by state agencies is so great, if profit seekers routinely swarm around the 'honey pot' of state agencies rather than around genuinely competitive market opportunities, the consequences are damaging to society. The entrepreneurial skills required for market competition are, in this respect, quite unlike the political skills required for regulatory closure.

All 'closure' is a response to existing incentives. Regulatory closure is an effect of the absence or weakness of economic governance that aims to guarantee universal rights of ownership, exchange, and legal adjudication. It is likely to prevent the development of those rights. When forming closed relationships, individuals and organizations aspire to ensure their own survival, even though their long-run 'objective' advantage may lie in a regulatory order that equally guarantees the rights of their competitors. When regulatory regimes are open rather than closed, all 'the participants expect that the admission of others will lead to an improvement of their situation' (Weber 1978: 43). Market freedom must mean openness to outsiders and newcomers (ibid.: 43–5). But if actors perceive a self-interest in monopolistic tactics, and the opportunity presents itself, they will try to form closed relationships.

These processes of 'closure' can extend against outsiders on a territorial or sectoral scale. For example, contemporary *dirigiste* strategies sometimes attempt to simulate competitive dynamics inside state-protected national economic sectors. Even within a monopolistic group, such as a national industrial sector or a business network in receipt of state subsidies, public agencies may deliberately create conditions for 'competitive struggle within the group' at the same time as they protect the group against outsiders (ibid.: 44). Weber calls this 'free competition for all the advantages which the group as a whole monopolizes for itself' (ibid.: 45). The general message could not be clearer: 'capitalism is retarded if [private] monopolies are protected by the state and stabilized with state subsidies' (ibid.: 351). Weber also explained the 'technical irrationality' of state economic planning. An administered economy is authoritarian, and it utilizes measures of consumption and want satisfaction rather than profitability to determine income distribution or the locations, products, and processes of economic enterprises. Instead, Weber favoured market freedom. It is almost always preferable that comparative profitability and price values should determine present and future consumption needs (ibid.: 100–13). In these and other ways, the economic reasons that Weber offers for the superiority of market capitalism complement his political critique of state-centred profit making.

Weber acknowledged the contribution that bureaucratic mercantilism had made to the development of capitalism in the Middle Ages and beyond. Today, however, the mercantilist or *dirigiste* form of state bureaucratization simply produces the 'paralysis of private economic initiative' (ibid.: lviii–lix). Weber identified the kind of situation that would become commonplace in the developing world after his lifetime and for the remainder of the twentieth century. The state often acquires control over strategic industries. It obliges private enterprises to use public service providers, whose revenues it appropriates to pay for administrative staff and state activities. The state protects national producers by restricting imports of selected goods that might compete with them. It creates bureaucratic mechanisms to regulate and to privilege some trades and professions. Much of the population becomes wholly reliant on the public economy and on state employment. If this form of bureaucratization continues, it will 'subdue capitalism'.

Representational dysfunction

Having explained the main dimensions of state dysfunctionality, we must briefly look at one specific form in which these problems can be transposed to the underdeveloped political sphere. Weber (ibid.: 297, 1395–7) described the negative situation as 'representation by the agents of interest groups' in the 'corporate state' where 'occupational groups' become 'drawn into the whirl of political power and party struggles'. The first problem is that economic progress can be slowed. Political representation on the basis of occupational interest groups such as business and labour erects a barrier against the market determination of economic action. Weber wrote of the naturally 'shifting sands of constantly changing operational units, trends in production and workforce, all of which are radically restructured in response to every new machine or market opening' (Weber 1994: 93). The institution of the corporate state cannot be efficiently 'adapted' to these perpetual transformations in modern economic structures. Technological and commercial restructuring pits 'corporations of interests organized by the state' against the 'living stream' of the '*real* economic interest groups' (ibid.: 98). Weber also pointed out that the interests of consumers – whose demands should influence the direction of production in a market economy – are not represented in the corporatist state. Ludwig von Mises, a friend of Weber, drew similar conclusions:

> [A] system in which only the wishes of the producers prevail ... might still have some meaning as long as conditions remain unchanged and as long as the distribution of capital and labour among the different lines of production correspond to some extent to the conditions of demand. But changes are always taking place. And every change in the conditions renders the system less workable.
>
> (von Mises [1940] 1998: 65)

Second, the principles of parliamentary democracy are undermined if the selection of representatives is 'not a matter of free choice' but rather if 'the body consists of persons who are chosen on the basis of occupations or their social or class membership', and if this leads to 'the development of powerful parties representing class interests' (Weber 1978: 297). When parties and party programmes systematically incorporate representations by organized economic groups – typically trade unions, chambers of commerce, financiers, professional associations, or farmers – parliament will be taken up with the substantive issues that concern these functional groups rather than with the *general* interest. Where a corporatist system is formalized, it would mean, in effect, the absence of formal equality in political rights.

> Parliament would become a mere market place for compromises between purely economic interests, without any political orientation to overall interests. For the bureaucracy this would increase the opportunity and the temptation to play off opposed economic interests and to expand the system of log-rolling with job and contract patronage in order to preserve its own power. Any public control over the administration would be vitiated, since the decisive moves and compromises of the interested groups would be made behind the closed doors of non-public associations and would be even less controllable than before. In parliament the shrewd businessman, not the political leader, would reap advantage from this situation; a 'representative' body of this kind would be the least proper place imaginable for the solution of political problems.
>
> (ibid.: 1397)

The corporatist subtype of parliamentary representation, which in one shape or another is a common characteristic of façade democracy, becomes a mechanism for perpetuating the political profit making and regulatory closure that typifies state action and government–business relations in precapitalist institutional orders. As Weber argued, corporatist interest intermediation through parliament – whether formal or informal – can simply mean that: 'Politics is penetrating into the economic order at the same time that economic interests are entering into politics' (ibid.: 299). With its enormous resources and capacity to influence and persuade, business is likely, in these circumstances, to exert disproportionate influence over the political and law-making process. Far from being the case that 'the state would then be the wise regulator of the economy', interest-group representation in parliament could easily lead to a situation in which 'bankers and capitalist entrepreneurs' acquire 'unlimited and uncontrolled command over the state' (Weber 1994: 104). Such a situation, coupled with the bureaucracy's determination to preserve its power, provides all the incentives for the most inefficient forms of state-activist organization of economic life. Yet the more activist the bureaucracy becomes, the more need there would be for it to be supervised. Bureaucracy's ability to escape supervision would rise in proportion to the growing influence of economic interests in parliament.

> The more the direct management of economic enterprises by the state bureaucracy were to grow, the more awkward would be the lack of an independent control organ that would have the power, as the parliaments do, to demand publicly information from the all-powerful officials and to call them to account.
>
> (Weber 1978: 1456)

This statement seems especially pertinent to the developing country where an activist state attempts to manage the economy, but where democratic representation is either absent or only primitively developed. Commentators who cheerfully look only at the short-run economic-growth effects may be deluding themselves about the durability of the arrangements. Similarly, political systems that lean towards managed interest-group representation rather than competitive, universal, and voluntarist representation will, in all probability, create common ground between the two forces in society that are most powerful and most keen to escape formal oversight and impartial regulation, i.e. negatively privileged monopolistic enterprises and an expansionary state bureaucracy. This, in turn, undermines the movement towards an effective division of institutional powers. 'Parliament must be much more sovereign in its powers' in order to regulate bureaucracy and the economic interests allied to it, 'on the principle that the needs of the masses must be represented' (ibid.: 105). Even rule by 'parliamentary cliques' would be preferable to 'rule by much more hidden and – usually – smaller cliques whose influence would be even more inescapable' (Weber 1994: 126).

Weber's analysis of the corporatist type of representational dysfunction therefore draws attention both to the risks of indefinitely postponing democratization and to the risks run by democratizing before market freedom, rule of law, and impersonal public administration have yet taken root. These problems illustrate the complexity of sequencing capitalist transition. Precapitalist – neopatrimonial or corporatist – economic interest-group representation in parliament can encourage the wrong kind of bureaucracy and slow the expansion of market freedom, thereby shackling the transition. By focusing on this defect, however, Weber's purpose is to reveal the indispensability of parliament's role. In the longer run, parliament is the institution from which other institutions must eventually derive their authority and legitimacy. It exercises overall public control of the state, reaches compromises among public interests, and deliberates and passes laws. As such, parliament becomes the ultimate source and sustenance of the highly developed capitalist rules and their mechanisms of enforcement.

Constrained state effectiveness

This section examines three general constraints on state administrative effectiveness in the economic sphere, each of which cautions against encouraging extensive state *discretionary* powers during capitalist transition. Each constraint identifies a cognitive or volitional characteristic of public officials – first, their bounded knowledge of economic life; second, an inherent tendency towards status-group closure; and third, structurally conditioned hostility towards markets and private enterprise. A necessary starting point for the discussion is to acknowledge the state's unrivalled power to impose its will. At all stages of its development the state has an incentive to exercise its control in order to maintain its authority. Constraints arise, however, for the reasons just given. The state's knowledge of markets is inferior to that of market actors. The danger of state power is magnified if the state is not yet impersonally regulated, since officials will be motivated by weak procedural discipline to pursue their private or group interests or to fall in with non-state interests. The problem grows even larger because bureaucratic groups find impersonal market freedom threatening, hard to control, and hard to understand.

Power invites the misuse, deliberate or unintentional, of power. No association or group can ever match the power of the state. Weber viewed state bureaucracy as 'the only really inescapable power'. He worried about the 'irresistible advance of bureaucratization' and the 'pervasive power of the bureaucrats', but he accepted the 'indispensability of the state bureaucracy', and recognized its 'inherent limitations' (Weber 1978: 1403, 1406). As the ultimate regulatory authority, and due to its sheer magnitude as a consumer and producer of goods and services, the state inevitably dominates economic life. The modern state-bureaucratic system of domination is 'superior to every kind of collective behaviour and social action opposing it' (ibid.: 987–9). It is inconceivable that this form of state power could ever be eliminated or replaced.

As Weber explained, public bureaucracy is the modern form of 'domination by virtue of authority, i.e. the power to command and duty to obey' (ibid.: 943). It is easy enough for the state to legitimize its power, because bureaucracy is an expression of valid legal authority and the right to issue commands. The official is 'legitimated by that system of rational norms' and 'obedience is owed to the legally established impersonal order', i.e. 'to the norms rather than to the person' (ibid.: 215, 954). So, the public's perception of state domination tends to be favourable. Most people feel that domination regulated by state rules will be less oppressive than domination based on private power in the market. Even so, the state has to continually reproduce its legitimacy and the 'habit of obedience' through 'organized activity directed to the application and enforcement of [its] order' (ibid.: 264). Moreover, with power also comes responsibility. If the state exercises its huge economic power ineffectively, the impact on society is so great that the state's natural legitimacy may be undermined.

Indeed, the first constraint on state effectiveness is the strong likelihood that the state will exercise its *bureaucratic* power poorly in the economy because its officials have no direct experience of the market. Public officials cannot know more about markets than entrepreneurs and the managers of firms. When public officials attempt to manipulate the market environment or to guide a market sector or an enterprise, or if they try to 'rule the market' through conduct rather than structure regulation, they are bound to make mistakes.

> Only the expert knowledge of private economic interest groups in the field of business is superior to the expert knowledge of the bureaucracy. This is so because the exact knowledge of facts in their field is of direct significance for economic survival.... For this reason alone authorities are held within narrow boundaries when they seek to influence economic life in the capitalist epoch, and very frequently their measures take an unforeseen and unintended course or are made illusory by the superior expert knowledge of the interested groups.
>
> (Weber 1978: 994)

Weber suggested that the private entrepreneur's greater knowledge and consequent 'relative immunity from subjection to the control of rational bureaucratic knowledge' is a reason for the often ineffectual and counterproductive state efforts to organize the means and ends of economic life (ibid.: 224–5). In theory, public administration acquires its 'domination through knowledge' (ibid.: 225). But if the knowledge of the bureaucrat who exercises control over official information is less in a particular economic field than the knowledge of market actors, then obviously the choice of best means to a desired end (whether or not the end is defined by the state) will be most optimally made by capitalists who know their own business. Adam Smith observed the same dilemma: 'What is the species of domestic industry which his capital can employ, and of which the produce is likely to be of the greatest value, every individual, it is evident, can, in his local situation, judge much better than any statesman or lawgiver can do for him' (Smith 2000: 485).

It is not only a question of inadequate *knowledge* of economic conditions. State officials cannot manipulate markets or market sectors with a reasonable level of certainty about outcomes because they have insufficient *incentives* to make the correct decision. If a government agency exercises poor judgement when deciding which market players will receive its subsidy, the agency will probably go unpunished. Incentives are different in the private sector where enterprises must continually innovate in order to adapt to changing market conditions. An error of judgement could bring about the extinction of the enterprise.

The second major constraint on state effectiveness – a behavioural one – links up closely with the problems of 'political profit making' and 'regulatory closure' discussed earlier. Organizational incentives for the misuse of state power coexist with interest motives that can lead state officials to pursue contra-capitalist economic policies, and with attitudinal characteristics that encourage intra-state closure. In his analyses of bureaucratic interests and intra-state politics Weber dealt extensively with the nature of *status groups*. A status order within the state may have contradictory effects, which, from the present viewpoint, can be divided into *positive* and *negative* status-group characteristics of a modernizing state. In the first place, the willingness of the governed to be dominated by state officials is positively rooted in a belief that the status order of bureaucrats is a true reflection of the existing legal order. Society's behavioural norms validate the rules of action of the formal power system. Officials enjoy high rank in modern society because of their formal education, organizational and decision-making power, professional ethics, and also their impersonal purposes. Even if bureaucrats display exclusiveness in their behaviour or style of life, citizens can accept this as harmless and natural self-identification, a bond based on merito-cratic specialization and the expectation of meritocratic promotion. The legiti-macy of state agencies depends on their inbuilt sense of duty, a functional division of labour, objective norms, technical rationality, and a strict separation of the public and private lives of officials.

As noted earlier, an ideal bureaucratic order 'levels' the internal status differ-entials by recruiting solely on the basis of technical competence. Weber argued that this levelling

> creates a favourable situation for the development of bureaucracy by elimin-ating the office-holder who rules by virtue of status privileges and the appro-priation of the means and powers of administration; in the interests of "equality", it also eliminates those who can hold office on an honorary basis or as an avocation by virtue of their wealth.
>
> (Weber 1978: 226)

Similar training and credentials create commensality of status throughout the public sector. Intra-state competition for prestige or esteem is then mainly competition between equals. In the ideal situation, officials are formally equal before law.

However, Weber was under no illusions about the 'economic consequences of bureaucratization'. State bureaucracy can be used by particularistic interests, which are not 'equal'. It is 'easily made to work for anybody who knows how to gain control over it' (ibid.: 988).

> The consequences of bureaucracy depend upon the direction which the powers using the apparatus give to it ... one has to remember that bureauc-racy as such is a precision instrument that can put itself at the disposal of quite varied interests, purely political as well as purely economic ones, or any other sort. There is also the possibility ... that bureaucratization of the administration is deliberately connected with the formation of status groups, or is entangled with it by the force of the existing groupings of social power.
>
> (ibid.: 989–90)

The potentially negative characteristics of a status order are apparent if one con-siders that 'stratification by status goes hand in hand with a monopolization of ideal and material goods or opportunities', and that 'material monopolies provide the most effective motives for the exclusiveness of a status group' (ibid.: 935). Notwithstanding the levelling process within the state, a bureaucratic status group always has a concrete interest in appropriating powers and privileges that exclude outsiders. The incentives for the monopolization of power by status groups within the state 'arise in the framework of organizations which satisfy their [economic] wants' (ibid.: 306). It is not uncommon, Weber observed, for the 'directing authorities' of state organizations to compete with each other 'to increase their own power and to provide the members under their authority with means of consumption and acquisition and with the corresponding opportunities for earnings and profits' (ibid.: 194). There is a clear tendency for 'officials to treat their official function from what is substantively a utilitarian point of view in the interest of the welfare of those under their authority' (ibid.: 226). That is how they protect their own advantages.

In all of these ways, even a modernizing and superficially democratic state can revert to patrimonial styles of authority. The status-group character of the bureaucracy combines easily with the remnant traditional character of rulership, and resists the trend towards the enforcement of impersonal procedural norms. We encounter this situation in developing-society bureaucracies where the exercise of public power gives the full appearance of being 'primarily a personal right of the official [who] makes ad hoc decisions ... according to his personal discretion' (ibid.: 1041). Weber draws a sharp contrast with the modern state: 'Instead of bureaucratic impartiality and of the ideal – based on the abstract validity of one objective law for all – and of administering without respect of persons, the opposite principle prevails' (ibid.). Even in the more advanced societies, public administrations are in varying degrees made up of status groups with vested interests competing to appropriate rights, functions, and privileges of public office. But the situation is especially acute in precapitalist states if the economic interests of bureaucratic strata can be satisfied by 'living off the exercise of political power', and if 'an expansion of power means more office positions, more sinecures, and better opportunities for promotion' (ibid.: 911).

The final constraint on state effectiveness is a particular source of irreconcilability between the interests of state actors and the market actors who drive capitalist transitions. Weber argued that the prestige of public office produces a hostile attitude towards private economic power. The antipathy of official bureaucracy toward the impersonal order of the market has its source in status-group mentalities. Weber's distinctions between *status* and *class* situations helps to explain the nature of status-group motives (ibid.: 305–7, 926–39). The life chances of social classes are created by *economic* struggles relating to acquisition of property and means of production. Class advancement occurs mainly through success in the market. Status groups, in contrast, are typically communities of interest that arise within *organizations* and whose life chances are determined by honour and convention relating, for example, to particular valuations of prestige. Status privilege is regulated by restrictions on entry to the group, by the monopolization of organizational powers, and by controls on consumption of goods and services. Conventions regulating status styles of life and the status mode of closure against outsiders create 'economically irrational consumption patterns', and can 'render exchange with outsiders impossible' (ibid.: 307, 638). Status groups have no vested interest in the *free* play of market forces.

> the market and its processes knows no personal distinctions: 'functional' interests dominate it. It knows nothing of honour. The status order means precisely the reverse: stratification in terms of honour and styles of life peculiar to status groups as such. The status order would be threatened at its very root if mere economic acquisition and naked economic power ... could bestow upon anyone who has won them the same or even greater honour as the vested interests claim for themselves.... Therefore all groups having interest in the status order react with special sharpness precisely against the pretensions of purely economic acquisition. In most cases they react the more vigorously the more they feel themselves threatened.... As to the general effect of the status order, only one consequence can be stated, but it is a very important one: the hindrance of the free development of the market.
>
> (ibid.: 936)

When a status order is dominant inside the state, the likely outcome will be attempts to fetter market freedom, and the consequent conflict between state and market interests. In precapitalist society, public administrators are typically 'distrustful of capitalist development, which revolutionizes the social conditions' (ibid.: 1109). Traces of these attitudes from the past remain even in the more advanced societies. The 'resentment against emergent autonomous economic powers', and the 'traditional status-oriented attitude of the bureaucracy toward rational economic profit', became 'the motives on which modern state welfare policies could rely' (ibid.: 1109). Throughout the developing world today it is possible to see how bureaucratic status groups continue to wield their power to shape clientelist networks, to regulate consumption of goods and services, to restrict the choices of consumers, to interfere with contractual claims in the market, and to limit the property rights of selected economic groups. The usual effect is that 'status groups hinder the strict carrying through of the sheer market principle' (ibid.: 930). When state bureaucracy acts as a status group it tends to be hostile towards competitive economic interests in the market, which it finds itself unable to control directly. These incentives to fetter market freedoms are either self-interested or moralistic.

> The main difference between the utilitarianism of the officials and the specifically bourgeois ethos has always been the former's abhorrence of the acquisitive drive, which is natural for a person who draws a fixed salary or takes fixed fees, who is ideally incorruptible, and whose performance finds its dignity precisely in the fact that it is not a source of commercial enrichment.
>
> (ibid.: 1108–9)

While noting the many internal constraints on effective state action, I have sought to explain why Weber viewed the legal-administrative function of the state as indispensable if capitalism is to prosper. Somehow, the state must create countermeasures to the incentives for negative collusion between state and economic interests. One aspect of the problem – the relative power of state and business – can be dealt with briefly. The issue is raised indirectly in one of Weber's many comments on the tendency of status groups to actively resist the spread of markets: 'The beneficiary of a monopoly by a status group restricts and maintains his power against the market, while the rational-economic monopolist rules through the market' (ibid.: 639). Rather like Joseph Schumpeter, Weber recognized that temporary economic monopolies perform valuable functions for capitalist economies if they are 'monopolies ... based solely upon the power of property [and] upon an entirely rationally calculated mastery of market conditions which may, however, remain formally as free as ever', and as long as they do not constitute 'restrictions on the formation of rational market prices' (ibid.).

At the same time, since 'control over economic goods' is one of the most important 'instruments' of power, it is necessary to recognize the consequences of private monopolies with respect to the balance of power between state and business (ibid.: 942). Weber discusses two relevant types of 'domination'. Modern public bureaucracy is 'domination by virtue of authority, i.e. the power to command and duty to obey'. A quite different type is 'domination by virtue of a constellation of interests'. Weber's main example of the latter form is 'monopolistic domination in the market' (ibid.: 943). Through skill, exclusive possession of goods, or some other concrete material advantage, the monopolistic enterprise can influence the conduct of other market actors who nevertheless remain formally free of any obligations of duty to the dominant enterprise. Typical examples of such domination include market closure through price fixing or through the appropriation of technologies. The danger, however, is that a 'constellation of interests' in the market can 'easily be transformed into formally regulated relationships of authority', which 'may be felt to be much more oppressive than an authority in which the duties of obedience are set out clearly' (ibid.: 946). The suggestion is that if legal-regulatory constraint on the exercise of state power is not adequate, a relationship of domination in the market that is protected and sustained by the state can be converted into a relationship of domination by virtue of an authority that is felt not to be legitimate because its origins lie in 'the very absence of rules' (ibid.).

Business is hardly powerless. A modern economy 'consists of a complete network of exchange contracts, that is, in deliberate planned acquisitions of powers of control and disposal' (ibid.: 67). The promise of 'future advantages which appear as objects of exchange in economic transactions' is the incentive for expanding economic transactions, and the 'power of capital' is derived from 'control over the means of production and over economic advantages' (ibid.: 69, 95). It is often observed that big business enjoys a privileged relationship with government. Corporations have influence over government among other reasons because they determine levels of economic activity, employment of factors of production, and can shape public preferences and set agendas of public debate. A modern state knows its own survival depends on a prosperous and dynamic business sector. Business can be privileged in another way if its influence in government depends on winning the personal support of politicians and regulators. While business remains structurally subordinate to the state, it can pursue its power within that structure.

In precapitalist society, where rulers govern through interpersonal networks and do not tolerate other centres of influence, it is likely that 'in the interest of [their] domination' the political elite 'must oppose the economic independence of the bourgeoisie' (ibid.: 1107). As the market expands during capitalist transitions, however, economic groups acquire more autonomy and may be able to exploit the evolving legal-administrative order to appropriate property and other economic advantages in ways that would not be possible in a modern society. As I will show in Chapter 3, Weber had no illusions about the motives of market interests that pressure for the creation of institutions that give them property and contract rights: 'The result of contractual freedom is in the first place the opening of the opportunity to use, by the clever utilization of property ownership in the market, these resources without legal restraints as a means for the achievement of power over others' (ibid.: 730). In the early stages of transition, 'formal legal equality' can be a source of exclusionary power benefiting existing property owners (ibid.: 699).

On the other hand, if domination is defined simply as having the power to impose one's own will on others (ibid.: 942), it is clear that business power is as nothing compared with the power of the state. Regardless of what resources they employ in pursuit of privileges, and irrespective of the fact that small numbers may give them concentrated lobbying power, business groups cannot organize their forces on anything remotely resembling the scale of state forces. Entrepreneurs are beholden to the bureaucrat *if* the latter seeks to influence the former against their will. *If* it desires to, the state can control business because it has the power to do so, and also because its dominance rests on legitimate and impersonal legal authority.

Yet power and domination do not equal 'strength' if this is defined in terms of state *developmental* effectiveness. Weberian theory can show why a state with extensive economic functions is likely to be weaker rather than stronger in the long run. State agencies have all the incentives to expand state functions, even if by doing so they actually diminish their regulatory power over business. Paradoxically, state power can supply all of the interest-group incentives that will weaken the state. The accumulation of state functions facilitates regulatory closure and stimulates the growth of a bureaucratic status order. Given these structures and motives of state power, any effort to 'strengthen' state capacity by increasing its discretionary powers of control over economic life inevitably produces serious state dysfunction.

As long as the motives of state officials continue to be a reflection of the characteristic motives of status groups throughout history, their interests will remain irreconcilable with the economic motives of market actors whose instincts and drive for competitive profit making are the most elementary causal force of capitalist transition. Once the nature of bureaucratic status groups is understood, it is easier to see why in societies where the structure of domination favours the discretionary authority of the state over private enterprise, the economic role of public agencies tends to prioritize functions of regulation that end up stifling entrepreneurship and profit making. Economic growth is hindered if public officials regard impersonal market transactions as inferior or threatening. On the other hand, if bureaucrats are free to develop economic interests of their own, corruption and political profit making will be the norm. Weber's observations on state bureaucracy suggest that the incentives of bureaucrats vary according to the nature of the tasks the state takes on or is asked to perform. *Neodirigiste* writings that advocate 'active' state economic roles have neglected the powerful logic of Weberian insights relating to inherent constraints on state effectiveness. In states with too many economic functions, bureaucrats are likely to develop definite economic interests while remaining hostile toward market freedom.

Weber suggested that the economic ignorance of state actors relative to private-market actors is a reason for limiting the scope and intensity of state economic functions. On the other hand, however, the official's limited experience of economic life and alienation from the market has the effect of restoring powers to business *in spite of* state power. In this particular respect the public bureaucracy is always 'weaker' than business, which is no bad thing. Whereas state rules of conduct can be made relatively predictable for market actors, the state cannot rely on predictable behaviour and outcomes in the market. When a state tries to engineer predictability in the market it weakens the adaptive efficiency of enterprises and undermines their incentives to innovate. The state is then also more likely to become a 'marketplace' for political profit making. The lesson, then, is that the need to regulate monopoly and to prevent abuses or misuses of market power has to be balanced by incentives to encourage genuine competition in the economic market. In practice, and for the practical reasons that I have sought to explain, this must mean a delimitation of state functions and a reduction of state tasks.

Separation of powers

I have already indicated that Weber proposed two broadly impersonal solutions to problems of state power and state–business closure. First, state bureaucracy should be oriented formally and legally to non-discriminatory procedures in order to prevent the appropriation of state authority by or on behalf of private interests. Second, the core functions of state bureaucracy should be confined to the legal regulation of economic life in order to reduce the incentives for the state to become actively engaged in economic action and in order to restrain state interests from fettering the expansion of markets.

I conclude this chapter by examining a third impersonal solution to state dysfunction – checks and balances, or the division of powers. Weber used the analogy of countervailing 'empires' to describe the institutionalized separation of powers in modernizing states. Democratic representation and judicial independence are viewed as society's method of '*limiting*' government power. The concurrent '*separation*' of powers is conceptually distinct in so far as it refers to competing powers within the state.

> Limitation of power exists where, due to sacred tradition or enactment, a particular *imperium* is restrained by the rights of its subjects. The power-holder may issue only commands of a certain type, or may issue all sorts of commands except in certain cases or subject to certain conditions.... The other kind of restraint ('separation of powers') exists where one *imperium* conflicts with another *imperium*, either equal or in certain respects superior to it, but the legitimate validity of which is fully recognized as limiting the extent of its authority. Both limitation of power and separation of powers may exist together, and it is this coexistence which so distinctively characterizes the modern state with its distribution of competence among its various organs.
>
> (Weber 1978: 652)

The legal system, bureaucracy, and parliament are separate 'spheres of competence' and power. The interaction of a plurality of state agencies in capitalist society exemplifies what Weber described as 'functionally specific separation of powers ... [in which] it is only by means of *compromise* between them that legitimate measures can be taken' (ibid.: 282). This need for compromise always means, in effect, that the 'constitutional separation of powers is a specifically *unstable* structure' (ibid.: 283). Yet another characteristic of the separation of powers is its '*objective* character' as distinct from the power of status groups or monocratic powers, which are 'more open to personal influences' and therefore 'more easily swayed' (ibid.: 283–4). Paradoxically, this *objective instability* created by separate spheres of authority within the state is able to 'introduce an element of *calculability* into the functioning of the administrative apparatus', one that is 'favourable to the formal rationalization of economic activity' and that is absent in centrally planned economies (ibid.: 284). The modern legal state has emerged only in countries where 'the political organization assumed the form of an institution with rationally dovetailed jurisdictions and a separation of powers' (ibid.: 653).

Only one dimension of the separation and limitation of powers is directly relevant in the present context – parliament's role in regulating the bureaucracy. Weber (ibid.: 271) argued that the power of state administration can only be 'limited' by 'agencies which act on their own authority'. The only agency able to continuously supervise and control is parliament. Weber's discussion of parliament's technical relationship with the bureaucracy was an extension of his broader effort to explain the non-discriminatory character of modern states.

> Bureaucracy inevitably accompanies modern mass democracy, in contrast to the democratic self-government of small homogeneous units. This results

from its characteristic principle: the abstract regularity of the exercise of authority, which is a result of the demand for 'equality before the law' in the personal and functional sense – hence, of the horror of 'privilege' and the principled rejection of doing business 'from case to case'.

(ibid.: 983)

Control of public bureaucracy, which is a primary function of democracy, consists of ensuring that bureaucracy continues to adhere to the parametric principle of legal equality by preventing 'the development of a closed status group of officials' and by expanding the 'influence of public opinion' (ibid.: 985). But since the 'overtowering' power of state bureaucracy provides all the *incentives* to sabotage the procedural ideal of 'equal rights of the governed', countermeasures are needed (ibid.: 985, 991). Political science and philosophy often dispute models of democracy according to their capacity to satisfy human needs or desires for equality, liberty, and justice. Weber also defended values of universal suffrage and individual freedom. But his principal interest was in the instrumental efficiency of political institutions. The political form of the state was, for Weber, a technical issue.

We are dealing here with simple questions of techniques for formulating national policies. For a mass state, there are only a limited number of alternatives.... In themselves, technical changes in the form of government do not make a nation vigorous or happy or valuable. They can only remove technical obstacles and thus are merely means for a given end.

(ibid.: 1383–4)

Of what, in practice, does the conflict between the parliamentary and administrative *imperiums* consist? Politicians depend on bureaucrats to 'continuously solve political problems' (ibid.: 1417). Yet the bureaucrats are difficult to control because 'such control is possible only in a very limited degree to [politicians] who are not technical specialists'. In many situations, 'the highest ranking official is more likely to get his way in the long run than his nominal superior, the cabinet minister, who is not a specialist' (ibid.: 224). The politician 'always finds himself, vis-à-vis the trained official, in the position of a dilettante facing the expert' (ibid.: 991). State bureaucracy will habitually 'hide its knowledge and action' so as to insulate itself from criticism (ibid.: 992). The 'official secret' is its 'supreme power instrument' (ibid.: 1418). The state bureaucracy 'naturally prefers a poorly informed, and hence powerless parliament' (ibid.: 993). Bureaucracy's continual fight to weaken parliament's supervisory power is accentuated, also, by status rivalries between the two spheres. Bureaucrats, who obtain their positions on the basis of impersonal qualifications are likely to resent the politician 'who seeks and gains power without legitimizing himself through a diploma' (ibid.: 1413).

Parliament can employ various methods for overcoming bureaucracy's resistance to supervision (ibid.: 1407–24). It can recruit heads of administrative agencies, or appoint them from among its own members. It can veto senior administrative appointments and force the resignation of officials if they lose the confidence of parliament. Administrative chiefs can be compelled to account to parliament for their actions. They can be forced to follow the operational guidelines laid down by parliament. Parliament is guaranteed the right to obtain information from public agencies. It is also able to impose discipline upon warring factions within the public bureaucracy. Indirectly, through the instrument of the ballot box, elected politicians are the rightful '*countervailing force*' against bureaucracy's natural 'desire to perpetuate the absence of controls' (ibid.: 1417, 1423). The 'possibility of public criticism' is one means of disciplining bureaucracy, and of maintaining 'the impersonal character of public office' (ibid.: 968).

Finally, the vital instrument of administrative control at the disposal of politicians is the parliamentary commission of inquiry with legal powers of investigation and sanction. Through it, parliament can 'force the administrative chiefs to account for their actions in such a way as to make [punishment] unnecessary' (ibid.: 1418). As Weber says, 'systematic cross-examination under oath of experts before a parliamentary commission in the presence of the ... departmental officials ... alone guarantees public supervision and a thorough inquiry' (ibid.). The parliamentary commission of inquiry at least permits specialists to openly debate the arguments for and against government action. As a result, politicians and senior officials are better informed. The democratic process is made transparent, and the public will become more appreciative of government's work. Weber admired the British parliament's use of the right of inquiry, the reporting of these committee proceedings in the national press, and, hence its contribution to the political awareness of the public. This is how 'the nation keeps itself informed about the conduct of its affairs by the bureaucracy, and continuously supervises it'. In Weber's view: 'Only the committees of a powerful parliament can be the vehicles for exercising this wholesome pedagogic influence' (ibid.: 1419).

Weber published these observations on representational development in 1917 in a widely read newspaper, 'the leftwing-liberal *Frankfurter Zeitung*' (Roth 1978: civ–cv). Nearly a century later, the developing world's façade democracies lack anything remotely equivalent in procedural quality to the kind of parliamentary commission of inquiry that Weber commended. Its institutional function is not even on the cards for the foreseeable future in a country such as China. In this sense, as in many others, surprisingly little has changed since Weber drew his foundational comparisons between precapitalism and capitalism.

State, law, and politics

The legal-regulatory, administrative, and representational conditions of the modern state described in this chapter are absent in precapitalist societies. The contorted vision of bureaucracy-led transition that is often found in contemporary *neodirigiste* writings could result, in part, from an understandable misinterpretation of history. In the original sequence of the evolution of organized state authority the consolidation of bureaucracy *preceded* formal law and free representation. Today, adherents of activist bureaucracy-first policies fail to recognize that state administration of the economy does not *start* to become modern until the impersonal formal-procedural norm is enforced in law, and does not *finally* become modern until it is supervised by a parliament that is itself run mainly along formal and impersonal lines. Bureaucracy cannot be of much service to society until this process is underway.

Each of the institutional spheres of capitalist society discussed here – economic regulation, law, public administration, and political representation – has a role in monitoring and regulating each of the other spheres. However, some of these interactive relationships are especially sharply drawn. Whereas law becomes the direct instrument for regulating markets, parliament becomes the direct instrument for regulating bureaucracy and, to a lesser extent, law. Thus, democratization eventually promotes further legal-administrative rationalization. When parliament supervises state bureaucracy it monitors the *procedural* norms of public administration. It aims to ensure that officials and the citizenry will continue to be equal before the law. Democracy is the ultimate constraint on the discriminatory powers of public administration.

> Democracy as such is opposed to the rule of bureaucracy, in spite and perhaps because of its unavoidable yet unintended promotion of bureaucratization. Under certain conditions, democracy creates palpable breaks in the bureaucratic pattern and impediments to bureaucratic organization.... For this reason, it must also remain an open question whether the power of bureaucracy is increasing in the modern states in which it is spreading. The fact that bureaucratic organization is technically the most highly developed power instrument in the hands of its controller does not determine the weight that bureaucracy as such is capable of procuring for its own opinions.
>
> (Weber 1978: 991)

This passage presupposes the development of democracy, which, in turn, presupposes prior law. We have still to examine in detail the ethical and legal preconditions for effective state-parametric regulation of the economy; a topic that requires a separate chapter. Before discussing the role of law, however, it can be noted that a Weberian theory of development supports – on purely pragmatic grounds of prior law – a policy sequence that may delay or suspend the full onslaught of political competition until the reciprocal conditioning of markets and state law has reached a more advanced stage. We have seen that an effective system of political competition depends *completely* on rule of law in much the same way that modern markets do. Without calculable procedural impersonality, value tolerance of competition, and formal state incentives for the continuous usurpation of monopolistic powers, real democracy does not exist. But political competition rarely generates its own impersonal rules, and, for practical reasons, is even less likely to be the origin of pressure for market freedom. As we have seen, the problems of negative privileges, political profit making, and regulatory closure, which the legal regulatory function of the modern state is intended to correct, can have their sources in both an underdeveloped bureaucracy *and* an underdeveloped parliament.

Thus free representation could not perform its institutional function in transitional societies unless and until the formal and enforceable rules of competition ensure that the political process is more or less honest and impartial. This would be impossible if 'democracy' were just a battleground for maximizing interest-group advantages or the control of clientelist retinues. In this sense, the construction of genuine democracy is an extension of precisely the same dynamic that produced capitalist law and administration.

> The 'progress' toward the bureaucratic state, adjudicating and administering according to rationally established law and regulation, is nowadays very closely related to the modern capitalist development. The modern capitalist enterprise rests primarily on calculation and presupposes a legal and administrative system, whose functioning can be rationally predicted, at least in principle, by virtue of its fixed general norms, just like the expected performance of a machine.
>
> (Weber 1978: 1394)

Modern parliament is little different. Its functioning can be 'rationally predicted' because its operating systems are identical in one respect – they are oriented to formal and impersonal procedural norms. Policies emanating from parliament can promote the rationalization of the economy and of the state. But it would appear to be difficult, if not impossible, for parliament itself to be 'rationalized' and for its members to *lead* society in the tasks of maintaining and developing market capitalism before economic evolution has given rise to a certain level and type of rule of law that can be extended to the representational sphere, and certainly not before some progress has been made in applying impersonal law to markets and state administration.

3   Law and economy

Weber's theories of capitalism provide compelling support for the argument that policymakers in developing countries should focus their initial reform efforts on economic liberalization and the construction of appropriate legal mechanisms to regulate markets. In the typical conditions of sequenced capitalist transition, the order of priorities gives proportionally less emphasis to building up state administrative and representational capacities. Weber's relevant writings deal with the intertwined evolution of markets, ethics, and law over long historical periods during which capitalism began to emerge through trial and error in parts of Europe. Yet there are reasons to suppose that the causal chains which Weber observed during the original transitions will be similar during necessarily telescoped phases of contemporary development.

The discussion of law in this chapter is relevant to debates on whether formal rules or informal norms and social relations are the foundations of economic trust. Trust between persons with shared morals improves market behaviour and substitutes for the formality of legal organizations. Weber (1978: 320) observed that in modern economies it is hardly ever necessary for partners in exchange to resort to third-party adjudication. Social convention may be 'far more determinative of ... conduct than the existence of legal enforcement machinery'. Ethical consensus compensates for the limitations of legal foresight and counteracts the many incentives to circumvent formal rules. However, in a complex social system made up of many organizations, reliable administration of law is the structure on which trust acquires incontrovertible force. Weber said: 'To the person to whom something has been promised the legal guaranty gives a higher degree of certainty that the promise will be kept' (ibid.: 667)

At issue is the advantage of procedural certainty. In advanced economic and political exchange the source of ultimate trust is law, unambiguously guaranteed by neutral state power. Legal trustworthiness improves the calculability of outcomes in economic relationships: 'Industrial capitalism must be able to count on the continuity, trustworthiness and objectivity of the legal order, and on the rational, predictable functioning of legal and administrative agencies' (ibid.: 1095). Maintenance of market freedoms requires something more solid than amorphous social virtues. A modernizing society needs a rule-compliant economy in which contracts can be upheld independently of the personal authority of power holders. Strongly developed interpersonal or communitarian networks based on localized trust tend – especially when overarching frameworks of impersonal law are absent – to begin excluding outsiders in the effort to monopolize economic opportunities. In this way, they become obstacles to economic development. In reliably regulated competitive markets, the nebulous microfoundations of informal trust have less significance. During capitalist transitions, communitarian ethics are typically abandoned as economic actors transit from closed markets to open markets. As producers and consumers move beyond the internal economy and into the external economies, so too are their attitudes toward competition revolutionized.

Proto-institutional ethic

The argument begins by recognizing the historical role that market forces play in capitalist development. The long-run institutional effect of the expansion of commerce was the evolution of an ethic of market freedom. This market-sustaining ethic was the embryo of capitalism. Informal regulation of market competition first evolved spontaneously as trade and the division of labour revealed the desirability of collective norms for economic exchange. Formal institutions responsible for law, administration, and political representation evolved long after the informal regulation of commercial life.

What is the market ethic? To answer this question we must distinguish two market situations. The 'free market' is not regulated by ethical or legal norms (Weber 1978: 637). Modern 'market freedom', in contrast, assumes secure property rights and formal universal rights to compete for profits. Market freedom is characterized by a competitive economic struggle unfettered by personal loyalties or communal obligations, by state intervention on behalf of individual enterprises, or by uncertainty about whether malfeasance will go unpunished. Between free market and market freedom is the 'market ethic' or 'capitalist ethic', namely a proto-institutional set of behavioural norms and beliefs about the value of market freedom that will eventually be formalized as legally regulated norms. Capitalist ethics do not prevail everywhere that economic activity is 'competitive'. They are not, for example, a characteristic of rent-seeking markets where competitive struggle is for politically created appropriations of profit opportunities. Similarly, capitalist ethics do not thrive in situations where the state authorities select firms or sectors for privileges to compete under protective – usually national – shelters.

Although best known as the author of *The Protestant Ethic and the Spirit of Capitalism* (1992), Weber's theorization of the modern market ethic can only be understood by emphasizing its secular dimension. The diffusion of the 'spirit of capitalism' was 'a sort of liberal enlightenment' that looked favourably on business success (ibid.: 70). Although there were 'correlations between forms of religious belief and practical ethics', it would be 'foolish and doctrinaire' to claim capitalism could only have evolved because of the Reformation (ibid.: 91). In northern Europe and the United States, Protestantism 'helped to deliver the spirit

of modern capitalism' (Weber 1947: 321). It was fortuitous historical circumstance that allowed religious belief to become the ideological carrier for a
rational 'ethos of the modern bourgeois middle classes'. Puritan sects were
simply bearers for the asceticism and vocation for hard, methodical, and honest
work that helped build the foundations of modern individualism. The Protestant
'style of life' coincided with the 'self-justification that is customary for bourgeois acquisition: profit and property appear not as ends in themselves but as
indications of personal ability' (Weber 1978: 1200).

Religious ideas were expressions of national character during the European
Middle Ages, but were themselves a product of geographic, political, and economic circumstance, and of the growth of cities, law, bookkeeping, and science.
Economic interests often lay behind the attitudes of Protestantism (ibid.: 583–9).
The liberal enlightenment gradually stripped economic life of any religious
content. In the twentieth century, declared Weber, the 'religious root of modern
economic humanity is dead' (1981: 368–9). The 'people filled with the spirit of
capitalism today tend to be indifferent, if not hostile, to the Church' (Weber
1992: 70). The ethic of capitalism is really founded in *social premiums* attached
to types of moral conduct that resulted from the spread of market relations.
Bourgeois ethics, according to Weber, are premiums placed on discipline, production, probity, and cautionary finance, which were founding principles of early
capitalism (1947: 313, 321). In capitalist society, money making and capital
accumulation are acceptable if 'done legally' as 'the expression of virtue and
proficiency' (Weber 1992: 53–4). Capitalists are governed by an impulse to
make money, but also by morals relating to methods of money making, as well
as the 'irrational sense of having done [the] job well' (ibid.: 71). 'Acquisitive-
ness' is not unique to capitalism, and has been 'at home in all types of economic
society' (ibid.: 58). In fact, 'absolute unscrupulousness' in 'the making of money
has been a specific characteristic of precisely those countries whose ... capitalistic development ... has remained backward' (ibid.: 57).

The important transition in the moral valuation of economic activity is the
gradual abandonment of the communitarian conventions of precapitalist society
in favour of universalistic economic norms. Communitarian norms are *interpersonal* rather than impersonal. A sharp separation between the ethics of 'internal'
and 'external' transactions holds back the development of capitalism. Weber
called this the problem of the 'double-ethic'. Traditional society frowns upon
those who profit from transactions with members of their own community, even
though economic dealings with outsiders – if permitted at all – are legitimately
conducted with 'complete ruthlessness' (ibid.: 57; 1981: 312–13). Economic
freedom within the community is deliberately limited, while external economic
exchange is undertaken in an atmosphere of suspicion and hostility. If a community's maxim is that 'brothers do not bargain with one another' then the
'market principle of price determination' will be absent (Weber 1978: 362).
Nationalism, which Weber described as 'the pathetic pride in the power of one's
own community, or [the] longing for it' (ibid.: 398), preserves the moral double
standard of hostility towards outsiders.

Thus, transition to market society entails a twofold ethical transformation. First, it destroys the ethics that subordinate economic exchange to social approbation by status, kinship, ritual, prohibitions on usury, or irrational limitations on the kinds of goods that can be exchanged. Second, the ethic that legitimizes cheating in exchange relations with people outside the community is eliminated. A condition of capitalist transition in the Western world was a 'lifting of the barrier between the internal and external economy, between internal and external ethics, and the entry of commercial principles into the internal economy' (Weber 1981: 313). 'Dualistic ethics' are abandoned as the marketplace gradually breaks down all economically irrational forces of traditional rulership that are obstacles to free exchange. Commercial principles are applied in the internal economy, while ethics of fair dealing are preserved and extended to the external economy. Weber (1978: 636) argued that when a market is allowed to 'follow its own autonomous tendencies' it creates impersonal communities where economic behaviour is no longer oriented to obligations of brotherhood or neighbourhood but rather to the matter-of-fact calculation of profits, exchange of commodities, and competitive survival. The principle that prevails, he repeatedly says, is that 'honesty is the best policy'.

> It is normally assumed by both partners to an exchange that each will be interested in the future continuation of the exchange relationship, be it with this particular partner or with some other, and that he will adhere to his promises for this reason and avoid at least striking infringements of the rules of good faith and fair dealing.
>
> (ibid.: 637)

The ethical trend is further intensified with industrialization and entrepreneurship. Weber's classic example is of the secular innovator in the textile industry, imbued with the spirit of capitalism, who sets out to profit systematically from new opportunities (1992: 65–9). The entrepreneur is an individual of strong character, self-control, and exceptional vision. Around him he sees leisurely business, friendly relationships among business competitors, and a traditionalistic approach towards profits, labour time, and customers. The entrepreneur is not driven by a desire to burst this world apart, and is not motivated simply by greed. He does not have the power to force others to act against their wishes. He can see there is not even a need to invest large amounts of capital in the new enterprise. He may be a young subcontractor who identifies new ways of exploiting the existing organizations and technology, and calculates how to gain an edge in a slow industry of moderate effort and monopolistic profit. He chooses his employees carefully, improves labour supervision, keeps his prices low, and increases turnover. He develops marketing methods that involve more direct and regular contact with customers, and adapts production to customer needs. He recognizes, also, that he must act ethically to secure the confidence of customers, workers, and business partners. As a 'first innovator' the entrepreneur encounters the mistrust, hostility, and moral indignation of monopolists whom he usurps. Once enough innovators have taken similar initiatives, and once the lag-gards have been swept up and the success of new methods is obvious to all, the effect of an economic ethic may be equivalent to that of a general social norm.

This is the process of economic rationalization. Markets exert pressures on labour and capitalists to be methodical and calculative. Consequently, market expansion can modify the attitudes of entire societies. Price determinations even-tually produce an impersonal self-binding regularity in the behaviour of eco-nomic actors. As Weber (1978: 585) said, 'rational economic association always brings about *depersonalization*'. People orient their actions to the impersonal market ethic, which they view as legitimate and binding. The ethic has a func-tion, recognized by most market participants, of preserving the action system. It is upheld by the likelihood of social disapproval and boycotts against violators. It requires a tolerance for the discipline, risks, and morals of market society. As the rewards become apparent, communitarian ethics are weakened. The clamour for protection against competition subsides as people develop a rational interest in regulated competition. 'The result', said Weber, 'is a regulated economic life with the economic impulse functioning within bounds' (1981: 356).

The ethical origins of capitalism raise the possibility that market ethics could be the content of modern capitalist ideologies. During the early capitalist trans-itions, Protestant theologians systematically interpreted reality and influenced normative and behavioural change. The dominant carriers of worldviews were religious intellectuals, and it was they who supplied the ideological motivations or justifications for economic action. It may be reasonable to expect that con-temporary ideologies could provide an irreligious cognitive and volitional frame-work for cultivating the ethics of modern capitalism. The carriers of the 'spirit' of capitalism today include entrepreneurs who develop an attitude for seeing every problem in economic and technological terms. Yet although the spread of an entrepreneurial spirit can help to change society, it is not the social function of entrepreneurs to transmit economic ethics to society. Intellectual professions are the carriers not only of informal morals and values in market society – some of which will be collectivized as formal-legal norms – but also of social-scientific knowledge that justifies capitalism. That ideologists have not always wanted or been able to perform this function effectively in the past does not mean that they could not do so better in the future.

This is an unusual way of looking at ethics, which are normally viewed as attributes of culture rather than ideology. Ethics are moral values, treated as valid norms. Initially, they emerged by spontaneous evolution. There is, therefore, some truth in Hayek's claim: 'Ethics is not a matter of choice. We have not designed it and cannot design it' (Hayek 1982: vol. 3, 167). Cultures, which are collective by nature, tend not to value individualistic ethics of market exchange. Resistance to the spread of economic competition is an innate characteristic of premodern society. Weber (1978: 638) pointed out, for example, that commercial ethics are 'alien' in rural communities, which fear commerce and equate it with cheating. However, since social order in all advanced societies now depends on market ethics, we must ask how this ethic will emerge in developing societies.

In this book I make a distinction between *design* and *emulation*. Whether people emulate a functional ethic, whatever its origins, is ultimately their free choice. The only question is: can people be persuaded to make the choice? Ideology, unlike culture, is also a matter of free choice, and the function of ideology is to inform and persuade. In Chapter 5 I will argue that ideologies have cognitive and volitional functions in breaking down cultural and interest-group barriers to the development of markets. At this stage we need only observe how Weber's conceptualization of ethics is relevant to ideology. An 'ethical standard', Weber (ibid.: 36) said, is 'one to which men attribute a certain type of value and which, by virtue of this belief, they treat as a valid norm governing their action'. In Weber's opinion, 'practical ethics' have never been determined by culture alone. On the contrary, he said, an 'economic ethic has a high measure of autonomy' (Weber 1947: 268). An economic ethic might well have cultural anchorages in society. Nevertheless, 'an ethic which rejects all cultural values is possible without any internal contradictions' (Weber 1949: 15). Moreover, ethics can be 'normative', and 'normative ethics' can conflict with institutional or political norms. In that sense, an ethic resembles ideology.

Since communitarianism constrains the development of market ethics in developing societies, an ideology that opposes communitarianism could begin life as advocacy on behalf of market liberalization. Market reforms can set in train a capitalist dynamic of proto-institutional change that speedily transmutes the formal institutions of society. Legal-administrative reform will be easier to implement if the economic ethics of many individuals are already favourable to it. The economic values that encompass mundane attitudes towards work, competition, and commerce might be starting points for this process. Ethical change takes shape in a growing tolerance for principles of conduct that are adequate for the development of market freedom, as the rewards for private discipline and private risk rapidly become apparent. The *practice* of market enterprise creates the *demand* for collective norms that will eventually govern economic exchange and contractual obligations, and minimize generalized risk.

Evolution of norms

Weber asked 'how anything new can ever arise in this world' (Weber 1978: 321). He struggled to answer the most complex question – how do informal norms emerge and then evolve into enforceable formal law? The chronology is imprecise. A continuum of multiple determinations, a patterning of action, and the knock-on effect of one variable upon another begins slowly and then picks up speed. Modern laws are the norms that have acquired a formal guarantee of enforcement by the coercive apparatuses of the state. Even so, the determination of action by law is not inevitable. 'Consensual action' based on informal custom or convention can be 'firmly embedded', and 'may continue to exist for centuries' (ibid.: 756). Weber well understood that 'legal obligation', though it may oppose traditional norms, 'frequently fails in the attempt to influence actual conduct' (ibid.: 320).

In conceptualizing normative change it is useful to adopt Weber's preferred method of analysis – begin by discovering the function of a norm, then work *backwards* to gain an understanding of the process through which norms are selected and survive. In Weber's words, 'we must know what kind of action is functionally necessary for 'survival' [and] the continuity of the corresponding modes of social action, before it is possible even to inquire how this action has come about and what motives determine it' (ibid.: 17–18).

One of the recurring 'Weberian' arguments in the present book is that modern impersonal norms, which are institutionalized in legal, administrative, and political organizations of capitalist society, increase the calculability and fairness of economic and political life, and ensure the survivability of the capitalist system. However, the mere existence or functionality of a procedural norm cannot guarantee that its instrumentality will be recognized or accepted automatically. Weber attempted to resolve the puzzle of normative evolution by systematizing a bewildering array of determinants of action (ibid.: 29–36, 311–25, 753–60). A legal order does not emerge simply because of its 'logically demonstrable correctness', or because of what people believe 'ought' to occur. Many determinants and motivations bear upon the evolutionary process, which Weber conceptualized as a 'continuum with imperceptible transitions' from 'custom' (norms of tradition, habit and imitation), to 'convention' (norms of consensus, fear of disapproval, and the informal boycott), and finally to 'formal law' (rights enforced coercively by administrative means). Law standardizes understandings that were originally arrived at through informal agreements.

'New norms' have sometimes 'emerged through explicit imposition from above' (ibid.: 760). However, most of the early changes along the continuum are influenced by people's 'subjective experiences' of the world, their 'conscious expectations', and the 'consensual understandings' within a group, association, community, or society about how individuals will or should act and react in specific circumstances (ibid.: 754–5). The processes of inventing, selecting, and injecting social norms into economic conduct, and the transformation of informal norms into enforceable legal obligations, occur if it was in the self-interest of individuals or groups – especially if self-interest combines with loyalties to members of the group or society.

Significant normative changes also happen by 'innovation' (ibid.: 322). Within society, often in response to a new situation, there arises 'a new line of conduct' or a new collective-action rule produced by a rational consensus among interested parties (ibid.: 755). Furthermore, normative or institutional innovation can be 'induced' by changes in the external environment. I will argue that global technological, economic, or political developments may provide the impetus for selecting capitalistic norms in developing societies. Evolutionism is explicit in Weber's method of exploring the adaptive efficiency of norms, as when 'the total structure of social action changes in response to external conditions' (ibid.). In addition, normative changes are more likely to 'survive' if they 'are adapted to the external environment' (ibid.: 322).

Of several kinds of [normative] action, all may have been well suited to existing conditions; but, when the [external] conditions change one may turn out to be better suited to serve the economic or social interests of the parties involved; in the process of selection it alone survives and ultimately becomes the one used by all so that one cannot well point out any single individual who would have 'changed' his conduct.

(ibid.: 755)

Above all, however, Weber emphasized the individualistic sources of innovation that produce 'collective action' by 'inspiration' or by a 'sudden awakening, through drastic means, of the awareness that a certain action "ought" to be done'. Innovation might also result from an 'empathy' that induces 'certain kinds of consensus' about the 'oughtness' of an innovation that ultimately generates a law and the corresponding machinery for its enforcement (ibid.: 322–3). Finally, and decisively, 'constant recurrence of a certain pattern of conduct' can create a perception that there now exists a 'legal obligation requiring enforcement' (ibid.: 323).

> Eventually, the interests involved may engender a rationally considered desire to secure the convention ... against subversion, and to place it explicitly under the guarantee of an enforcement machinery, i.e. to transform it into enacted law. Particularly in the field of the internal distribution of power among the organs of an institutional order experience reveals a continuous scale of transitions from norms of conduct guaranteed by mere convention to those which are regarded as binding and guaranteed by law.
>
> (ibid.: 323)

The higher the level of 'rationalization' in society or economy, the more likely it is that these types of pressure will produce the normative and legal changes characteristic of capitalist transitions. Weber adds more intentionality and discontinuity to his evolutionary schema by describing how the invention and imitation of norms, and their conversion to law, can be a controlled process of deliberate enactment (ibid.).

> More frequent ... is the injection of a new content into social actions and rational associations as a result of individual invention and its subsequent spread through imitation and selection. Not merely in modern times has this latter situation been of greatest significance as a source of economic reorientation, but in all systems in which the mode of life has reached at least a measure of rationalization.
>
> (ibid.: 755–6)

Market participants do not necessarily recognize immediately the need for legal enforcement by the state (ibid.: 756). Nevertheless, it is clear that their informal agreements on the rights and wrongs of a mode of transaction make it likely that 'the function later [will be] fulfilled by the legal guarantee of a norm' (ibid). In these ways, the economic orientation of society evolves in continuous transition towards institutional capitalism.

Enforcement of rules

The custom–convention–law continuum is how Weber explained the transition from interpersonal market ethics to the formal enforcement of impersonal economic rights by the state. It can be noted that there are obvious conceptual as well as terminological similarities between Weber's writing on this subject and much later analyses of the evolution of law in new institutional economics, even though the latter derives some contrary lessons about the origin, nature, and potential of state institutions in modernizing societies (North 1990).

Wherever there is simple small-scale exchange among people who share common values there will be little need for 'third parties' to enforce the market rules. If transactions are local and directly between persons who know each other or who belong to the same group or network, the security of established custom may provide adequate normative regulation. Weber (1978: 319) defines 'custom' as 'typically uniform activity which is kept on the beaten track simply because men are accustomed to it and persist in it by unreflecting imitation'. Economic exchange in traditional society is governed by 'custom', i.e. 'rules devoid of any external sanction' (ibid.: 29). Custom produces 'dependency relationships' among unequal partners, mutual obligations of reciprocity, and clientelist transactions between economic units (ibid.: 1010–11). Market regulation by custom can involve 'accepted limitations on exchange' (ibid.: 82). Often, the 'effects of conformity with long-standing customary norms in the economy can be similar to those that result from motivations of self-interest when the parties to an exchange have identical expectations about each other's behaviour' (ibid.: 29–30).

However, as the quantity, distance, and complexity of economic exchanges grow so does the demand for guarantees that rules of exchange will be 'binding and protected against violation by sanctions of disapproval' (ibid.: 34). Economic groups devise many informal means for expressing disapproval and constraining undesirable behaviour without the need for external coercion by a third party. 'Convention', which is not based solely on self-interest or on tradition, is a non-coercive means of coordinating transactions. Convention represents belief or interest in the legitimacy of the economic order governing the action. A market ethic can be supported by convention. Ethics and conventions are similar in that neither requires an external enforcement agency. In Weber's words, a 'system of ethics' is 'likely to be upheld to a large extent by the probability that disapproval will result from its violation, that is, by convention' (ibid.: 36). Convention is, in other words, an 'order' that is felt to be binding for social or economic relationships and can 'determine the course of action'. On the other hand, individuals can be subject to 'contradictory systems of order' (ibid.: 32). Conventions are especially important in economic life when there exists 'social disapproval of treating certain utilities as marketable or of subjecting certain objects of exchange to free competition and free price determination' (ibid.: 82–3).

It is impossible to precisely pinpoint the transition from custom to convention, or from convention to law. Weber suggests, as a near approximation, that coercive legal order first becomes apparent when a boycott or other punishment of transgressors is 'formally threatened and organized' (ibid.: 34). As soon as there is a 'coercive apparatus' to enforce the compliance with norms it must be assumed that norms have become laws (ibid.: 312). Nevertheless, there is an ongoing interaction between law, custom, and convention. Each may be the 'source' of the other (ibid.: 332). More or less identical objectives of market regulation can be achieved by means of formal or informal prohibitions (ibid.: 82–3). Yet law is different from custom and convention in one vital respect. Laws have an *autonomy* from the social environment that is not given to either custom or convention. They can be created for purely *technical* reasons unrelated to the preexisting customs or conventions, that is, without any normative precedent at all. For example: 'Legal rules ... may have been established entirely on grounds of expediency' (ibid.: 36).

Legal order presupposes a coercive but legitimate state, the existence of a group of persons who specialize in legal design, and a 'staff' to enforce the laws. 'Today', says Weber, 'the most common form of legitimacy is the belief in legality, the compliance with enactments which are formally correct' (ibid.: 37). Custom and convention never achieve the intensity of legitimacy or authority that is characteristic of laws. How is law selected, and when does law take precedence over custom or convention? In Weber's view, the 'institutional order is a product of evolution' in which law, political community, and market rationality become intertwined (ibid.: 905). Only the political community, i.e. the nation state, is uniquely able to legitimize the threat of physical violence in order to guarantee the legal order (ibid.: 902–4). The motives for forming political communities can be economic, territorial, social, or moral. Political communities can be economic entities defined by territorial borders. Internally, they regulate the interrelationships of their members. The reasons for establishing a legal order or a political community are almost identical. In each case, interest groups have worked together to seek the protection of 'those rationally regulated guaranties which none but the political community was able to create' (ibid.: 904). Weber described this process as the 'nationalization of all legal norms', which produces the 'rational consociation' of the modern state (ibid.). His depiction of the transition towards nationalized legal norms emphasizes a process of selection through which *'expansion of the market'* and *'public peace'* become objects for individual invention and collective action.

Weber viewed peace and prosperity as interwoven ends in the transition to capitalism. Market exchanges create the pressures for establishing legal guarantees of public peace by means of institutions that reconcile disparate interests. In Weber's words, a market 'transcends the boundaries of neighbourhood' and was the first 'peaceful relationship' that communities ever had with the 'world outside' (ibid.: 637). Among people who regularly engage in market exchange, the continuity of relationships and assurances of future contracts elicit an attitudinal disposition towards good faith anchored in law. In the following passage Weber describes how bourgeois interests in public peace and property rights patterned the evolution of the modern state.

If the coercive apparatus is strong enough, it will suppress private violence in any form. The effectiveness of this suppression rises with the development of the coercive apparatus into a permanent structure.... Subsequently, it engenders, more generally, a form of permanent public peace, with the compulsory submission of all disputes to the arbitration of the judge, who transforms blood vengeance into rationally ordered punishment, and feuds ... [into] rationally ordered legal procedures. Thus the political community ... [is] transformed into an institution for the protection of rights. In so doing it obtains ... decisive support from all those groups which have a direct or indirect economic interest in the expansion of the market community ... [The] groups most interested in pacification are those guided by market interests.... And as the expansion of the market disrupted the monopolistic organizations and led their members to the awareness of their interests in the market, it cut out from under them the basis of that community of interests on which the legitimacy of their violence had developed. The spread of pacification and the expansion of the market thus constitute a development which ... finds its culmination in the modern concept of the state as the ultimate source of every kind of legitimacy of the use of physical force; and that rationalization of the rules of its application which has come to culminate in the concept of the legitimate legal order.

(ibid.: 908–9)

For reasons of inconvenience or neglect, Weber's argument about the interlinked development of markets, law, and nation states is often lost in the secondary literature. The legitimacy of the modern state grew first from efforts at *pacification* that were a direct *consequence* of the expansion of markets, and then subsequently from legal adjudication. This was, in effect, the *sequence* of transition.

The ever-increasing integration of all individuals and all fact-situations into one compulsory institution [of the state] which today, at least, rests in principle on formal 'legal equality' has been achieved by two great rationalizing forces, i.e. first, by the extension of the market economy and, second, by the bureaucratization of the activities of the organs of the consensual groups. They replaced that particularistic mode of creating law which was based upon the private power or the granted privileges of monopolistically closed organizations.

(ibid.: 698)

This introduction to Weber's thinking on the relationship between economic and legal development allows us to see why the crucial policy sequences of capitalist transition in developing societies might today also be market-led and law-led. Market interests create demand for the legal-administrative mechanisms that capitalist economies require. Nevertheless, it would clearly be a mistake to over-idealize the role of law in capitalist transition. Weber himself emphasized that the process by which law protects economic interests is not without many dangers. For example, monopolistic groups may exploit legal rights for their own advantage. The following section explains why, even so, the dominant pattern of change during capitalist transitions is the progressive usurpation of monopolies.

Property and contract

Let us first consider how Weber conceptualized legally acquired property rights in the development of modern capitalism. It was Weber's view that market interests drive the evolution of legally protected property. Again, this is the *sequence* of transition.

> The organization of economic activity on the basis of a market economy presupposes the appropriation of the material sources of utilities on the one hand, and market freedom on the other. The effectiveness of market freedom increases with the degree to which these sources of utility ... are appropriated.... All parties to market relations have had an interest in this expansion of property rights because it increased the area within which they could orient their action to the opportunities of profit offered by the market situation. The development of this type of property is hence attributable to their influence.
>
> (Weber 1978: 112–13)

Whenever Weber discussed property rights he spoke simultaneously of their liberating effect on economies as well as their potential to constrain economic freedom. There is always a chance that formal freedoms of contract and property, rather than empowering all those who aspire to profit making, might only serve the interests of those who have economic power at the time when laws to protect property are enacted.

> The result of contractual freedom ... is in the first place the opening of the opportunity to use, by the clever utilization of property ownership in the market, these resources without legal restraints as a means for the achievement of power over others. The parties interested in power in the market thus are also interested in such a legal order. Their interest is served particularly by ... 'legal empowerment rules' ... [that] create the framework for valid agreements which, under conditions of formal freedom, are officially available to all. Actually, however, they are accessible only to the owners of property and thus, in effect support their very autonomy and power positions.
>
> (ibid.: 730)

Guaranties of property became formal rights because of the influence exerted by existing property owners. Nevertheless, the very same rights subsequently empowered all future owners of land and capital. Weber conceptualized property rights as 'appropriation'. In general terms, 'rights' will be 'appropriated advantages' (ibid.: 44). Advantages, which may be 'real or imagined', often refer specifically to utilities, and, in particular, to the 'calculable chances of having economic goods available or of acquiring them under certain conditions in the future' (ibid.: 68–9, 315). During the evolution of the state, some rights were selected for formal legal enactment 'guaranteed by the coercive power of the political authorities' (ibid.: 315). In the 'purest type of ... formal order ... all non-human sources of utility are completely appropriated so that individuals can have free disposal of them, in particular by exchange, as in the case of the modern property system' (ibid.: 75). The calculable expectation that property rights will be upheld by states is an institutional precondition of capitalism, and is the legal foundation of modern economies.

> Today economic exchange is quite overwhelmingly guaranteed by the threat of legal coercion. The normal intention in an act of exchange is to acquire certain subjective 'rights', i.e. in sociological terms, the probability of support of one's power of disposition by the coercive apparatus of the state. Economic goods today are normally at the same time legitimately acquired rights; they are the very building material for the universe of the economic order ... [At the least] the interference of legal guaranties merely increases the degree of certainty with which an economically relevant action can be calculated in advance.
>
> (ibid.: 329)

When Weber spoke of 'property rights' he meant legal appropriations of ownership, use, or disposal of all factors of production – land, labour, technology, or capital. In a capitalist economy there must be 'appropriation of the means of production by individual units, that is by "property"' (ibid.: 93). Property is of most advantage to the entrepreneur who makes investments of capital in productive enterprises that provide good returns. The legal guarantee greatly increases the degree to which entrepreneurs can calculate the consequence of their actions. A formal and impersonal system of property rights provides continuous incentives for innovation and entrepreneurship by protecting the entrepreneur from unlawful market closure by rivals and from proprietary encroachments by the state.

> It is the most elemental economic fact that the way in which the disposition over material property is distributed among a plurality of people, meeting competitively in the market for the purpose of exchange, in itself creates specific life chances.... The mode of distribution gives to the propertied a monopoly on the possibility of transferring property from the sphere of use as 'wealth' to the sphere of 'capital', that is, it gives them the entrepreneurial function and all chances to share directly or indirectly in the returns on capital.
>
> (ibid.: 927)

Property is the source of economic power. Property rights are inseparable from the power context and the conditions that do or do not permit property rights to be appropriated by individuals and groups. Property rights enable the entrepreneur to better predict how effectively a power will endure for so long as the entrepreneur can remain competitive.

> To the person who finds himself actually in possession of the power to control an object or a person the legal guaranty gives a specific certainty of the durability of such power. To the person to whom something has been promised the legal guaranty gives a higher degree of certainty that the promise will be kept. These are indeed the most elementary relationships between law and economic life.
>
> (ibid.: 667)

The central issue relates, then, to how economic rights are appropriated, how they are created and protected, and how the corresponding power is utilized. Economic rights may be utilized positively or negatively. Appropriations of economic advantages can be the sources of monopolistic closure by privileged groups. Without state-regulatory countermeasures, economic actors will simply appropriate opportunities for profit by protecting themselves against competition. Yet, economic rights are also the foundation of market freedom. The security they afford energizes the entrepreneur whose upward mobility is through the market rather than through their connections with the state. Formal legality of economic relations in capitalist society is the only real guarantee of the possibility of such mobility. A property right empowers entrepreneurs by enabling and permitting them to usurp monopolies. However, because laws are made politically by governments, formal economic rights cut both ways. Rules that become written law are not always the most efficient ones. If the political process is impersonal, the laws and enforcement procedures will tend also to be impersonal. But if interest groups can determine political decisions, the laws will reflect those interests. Depending on how the right is defined, and how much power the state can apply to the enforcement of law, a property right can favour a small number of owners:

> where the protection of rights is guaranteed [only] by the organs of the political authority, the coercive apparatus may be reinforced by pressure groups.... The law of the state often tries to obstruct the coercive means of other associations.... But the state is not always successful. There are groups stronger than the state ... [The] state has been forced, at least partially, to trim its sails.
>
> (ibid.: 317)

In ancient times, 'legal procedure' was used to 'legalize' the 'unequal distribution of economic power' (ibid.: 812–13). Even in modern economies, where rights can seem to be equal among all citizens, legally privileged individuals or groups are often still able to appropriate them. There is a distinction, therefore, between 'alienable free property' that can be openly exchanged in the market, and appropriated property rights monopolized – e.g. by inheritance – within pre-defined groups of persons for their own benefit. Weber offers the example of a stock exchange that might remain 'closed to outsiders' while allowing its own members 'perfectly free competition for all the advantages which the group as a whole monopolizes for itself' (ibid.: 45). A negative, i.e. inherently unequal appropriation is termed a *'closed* economic relationship' (ibid.: 341–3). Before modern capitalism, privileges gained through 'closure' were typically the source of property in natural resources, as well as of legal orders designed to limit market competition. Weber points out that various 'stages of internal closure' have historically preceded the more expansive individualistic phases of transition, which set the stage for modern capitalism.

> If the appropriated monopolistic opportunities are released for exchange outside the group, thus becoming completely 'free' property, the old monopolistic association is doomed. Its remnants are the appropriated powers of disposition which appear on the market as 'acquired rights' of individuals.
>
> (ibid.: 343)

'Closure' is encountered in all societies, traditional or modern. Although open economic relationships can subsequently become closed again, Weber was most interested in the *'sequence* to the full appropriation of all the material means of production' (ibid.: 639). Of his many statements on the subject, one passage, above all others, captures Weber's view of the prerequisite condition of a genuinely capitalist economic environment: 'Complete appropriation of all material means of production by owners and the complete absence of all formal appropriation of opportunities for profit in the market; that is, market freedom' (ibid.: 161). More than anything else, it is this condition of 'market freedom' that defines capitalist economies.

The historical sequence begins with monopolistic closure of the market by status groups. Then, under pressure from the expansion of the money economy and a division of labour, and the growing demands for a share of profits, some market participants become interested in 'the possibility of using their vested property rights for exchange with the highest bidder, even though he may be an outsider' (ibid.: 638). They create political pressure for the creation of universalistic legal freedoms that will enable them to secure means of production, investment, and exchange through the market without monopolistic restrictions. Although their self-interest motive may be to create new avenues of closure, the impetus for action is the attempt to *break up* the existing monopolies.

The sequence culminates when those who have 'a stake in the capitalistic system' finally get 'the upper hand', destroying existing appropriations and achieving 'free competition' (ibid.: 639). Monopolies that are created as a consequence of this process will be 'capitalistic' ones. The new monopolies do not – as was the case previously – exclude market competition. Now, they 'are based solely on the power of property' and must depend 'upon an entirely rationally calculated mastery of market conditions'. The market is, only then, formally free without 'restrictions on the formation of rational market prices', but with 'guaranties for the observance of market legality' and 'market peace' (ibid.). In order to ensure their survival capitalist interests willingly give up their right to monopolistic privileges.

In the new circumstances, economic rights become positive rather than negative rights. When all economic goods are legitimately acquired rights guaranteed by the state, legal property rights can provide a universe of possibilities for equalizing the commercial opportunities in society. In modern law: 'Every right is thus a source of power of which even a hitherto entirely powerless person may become possessed' (ibid.: 667). Rights that are protected by formally enacted law benefit existing power holders, but they also open up 'individual opportunities and liberating capacities' (ibid.: 813). In the modern society, state coercive powers protect legitimate profits acquired by businesses in an exchange economy from predatory businesses that have profited illegitimately from appropriations of political power, or that employ the force of violence (ibid.: 204–6).

Legitimate appropriations in a competitive market economy include production units, management powers, credit instruments, supply chains, and marketable goods (ibid.: 144–50). The 'legal expression' of 'free competition' requires that 'the modern state guarantee only claims on concrete usable goods or labour services'. The state should not employ its authority 'for the exercise of direct coercion in favour of the owner or purchaser of [an entire] "market"' (ibid.: 329). Today, government–business relations in the developing countries often continue to involve vying for entitlements to *whole* markets. Such appropriations are common in societies where processes of political profit making encourage government *protections* to be exchanged for performance targets, contributions to public funds, provision of vital infrastructure, or, more simply, bribes.

Further examples of how economic factors determine the evolution of law are found in Weber's studies of the institutionalization of formal contractual rights. Contractual rights appear as agreements made to secure a specifiable outcome of economic exchange. In traditional society, exchange agreements tend to be informal and fraternal or clientelist. Agreement may be marked by a change in the status of the parties to the agreement (ibid.: 672). A person may become a protector, a client, a comrade, or a new member of the family. Such agreements are arbitrary, and corresponding powers of negotiation are typically unequal. Weber argued that a system of formal legally binding contracts emerged because of the demands from business for impersonal, calculable, and unambiguous contracts (ibid.: 847). In the modern contractual society, freedom of economic association is formal and therefore predictable. Contractual agreements are unambiguous claims and obligations that are legally binding on the market participants. Exchange is a 'legal transaction', which involves 'the acquisition, the transfer, the relinquishment, or the fulfilment of a legal claim' (ibid.: 668). In determining the rules by which contracts are drawn up and administered, the state provides legal security for transactions.

Legal reforms relating to economic contracts were a response to the growing complexity of production and commerce. Purposive contractual rights resulted from the dissolution of the household economy in many parts of Europe during the Middle Ages, and its replacement by the legally autonomous capitalistic corporation subject to what Weber calls formal 'associational contracts' (ibid.: 375–80, 705–29). Weber illustrated this by describing the typical developmental pattern of a Mediterranean household business. Initially it was regulated by domestic rules under a family authority that did not separate household funds from commercial capital. By taking advantage of emerging opportunities for profit making and capital accumulation the household evolved into a business organization interested in acquisition and trade. It began to act as an 'enterprise'. Business gradually became a separate vocation. Business partners were found outside the household, and new distinctions were made, for example, between domestic servants and employees, and between private debts and commercial debts.

The upshot was that business assets were increasingly disconnected from the private property of household members. Indeed, the private economy was 'bureaucratized' in this way at more or less the same time that public office was formally severed from the private property of the public official. Commercial law first developed in medieval Europe. The key legal innovation was 'the concept of the juristic person', which gave 'legal personality' to economic organizations (ibid.: 706–7). Corporations became legal entities distinct from the private assets of their members. The need for legal contracts arose from having to distinguish between business capital and personal wealth, and to take account of the fact that members of a family enterprise could simultaneously belong to other commercial organizations. Weber observes that 'the separation of the household and business for accounting and legal purposes' exerted pressure for 'the development of a suitable body of laws, such as the commercial register, elimination of dependence of the association and the firm upon the family, separate property of the private firm or limited partnership, and appropriate laws on bankruptcy' (ibid.: 379).

In sum, a process of interest-group closure against outsiders that is intended to exclude competitors evolves by stages into more inclusive appropriations that open up economic opportunities to all people. When guaranties of property first became formal rights they were not neutral. They expressed the power and influence of existing owners. Later, the same rights empowered new owners of land and capital. In the modern contractual society, economic rights are secured in a system of formal codes or precedents operating independently of political party, economic enterprise, or public agency. Such rights cannot be attached to a specific individual or social group. They are, as Weber said, 'the one sure guaranty of adherence to *objective* norms' (ibid.: 867). Formally impersonal laws upheld by the state enable (empower) appropriations of property and contract rights by all market actors equally, and they ensure that the conditions of economic life will be relatively predictable. Capitalist transition is, at least initially, the process of creating that situation. Property and contract laws, company law, and the legal 'detachment' of the person from the organization, explain 'the qualitative uniqueness of the development of modern capitalism' (ibid.: 379–80). All of this occurred 'in consequence of a growing exchange economy' and increasing interest in obtaining means of investment, production, and labour in the marketplace (ibid.: 706). Exchange of goods and services were thereby emancipated from the particularistic restrictions of kin, community, or status group.

Economic reasons of law

In later chapters dealing with contemporary transitions to capitalism we will observe the desirability, in purely ideal terms, of establishing effective legal frameworks for the regulation of private enterprise before or during processes of market liberalization. As in the past, however, the reverse has usually occurred in practice. It is the evolution of markets that provides the impetus for the evolution of market-sustaining legal rights. Like the ethical norms that precede them, legal mechanisms for the adequate regulation of economic action almost always follow from the expansion of markets. *Market interaction makes visible the need for particular regulations.* Weberian theory suggests that market freedom is created first by economic forces, second by norms, and third by law. We frequently have cause to observe today that effective regulation of the economy is almost always a step behind continually evolving market dynamics, even in the most advanced capitalist societies.

If it is true that the modern state evolves in response to the rationalizing force of markets, then policymakers might take the wrong route by attempting to create a regulatory order before they have significantly liberalized markets. It seems reasonable to assume this is the case if we note, furthermore, that policymakers and public administrators in precapitalist countries do not yet have enough state infrastructure and resources, and do not yet display enough cognitive or volitional rationality to permit the construction and enforcement of sophisticated laws that would foster desirable market behaviour in societies where competitive markets have barely begun to emerge. If the significance of preemptive legal reforms in developing countries pales alongside the decentralized and autonomous economic determinants of a rising legal order, this has important implications for policy during contemporary structural reforms. At stake would be choices about the best sequence for capitalist transition.

The theoretical question has to do with the direction of causality. Weber's studies usefully reveal complex inter-determinations between markets and law. The simple conclusion we could draw from them is that the economy first determines the law, and that the law subsequently determines the economy. Nevertheless, in his voluminous writing on the relationship of law to the economy, Weber consistently depicts causation running both ways. It is inconceivable that history will always move in one direction rather than another. Markets generate evolutionary pressures that determine human action, but then so does law. The relationship is really one of reciprocal conditioning, with the possibility that some institutional or economic forces will be greater in particular phases of the transition.

It is to be emphasized once and for all that a concrete result cannot be viewed as the product of a struggle of certain causes favouring it and other causes opposing it. The situation must, instead, be seen as follows: the totality of *all* the conditions back to which the causal chain from the 'effect' leads had to 'act jointly' in a certain way and in no other for the concrete effect to be realized. In other words, the appearance of the result is, for every causally working empirical science, determined not just from a certain moment but 'from eternity'.

(Weber 1949: 187)

Yet it remains legitimate to speak of 'driving forces' in a causal chain of capitalist transition if we keep in mind that the explanation of the 'adequacy of causation' is only 'conceptual', i.e. it is based on 'abstraction of certain components of the real causal chain' and on 'judgements of objective possibility' (ibid.: 188). Weber himself was more often inclined to speak of one condition or factor being 'favourable' rather than 'necessary' for the development of another (Kalberg 1994: 152). In the present context, it is then possible to explore why some causes provide more *adequate* explanations of phases of change during a capitalist transition than others. The importance of causation in policy making cannot be ignored. This section aims to explain why market freedom is both a developmental cause and consequence of legal regulation.

Even were we to leave aside theoretical issues of causation, the empirical and logical outcomes would still be plain to see. Law is indispensable in capitalist society, and the state's fundamental function is to regulate property and contract rights. Business 'requires a promptly and predictably functioning legal system, i.e. one which is guaranteed by the strongest coercive power' (Weber 1978: 337). Entrepreneurs are 'intensely interested in systematized, unambiguous, and specialized formal law which eliminates both obsolete traditions and arbitrariness and in which rights can have their source exclusively in general objective norms' (ibid.: 814). Law is 'the one sure guaranty of adherence to objective norms' (ibid.: 847). Only law is able to guarantee that a business environment will stay relatively secure through time. In a capitalist economy, law and market are joined at the hip: 'There exists ... an intimate connection between the expansion of the market and the expanding measure of contractual freedom ... guaranteed as valid by ... the total legal order of those rules which authorize such transactional dispositions' (ibid.: 668). Market exchange is symbiotically a 'legal transaction' for 'the acquisition, the transfer, the relinquishment, or the fulfilment of a legal claim'. With 'every extension of the market, these legal transactions become more numerous and more complex' (ibid.). Protections for private contracts and property are, in the end, just 'the legal reflex of the market orientation of our society' (ibid.: 672). Weber leaves us in no doubt that he believes changes in economic life impact directly on the evolution of the legal system.

Obviously, legal guaranties are directly at the service of economic interests to a very large extent. Even where this does not seem to be, or actually is not, the case, economic interests are among the strongest factors influencing the creation of law.

(ibid.: 334)

Indeed, the destruction of the precapitalist 'bearers of laws' and 'legal guaranties', says Weber, 'has been the result of the development of the market' (ibid.: 337). Consensus among market interests has always and everywhere 'influenced the systematization of law' and 'intensified the institutionalization of the polity' (ibid.: 655). The causal relationship is stated in the clearest terms:

> the constant expansion of the market ... has favoured the monopolization and regulation of all "legitimate" coercive power by one universalist coercive institution through the disintegration of all particularist status-determined and other coercive structures which have been resting mainly on economic monopolies.

(ibid.: 337)

Even when law has been systematized, market interests continue to influence which aspects of the legal corpus will be implemented, and which will not.

> A legal order can ... be characterized by the agreements which it does or does not enforce. In this respect a decisive influence is exercised by diverse interest groups, which varies in accordance with differences in the economic structure. In an increasingly expanding market, those who have market interests constitute the most important group. Their influence predominates in determining which legal transactions the law should regulate by means of power-granting norms.

(ibid.: 669)

On the other hand, although capitalist interests demand a system of formal legal guarantees, and although the rationalizing force of the market leads in this direction, these factors alone do not *produce* the modern features of present-day law: 'Economic conditions have, as we have seen, everywhere played an important role, but they have nowhere been decisive alone and by themselves' (ibid.: 883). The influence of market interests upon the creation of law is indirect in the sense that it is only as a consequence of 'certain rationalizations of economic behaviour, based upon such phenomena as a market economy or freedom of contract, and the resulting awareness of underlying, and increasingly complex conflicts of interests to be resolved by legal machinery' (ibid.: 655).

It is always legal professionals who interpret these signals and who codify the content of law. Legal education and legal training influence the rationalization of law and remain relatively autonomous from the 'economic and social conditions' (ibid.: 776). The development of legal techniques has a 'high degree of independence' from the development of the economy (ibid.: 650). Weber underlines the fact that legal institutions shape economic action: 'The structure of every legal order directly influences the distribution of power, economic or otherwise, within its respective community' (ibid.: 926). Legal theory and practice evolve independently of the economy and under the control of professional groups of lawyers whose formulations do not necessarily coincide with the interests of rulers or the owners of economic assets.

> To be sure, economic influences have played their part.... On the other hand, we shall frequently see that those aspects of law which are conditioned by political factors and by the internal structure of legal thought have exercised a strong influence on economic organization.
>
> (ibid.: 655)

The partial autonomy of law and legal professionals helps explain why capitalism has coexisted with at least two legal traditions of European origin, Anglo-Saxon common law and continental Roman law. Drawing on Weber's legal studies, Talcott Parsons (1999: 173) took the view that common law, with its well-developed property and contract rights, procedural propriety and consistency, adaptive efficiency, and guaranties of judicial independence, had been 'a fundamental prerequisite' of the industrial revolution in England. Yet, although Weber also perceived a good fit between capitalism and common law in nineteenth-century England, he did not draw general conclusions about the superiority of common law. Having compared the character and qualities of each, Weber concluded that 'once everything is said and done about [the] differences in historical developments, modern capitalism prospers equally well and manifests essentially identical economic traits under legal systems containing rules and institutions which considerably differ from each other' (Weber 1978: 890).

Weber also makes the point that in practice neither common nor continental law are pure cultural types, since in most cases legal systems are hybrids conditioned by the responses of legal professionals to particular political histories and the structures of domination in each society (ibid.: 977). Even English common law, which in some respects was less formal, had absorbed influences of Roman law in its 'systematic structure', 'definitions', and 'legal principle' (ibid.: 855). In the early stages of the transition to capitalism when property rights were still privileges, the costliness of common law, which effectively denied non-propertied classes easy access to justice, may have provided 'support for the capitalistic system' (ibid.: 814, 892). However, the *decisive* factor was that law should be formally calculable with respect to property and contract rights. 'Capitalistic interests', said Weber, 'will fare best under a rigorously formal system of adjudication, which applies in all cases' (ibid.: 814).

> Juridical formalism enables the legal system to operate like a technically rational machine. Thus, it guarantees to individuals and groups within the system a relative maximum of freedom, and greatly increases for them the possibility of predicting the legal consequences of their actions. Procedure

becomes a specific type of pacified contest, bound to fixed and inviolable 'rules of the game'.

(ibid.: 811)

In this respect, formalistic Roman law could be adjusted to the needs of capitalism, as could more adaptive but nonetheless also formalistic common law drawing on precedent, which produces 'a practically useful scheme of contracts and actions oriented towards the interests of clients in typically recurrent situations' (ibid.: 787). As Swedberg (1998: 255) notes, Weber believed that 'English common law was calculable'. The strict application of precedent produces a 'calculable schemata' (Weber 1994: 148). But, since even 'primitive procedures for adjusting conflicts of interest between kinship groups are characterized by rigorously formalistic rules of evidence', it is clearly not formalism per se that determines the calculability, objectivity and impartiality of law (Weber 1978: 811). Legal formalism can be turned to any end, not just capitalism's ends. In transitions to capitalism the *decisive* factor is that functionally equivalent common- and Roman-law systems are equally and similarly 'freed' from patrimonial forms of justice (ibid.: 891). Legal power and legal procedure in patrimonial society are personalistic, ambiguous, and arbitrary. Particularistic forms of justice, Weber frequently observed, are preferred by groups that resist capitalism. Among all the types of 'despot' and 'demagogue' there is always encountered 'the inevitable conflict between an abstract formalism of legal certainty and their desire to realize substantive goals' (ibid.: 811).

Transitional law

Weber's analyses of the relationship between law and economy raise many issues of relevance to policy decisions about reform sequences in contemporary transitional societies. First, the particular content and mechanisms of law, which vary between countries and cultures, are less important than the expectation that law will be *enforced*. Economic actors can adapt to different systems of law that are broadly compatible with capitalism with respect to property and contract rights, as long as the procedures and outcomes of legal adjudication are more or less calculable and impersonal.

There is also a related issue of 'access' to law. A design characteristic of modern capitalism is that legal systems guarantee equal treatment for plaintiffs and defendants by the judiciary and more or less equal access to law irrespective of a person's relative economic or political status. Equality before the law in advanced societies with a formal separation of powers is never perfect, yet the system is continually under review and subject to scrutiny by diverse groups and sectors. In precapitalist society, in contrast, law and legal systems remain in various respects exclusionary by design or by intent. Either that, or the costs, time, quality, administrative complexity, or uncertainty of inefficient legal adjudication has the unintended effect of excluding sectors of the population from law.

Underdevelopment of law is not necessarily or solely due to the absence of economic incentives to improve legal systems. Regardless of the pressures exerted by market interests, it is the legal professionals, legislators, and administrative heads who perform a leadership function in the design of substantive law and in social innovations relating to the enforcement of law. Even a strategy to emulate the laws or legal institutions of more advanced societies will still require some expert professional adaptations to fit new techniques to the existing machinery of law. In the following passage, Weber compares legal development with technological development. The economic determination of law is contingent on prior legal structure and legal agency – which supplies the legal techniques – in the same way that entrepreneurs depend on the inventors of technologies.

> Like the technological methods of industry, the rational patterns of legal technique to which the law is to give its guaranty must first be 'invented' before they can serve an existing economic interest. Hence the specific type of techniques used in a legal system or, in other words, its modes of thought are of far greater significance for the likelihood that a certain legal institution will be invented in its context than is ordinarily believed. Economic situations do not automatically give birth to new legal forms; they merely provide the opportunity for the actual spread of a legal technique if it is invented.
>
> (Weber 1978: 687)

The logic of using law as a policy instrument to achieve regulatory outcomes becomes especially strong once the legal system has developed to a point of critical mass, i.e. when there are sufficient lawyers, legal scholars, judges, an organic complex of courts of law, a legislative assembly subject to more or less democratic processes, and relatively rational bureaucracy for administrating law. Once the institutional foundations of the parametric state are established, it would sometimes – perhaps often – be possible for law to outweigh economy in the scale of causal primacy. Prior to that point, however, market expansion continues in fundamental ways to drive the development of economically relevant law. It is important to remain aware that premature and inappropriate law making could hinder capitalist transition by placing obstacles in the way of the development of competitive economic enterprises and market freedom. The causality dilemma applies equally to all developing countries. Laws are the product of states, yet in precapitalist societies the modern state is a 'work in progress'. This is why the sequence of causation in developing societies tips back towards the economy, and why market liberalization is usually a precondition of progress in the legal sphere. A strong argument exists for structural economic reform to take precedence over institutional reforms when difficult choices must be made about reform sequencing.

Weberian analysis suggests, furthermore, that developing countries should beware the power of law almost as much as they should beware the power of public bureaucracy. Since 'purposes' of law may be 'prescriptive, prohibitory, and permissive' (ibid.: 667), laws can be used to create and uphold *positive* privileges, such as the universal economic freedoms given by well-defined property and contract rights, or *negative* privileges based on particularistic dispensations of state favour, patronage, or monopoly rights. Laws are given their 'purpose' by the state. Whereas pervasive states tend to be prescriptive, parametric states tend to be permissive. Since law is a coercive state power, the deleterious effects of negatively designed or negatively interpreted law will be far-reaching. The 'prevailing norms controlling the operation of the coercive apparatus' can 'induce the emergence of certain economic relations which may be either a certain order of economic control or a certain agreement based on economic expectations' (ibid.). Experiences of state activism in many countries show that, depending on how they are designed and applied, economic laws can be as harmful to economic development as the inappropriate administrative interventions examined in Chapter 2.

In addition, there is always a danger that legal reforms in underdeveloped polities will generate excessive legalism that raises the costs of economic and administrative transactions. As we have seen, Weber's vision of the legal underpinnings of capitalist transition seeks to create conditions that will minimize this problem. Rather than law for the sake of law and politics, it is mainly a case of law for the sake of market expansion and efficient administration. It is neither necessary nor desirable that market interests regularly engage in litigation. Legal guaranties and a credible threat of enforcement reduce the need for recourse to law because everyone is relatively informed about the likely formal consequences of a breach of contract. In 'a stable private economic system of the modern type ... we see that in most business transactions it never occurs to anyone even to think of taking legal action' (ibid.: 328). An overabundance of superfluous laws reduces market dynamism and can force businesses to escape into the informal economy. In the more advanced economies, law has the purpose of improving market competition and extending the formal economy. People obey the law because they see it is in their self-interest to do so, and, to a lesser extent, because they have been educated to view its formalism as ethical or conventional and are afraid of the social disapproval that would follow if they disobeyed the law.

Background law is the solid structure that permits market ethics to operate more or less effectively. Only then can impersonal economic exchange be widespread and recurrent without the need for repeated third-party arbitration. The law–economy nexus promotes capitalist transitions if the state keeps laws and the legal system within boundaries that do not hamper market dynamism. In economic terms, the legal-regulatory order is ideally parametric and restricts itself to such non-discriminatory rules as are necessary for promoting the general economic good. Legalism is limited when economic applications of law are confined mainly to universal property and contract rights and the creation of regulatory conditions conducive to reproducing market freedom.

A common obstacle to transition is simply that law and the legal system, even when they have the external appearance of being formal, impersonal, and machine-like, can be captured by interests. Obvious instances are when legal officials become personally involved with private economic interests that seek to influence law making or the administration of justice. Risks similarly arise when law making and adjudication are absorbed directly into government or administrative processes in such a way that they reflect the interests of narrow political or economic constituencies. It is difficult to undertake meaningful legal reform in underdeveloped polities where clientelist and personalist mechanisms of representation admit particularistic, populist, or criminal demands. In Weber words, 'lawmaking and lawfinding are substantively irrational to the extent that decision is influenced by concrete factors of the particular case as evaluated upon an ethical, emotional, or political basis rather than by general norms', and to the extent that it 'accords predominance to ethical imperatives, utilitarian and other expediential rules, and political maxims', which, because they are 'substantive' and not 'abstract', lack the necessary 'logical rationality' and 'legal formalism' (ibid.: 656–7). To reiterate the core Weberian argument, effective law making and administration of law requires the enforcement of impersonal procedural norms.

Reformers in transitional countries can also heed Weber's warning that 'the threat of coercion supporting the legal order' may in practice only have 'a limited measure of success' in the economic sphere (ibid.: 334–5). Law may be inappropriately designed or ineffectively enforced even when political leaders genuinely intend to create a legal system compatible with capitalist economic policy. First, the level of 'education' and 'pacification' in a society may not yet have progressed to the point where the general population is willing to acquiesce in state efforts at 'enforcing economic conduct'. Second, it is hard for the law to manipulate economic variables, not least because the 'economic capacity of persons' is constrained by the nature of the stock of goods, existing habits, and 'the interdependence of the individual economic units in the market'. Third, some economic interests may be strong enough to resist new laws, and 'it is often not difficult to disguise the circumvention of a law in the economic sphere'.

Finally, and perhaps most importantly, reformers should keep in mind the perennial and ubiquitous difficulty of natural constraints on state knowledge, a problem which goes to the heart of other caveats discussed in this section. By deliberately keeping law to an essential minimum within practicable (enforceable) parametric boundaries state officials are more certain to avoid creating laws or legal techniques that will slow the expansion of markets, and are more likely to reduce incentives for market interests to circumvent or ride roughshod over necessary laws that protect property, constrain monopolistic closure and fraud, and defend against generalized public risk. Like their counterparts in the sphere of public administration, legal professionals and legislators are bound to have a poorer understanding of economic facts than market actors. Since their knowledge is limited, their laws may not have the intended effect. More complex substantive laws will mean even more unintended consequences that need to be rectified.

It is obvious that those who continuously operate in the market have a far greater knowledge of the market and interest situation than the legislators and enforcement officers whose interest is only formal. In an economy based on all-embracing interdependence on the market the possible and unintended repercussions of a legal measure must to a large extent escape the foresight of the legislator simply because they depend upon private interested parties. It is those private interested parties who are in a position to distort the intended meaning of a legal norm to the point of turning it into its very opposite.

(Weber 1978: 335–6)

In conclusion, although Weber recognized the relative autonomy of the legal profession and the independent force of legal developments during capitalist transitions, on balance his analysis of the relationships between law and the economy puts the stress on economic changes that create pressures for the construction of economically effective laws and legal systems. Legal professionals employed by the state created the relevant laws, yet they would not have done so but for the expansion of markets, market ethics, and the demands of market interests. A clearly understood legal order for the proper regulation of legitimate, formally equal property and contract rights is indispensable if capitalist transition is to gain momentum and be sustained. Last but not least, legal-regulatory reform applied to the economic sphere is likely, in turn, to facilitate the enforcement of impersonal procedural norms in the administrative and representational subsystems of the developing state. Separation of powers, and systematic interaction between the institutional subsystems, improves the quality and relevance of law. These are preconditions and sequences of capitalist transition.

Economy, law, and politics

In this and the preceding chapter I have examined Weber's views on the necessary interrelationships between market ethics, law, administration, and representation in the development of capitalism. Taking these elements together, we gain an impression of the transitional priorities. Weber's portrayal of capitalism – in terms of calculable market freedom, parametric legal-administrative regulation of the economy, generalized rule of law, impersonal state administration, the formal division of powers, modern parliament as a counterweight to bureaucracy, and the requirement throughout for strong leaders – lends support to the *market*-led and *law*-led policy sequence proposed in the present study. This is the path that countries take when they lay foundations for durable economic growth, when they formalize and depersonalize state organizations, and when they reduce the scope for political profit making and regulatory closure.

It is also the path that countries follow when they eliminate systematic interest-group closure in the representational system. It seems fitting to end by tying together these threads of the capitalist sequence with reference to the final link in the causal chain. Societies in transition to capitalism have no choice but to build systems of free representation at some proximate phase in the process. Weber (1978: 296–7) describes the historical 'transition' as follows. First, the evolving *'economic order'* of modern capitalism had the effect of 'undermining' the precapitalist status order, and made it possible for a new breed of *political* individual 'to pursue their career regardless of their social position'. Second, once it became apparent that 'calculability and reliability in the functioning of the legal order and the administrative system is vital to rational capitalism', emerging market interests recognized the need to 'impose checks' on precapitalist rulers 'by means of a collegial body in which the bourgeoisie had a decisive voice, which controlled administration and finance and could exercise an important influence on changes in the legal order'. It subsequently became obvious that the 'formal rationalization of the economic order and the state, which was favourable to capitalist development, could be strongly promoted by parliaments'.

These descriptions are consistent with Weber's implicit argument throughout *Economy and Society* (1978), namely that the first links in the causal chain of capitalist development are market expansion, law, and then administration. The final link is full democracy. With the available knowledge, these are sequences that can be purposefully telescoped during the contemporary transitions. It may well be true that Weber did not have this constructivist objective clearly in mind, or that he did not consider it either necessary or desirable. However, the present more extreme disparity between highly developed capitalist societies and the residual, routine institutional underdevelopment in much of the rest of the world justifies making these linkages more explicit in a policy-based approach.

It will be difficult for genuine and useful parliamentary representation to emerge in the absence of market freedom and rule of law. In the primitive representational condition that Weber called 'negative politics', the institutional incentives remain for 'big business' to support 'the retention of an unsupervised bureaucracy', 'parliamentary mediocrity', a 'system of handouts' and 'unofficial patronage', 'cruder or finer forms of capitalist recommendations', and 'capitalist exploitation of connections' (ibid.: 1429–30). Democracy's consolidation depends on other conditions being met.

> There can be no doubt that only the presence of absolutely compelling political circumstances will change anything at all in this respect. Parliamentary governance will not arrive on its own. Nothing is more certain than that the most powerful groups work against it.
>
> (ibid.: 1430)

The argument I will expand on further is that recurrent development crises and the sequenced evolution of markets and market regulation are most likely to give rise to conditions ripe for 'positive politics' in the administrative and representational fields. Weber's entire discussion of politics is dominated by the pragmatic theme of effective leadership. 'For a rational politician the form of government appropriate at any given time is a technical question which depends upon the political tasks of the nation', and it is always the case that the 'vital interests of the nation stand, of course, above democracy and parliamentarism' (ibid.: 1383). Even in precapitalist societies with only a rudimentary 'bureaucratic-rational' government, 'the wide latitude of the ruler's unrestricted discretion can reinforce the anti-traditional power of capitalism' (ibid.: 1094). Drawing the logical inferences from Weber's views on essential state factors of capitalist transition, if there were to be a stark choice between increasing political competition within the precapitalist equilibrium, or empowering leaders during times of crisis when social volatility, populism, and heightened distributional pressures might impede reforms, then market expansion and rule of law must be priorities in generating pressures to rupture the precapitalist equilibrium. As the next chapter will show, these are tasks that more or less rational and autonomous technocrats may be more likely to accomplish during critical periods when they obtain some temporary shelter from political competition.

4   Development in disequilibrium

This chapter outlines a theoretical framework for understanding institutional change during capitalist transitions. A central argument will be that the reciprocal conditioning of economic and institutional change is frequently a discontinuous rather than incremental process. Recurrent instability is a feature of both institutional and economic life during capitalism's development. The economist, Joseph Schumpeter, gave a strong sense of this when he described the 'jerks and rushes' of industrial progress and its associated 'social and cultural' transformations.

> We must recognize that evolution is lopsided, discontinuous, disharmonious by nature – that the disharmony is inherent in the very *modus operandi* of the factors of progress. Surely, this is not out of keeping with observation: the history of capitalism is studded with violent bursts and catastrophes which do not accord well with the alternative hypothesis we herewith discard, and … [we] come to the conclusion that evolution is a disturbance of existing structures and more like a series of explosions than a gentle, though incessant, transformation.
>
> (Schumpeter 1964: 76–7)

Schumpeterian analysis of institutional development – which I propose as an alternative to the Hayekian paradigm of incremental institutional change – focuses on human agency that speeds up and guides capitalist transitions. Institutional change during capitalist transition resembles the advanced *economic* process of capitalism in the sense that both depend on entrepreneurial innovations fashioned by exceptional and motivated leaders who seek temporary shelter from competition until such time as the rewards of innovation can be harvested. In addition, the reciprocal determination of institutions and economies during the evolution of capitalism means that economic agency and institutional agency are similarly subject to recurrent structural pressures that generate and resolve crises. The modern era is patterned by periodic crises, which are unavoidable elements of cycles of innovation and competition that drive successive industrial revolutions in the heartlands of the world economy. Institutions influence and absorb these upturns and downturns. Crises, in turn, have a tendency to induce institutional innovations.

A typology of change

What follows is a typology of four distinct forces of institutional change, which will be fleshed out in later sections. A useful theory of institutional construction must explain external forces acting upon institutions as well as internal forces driving change within institutions. It should be possible to analyse the variable intensity of these forces at different stages in their evolution. In particular, it is necessary to distinguish long-run internal equilibrium tendencies that maintain slow evolutions, from external or internal disequilibrium episodes that intensify the forces of change. These factors of institutional change may be present *together* in a single society at any point in time. Yet from a public-policy perspective it is useful to disentangle the sources and effects of each of the main variables in order to see how they might be harnessed to development strategies.

Routine equilibrium change

Routine equilibrium change is a very gradual aggregation of countless small-scale changes that incrementally modify the institutional system. It is not organized change. Institutions of the now more advanced capitalist societies evolved over centuries through a process of piecemeal and cumulative experimentation, elimination, and selection. The most competitive or efficient institutions survived. The functions of these institutions were slowly learnt; they were not designed. Incremental change is punctuated only rarely, for example during wars, when changes are big or rapid enough to upset the equilibrium.

Incremental progress may be interspersed by periods of static equilibrium resulting from stalemates between opposing interests or ideologies, or from strong cultural resistance to change. Many scholars believe that behaviour in incrementally evolving institutions is heavily weighted by informal rules of conduct handed down from previous generations; informal rules that may have congealed as formal institutions, but which constrain future change. As I have already shown, however, 'cultural' constraints on change can be exaggerated or confused with 'political' constraints. A more general and valid point is that in the societies that pioneered transitions to capitalism, the legal, administrative, and political institutions evolved because there was – at times – sufficient freedom to learn through trial and error. This process can be thought of as a 'moving equilibrium' of institutional adjustments.

External disequilibrium change

External disequilibrium change is the result of discontinuous pressure emanating from outside the national territory, which reshapes the domestic environment in which capitalist transition actually occurs. The contemporary transition is different from the original evolutions of capitalism because it occurs in a global environment where capitalism already exists in the most advanced societies.

Capitalism is continually revolutionizing technologies and the economic conditions of production, and always exerting pressures upon institutions to adjust to economic innovations. On a world scale these forces impact on the nature, pattern, timing, and pace of institutional change in all developing countries that maintain at least partly open economies. Exogenous forces operate alongside the endogenous drivers of developmental change.

The only 'external force' discussed in this chapter is the Schumpeterian long wave of techno-economic change, which generates upswings and downswings in the core economies of the international trading system, and which can itself be a catalyst for institutional adjustment in peripheral countries. The external force is systematic, in the sense that it repeats regularly. In the past, mercantilism, colonialism, and imperialism might have qualified for inclusion in this category – over long periods of time they exerted recurrent external pressures for institutional change in large parts of the global periphery. Other external but non-systematic forces are excluded from the present analysis. Contemporary conditionality attached to international credit or foreign aid, or political or military interventions (including *in extremis* interventions to deal with violence or disaster), are comparatively less durable, effective, or reliable means of inducing institutional change in developing countries. Reforms 'imposed' by outsiders create dependency and are eventually regarded as illegitimate. Commitments by outsiders are rarely maintained. Compliance with external conditionality is similarly difficult to achieve or sustain.

Internal disequilibrium change

Internal disequilibrium change is autonomous policy innovation in the domestic context. It is the main mechanism of contemporary capitalist transition. Endogenous initiatives resolve endogenous development problems. In most cases, an internal crisis creates the opportunity to construct new institutions or reform existing ones. In Chapter 7 I will describe this ambitious form of change as a recursive 'crisis-induced policy sequence' typically linked to the development reversals of populism, activism, and neoliberalism. The key conditions of change (described in this chapter) are leadership by exceptional individuals, a complex mix of motives, and temporary shelters from political competition. Other favourable conditions include appropriate knowledge of capitalism and capitalist transition, or, at a minimum, firm commitments to liberalize markets and modernize institutional subsystems by rapid small steps. Ideally, reforms will be designed to achieve parametric regulatory competencies and bring about market freedom and the impersonality of the state. Policymakers continually innovate and fine-tune reforms in response to concurrent changes in the internal and external environments. This is a highly pressured situation of fast learning, with change being characterized by disproportionalities, tensions, conflicts, and bottlenecks.

Routine disequilibrium change

Routine disequilibrium change refers to the paradoxical 'continual discontinuity' of institutional innovation in the most dynamic capitalist societies. Capitalism eventually 'stabilizes' in perpetual disequilibrium. A number of factors combine to produce this situation. In order that societies can hold on to their advantages in a world of relentless economic experimentation and periodic large-scale technological transformations, the institutions of society learn to adapt continually. The most important institutional function is to readjust the regulation of markets as a requisite for sustaining a competitive and growing economy.

In addition, when sufficient institutional capacity and 'intelligence' has been created the state may play supportive roles in activities that enhance national competitiveness and the dynamism of social order; roles that it could not have performed efficiently and dispassionately during the transition to capitalism. It might, for example, collaborate with private enterprises in research and development, or spearhead best-practice methods for public and private delivery of services in infrastructure, education, or health. Furthermore, political and economic freedoms intensify and 'institutionalize' methods of trial and error, which facilitate adaptation throughout the social system. Finally, the routine impersonality of state procedural norms induces ever-greater fluidity in decentralized interactions of organizational subsystems of the state, thereby increasing the disequilibrium pressures upon each subsystem to adapt efficiently. It can be noted that an advanced hyper routine of 'continuous disequilibrium change' is not the same thing as the – usually concurrent – pattern of slower evolution in a moving equilibrium.

This preliminary four-part typology could suggest that disequilibrium changes are subject to many constraints and run the risk of failure, while routine equilibrium change allows a *sure and steady* surmounting of constraints. On the other hand, equilibrium change seems much too slow to be of practical interest to developing countries today. A country that does not want its capitalist transition to be prolonged indefinitely has little choice but to explore the viability of shorter-run disequilibrium transitions, when autonomous policy actors can respond to reform stimuli and implement a rapid-change sequence. In this sense, there are similarities between external and internal disequilibrium change. Both types are shaped by three critical factors discussed in this chapter – the quality of leaders, their motives, and their methods of exercising power.

Institutions: made or grown?

These 'Schumpeterian' ideas about disequilibrium endogenous and exogenous change suggest a promising line of enquiry. However, they are completely absent from the mainstream of institutional theory. Instead, debates about institutional change have long revolved around one central question: are institutions 'made' or do they 'grow'? Made institutions are purposefully *designed* and *constructed*, by implication during the working life of their creators. Grown institutions evolve *incrementally* and *spontaneously* over generations. Much writing on institutional change adopts a position that leans towards one or other side of the debate whilst also recognizing, to some degree, that institutions really change through a combination of conscious organization and spontaneous selection. It is probably true to say that a realistic evaluation of the feasibility of capitalist transition will emerge from the confluence of ideas about 'made' and 'grown' institutions.

Our schema of four types of institutional change seems able to incorporate all sides of the debate. The first type evolves incrementally in stable or moving equilibrium. The second and third types are constructed in discontinuous disequilibrium. The fourth evolves in continuous disequilibrium. Despite the obvious potential for accommodation, institutional theory has hitherto given the impression of an irreconcilable conflict between incrementalism and constructivism. Incrementalism, which is by far the most influential viewpoint in institutional theory, lays stress on the factors of cultural heritage that constrain institutional reform. The leading advocate of incrementalism, Nobel Laureate Douglass North, argues that successful institutional change is necessarily gradual, continuous, and stable (North 1990). Short-run, policy-led institutional transformations are seen as impractical and rare.

The inevitable effect of incrementalist theory is to dampen enthusiasm for radical reform proposals. In this section I examine Friedrich Hayek's thesis of spontaneous social order, which is a major influence on incrementalist thinking. By singling out culture as the constraint on institutional change North follows in the tradition of Hayekian spontaneous order where rules are the result of cultural evolution. North argues, for example, that even after 'discontinuous change', i.e. 'a radical change in the formal rules as a result of conquest or revolution', many of the informal rules, which represent a 'deep-seated cultural inheritance', will resist the new formal rules (ibid.: 89–91). Very similarly, Hayek says that norms and 'rules of conduct' are 'part of a cultural heritage which is likely to be fairly constant' (1982: vol. 2, 17–19). In Hayek's words: 'Even when as a result of revolution or conquest the whole structure of government changes, most of the rules of just conduct ... will remain in force' (ibid.: 135).

In Hayek's writing one finds the fullest development of an important idea, namely that the great institutional edifices of modern societies, such as the state and its legal system, were unplanned and evolved by slow and continuous adaptations that were the cumulative outcome of innumerable small-scale and individual changes to social rules. The knowledge each individual has of social institutions is inherently limited. Knowledge is dispersed throughout society and cannot be effectively controlled at the centre (by the state). Full knowledge is not, therefore, available to putative designers and builders of institutions. Instead, institutional change results from competing ideas and interests that incrementally shape fragments of what eventually becomes the recognizable multi-stranded 'organic' social order of liberal capitalism.

Hayek himself traces the 'evolutionary approach' back to Adam Smith, David Hume, Edmund Burke, and Carl Menger. The eighteenth-century Scottish philosopher, Adam Ferguson, proposed an idea that Hayek built on: 'Nations stumble upon establishments, which are indeed the result of human action, but not the execution of any human design' (in Hayek 1982: vol. 1, 150). Hayek criticizes what he terms 'constructivist rationalism', namely the belief that 'social institutions are, and ought to be, the product of deliberate design' (ibid.: 5). In reality, 'man has never invented his most beneficial institutions' (Hayek 1982: vol. 3, 163). Capitalist society was the result of the muddling efforts of millions of individuals who could have no conception of the political and economic orders that their pursuit of self-interest in localized agreements would produce. The successful institutions were selected once they had grown, and they survived because they remained competitive. In other words, social evolution is microscopic. The human hand is barely visible. Discrete policy interventions are mere incidents in the process of institutional change.

Although we can quibble about the wider implications of this analysis, Hayek's explanation of the *rules* of liberal society remains absolutely vital for our understanding of ideal capitalism. The procedural foundations of liberal-capitalist societies are principles of 'just conduct' resting on 'universal *negative* rules' relating to 'peace, freedom, and justice' (ibid.: 131). Negative rules repress some types of behaviour, but they do not dictate outcomes. Nor do negative rules impose duties on people. Their purpose is to prevent actions that will cause harm or threaten the peaceful coexistence of individuals, such as actions that would undermine the impersonality of market exchange. Negative rules are oriented not to 'ends' but rather to ensuring that all but the 'means' of 'just conduct' are prohibited (Hayek 1982: vol. 2, 67–73, 107–32). A capitalist market order punishes malfeasance and prohibits permanent monopoly as the means of profit making. But it must also reject any outside authority, i.e. government, that uses a political or moral conception of '*social* justice' to determine distributive entitlements to the fruits of economic exchange.

Hayek does accept that informal rules, which are founded in custom and evolve slowly by trial and error, are eventually organized by the state as formal institutions. Even in the spontaneously grown social order, a time will arrive when society formalizes the mechanisms that enact and enforce evolved rules of conduct. Courts of law, constitutions, and government agencies administer rules that are systematized in legal codes. Moreover, a legal order is constantly changed by the courts and legislation. Within the boundaries of a 'given cosmos of rules' the tinkering of judges and legislators is part of the spontaneous process of selection and adaptation (Hayek 1982: vol. 1, 88, 100, 119). A modern system of law, says Hayek, 'is the outcome of a process of evolution in the course of which spontaneous growth of customs and deliberate improvements of the particulars of an existing system have constantly interacted' (ibid.: 100). In such statements, Hayek almost gives the impression that institutional construction and spontaneity coexist. His analysis becomes problematic to a theory of capitalist transition, however, at the points where he departs from what is essentially a Weberian argument about the transition from informal norms to formal law.

Explicitly *against* Weber, Hayek sought to argue that an institutional order cannot be organized and made 'valid' or 'binding' for the simple reason that an institution cannot exist as an organization (Hayek 1982: vol. 2, 170 n50). An 'organization' is an artifice, a constructed exogenous arrangement, whereas the 'spontaneous order' is endogenous and self-generating (Hayek 1982: vol. 1, 37). Despite his tolerance of legal tinkering and improvements to state policies, Hayek's central claim was that spontaneous order is incompatible with planned organization (ibid.: 46–54). His framework of analysis makes it essential to assume that in capitalist society organizations operate within a *self*-organized social order. The 'structure of modern society has attained that degree of complexity ... which far exceeds any that could have been achieved by deliberate organization' (ibid.: 50). Organizations can attain the limited ends of a corporation or association 'by direct commands', but not the ends of institutions. Thus, 'a combination of spontaneous order and organization it can never be rational to adopt' (ibid.: 51).

Hayek would seem to be saying that you should not apply the methods of an organization to the construction or substantial modification of an institutional order. There may be enough knowledge to build organizations and to design some government policies, but certainly not enough to build an institutional order. Constructivists commit the error of believing that government could, by its authority and knowledge alone, build regularities of conduct, or create and then maintain the social order. Although property rights have a vital institutional function in capitalism, this fact alone does not justify the risks of devising a system of property rights by fiat. Man is not intelligent enough to fit together the pieces for a purpose. Attempts to do so will have unpredictable consequences.

Moreover, as Hayek repeatedly says, all efforts to design or build institutions entail 'the pursuit of known common goals', which necessarily involve 'commands' and 'compulsion'. It is inevitable that this will suppress the intellectual and political freedoms that are needed for social and scientific progress. The pursuit of common ends leads to nationalism and socialism (Hayek 1982: vol. 2, 111). In contrast, capitalist society evolves as individuals learn to obey and test the abstract moral rules of just conduct. These rules are cultural; they have their source in custom and tradition. They evolve only when self-interested 'rule-breakers' and 'innovators' modify the 'practices' of rules. If successful, the modifications are subsequently selected and legitimized with 'the approval of society at large' (Hayek 1982: vol. 3, 61, 167).

> That neither what is instinctively recognized as right, nor what is rationally recognized as serving specific purposes, but inherited traditional rules, or that what is neither instinct nor reason, should often be most beneficial to the functioning of society is a truth which the dominant constructivist outlook of our times refuses to accept.
>
> (ibid.: 162)

Hayek's critiques of state planning have helped to expose the limitations of human organization, foresight, and knowledge. He also offered a most convincing defence of competition, both in markets and in ideas. The question in the present context, however, is whether his critique of constructivism remains relevant to the study of capitalist institutions, which manifestly have concrete functions and organizational forms in the advanced societies, and which – given that there *does* now exist knowledge of how these institutions function – could presumably be 'constructed' in developing societies. Is there any remaining justification for denying that rationally motivated 'modern realists' can ever gain accurate knowledge of institutional functions in order to emulate or redesign them for developmental ends? Hayek's vision can appear doctrinaire to the well-intentioned policy practitioner who wants to 'transfer' knowledge of successful institutional elements of evolved capitalism to the developing countries.

Even with respect to institutional change in advanced capitalism, Hayek may have gone too far in his critique of constructivism. We would expect James Buchanan – founder of public choice theory, and pioneer of economic methods for the analysis of collective-action pathologies – to be supportive of Hayek. Indeed, Buchanan is bullish in his praise for the spontaneous *market* order – 'To the extent that markets work, there is no need for the state. Markets allow persons to interact, one with another, in a regime that combines freedom and order, provided only that the state supply the protective legal umbrella' (Buchanan 2001: 243). Buchanan also, like Hayek, favours the constitutional 'generality principle'. Government should strive to be non-discriminatory in its actions. Political decision making works best when it is guided by universal norms that apply equally to all persons and groups without privilege or favour. In *The Constitution of Liberty*, Hayek (1960: 188) approved of the framing of constitutional doctrine in the United States, which enshrines a distinction between desirable 'general' law – not to benefit particular persons or groups, and binding on everyone in similar circumstances – and 'special' legislation made for interests. In his writings, Buchanan extends the generality principle beyond law to the sphere of political action, on the grounds that politics requires similar rules.

Buchanan parts company with Hayek, however, over the latter's 'attribution of invisible-hand characteristics to the evolution of legal institutions' (Buchanan 2001: 101). Just as the market requires the umbrella of law to discourage monopoly and rent seeking, so politics and policy need the umbrella of a constitution that lays down general decision-making rules about uniformity and non-discrimination. In both cases, deliberate design or reform of a legal or constitutional framework is required. Buchanan calls his approach '*constructivist*', though subject to the difficult contractarian caveat that institutional constructions are not imposed but rather are agreed on as if they were a fair-exchange contract among affected persons (ibid.: 103). Spontaneous *institutional* evolution, says Buchanan, is not necessarily 'efficient' in the same way that the operation of markets is efficient when constrained by appropriate institutional structures (ibid.: 107). Institutional evolution is only efficient within the constraints of constitutional rules. Buchanan's 'constitutional revolution' proposes continuous redefinition or creation of 'newly defined rights' that will 'keep pace' with change in society, the economy, and the natural environment (Buchanan 2000: 226–7).

The historically determined institutions of legal order need not be those which are 'best'. Such institutions can be 'reformed', and can be made more 'efficient'. The discussions of such potential reforms should, of course, be fully informed by an understanding of the principle of spontaneous order ... [But] explicit and deliberately designed proposals for reform can be, and should be, advanced by those whose competence offers them an understanding of the principle of spontaneous coordination. Framework proposals for change can be, and should be 'constructed'.... The economist can, and should, suggest the enactment of a rule, a law....

(Buchanan 2001: 102, 105)

A good institutional design will incorporate knowledge of the spontaneous processes. But, legislators must be willing to modify legal institutions according to constructivist criteria. On this point, Buchanan (2001: 107) argues that Hayek's thesis is 'logically inconsistent':

Hayek is so distrustful of man's explicit attempts at reforming institutions that he accepts uncritically the evolutionary alternative. We may share much of Hayek's scepticism about social and institutional reform, however, without elevating the evolutionary process to an ideal role. Reform may, indeed, be difficult, but this is no argument that its alternative is ideal.

(Buchanan 2000: 211)

Hayek's analysis of 'rules of just conduct' can tell us how proven institutional strengths of an evolved market society are *maintained*. The problem I highlight is that Hayek offers no guidelines for replicating those institutional patterns in transitional societies. Must the latter go through the evolutionary process from beginning to end just as the advanced societies did? Hayek analyses the known functions of capitalist institutions. It is important to understand that, in their *origins*, these institutions were not consciously created for any known purpose. Less convincingly, Hayek says they are *still* not manifested in organizational forms that can be manipulated. Moreover, since policy outcomes cannot be foreseen, and since common purposes destroy the spontaneity of social order, state intervention will do more harm than good. Cannot organized actors in developing societies apply their knowledge of capitalist orders when constructing equivalent institutions? Cannot state technocrats who study the institutional frameworks of Western Europe or North America then 'know the desirable direction of progress'? Hayek seems to say this would be impossible:

progress cannot be dosed.... All we can do is to create conditions favourable to it and then hope for the best. It may be stimulated or damped by policy, but nobody can predict the precise effects of such measures.... Guided progress would not be progress.... To confine evolution to what we can foresee would be to stop progress.

(Hayek 1982: vol. 3, 169)

As a critique of socialism, this argument had a persuasive logic. Hayek helped to expose the sicknesses of socialist hyper constructivism. Socialism was doomed to failure. It presupposed 'a system of common concrete ends' defined by political authorities (Hayek 1982: vol. 2, 99, 136). Socialism was conceived as 'the organization of society *as a whole*' (Hayek 1982: vol. 1, 53). State institutions attempted to take command of all the nation's resources and to manage all but the smallest details of social, political, and economic organization. Socialism and *dirigisme* were indeed the models that most often inspired mid-twentieth-century constructivists. The catastrophes wrought by these models, which were evident long before the collapse of the Soviet Union, go a long way towards explaining the discredit brought upon constructivism by writers such as Hayek.

There is, therefore, a paradox in the perception nowadays that post-socialist transitions are the new frontier for constructivist theory. One question is equally relevant both to post-socialist transitions and the 'normal' transitions from pre-capitalism to capitalism – *what must be the sequence of change*? Should a country move quickly to create markets, or should it first establish the rule of law or a representative democracy? In another sense, however, the twentieth-century preoccupation with socialist and post-socialist countries has been a distraction from the problems Weber and others wrote about at the beginning of the century, and which still concern countries that did not choose a socialist detour. Post-socialist countries try to build capitalism in a society that long existed without markets, private property, or democracy. Their institutions were scientifically designed and constructed alternatives to democracy and market capitalism, engineered or re-engineered not to speed up capitalist transitions but to perform reverse functions. Normal precapitalist countries, the majority in the developing world, did not sustainedly or purposefully deviate from a slow capitalistic evolution despite episodic *dirigisme*, populism, or corporatism. If socialism was the long detour from capitalist transitions, it follows that post-socialism was in some respects a continuation of that detour.

Social science has a chance to return to an earlier concern with capitalist transition as the fundamental challenge for developing countries in general. Hayek's pessimism, which originates in a critique of socialist and *dirigiste* planning, may no longer be justified, now that – thanks in no small measure to his own work – we know far more about the institutional order of capitalism. The reworking of that knowledge is the key challenge in any analysis of feasible capitalist transition. Post-socialism is one thing. The starting point for most countries is another.

Schumpeter's innovation

This section will examine Joseph Schumpeter's theory of economic development. In essence this theory depicts a wave-like process by which unproductive equilibrium routines give way to disequilibrating entrepreneurial innovations and subsequent socioeconomic adjustments to recurrent periods of 'creative destruction' brought on by intense competition for the fruits of innovation. My own interest lies mainly in the implications of this theory for the study of institutional progress. Later in the chapter I will discuss Schumpeter's neglected argument that institutional change is analogous to economic change (Schumpeter 1991). Both proceed from equilibrium to disequilibrium, and both are driven either by external factors (e.g. crises) or by internal leadership. The implication is that institutional progress may be subject to similar 'motive forces' of innovation. The dynamics of institutional development may resemble the dynamics of economic development. Institutional innovations, like economic innovations, are products of creative leadership, motivated action, and imperfect competition.

By way of introduction, it should also be noted that Schumpeter was aware of the incrementalist approach to understanding change in history, which he called 'microscopic'. The following important passage reveals that his preferred method of analysis was 'macroscopic'.

> [A] point properly pertaining to the realm of general methodology must be touched on in order to eliminate an apparent contradiction between our way of looking at economic or social change and the principle of historic continuity which tends to assert itself in historical analysis.... Our theory of the mechanism of change stresses *discontinuity*. It takes the view that evolution proceeds by successive revolutions, or that there are in the process jerks or jumps which account for many of its features. As soon, however, as we survey the history of society or of any particular sector of social life, we become aware of a fact which seems, at first sight, to be incompatible with that view: every change seems to consist in the accumulation of many small influences and events and comes about precisely by steps so small as to make any exact dating and any sharp distinction of epochs almost meaningless.... Cooperation of many minds and many small experiences acting on a given objective situation and coordinated by it slowly evolve what appears as really new only if we leave out intermediate steps and compare types distant in time and space. The decisive step in bringing about a new thing or ultimate practical success is, in most cases, only the last straw and often relatively insignificant in itself. Needless to say, this holds true also of the process of change in social institutions.... Now it is important to note that there is no contradiction whatever between our theory and a theory of history which bases itself on these facts. What difference there is, is a difference of purpose and method only....
>
> (Schumpeter 1964: 181–2)

Schumpeter is thus able to show that the difference between an emphasis on continuity or on discontinuity is not only one of historical method but also of the purpose of the analysis. If the purpose is to see how developing countries might today undergo transitions to capitalism then we require not only knowledge of spontaneous processes but also of the motives for innovations that generate 'successive revolutions' during which societies 'jerk and jump'. Hayekian microscopic analyses of institutional change tend to lose sight of the turning or tipping points and conscious human agency. Macroscopic analysis, on the other hand, will tend to bring the discontinuities of the recent past, present, and even the probable near future, more sharply into focus.

A Schumpeterian perspective is not completely at odds with Hayek's evolutionary analysis. Schumpeter's 'creative destruction' and Hayek's 'spontaneous growth' are both equally incompatible with centralized economic planning. Yet, Schumpeter's emphasis on discontinuity and individual agency is self-evidently not reconcilable with a thesis of equilibrium evolution. Hayek (1982: vol. 1, 36) said that a spontaneous order is always an 'equilibrium set up from within', never an order created exogenously, i.e. 'by forces outside the system'. Schumpeter, on the other hand, recognized the potential of equilibrium change as well as internal and external disequilibrium change, all of which can be 'sequences' of a kind in the development of institutions and economies. Although Schumpeter's macroscopic analysis is not strictly speaking a form of constructivism, I hope to show that its extension to the study of innovation, leadership, and competition can reveal much about the process of institution building in developing societies.

If we also compare Schumpeter with Weber, we see a quite different but complementary perspective within the field of economic sociology. Weber focused on the causality interfaces of market expansion and institutional development during original capitalist transitions, and defining functions and processes of the modern state (see Chapters 2 and 3). Schumpeter gave much less attention to the state and the origins of capitalism. His main interest was the autonomous economic process of modern capitalism, and the intrinsic dynamism of market competition in capitalist economies. On the other hand, we will see that Schumpeter and his followers study the interconnections of economic and institutional change during the evolution of capitalism. There is a strong suggestion that a similar dynamic of change is at work in economic and institutional fields.

The first task, however, is to explore key structure–agency dimensions of Schumpeter's economic theory with a view to later incorporating the most useful elements in an equivalent institutional theory. In *The Theory of Economic Development* (1983), *Business Cycles* (1964), and *Capitalism, Socialism and Democracy* (1947) Schumpeter explained some fundamental characteristics of the capitalist economy, and advanced his central thesis that technological innovation and market competition lead to recurrent industrial revolutions and long-run prosperity. Our starting point is Schumpeter's division of the economic process into three 'classes', which arguably can be viewed as possible sequences of economic development (Schumpeter 1983: 218).

1   The routine circular flow of stable or moving equilibrium in market economies.
2   Real economic development arising from disequilibriating processes of product and process innovation in conditions of imperfect market competition.
3   Recurrent crises that change the course of development and lead to a resto-

ration of equilibrium tendencies until such time as the impulse for change recurs.

Schumpeter argued that innovation is necessarily absent in market equilibrium. On the other hand, he accepted that economies may approach equilibrium while still undergoing change. 'Equilibrium' refers to a system whose energies are evenly balanced. In theoretical equilibrium, everyone 'lives and works in an unchanging physical and social institutional environment' (Schumpeter 1964: 15). If the 'pattern of consumption and production is trimmed to perfection', individuals and organizations have no reason to radically modify their behaviour (ibid.: 20). In a neoclassical equilibrium tending towards perfect competition, people can learn the self-reproducing routine by which preferences translate into timely small adjustments of product quantities, prices, incomes, and credit. Firms routinely adjust by calculating from available data, and make rational predictions about changing prices and quantities of goods. Tendencies towards equilibrium are 'actually operative in the reality around us' (ibid.: 25). The routine allows steady increments in productive resources, as well as adaptations in consumer demand and in methods of supply. In other words, the 'circular flow' suggests slow-moving short-run adjustments of a system-maintenance type.

With markets in relative equilibrium, each economic actor can be more or less certain how others will react. This might account for stable conditions in advanced economies. Nevertheless, neoclassical assumptions about costless information, effective foresight, predictable institutional conditions, impersonal markets, stable preferences, and utility-maximizing behaviour are not realistic. Schumpeter pointed out that all sorts of 'lags' in the reactions of economic players prevent a smooth meshing of the gears of competition. The wider environment of economic action also constantly changes the course of the circular flow. In Schumpeter's view, the equilibrium concept is useful only as a *heuristic* device that allows the researcher to explore how elements of a system might react to one another when major changes occur outside or within the system. By knowing what an ideal equilibrium looks like, the analyst can estimate the impact of change upon variables such as investment, prices, or employment, and can judge how far the change will depart from stable market routines. The circular flow only identifies potential balances between economic variables; it makes no claim to explain the real world. Equilibrium is a benchmark against which the relative impact of fluctuating empirical phenomena may be identified.

> [The] concept of a state of equilibrium, although no such state may ever be realized, is ... indispensable for purposes of analysis and diagnosis, as a point of reference. Actual states can conveniently be defined by their distance from it.
>
> (ibid.: 43)

None of this substantially modifies the patterns of production and consumption. A balanced system 'that at every given point of time fully utilizes its possibilities to the best advantage' will not be as good for development as a system that experiences disturbances and continually struggles to improve its performance (Schumpeter 1947: 83). Instead, *real* economic development (the second class of change in Schumpeter's schema) occurs in disequilibrium, when a disturbance forces the system to depart from the circular flow. *The cause is innovation.* Continual product and process innovation is the 'outstanding fact in the economic history of capitalist society' (Schumpeter 1964: 61). 'New Combinations' of materials and forces of production, and new ideas that change the way something is produced, sold or consumed, transform economies by generating new industries, firms, ideas, goods, methods, and organizations.

Schumpeter's theory of innovation deals with three dimensions of entrepreneurial agency – *leadership, profit motive, and imperfect competition.*

First, innovation leaders are more important as agents of change than the owners of capital and property, because innovators build the roads that capitalists will walk along (Schumpeter 1983: 75–85). Today, we find that large firms often lead in technology development and routinely cultivate entrepreneurial aptitudes within the firm (Baumol 2002). When Schumpeter studied the innovation process, leaders were typically individual entrepreneurs, daring and intuitive 'new men' in young firms who took bold initiatives and stepped 'outside the routine'. Innovators swim against the stream and defy constraints on change. They persuade investors – who take a commercial view of the viability of an enterprise and the profitability of innovations – to bear the risks of a new idea and to provide the finance for entrepreneurial plans (Schumpeter 1983: 89). Innovation is a *behavioural characteristic* of capitalism. The psychology of innovators differs from managers who maintain an established business. Schumpeter said: 'Everyone knows that to do something new is very much more difficult than to do something that belongs to the realm of routine' (1964: 72–3). Innovators move production into new channels where the means and ends of economic activity are not calculable. They break conventions, conquer social resistance, and usurp older firms. They win new customers. The neoclassical equilibrium routine does not need this kind of leadership (Schumpeter 1983: 84).

Second, there is the question of what motivates the leaders of innovation. The usual motive of economic action is 'satisfaction of wants'. Related motives include status rivalry, or the power gained as a result of successful entrepreneurship. Schumpeter believed that noble ambitions and work ethics also influence innovation – 'the will to conquer: the impulse to fight, to prove oneself superior to others, to succeed for the sake, not of the fruits of success, but of success itself', and 'the joy of creating, of getting things done, or simply exercising one's energy and ingenuity' (1983: 92–3). Nevertheless, it is clear that *profit* is the main motivator of economic innovation. In capitalism, the profit motive coincides with institutional incentives that channel economic action away from politically generated profits and towards market competition and business innovation (Schumpeter 1964: 105–6). Without profit the entrepreneur would not exist.

Third, it is necessary to examine the type of competition that encourages innovation. Innovation and competition are directly linked in economic life. As

Schumpeter said, 'the new does not grow out of the old but appears alongside of it and eliminates it competitively' (1983: 216). Competition spreads the benefits of a useful innovation by improving products, creating mass markets, and lowering costs. What was unusual, at least compared with neoclassical theory, was how Schumpeter conceptualized competition. First, the driving force of economic evolution is not *price* competition but rather 'competition from the new commodity, the new technology, the new source of supply, the new type of organization' (Schumpeter 1947: 84). Furthermore, Schumpeter argued that successful innovation requires 'imperfect competition', i.e. a temporary shelter from competition:

> perfectly free entry into a new field may make it impossible to enter it at all.... As a matter of fact, perfect competition is and always has been temporarily suspended whenever anything new is being introduced – automatically or by measures devised for the purpose – even in otherwise perfectly competitive conditions.
>
> (ibid.: 104–5)

The explanation for the diminishment of competition during an innovation cycle lies with how innovators understand their future profit. Entrepreneurs know the special premium from innovation cannot last. Competitors who emulate that innovation are bound rapidly to reduce the level of profit (Schumpeter 1964: 79–80). The mere threat of competition can elicit behaviour that corresponds to ideal competition (Schumpeter 1947: 85). But, the lure of monopoly, even if it is only temporary or partial, is also a tangible incentive to compete. Monopolistic profits are 'prizes offered by capitalist society to the successful innovator' (ibid.: 102). Schumpeter was adamant that the monopolistic position of the innovator is temporary and should not receive state support. The monopolist will be 'surrounded by a sufficiently broad zone of competition' (1964: 33). In fact, a monopolistic position cannot generally be sustained unless government intervenes to support it.

> [Pure] cases of long-run monopoly must be of the rarest occurrence and ... still rarer than ... perfect competition. The power to exploit at pleasure a given pattern of demand ... can under the conditions of intact capitalism hardly persist for a period long enough to matter for the analysis of total output, unless buttressed by public authority.
>
> (Schumpeter 1947: 99)

By monopolistic 'shelters' Schumpeter meant business practices that allow entrepreneurial firms to protect *themselves* from competitors during periods of major industrial restructuring. He was critical of state-administered protections, such as import tariffs, subsidized credit, and other political supports that lead to 'weakness' and 'industries of doubtful value' (Schumpeter 1964: 7). Only market competition can stimulate true entrepreneurship and maintain the climate of innovation and change. Tactful and reserved state regulation is required. The state should not limit the investment opportunities of entrepreneurs, and should not try to stabilize capitalism by reducing the risk taking on which innovation thrives (Schumpeter 1947: 91). State economic action must be confined only to 'matters that can be successfully handled by a government'. This will mean 'a corresponding limitation of the activities of the state' (ibid.: 291–2). Acceptable and lawful strategies by which business can create 'temporary shelter' from competition include patents, insurance, hedging, secrecy, inflationary prices, investment strategies that give the firm time to build up its customer base, arrangements to access corporate seed capital, legal agreements to avoid cut-throat competition, or cartelization (ibid.: 87–106).

We turn now to Schumpeter's third and final class of economic process – disturbances that change the direction of development. The disequilibrium effect intensifies as the cumulative consequences of competition and product and process innovations force societies and economies into major structural adjustments. The large-scale global changes that Schumpeter sought to explain simply could not be caused by single innovations that are 'evenly distributed through time' (1983: 223). Rather than orderly and stable change, Schumpeter observed that innovations arrive 'discontinuously in groups or swarms'. The whole process 'proceeds by jerks and rushes' (1964: 75–6). The bunching of supplementary innovations upsets all of the existing routines of market signalling. Entire economies are compelled to adapt as disturbances gather momentum and spread through the system. Some industrial sectors advance as others fall behind. New opportunities arise for some firms, but they spell death for others. Indeed, the 'incessant rise and decay of firms and industries ... is the *central fact* about the capitalist machine' (ibid.: 70).

The Schumpeterian sequence of economic change can be summarized as follows. A wave of innovations brings a surge of profit, investment, and employment opportunities. The resulting economic boom raises business expectations. Responding to the growth surge, firms undertake a second wave of investments. The profit opportunities and growth possibilities give signals to swarms of imitators. New entrants adapt the original innovations, and develop derivate technologies in downstream or upstream industries. Innovations in separate industrial sectors impact on one another, and new products are created to meet changing demands. A classic example was the interrelated innovation pattern based on petroleum, automobile, glass, and rubber industries during the global postwar economic upswing of the 1950s and 1960s.

At the midpoint of the economic cycle the growth trajectory is slowed by crisis. Once the Schumpeterian bandwagon starts to roll, 'some people fall off and profits are gradually competed away until recession sets in' (Freeman 1985: 606). When the 'innovations are completed and investment subsides ... an avalanche of consumer goods pours onto the market with dampening effects on prices; rising costs and interest rates squeeze profit margins, and the economy contracts' (Elliot 1983: xxvi–xxvii). The boom created by innovations is followed by market saturation, increasing competition for credit, and, finally, the exhaustion of technical advance in the lead economic sectors. Crises signal the end of a period of prosperity. They are, in part, a consequence of previous prosperity; a cost that must often be paid for economic progress (ibid.: xxvii). Capitalism is sensitive to the disharmonies caused by innovation, but could not exist without them:

> without innovations, no entrepreneurs; without entrepreneurial achievement, no capitalist returns and no capitalist propulsion. The atmosphere of industrial revolutions – of progress – is the only one in which capitalism can survive. ... In this sense stabilized capitalism is a contradiction in terms.
>
> (Schumpeter 1964: 405)

Schumpeter did not believe that the depression of the 1930s represented a 'breaking down' of 'the propelling mechanism' of capitalism (Schumpeter 1947: 64, 111). Recessions and depressions are not capitalism's failure. Although knowledge of economic cycles can be engaged to plan for the likelihood of downturns, risk avoidance would be dangerous. Private moral hazard would develop if the historical promise of eventual recovery encouraged businesses to 'anticipate the coming boom' and postpone the liquidation of assets, when what is required is the spontaneous corrective behaviour that ensures survival (Schumpeter 1983: 243). Government must not presume that it has 'sufficient power and insight' to plan innovation and 'minimize the disturbance' it causes (Schumpeter 1964: 280).

Schumpeter argued that 'disharmony is inherent in the very modus operandi of the factors of progress' (ibid.: 77). The most pathological crises contain their own 'restorative tendency' (ibid.: 130). During crises, the fruits of a preceding period of innovation can be harvested. It becomes cheaper to adopt new technologies. Downturns are the time to restructure inefficient business, to eliminate 'dead wood', recruit intelligent minds, find solutions to recurrent problems, and lay the groundwork for a future round of innovation. Recovery is a 'painful process of modernization, rationalization and reconstruction' (ibid.: 110). Fundamental 'reorganization and adaptation' are the means of overcoming 'maladjustments and rigidities' (ibid.: 130–1). The 'organic process' of economic evolution, said Schumpeter, is a 'perennial gale of creative destruction' that destroys and recreates economic structures (1947: 83–4).

Such crises are intrinsic to the innovation mechanism of capitalism. Schumpeter aimed to provide 'a reasoned history, not of crises only, nor of cycles and waves, but of the economic process in all its aspects' (1964: 177). He was highly critical of economists and historians who offer superficial explanations of crises and neglect underlying economic or institutional processes.

> Historians of crises primarily talk about stock exchange events, banking, price level, failures, unemployment, total production and so on – all of which are readily recognized as surface phenomena or as compounds which sum up underlying processes in such a way as to hide their real features.
>
> (Schumpeter 1964: 178)

Many economists ... focused their attention on the spectacular breakdowns that came to be referred to as 'crises'. And those crises they failed to see in their true light, that is to say, in the light of the cyclical process of which they are mere incidents. They consider them without looking beyond and below, as isolated misfortunes that will happen in consequence of errors, excesses, misconduct or of the faulty working of the credit mechanism.

(Schumpeter 1947: 41)

There seemed to be a natural confluence between Schumpeter's economic theory and historical data on long-term global economic fluctuations. In the 1920s, Nicolai Kondratiev detected 60-year cycles of economic growth and industrialization dating from 1780. Kondratiev attributed them to factors such as savings rates, infrastructural investments, supply of credit, capital concentration, and long-term commodity price fluctuations. Schumpeter wrote approvingly that the trajectory of these long waves of industrial revolutions in the nineteenth and twentieth centuries revealed 'the nature and mechanism of the capitalist process better than anything else' (Schumpeter 1947: 67–8). The timing of Kondratiev cycles more or less matched Schumpeter's own analysis of 30- to 50-year industrial cycles defined by the periods during which clusters of innovations are absorbed in the economic system. He concluded that there exists 'one class of crises, which are elements, or at any rate regular if not necessary incidents, of a wave-like movement of alternating periods of prosperity and depression, which have pervaded economic life ever since the capitalist era began' (Schumpeter 1983: 223).

Disagreements remain about the timing, diffusion, and magnitude of technological breakthroughs that seem to mark out historical upswings and downswings in global economic activity (Reijnders 1990). Schumpeter's critics point to the inadequacy of statistical data. Schumpeter himself acknowledged that over long time periods there are bound to be gaps in the evidence. He argued, nevertheless, that the statistics are 'merely part of the material', since 'even our scanty information suffices' to show that changes in economic structure are cyclical in nature (Schumpeter 1964: 177–82). Present-day Schumpeterian scholars are more likely to provide evidence for long waves that is *qualitative* rather than quantitative (Nelson 1996). In a recent periodization of long waves, for example, Freeman and Louçã (2001: 139–51) argue that 'structural and qualitative changes in the economy', 'new industries and the adoption of new technologies', and the changing relative costs of key inputs all suggest that long waves are characterized by 'monumental organizational and institutional changes'.

This brings us, finally, to how Schumpeter viewed the *reciprocal conditioning* of economic and institutional forces. Although large-scale economic change exerts pressures upon institutional systems to adapt to new circumstances, institutions also determine the possibilities for economic change. Typical socioeconomic adjustments to industrial change include public and private investments in infrastructure, changes in the global location of leading economic activity, the rise and decline of firms, innovations in fields as disparate as management practice, architecture, and construction methods, and social policies influencing everything from education to welfare (Schumpeter 1947). Institutions cope with the global disequilibria generated by technological and economic revolutions. But cyclical institutional adjustments are not only 'organizational'. They are also affected by the relative behavioural influences of interests, social values, public emotions, and ideologies. The process of creative destruction extends to social structures and social norms over a wide area, and can change the course of institutional development.

> No therapy can permanently obstruct the great economic and social process by which business, individual positions, forms of life, cultural values and ideals, sink in the social scale and finally disappear.
>
> (Schumpeter 1983: 255)

> Our cyclical schema ... stresses that kind of economic change that is particularly likely to break up the existing patterns and to create new ones, thereby breaking up old and creating new positions of power, civilizations, valuations, beliefs, and policies.
>
> (Schumpeter 1964: 279)

The tendency, however, is for social institutions to *lag behind* changes in the economy. Crises create opportunities and motivations for resolving disproportionalities. Yet despite pressures exerted upon them by developments in technologies and markets, the response of institutions to economic change is rarely proportional to the pressure.

> Social structures, types and attitudes are coins that do not readily melt. Once they are formed they persist, possibly for centuries, and since different structures and types display all different degrees of this ability to survive, we almost always find that the actual group and national behaviour more or less departs from what we should expect it to be if we tried to infer it from the dominant forms of the productive process.
>
> (Schumpeter 1947: 12–13)

The inverse of this relationship is apparent when institutions become 'external factors' weighing upon the economic process (Schumpeter 1964: 279). Economic evolution can then be '*institutionally conditioned*' (ibid.: 278). Schumpeter described his economic model as 'strongly institutional in character' (ibid.: 120). The 'institutional pattern of capitalist society' shapes adaptations by economic agents of change (ibid.: 105–6). Institutional change cannot be predicted only by observing economic conditions (ibid.: 283). Like other 'external factors' acting upon the economic process, e.g. wars, natural disasters, or other mishaps, institutions could themselves be the immediate origin of economic crisis:

it would be quite possible for the real causes of crises to exist outside the purely economic sphere, that is for them to be consequences of disturbances which act upon the latter from outside.... A crisis would then simply be the process by which economic life adapts itself to new conditions.

(Schumpeter 1983: 218)

It is only comparatively recently that Schumpeterian scholars have examined the 'coupled dynamics' of economic, social, and institutional change (Dosi 1990). Christopher Freeman and Carlotta Perez portray long waves as 'a succession of techno-economic paradigms associated with a characteristic institutional framework [that] emerges after a painful process of structural change' (Freeman and Perez 1988: 47). Paradigm change occurs once there has been a transformation in 'common sense' about profit opportunities and the organization of production, and once it is perceived that 'carrier technologies' have potential to be diffused throughout an economic system. The scale of restructuring in each upswing might be manifested institutionally by changes in the regulation of national and international markets, the organization of credit systems, legal frameworks for property and contract rights, forms of political representation, education priorities, and changes in the balance of private- and public-sector activity (Perez 1985). Crises play a fundamental role at the intersection of old and new paradigms by *revealing* the 'mismatch' between institutional change and techno-economic change. Because change is not easily absorbed in societies, economic and institutional systems usually experience very different rates of change. Institutions tend to 'suffer from a high degree of natural inertia, strengthened by past successes and upheld by vested interests' (ibid.: 37).

Boyer (1988) calls Schumpeterian crises 'structural', by which he means 'the very functioning of [economic] regulation comes into contradiction with existing institutional forms, which are then abandoned, destroyed, or bypassed'. Unless institutions, economic policies, and business management systems are reformed, 'the system can no longer reproduce itself in the long run, at least on the same institutional and technological basis' (ibid.: 76). Structural crisis differs from the more frequent and self-correcting crises that are symptomatic of demand-and-supply lags in the business cycle.

The downswing of Schumpeterian long waves may be responsible for largely *unavoidable* crises that create the conditions for further economic and institutional progress. In Chapter 6 I will examine 'development' crises, which, though they are also 'structural' in Boyer's meaning of the term, are easier to *avoid* by pursuing different policies. On the other hand, both types – long-wave crises and development crises – are equivalent in so far as the intensity and duration of the disproportionality between institutional and economic change can be reduced where institutions are efficient. Schumpeter argued, for example, that exceptionally adaptive societies can sometimes achieve 'almost perfect parallelism between economic and institutional development' (Schumpeter 1991: 443).

Institutional innovation

We can now examine Schumpeter's final innovation, which dealt with institutional rather than economic theory. At the time of his death in 1950, Schumpeter was about to embark on a lecture series that would explain the nature of institutional change and provide a more detailed account of the relationship between economic and institutional change. His proposals for the Walgreen Lectures, which were to be titled 'American Institutions and Economic Progress' (Schumpeter 1991), are so brief and sketchy that it is impossible to be certain how Schumpeter's analysis would have developed. The lecture notes that survive do, however, suggest a radical new method for understanding institutional change. The Walgreen Lectures would explain the 'interaction' of 'economic and political factors' (ibid.: 438).

Schumpeter repeats his earlier arguments about institutional and reverse causality. 'Economic life is never uninfluenced by institutional factors', and 'institutional patterns shape the economic process'. On the other hand, 'economic evolution will shape human values, attitudes, legal structures, administrative practice, and so on, to some extent' (ibid.). Moreover, 'lag phenomena' or 'discrepancies' between institutions and economic processes 'are among the most important explanatory factors of human history' (ibid.: 440). Some elements of Schumpeter's institutional analysis in the Walgreen Lectures are conventional, while others are unhelpful. The claim that 'group motives' can 'determine the possibilities for economic and institutional change' states the obvious (ibid.: 440–1). In addition, Schumpeter's definitions of 'institutions' are imprecise and all-encompassing, including informal and formal institutions, market institutions, attitudes of mind, and 'patterns of behaviour'.

Yet the Walgreen Lectures also suggest something completely new – a three-part schema for the theorization of institutional change that mirrors his theory of economic change. The economic theory, as noted earlier, takes in (1) the 'circular flow', (2) real development resulting from innovations, and (3) crises that change the course of development. In observing this process of 'economic progress', says Schumpeter, 'we were of course aware all the time that economic life is never uninfluenced by institutional factors, but we simplified matters by the device of "freezing" political and social conditions'. Now, Schumpeter proposed to 'do exactly the same in reverse: assuming the economic process to run along as depicted, we shall investigate the manner in which social institutions change in time' (ibid.: 438–9). In three short paragraphs, Schumpeter outlines the equivalent types of institutional change.

1 The 'routine business' of an institution 'may best be analysed by analogy with an economic concept ... the concept of a stationary state'. Thus, 'even a routine activity induces of itself a slow process of institutional change'.
2 Routine change in the 'stationary state' contrasts with deliberately adaptive 'autonomous institutional change' led by groups of political, administrative, and ideological agents, whose motives and interests may be 'entirely

different from those of the people for whom these groups speak'. The motives of these groups suggest 'an interesting analogy with the economic concept of profit'.

3   Further change involves the 'responses' of leading agents 'to the impact of factors *external* to the given institutional pattern'. For example, 'any major war or any major economic crisis affects a country's institutional pattern for good'.

Much as in the theory of economic change, the typology of institutional change presented in the Walgreen Lectures could be conceptualized as 'three corresponding pairs of opposites': (1) opposition of routine equilibrium to discontinuous change; (2) opposition of static and dynamic methods of analysis; and (3) opposition between two agents of change – managers of the equilibrium and radical innovators (Schumpeter 1983: 82). The emphasis given to institutional innovators is especially interesting. Schumpeter writes of the 'indeterminate' influence of the 'leading personnel' and 'exceptional individuals' in society. He also says that 'factors of economic and institutional progress' are shaped by 'the qualities of the human material, the intelligence, foresight, endurance, and so on, that are at any time present' (Schumpeter 1991: 442).

It would seem, therefore, that Schumpeter proposed to utilize pattern variables of economic evolution as the basis for an equivalent and original conceptualization of institutional change, and to suggest that a similar dynamic of change may operate in both the institutional and economic spheres. One significant aspect, which nevertheless remains unexplained, is that the *motive* for institutional change is analogous to profit making.

Picking up where Schumpeter left off, we can try to specify this dynamic and to expand the analysis to take account of the problems faced by developing societies in transition to capitalism. My argument will be that Schumpeter's hints about the nature of institutional change can clarify the interconnected institutional and economic patterns of capitalist transition. Moving from theoretical logic into concrete analysis, three sequences should be examined:

1   An equilibrium of institutional routines.
2   Disequilibriating processes of internal policy innovation giving rise to real institutional development.
3   External disequilibriating economic processes influencing the timing and pattern of institutional development.

To simplify matters, my discussion in the following two sections conflates the sequence by merely separating the equilibrium routines from the disequilibrium forces. The final section of this chapter incorporates a fourth process, which Schumpeter did not recognize, namely disequilibriating innovations that are routinized in capitalism. In general terms, it can be noted that the 'disequilibrium' elements of Schumpeter's schema deal with external forces acting upon institutions and internal forces driving change within institutional spheres. The theoretical approach I propose also distinguishes equilibrium tendencies that maintain a slow evolution from disequilibrium episodes that intensify the forces of change. This method of utilizing Schumpeterian economic theory to explain institutional change is not a gratuitous application of economic theory to social and political analysis. I believe that Schumpeter's intention was to show that economic and institutional changes are part of a single process. His schema draws attention to interlinked conditions of contemporary capitalist transition.

The insights I will draw from a reformulation of Schumpeter's approach may be summarized as follows: (1) Neither institutional equilibrium nor economic equilibrium are good for development. (2) Particular qualities of leadership and entrepreneurship are indispensable in both institutional and economic fields. (3) Combined interest and ideology motives in the institutional sphere may acquire a potency that approaches but does not equal the economic profit motive. (4) Imperfect political competition can facilitate institutional innovations. Furthermore, I note that Schumpeter's stress on recurrent instability in capitalist economic and institutional change renders it radically different from incrementalist theory. Douglass North has written that: 'Instability is one thing; the process by which change and adjustment take place is something else' (North 1981: 31). Adopting Schumpeter's approach, we must arrive at the opposite conclusion. A Schumpeterian theory of institutional change calls attention to the unavoidable but necessary instability of contemporary capitalist transitions.

Equilibrium routines

Central to this explanation is the co-evolution, or reciprocal conditioning, of institutions and economies. How, and at what point in their evolution, does each influence the course of change in the other? We find that although economic disequilibrium normally creates the right conditions for disequilibrium forms of institutional change, institutions can also be incubators for disequilibrium pressures that shape economic development. Autonomous institutional processes are like economic processes if they give rise to entrepreneurial policy innovations fashioned by exceptional and well-motivated individuals who, in the short run, seek shelter from political competition. A similar analogy may be appropriate where the properties of a social or institutional equilibrium resemble those of economic equilibrium, i.e. when there is little or no endogenous pressure for radical change.

If institutional equilibrium were to operate along the lines that Schumpeter described for economic equilibrium, the following conditions might exist. In the stationary state, the interactions between institutional subsystems of market regulation, law, administration, and political representation produce continuous and self-adjusting compromises between public decision makers about policy formulation and implementation. Evenly matched countervailing pressures maintain the institutional system. Policy 'supply and demand' is balanced because the revealed policy preferences of state actors and citizens translate efficiently into routine timely changes to policy output. All policy-making variables are simultaneously regulated by each other, so expectations are stable. Policy output remains optimal. If the system is disturbed by a change in the external environment, the internal adjustment mechanisms spontaneously restore the equilibrium.

Routine institutional change bears some resemblance to the political process as depicted in early pluralist theories of advanced democracies, where government is a responsive 'weathervane' or 'neutral broker' among more or less freely competing pressure groups. In a liberal democracy, citizens, interest groups, political leaders, and policymakers can articulate preferences fluidly through a competitive mass media and a system of free and more or less perfectly competitive political representation.

In this way, an equilibrium model of the production and consumption of public policy in political markets might be made equivalent to a model of the production and consumption of tradable goods and services in economic markets. 'Efficient' institutional equilibrium would be possible only in a completely competitive world. In the unlikely situation that procedurally perfect political competition determines the selection of policies and leaders according to their demonstrable relative and objective fitness, we might find that institutional adjustments would be more or less instantaneous. Everyone has enough information to accurately calculate the means and ends of policy. The private interests of institutional actors mesh seamlessly with the public interest of citizens. One policymaker's behaviour is as predictable as any other. No single individual or group can determine the costs or monopolize the benefits of public policy. Routine adjustments of policy permit rapid recoveries from the consequences of any miscalculations in policy strategy.

Although this is not a realistic portrayal of even the advanced societies, it can be recognized that there are objective tendencies within the modern state pointing in this direction. In the motivational situation of the ideal Weberian bureaucracy, for instance, officials perform their institutional duties well because all of them are accustomed to a highly evolved impersonal structure of rule incentives and rewards. They have a safe expectation that others will adjust predictably in a similarly prompt and rational manner. Within the state, these uniformities and continuities of attitudes and actions increase the accuracy of expectations. When one person can be sure of how everyone else will act, nobody has any reason to radically modify their behaviour. Universal familiarity with often-repeated adaptations of similarly motivated citizens and policymakers facilitates efficient means-end policy making. It is easy to see, in addition, why most of the relevant actors have a subjective interest in maintaining or restoring this equilibrium tendency.

The precapitalist equilibrium preceding capitalist transition obviously bears little resemblance to the ideal equilibrium. Although its efficiency potential could also be narrowly defined in terms of the survivability of political rulers, a precapitalist neo-patrimonial institutional equilibrium will clearly be less 'efficient' in most ways than the pluralist ideal type of modern society. The equilibrium in precapitalist society is certainly 'stationary' rather than 'dynamic' with respect to processes of capitalist transition.

Talcott Parsons (1991) developed a sociological theory of equilibrium to explain stable capitalist society. He viewed social values as the primary structural factors of equilibrium in society. Value systems are shared conceptions of the type of society that is deemed moral and desirable, and they are institutionalized in organizations and internalized by individuals. Institutionalized value patterns, according to Parsons, are the backbone of the social system. They effectively mediate people's motivations. The 'total equilibrium of a social system' is attained by institutionalizing universal values that *structure* the motivations of actors (Parsons 1954: 239–40). Policy making will be routinely oriented to calculating value factors that sustain social equilibrium. Equilibrating processes 'integrate' the social system. *Dis*equilibrium, on the other hand, results from 'deviance'. Advanced societies possess the institutional mechanisms to forestall or correct individual deviance. It should be noted that Parsons was mainly interested in evolutionary changes that maintain the liberal-market society that is already pluralistic, consensual, and achievement-oriented, and where value systems of free enterprise and free political representation are solidly institutionalized.

Unlike Schumpeter, Parsons described social and economic upheavals as 'short-run *losses* in adaptation' (Parsons 1999: 159). The 'moving equilibrium' is an adjustment mechanism in advanced societies that do not experience major disintegrative forces (Parsons 1991: 520). Institutional socialization counteracts disintegrative tendencies that could upset the boundary-maintaining system (ibid.: 204–5, 481). On the other hand, as in Schumpeter's notion of equilibrium, a healthy system is continually 're-equilibrating' itself and 'forestalling deviancy tendencies' (ibid.: 298). Parsons used the term 'strain' when describing a disturbance in expectations that actors have about one another's conduct – 'Strain in this sense *always*, i.e. by definition, sets up re-equilibrating processes' (ibid.: 491). In normal boundary maintenance, social systems can cope with fluctuations in the external environment by adjusting the socialization process and by institutionalizing functional values at a rate that maintains a constant pattern of change (ibid.: 481–96).

What, however, if societies do not possess the prerequisite value system for efficient adaptation? The limitations of Parsons's formulation are most evident when one examines the necessarily *conflictual* capitalist transitions in developing societies where there is little if any consensus about values of economic freedom and political freedom. In precapitalist equilibrium, the values that balance the social system are qualitatively different from those operating in the advanced equilibrium. In the former, competition is restricted. At best, equilibrium balance is managed by the state for the purpose of distributing advantages among competing clientelist or rent-seeking groups whose 'competitive efficiency' is measured by relative success in obtaining or controlling privileges. Developing societies by definition lack the institutionalized intra-state separations of impersonal powers that guarantee formal freedoms for all persons to test policies, leaders, ideas, and to test products and services, through mechanisms – political and economic – of 'free' competition.

Weber, on the other hand, clearly identified precapitalist 'traditional' equilibrium as overwhelmingly *negative* for development. Stable conditions of policy selection in the precapitalist society facilitate particularism – they sustain social order without social mobility. The institutions for maintaining the social system are characterized by arbitrary rulership powers and case-by-case decisions. Their rule procedures and enforcement mechanisms are *predictably* 'closed' rather than 'open'. Relationships between state rulers and citizens are interpersonal as opposed to impersonal. Positions are obtained by personal privilege, and procedural incentives are structured to facilitate profit by political connection. People can therefore only place their trust in informal social networks. Such a system can stabilize precapitalist equilibrium for very long periods.

> Both tradition and arbitrariness affect very deeply the developmental opportunities of capitalism. Either the ruler himself or his officials seize upon the new chances of acquisition, monopolize them and thus deprive the capital formation of the private economy of its sustenance, or the ubiquitous resistance of traditionalism is reinforced by them so as to hinder economic innovations that might endanger the social equilibrium.
>
> (Weber 1978: 1094)

Viewed positively, equilibrium is a natural condition to which societies and economies gravitate after periodic change. However, a strongly institutionalized circular flow will be ruinous in precapitalist societies where opportunities for discontinuous political and economic restructuring arise recurrently because of crisis. Freeman and Louçã (2001: 52–3) point out that Schumpeter's way of seeing equilibrium could encompass both these viewpoints. The 'mechanism of equilibration' accounts for 'the resistance to change in the economic system, namely the defence of established business and institutional traditions'. On the other hand, equilibrium is also the mechanism for the 'absorption of change', since the imitation of successful innovations later plays a role in 'restoring equilibrium after innovation'.

Parsons focused on institutionalized change as a moving equilibrium of value socialization in the United States. Yet he was not uninterested in how a 'balanced' society comes into being. He recognized a degree of voluntarism in the socialization process. Parsons's view of institutional innovation – like Weber's analysis of normative evolution (see Chapter 3) – resembles the Schumpeterian leadership process. During the modernization of societies an 'instrumental consensus' can evolve among key acting units about the values, norms, and policy actions that are good for society (Parsons 1999: 257). Policy units process knowledge, make choices, perform tasks of goal selection, goal attainment, adaptation, and pattern maintenance. Especially interesting is Parsons's comment that in the most 'creative societies' there may arise a 'developmental breakthrough', i.e. an innovation that raises society's 'adaptive capacity' and increases its ability to compete with more advanced societies (1966: 23). The argument can be made more strongly. In the contemporary developing societies a more or less rapid transition to capitalism *requires* the disintegration of the primordial routine. This applies to countries trapped in a precapitalist equilibrium, or in a regressive populist-correction cycle, but also to more 'creative' developing societies that transit through alternating periods of decay and progress (see Chapter 6).

Parsons recognized that 'severe dislocations of the previous social organization' accompany institutional innovations (1999: 159). Economic, technological, or scientific developments, or a change in the environment, can disorganize a society. If their effect is large enough to disturb the expectations of many actors in society, there may emerge the impulse for major social change. They could conceivably bring about 'the progressive increase of strains in one strategic area of the social structure which are finally resolved by a structural reorganization of the system' (Parsons 1991: 493). Struggles between vested interests have a major role in situations of 'strain'. A developmental breakthrough may threaten to destroy the mechanisms for motivating and rewarding groups in society that hitherto maintained controls over economic resources and levers of political power, and which seek to defend existing structures. 'Fundamentalist' forces can choke off change, and can restabilize the institutional pattern (ibid.: 516–20). Change only occurs if progressive sectors confront traditional forces and reorganize the system.

The innovations of policy actors who are motivated by knowledge of capitalism will obviously not be accommodated easily by the precapitalist polity, by the value system, or by groups with vested interests in the existing order. In traditional society the dominant motivational forces are incentives to service higher-status individuals in exchange for rewards. Innovations that threaten that equilibrium are slow to emerge. Conflicting impulses within the social system may produce a *stalemate* equilibrium. They constrain radicalism until such time as pressures for change reach boiling point. The positive aspect of the *moving* equilibrium is that change is slow and steady, with less likelihood of big errors. If countervailing interests and structural pressures can adjust more or less harmoniously, then solutions can be tried and tested without severe disruption. There is no question that this form of incremental change does account for much of the long history of institutions.

Nevertheless, in many developing societies the norm is non-evolutionary equilibrium. Societies can also become locked into local problems of disproportionality between static institutions and an autonomously evolving economy. These societies can seem to reproduce their underdevelopment *indefinitely* even while the world around them may be changing rapidly. Precapitalist equilibriums of all kinds have a tendency to reinforce themselves, to slow change. In the more dynamic developing societies, on the other hand, recurrent discontinuities create opportunities for 'disequilibrium' institutional innovation.

Disequilibrium transitions

We now turn our attention to how disequilibrium institutional change occurs. A neo-Schumpeterian analysis of the causes and consequences of institutional disequilibrium reveals the potential for states to intervene, especially during crises, to enable capitalist transition. The essence of the argument is that economic crises motivate institutional problem solving, but that positive outcomes depend on the kinds of incentives for action that also characterize successful economic innovation.

Hirschman's novel thesis that development practitioners learn the arts of policy making by coping with disequilibria neatly complements a neo-Schumpeterian way of conceptualizing change *strategies*. Hirschman (1984: 96) advocated 'unbalanced' economic growth in developing countries. Rather than aim for optimal combinations of resources or factors of production, countries would do better 'skipping stages' and 'inventing sequences', even if they run the risk of getting them the 'wrong way around'. Hirschman believed that policy-makers are generally more effective when they embrace 'disproportionalities' and 'pressure mechanisms' than when they search for hidden rationality in chaotic processes (ibid.: 93–4, 105). Decision makers develop their competency for understanding and modifying the means and ends of policy better when they work in a hothouse environment, which forces them to *learn* to cope with recurrent tensions, bottlenecks, shortages, and instability. Societies move forward, says Hirschman, by 'sailing against the wind' (ibid.: 108). Sabel (1994: 148) similarly argues that there may be benefits to be had from 'perturbing' the status quo of markets or organizations in order to 'induce disequilibrium learning'.

What applies to the disequilibrium market conditions of entrepreneurship might also apply to institutions or organizations when subject to disequilibrium pressures to innovate. Further support for the 'imbalance' hypothesis is found in Weberian theory. As Randall Collins says, the development of capitalism always involved 'tensions between opposing elements' and continuous 'institutionalized strife', subject to the important caveat that a disproportionate development of one institutional sphere may in fact impede capitalist transition (Collins 1986: 34–6). A productive 'tension between opposing elements' avoids any single element becoming dominant.

In previous chapters I have discussed positive pressures and tensions between institutional subsystems of market regulation, law, administration, and representation in capitalist society, which are eventually manifested in formal divisions of power with checks and balances. Capitalism's institutional system works well as long as its subsystems 'harmonize' by reciprocal adherence to a common procedural norm. If subsystems are to 'learn' from competitive disequilibrium between subsystems they must share a common normative language. Formality and impersonality offer the only practical guarantees that subsystems will remain focused on universal as opposed to particularistic functions. This process of procedural harmonization among subsystems is not 'planned'. Holistic planning would eliminate the hothouse of disproportionality. For the same reasons, policymakers who pursue capitalist transitions should distinguish disequilibria that are useful for efficient adaptation from disequilibria that cause recurrent crises.

The task in this section is not unlike Nelson and Winter's engagement of Schumpeterian economic theory to understand organizational evolution, when 'processes of change' are introduced into an 'unrealistically quiet and static condition' (Nelson and Winter 1982: 98). I will explore how agencies of change can be introduced into a static precapitalist institutional equilibrium. The important factors are the Schumpeterian triad of entrepreneurial preconditions – *leadership*, *motives*, and *imperfect competition*.

Policy leadership

Policy leaders play the critical role in discontinuous disequilibrium change. As Schumpeter said, institutional progress depends on entrepreneurial leadership by 'exceptional individuals' (Schumpeter 1991: 442). Policy innovators are individuals whose role in institutional life is equivalent to the entrepreneurial leaders of technological innovation. Their functions are the management or innovation of policy formulation and implementation. If modern economic action is characterized by the peaceful appropriation of control over private resources that provide advantages in the satisfaction of private wants, then, by analogy, modern institutional action involves the appropriation of control over state resources for the purpose of satisfying public wants.

With respect to institutional theory, policy making involves 'instrumental' rather than 'incremental' change. In political terms, policy is always a process of struggle, competition, and compromise. The institutional location of peak policymakers is the position that allows them to wield legitimate power and to access the knowledge data and organizational resources required to calculate actual and potential patterns of economic and institutional change. Their role in organizations gives policymakers the power to shape the goal and process of change. This is an elite group of individuals who owe their positions to achievement or ascription. Either they wield state authority, or their opinions carry weight in government or law making. They may act autonomously, or they may be the carriers of vested interests.

Policy leaders differ from bureaucrats in much the same way that entrepreneurs differ from business managers. In psychosocial behavioural terms the difference between an innovation in business and in government is not enormous. Bold institutional reforms require daring leaps of faith but also sound technical expertise and the skills to calculate optimal means for pursuing a goal. Policy innovators swim against the stream. They 'break the mould' by circumventing dysfunctional values and by overcoming resistance from vested interests. Like the industrial entrepreneurs who depend on bankers and financiers, policy entrepreneurs must convince politicians and other elite groups to bear the political and economic risks. They must persuade these stakeholders of the viability and cost–benefit of the reform enterprise.

Policy motives

Appropriate motivation is the second, and more complex, factor of entrepreneurial agency. In the Walgreen Lectures Schumpeter pointed out that routine change in the stationary state contrasts with deliberately adaptive 'autonomous institutional change' led by groups that perform the role of political, administrative, and ideological agents of change in society. Their 'habits of mind and interests' might be 'entirely different from those of the people for whom these groups speak' (Schumpeter 1991: 439). As noted earlier, Schumpeter alluded to the existence of a motive in the institutional sphere equivalent to 'profit' in the economic sphere, but did not identify it. Profit is not the only motive driving innovation in economic life, but it is the overriding and indispensable motive. Therefore, a special problem arises when we try to identify the dominant motive for an *institutional* policy innovation.

There appears to be nothing of a regular nature in the institutional field that can be functionally equivalent to competition for profit in the economic field. If profit were the main motive for state policies we could not hope for anything other than perpetuation of the status quo in precapitalist society. Business would compete for government-regulated 'profit rents' from permissions and subsidies to trade or produce rather than undertake risky ventures in genuinely competitive markets. State officials would be predators selling public services to the highest bidder or diverting public resources into slush funds, patronage networks, and crony firms. Profiting from political connections is obviously not a desirable motivator of public policy.

One way around the problem is to recall Schumpeter's observation that a single economic entrepreneur may display various forms of behavioural motivation simultaneously. A broadly similar range of motivations are encountered in economic and *non*-economic action. In Chapter 5 I will discuss four types of relevant policy interest, which are summarized here. An '*ideal*' interest in moral values can be satisfied by pursuing the objectives of a policy action or by the behaviour that is adopted to achieve the goal. '*Material*' interest is satisfied by economic advantages gained through policy action, which may benefit the policymaker or a group, organization, or nation. '*Procedural*' interest can be satisfied by the ease of undertaking the policy action. '*Status*' interest can be satisfied by the prestige or power obtained from a position or role in the state. In other words, the attitude of policymakers towards institutional reform must be studied in terms of complex 'sets' of interests. When policymakers compete and compromise about institutional policy during capitalist transitions they do so in the context of an ongoing *public* as well as *personal* struggle between status, ideal, material, and procedural interests. They calculate their own motives and the motives of others who react to the policies. Institutional change happens only when sufficient numbers of competing individuals with influence inside the state compromise about content, technical means, and behavioural standards of policy.

Parsons clarified the issue – 'the cardinal fact of institutional behaviour' in the advanced society is that 'self-interested elements of motivation and disinterested moral sentiments of duty tend to motivate the same concrete goals' (1954: 240). If individualism is 'institutionalized', as arguably it has been in the most advanced societies, it is possible for utilitarian interest to coexist with shared conceptions and commitments to a good society, which are internalized as social values (Parsons 1999: 273, 318). Through learning, conformity, and self-motivation, a stable polity can reflect 'the interlocking of so many motivational elements in support of the same goals and standards' (Parsons 1954: 240). In contrast, the underdeveloped polities do not enjoy such harmonies of interest. In the precapitalist equilibrium it is difficult to reach agreement about policies that aim to confront traditionalist forces for the purpose of reorganizing the institutional system. The self-interested and disinterested motives identified by Parsons will not mesh seamlessly.

Weber explained why material interest in bribes, patronage, or sinecures will never be the sole motivator of political action even in precapitalist states. Politicians and officials are just as likely to want to conform to social values and conventions. They may value power, status, prestige, and public approval for their own sake. Status motivates both public policy and private enterprise – 'struggle for personal power, and the resulting personal responsibility, is the lifeblood of the politician as well as of the entrepreneur' (Weber 1978: 1404). The 'chain of motivation' of social action is 'subject to opposing and conflicting impulses', and 'only the actual outcome of the conflict gives a solid basis of judgement' (ibid.: 10). Furthermore, if the desirable kinds of policy motives *are* present in the *upper* echelons of the state, the safeguard against undesirable behaviour by lower-ranking officials will be the power to command and the duty of obedience 'regardless of personal motives or interests' in public organizations with clear hierarchical lines of authority (ibid.: 943).

So, we come to the question – can any 'interest' motive of institutional policy resemble the profit motive of economic action? By disaggregating the policy-maker's interests it is possible to recognize that self-interest is not only a utilitarian calculus of material advantage. A *mixture* of ideal, status, material, and procedural self-interest energizes innovation and shapes behavioural commitments in the policy field. Why, then, do so many political scientists and sociologists dislike the idea that self-interest routinely motivates policy action? Herbert Simon cautions against any idealization of policy motivations.

> In our formation of public policy ... it is probably reasonable to assume, as a first approximation, that people will act from self-interest. Hence a major task of any society is to create a social environment in which self-interest has reason to be enlightened ... [We] should be sure, first, that our social institutions are framed to bring out our better selves, and second, that they do not require major sacrifices of self-interest by many people, much of the time.
>
> (Simon 1983: 105)

A healthy dose of cynicism is needed. How can a policymaker who acts from private interest construct institutions that will satisfy the public interest? If they build institutions in the public interest, will this be the happenstance of unintended consequences, much as occurs when the pursuit of a private economic interest benefits the whole society? Individualistic theories view the formation of modern states as an outcome of voluntary social contracts between individuals who cooperate in their self-interest, or as coercion exerted by one interested group of individuals over others. Public choice theory contributes one side of the relevant story by unpacking states into their individually motivated acting units. Policymakers, it is argued, can weigh up the broad costs and benefits of their decisions even if at the same time they are bound to want to maximize their personal gratification or narrow need-fulfilment. Party competition and voting, political calendars, public policy, constitutional reform, the growth of government, and the supply of public goods and services are all influenced in significant measure by pure self-interest and, in particular, the politician's overriding motivation to survive in office. And, although politicians rely on bureaucrats to deliver the services that will win them votes, the bureaucrats themselves relentlessly maximize their budgets and compete to accumulate policy functions and public resources. Such theories might conceive the political process somewhat narrowly (public choice theory does not preclude altruistic motives, but tends to neglect the role of ideology). However, if the choice is between ignoring self-interest in the public sector or giving it due recognition, the latter is by far the wiser approach. Drawing on insights about how private preferences translate – positively or negatively – into public action, public choice theorists have produced important proposals for economic and constitutional policies that are intended to mitigate negative self-interest and harness positive self-interest.

On the other hand, if institutions are viewed solely through the lens of public choice theory there is a danger of creating a wholly cynical view of the policy process. With some justification, critics of public choice theory point out the tendency to pre-judge politicians and bureaucrats as incompetent, venal, egoistic, myopic, or cowardly. More attention should be paid to positive policy experiences. In an empirical study, Grindle and Thomas (1991) find that preferences and actions of policy elites in developing countries can be shaped by broadly beneficent pressures, choices, motives: (1) personal goals or ideological biases that motivate work for the betterment of society; (2) professional specialization in fields oriented to the provision of social services and public goods; (3) experience and skills that permit policymakers to anticipate and avoid unintended consequences; and (4) organizational loyalty and a sense of responsibility based on position or reputation. Studies like these find that policy elites can adjust pragmatically to changing environments and constraints. Some officials routinely take account of their own relative power or autonomy, institutional legacies, administrative competence, economic conditions, and international circumstances. Policymakers are not inevitably immobilized by bureaucratic power struggles or wider conflicts among societal elites. Good results often come from accommodating social interests through bargaining and compromise.

If not interest, then perhaps a certain pro-capitalist ideology can approximate the motivational strength of economic profit. The power of ideology to shape institutional transitions is considerable. Ideology can have a causal purity not shared by the amorphous 'interest'. Although interest groups often utilize ideology as a means of self-identification, ideology is never reduced to simple interest motivation. When it operates at the heart of political decision making, ideology can change people's perceptions of their self-interest and of the public interest. There is no romance in viewing ideology as a practical motivator of capitalist institutional change. Socialism's phenomenal influence in the twentieth century remains a fresh-enough reminder of the potential power of ideology. The 'logic of political survival' should not be understood purely as the expression of self-interest. It can also be ideological. I make the following claims for ideology.

- Ideology, like ethics, is a free choice that defines how values and interests are selected and pursued. If people choose ideology, ideology must persuade.
- Ideology is a volitional force initially generated by intellectuals. It can be a force of capitalist transition, or a source of resistance to it.
- Ideology is cognitive and knowledge-based. Science can eliminate the errors of ideology by testing for consistency, adequacy, and distortion.
- Carriers of ideologies, including policymakers, rationalize means-end problems and explain experience. Their ideas can be internalized by citizens.
- Developmental ideology is an educational mechanism that shapes policy and the procedures for carrying out policy. Ideology can be designed and constructed.

What role could an ideological breakthrough have during a crisis? Schumpeter (1964: 117) wrote of the volatility of 'waves of optimism and pessimism' in times of crisis, and the 'intellectual attempts to stem the tide'. Crises modify the ideological climate and justify a radical response by political regimes. During crises, emotions run high. There is no certainty about the nature of the ideological reaction to crises, which may be sincere or insincere. In *Man and Crisis* (1958), the Spanish philosopher Jose Ortega y Gasset distinguished between *incremental* history, when the ideological and normative convictions of society undergo smooth change without causing damage to society's skeleton framework, and, on the other hand, crises. A common response to crisis in the past has been to seek salvation in doctrines of socialization or collectivization in the effort to recreate the sort of conviction that society seems to lose as a consequence of the crisis. People 'falsify themselves to themselves; that is to say, they wrap themselves up in artistic styles, in doctrines, in political movements which are insincere and which fill the lack of genuine convictions' (ibid.: 86). Societies in crisis become disoriented. The 'map which permitted man to move within his environment' is lost. People are easily 'shoved about and confused'. They know that 'traditional norms and ideas are false and inadmissible ... but the truth is that there are no new positive beliefs with which to replace the traditional ones' (ibid.).

Unreality, autarky, and communitarian ideals have been typical mass responses to crises. Since these responses are in part ideological, it is reasonable to assume that alternative ideologies could, in the right circumstances, produce different reactions. Ideology has the unique quality of being a cognitive innovation as well as a motivator of institutional innovations. In this sense, the analysis of ideology can take its place alongside other forms of innovation in a Schumpeterian model of discontinuous evolution. First, the source of ideology is an innovation that modifies the stock of knowledge or revolutionizes selections from existing knowledge. Second, the transmission of knowledge is revolutionized by ideological innovations, i.e. new ways of formulating, communicating, and applying ideas that will convince and persuade. Finally, ideologies routinely inform and motivate policy innovations. The intellectual entrepreneurs of ideologies create knowledge or interpret knowledge in new ways. Policy entrepreneurs apply that knowledge to finding new solutions to new problems.

The view of crises as opportunities for reform assumes that societies learn from the shock of severe disturbance. Crisis forces everyone to try to understand the working of a system that was hitherto taken for granted. Disruptions to the equilibrium pattern of an economic or institutional order engender the motivation to seek out knowledge about the mechanisms that have malfunctioned. The demand for future crisis avoidance is a powerful pressure on public policy. In that context, design or redesign of an ideology is induced by awareness that something ought to occur. Successful ideologies are invented and then selected. They survive in competition with other ideologies if they are well adapted to the environment, which is not the same as saying they survive because of their objective efficiency (socialism is a case in point). Ideological innovations often arise as a result of a change in the internal or external environment. Crisis creates the demand for new ideas that claim to explain the system in crisis and that offer alternative systems as solutions to crisis. Finally, ideology helps to break the deadlock between 'interests' during crises. A theory of ideological motivation complements the theory of discontinuous institutional and economic innovation because ideology similarly involves rational enquiry, innovation, design, and the transmission of whatever is 'new'.

Imperfect political competition

The final Schumpeterian factor of entrepreneurial agency is imperfect competition. Creative destruction in the institutional field is likely, at some stage in the process, to involve restraints on political competition. In developing societies, policymakers who guide capitalist transitions seek shelter from the political forces that defend the precapitalist equilibrium. The analogy with temporary monopolistic profit making is plain to see. Just as shelter from market competitors provides incentives for economic innovation, an institutional innovation is more likely to produce results if policy entrepreneurs can be insulated from competitors while they formulate and implement reforms.

The idea of leadership autonomy is explored in Schumpeter's own analysis of delegated political authority (Schumpeter 1947: 269–302). The 'democratic method', as he defined it, is an 'institutional arrangement for arriving at political decisions in which individuals acquire the power to decide by means of a competitive struggle for the people's votes' (ibid.: 269). Within the zone of 'free competition' there will be 'differences of opinion'. Voters 'have the opportunity of accepting or refusing the men who are to rule them', but this 'cannot mean that the people actually rule' (ibid.: 284–5). 'Competition for leadership' in politics is analogous to competition in economic life. In both cases, 'competition is never completely lacking, but hardly ever is it perfect' (ibid.: 270–1). Even the democracies of Europe and North America 'recognize with practical unanimity that there are situations in which it is reasonable to abandon competitive and to adopt monopolistic leadership'. Political competition has particular disadvantages 'in troubled times' (ibid.: 296). However, by the same standards that apply in markets, monopolistic policy innovation is justified only if policymakers do not prolong the sheltering that shields them from political competition.

There are further ways in which imperfect economic and political competition resemble each other. The separation of government from business facilitates the timely lowering of barriers to economic competition. Monopoly is a result of competition among firms, and it remains subject to competitive pressures for as long as the state does not protect it. Monopoly is a manageable risk only if the surrounding environment remains competitive. Similarly, the formal representational system separating the state from citizens facilitates an eventual lowering of the barriers to political competition. Often because of a preceding crisis, technocrats first obtain their shelter with some legitimacy and significant support among a population. Later, if their ideas no longer remain competitive against the alternatives, the state need not prevent the resumption of politics. The role of competition for political leadership, and the electorate's role in producing government, can be created or restored. In time, as Schumpeter recognized, the polity needs rules of competition, checks and balances, a division of power, ideological pluralism, and legal safeguards against permanent political monopoly.

If the analogy with economic monopoly is to be convincing, imperfect policy competition must be *procedurally* consistent with the kinds of restrictive business practices identified in Schumpeter's economic theory. It is possible to envisage innumerable more or less legitimate monopolistic restrictions on political competition devised by the state's peak policy agencies, with the objective of minimizing the political obstacles to institutional reform. Aside from outright suppression of political dissent, manipulative government action in support of sheltered policy reform could include the following: (1) permit official secrecy about government's intentions; (2) insulate leaders from political criticism; (3) recruit the 'best brains' for policy agencies; (4) tolerate the short-term risks of losing public support during fast phases of reform in the expectation of medium-term gains from reform; (5) cushion targeted groups from short-term disadvantage while building political support; (6) pay off lobby groups or raise the cost of lobbying and political cartelization; (7) adjust the price of public goods and services in ways that win public support; (8) sequence reforms in ways that will help to maintain public support; (9) seek external finance and technical expertise to assist the implementation of reforms; (10) establish unofficial relationships between state agencies and citizen or business groups to obtain information or intellectual assets; (11) utilize constitutional means to legislate by executive decree.

Measures like these have drawbacks and could be misused by undisciplined sectors of the state as means to sustain the precapitalist equilibrium. In the right hands, however, they can buy time to prove the fitness of policy ideas. As long as the monopolistic phase is not prolonged, policymakers should be able to maintain their flexibility and exercise their entrepreneurial talents. 'Political shelter' is especially beneficial for the policy actors who are charged with carrying out the difficult first phase of reform, which triggers a sequence of further reforms. Once the initial reforms have shown clear signs of success, these or subsequent policymakers can imitate those breakthroughs in new areas, or pursue further avenues of reform while drawing on lessons learnt during the first innovations. Exactly as occurs in the economic process, once the competitive process of secondary institutional innovations has gained momentum, the 'consequences begin to make themselves felt all over the system in perfectly logical concatenation' (Schumpeter 1964: 106–7).

There is ample historical evidence to support the claim that developmental breakthroughs require strong political control at the centre. Developmental breakthrough can be the policy innovation that ruptures a precapitalist routine and creates the possibility of capitalist transition. However, since authoritarian regimes are just as likely to maintain or recreate the precapitalist routine, a favourable match between the concentration of political power and capitalist transition is not assured. One particularly important reason why democracy has not played handmaiden to capitalism in the past is that increases in political pluralism in transitional societies raise unrealistic popular expectations for redistributions of wealth and power (Huntington and Dominguez 1975). The resulting instability may provoke a backlash from conservative forces, and then a classic populism–correction–populism cycle might ensue. Because entrenched interest groups attempt to maintain the precapitalist equilibrium, state authority is needed to overcome the barriers to reform. Huntington's insight is valid. The 'change or destruction' of 'traditional social forces, interests, customs, and institutions', and the capacity to '*innovate policy*', necessitates 'the concentration of power in the agents of modernization' (Huntington 1968: 142). In especially difficult circumstances, or in societies where charismatic caudillos are the political norm, this could mean the 'concentration of authority in a single individual within those institutions' (ibid.: 156). Again, there is no guarantee that such power will not be misused. However, it remains the case that good leaders in imperfect polities can protect against the central problem of *political* order in development, namely that distributive demands will outrun the economic potential to satisfy them.

One of the more dependable logical 'laws' of social science is that economic growth eventually generates citizen demands for fuller political participation and more effective representation by leaders. As one scholar writes, 'the consolidation of a market economy increases the likelihood that democratic politics can similarly emerge' (Dominguez 1998: 54). Of more immediate interest in the present context, however, is the difficulty of initiating reforms that will open up markets when state power is not sufficiently consolidated. *Market*-led economic growth is likely to be more rapid in the early stages of development if political elites are strong and detached enough to mobilize human and physical resources, regulate conflicts, and secure property rights. Indeed, the same correlation tends to hold between state autonomy, authoritarian politics, and rapid *state*-led economic growth (White and Wade 1984). It would appear in general terms that an effectively 'strong' developmental state could be either 'pervasive' or 'parametric' in the terms defined in Chapter 2. The authority of the state is simply a technical instrument to eliminate obstacles – it can be engaged for different purposes.

Adrian Leftwich (1996: 284) describes an ideal 'developmental state' as one that can 'concentrate sufficient power, authority, autonomy, competence and capacity at the centre to shape, pursue and encourage the achievement of explicit developmental objectives'. The regime in charge of state policy is led by a compact of technocrats and politicians who insulate themselves from special-interest groups. Peak administrative staff are ideally well trained and technically competent. For a critical period, intra-elite disputes, patronage, or corruption do not weaken the reform thrust. The state maintains arm's-length relationships with non-state actors, which facilitates the definition of strategy and the implementation of policy. State autonomy can also be sustained by exploiting national security threats, one-party rule, and the availability of independent sources of state revenue. Civil society remains weak until such time as economic growth creates conditions that strengthen civil society. Meanwhile, there is no serious challenge to the state's power to force business groups to comply with the development strategy. A developmental state is more likely to maintain its domestic political legitimacy for as long as economic growth continues alongside complementary social and infrastructural reforms (for example, in housing policy).

In theory, then, the dynamic of institutional change in a 'politically restricted' developmental state may be analogous to the economic restrictions of private enterprises that create self-regulating lawful shelters from competition during the time it takes to reap the profit from innovations. Consistent with the Schumpeterian model, moreover, electoral politics and technocracy are not mutually exclusive. Since the 1980s, numerous democratically elected as well as soft authoritarian governments in East Asia and Latin America have appointed qualified technocrats to undertake thoroughgoing reforms. The unorthodox and Machiavellian *motivational situation* of a relatively autonomous 'change team' of 'reform- mongering' policymakers during crises frequently explains the success or failure of such regimes (Hirschman 1968; Waterbury 1992).

Policy elitism is not a universal requirement of institutional restructuring in a capitalist direction. However, this was the path taken in the now more advanced societies at critical stages in their development. Technocracy was also the common means of proto-capitalist restructuring in developing countries during the twentieth century. Technical specialists appointed by authoritarian regimes or imperfect democracies in developing societies have received temporary shelter from politics to build the institutions of a market society. If they have failed it is often because of poor knowledge and correspondingly weak ideology relating to the procedural goals and sequences of capitalist transition.

Disequilibrium routines

Until now I have discussed institutional changes during transitions to capitalism. The nature of institutional change in the more advanced societies needs also to be briefly examined in the light of an apparent error in Schumpeter's analysis. In *Capitalism, Socialism and Democracy* (1947), he claimed that capitalism was losing its evolutionary momentum and would be replaced by socialism. There are plausible reasons why a thesis of capitalism's self-destruction might hold true. One, which will be examined in the next chapter, is the inevitable intellectual hostility to capitalism. Schumpeter's less convincing argument, however, is that *economic* 'innovation itself is being reduced to a routine' (ibid.: 132). Because technological and economic progress had been 'automatized', he claimed, the developmental impulse of capitalism was crumbling.

> Technological progress is increasingly the business of teams of trained specialists who turn out what is required and make it work in predicable ways. The romance of earlier commercial adventure is rapidly wearing away, because so many more things can be strictly calculated that had of old to be visualized in a flash of genius.... Since capitalist enterprise, by its very achievements, tends to automatize progress ... it tends to make itself superfluous – to break to pieces under the pressure of its own success. The perfectly bureaucratized giant industrial unit not only ousts the small or medium-sized firm and 'expropriates' its owners, but in the end it also ousts the entrepreneur and expropriates the bourgeoisie as a class which in the process stands to lose not only its income but also what is infinitely more important, its function.
>
> (Schumpeter 1947: 132–4)

Schumpeterian economists have questioned that conclusion. Rosenberg (1994: 55) notes that Schumpeter focused on 'the earliest stages in the innovation process', and failed 'to consider the degree to which commercial success is dependent upon subsequent stages in the carrying out of an innovation'. Nelson (1996) accepts that research and development of technologies was to some extent 'socialized' in the twentieth century, but only in the sense of organized cooperation and coordination among firms and between government and firms. Innovation is institutionalized in corporations, scientific establishments, engineering professions, and universities. Some of it is supported by strategic government initiatives and public funding. This socialization of innovation may have reduced wastage and increased the complexity of innovation. Nevertheless, Nelson rejects the idea that technology innovation is now 'explicitly planned and coordinated ... across a broad field of activity' (ibid.: 80). Capitalism continues, as ever before, to recreate an uncertain, messy, and dynamic business environment favouring 'experimental tinkering' over planning (ibid.: 52–83). In practice, science and technology development remains, and must remain, a competitive, pluralistic, and flexible sphere of economic activity.

Even if Schumpeter's theory that innovation has been routinized by firms were correct, it need not follow that routinization dulls competition or entrepreneurship. Schumpeter himself recognized that the vitality of the 'entrepreneurial function … consists in getting things done' (1947: 132). Although the conditions for it have changed in some respects, innovation does continue to 'get done'. Baumol (2002) has shown that modern oligopolistic firms in competitive economic sectors reduce uncertainty by approaching innovation as they would a profit-making investment in plant and equipment. Large corporations devote 'a substantial staff and facilities largely or exclusively to the creation of new products and processes' (ibid.: 35). Baumol describes the routine of innovation by oligopolistic firms as akin to the arms race between nations. Innovation management requires standardized procedures, as well as directives about what should be invented and the release of new products. Innovation leaders work discreetly in technical and marketing departments. Competition pressures are simulated within private industrial and commercial firms in order to reward innovation. Although entrepreneurs may no longer be the sole protagonists of economic progress, they still play an important role in the economy. Individuals will often supply the 'heterodox, breakthrough innovations', while large firms provide 'the enhancements to those breakthroughs' (ibid.: 72). Small companies continue to be the source of novel innovations. Despite organizational changes in the management of innovation, the economic environment remains competitive.

What might the implications be for the method of analysing institutional innovation in advanced capitalism? It seems clear that Schumpeter was influenced to some extent by the widespread disenchantment with the workaday impersonality of capitalist life, which, as I discuss in the next chapter, has been a reason for disorientation among intellectuals about the 'empirical realities of the world and its institutions' (Weber 1978: 506). Perhaps Schumpeter's dubious prediction about the future of capitalist economies stems in part from his opinion that the depersonalization of economic and administrative life 'blots out personality' and 'vision' (Schumpeter 1947: 133–4). He wrote that the functions of 'individual leadership acting by virtue of personal force and personal responsibility for success', which previously energized the bourgeoisie, are now served by 'more impersonal methods'. The 'leading man … is becoming just another office worker' (ibid.: 133). Like many others before and since, Schumpeter seems to have confused the spread of impersonal procedures in the leading organizations of society with a loss of personal responsibility, leadership, and creativity. Yet the one does not necessarily follow from the other. Impersonal institutions can also create secure and predictable regulatory environments – free of patronage and privilege – which encourage personal risk taking and innovation. Whatever the reasons, Schumpeter clearly failed to predict that routine technological and economic innovation would continue to gather greater force and speed.

Given Schumpeter's misgivings about the future of modern capitalism it is not surprising that his (three-part) theoretical schema of 'institutional change' in the Walgreen Lectures did not consider the possibility of a (fourth) scenario in which institutional innovation becomes routine in the advanced society. Arguably, today we are witnessing the paradox of *stable instability* or *continuous discontinuity*. Economic and technological disequilibrium has become a pattern to which institutions in the advanced countries routinely adjust. If correct, this observation would be consonant with the argument that all of the institutions of modern society are subject to 'construction' imperatives (Coleman 1993). Continuous change in economic and institutional life is disconcerting. People often see it as unsustainable and anarchic rather than as a potentially permanent condition of progress and order. Yet, if Schumpeter had accepted the possibility of dynamic routines of economic innovation continuing into the future, he might also have recognized that they would appear in societies where market freedom and political freedom, and the discipline of adaptive trial and error, are institutionalized in calculable, formal, and impersonal regulatory orders. Weber (1978: 1118) could have had this in mind when he wrote of a '*modern routinised capitalism*'. That seems a useful description. At least it is a logical possibility, and one that is commensurate with the *non*-routine disequilibrium dynamics of capitalist transitions.

Other writers have implicitly acknowledged the possibility of continuous discontinuity while continuing to frame their argument in conventional equilibrium terms. Echoing Schumpeter's terminology, Herbert Simon (1983) discusses the evolutionary survival of social actors and social phenomena, and the formation of 'public policy', as functions of the feedback mechanisms of markets and political institutions, which keep 'the evolving system in the neighbourhood of its equilibrium' (ibid.: 39). Simon goes on to say that there can never exist a 'steady state' society 'in which all the problems have been solved' (ibid.: 106). Nevertheless, the nature of institutional evolution does seem to suggest that some societies are obviously much 'fitter' than others. 'Fitter', in this context, means that such societies possess the flexibility to adjust to continual change.

> The Darwinian process is a process of generating certain possibilities and then testing them and retaining the better ones.... If we have a landscape of evolving, elaborating niches – so that hills spring up everywhere so to speak – then we can conceive of a process of evolution that doesn't lead to anything one could call an optimum, or even a stable equilibrium. Evolution in such a world continually opens up new possibilities, new combinations.... It follows that the teleology of the evolutionary process is of a rather peculiar sort. There is no goal, only a process of searching and ameliorating. Searching is the end.
>
> (ibid.: 68)

Routine equilibrium adjustment is how evolutionary theories of incremental institutional change explain the continual renewal of liberal institutions in countries like the United States. Parsons (1991) discussed the survival of desirable normative patterns in an integrated society. While an institutional 'moving equilibrium' maintains orderly routines of adaptation, the social system will re-equilibrate itself and adjust to periodic strains. Hayek (1982: vol. 1, 63) identified the same phenomena in terms of the continual testing of institutional rules by individual trial and experiment. Thus, policy agents can only guess at 'how adaptation to altered external circumstances will be brought about', or 'in what manner the restoration of a disturbed equilibrium or balance can be accomplished'. Routine competition supplies feedback mechanisms or discovery procedures that generate more effective institutions. North (1990: 99, 136) shows that legal and administrative institutions in the United States have been more 'adaptively efficient' than Latin American institutions. The latter reinforced 'disincentives to productive activity', whereas the former 'rewarded productive activity of organizations and their development of skills and knowledge'. In adaptive societies there exists 'an efficient feedback mechanism to identify choices that are relatively inefficient and to eliminate them'. Failed institutions as well as failed economic units are routinely eliminated. As North (2005: 169) says, there emerges 'an ongoing condition in which the society continues to modify or create new institutions as problems evolve'. As I have argued in this chapter, neither North, Parsons, nor Hayek adequately explored the preceding *non*-routine processes that could have enabled developing countries to become more adaptively efficient over the last 100 years. It is that potential for 'jerking and jumping' disequilibrium transition to capitalism that I have sought to identify and explain.

This chapter has examined a Schumpeterian model of autonomous, discontinuous, and disequilibrium institutional change that could be appropriate for developing countries. Arguably, if this form of institutional transition were more widely followed in developing countries more of them might today be further along the road to capitalism. Most important is that the strong logic of this model shows why successful institutional change need not be a prolonged and purely spontaneous process. Hayekian theory does not offer a complete panorama of the possibilities for capitalist transition. The followers of Hayek in the 'growth versus design' debate continue to prefer the microscopic mode of analysing historical *and* contemporary institutional change. My objective has been to flesh out Schumpeter's claim that real development – the creation of 'new combinations' – is likely to occur macroscopically in disequilibrium conditions. In this regard, the process of capitalist transition is distinctive. Capitalism's development is punctuated by discontinuity during periods of instability. Institutional progress in contemporary developing countries telescopes the changes in shorter time frames.

There is, nevertheless, a subsequent scenario, only briefly outlined here, that fits more easily with the microscopic perspective on change in advanced societies. When development reaches a certain threshold within a social system, i.e. once it has run past the social system's indefinable point of capitalist transition, and after several cycles of institutional crisis, discontinuous creative destruction may give way to a calmer situation in which smaller-scale innovations maintain a new disequilibrium routine of selection and adaptation. We may then speak of a transitional mode of periodic radical change mutating into the 'normal' pattern of very advanced capitalist society. The minimally destructive, regular, small-scale, timely adjustment does not replace the large-scale techno-economic cycles of economic history, which are bound every now and then to throw up a cataclysmic series of events. For the most part, it is simply that adjustment to 'long waves' becomes a learnt innovation routine for matching institutions to the economic pattern.

5   Carriers of change

When motivated policymakers in developing countries set out to achieve a capitalist transition they need knowledge of the capitalist institutions that can be emulated, and knowledge of sequences and dynamics of institutional change. How is such knowledge created and how is it made available in the world? Can leaders and citizens in the developing countries be persuaded to take the capitalist path? What resistance will be encountered? What cognitive capacities are required?

This chapter applies positive ideas about the agencies of change to a critique of approaches that emphasize interest-group, cultural, or cognitive constraints on reform. The objective is to restore two interlinked cognitive and volitional variables – ideology and rationality – to the centre of the analysis of capitalism and capitalist transition. The major political and economic systems of the world in the past century were shaped, for better or worse, by the ideas of intellectuals who knew the power of ideology and realized the potential of rationality. Hayek, for one, understood that 'ideology may well be something whose widespread acceptance is the indispensable condition for most of the particular things we strive for'. Ideology is 'the indispensable precondition of any rational policy, but also the chief contribution that science can make to the solution of the problems of practical policy' (Hayek 1982: vol. 1, 58, 65). I will argue that ideology must be cognitive, rational, and scientific in order to motivate capitalist policy. Good policy, also, needs to be rationally formulated and implemented. Since these requirements of the transition to capitalism assume a preexisting level of knowledge of capitalism, it will be important also to take a hard look at how the social sciences interpret capitalism.

Some summary definitions of the basic terms – ideology and rationality on one hand, and interest and culture on the other – will serve to introduce the argument. The *Oxford English Reference Dictionary* explains 'ideology' simply as 'the system of ideas at the basis of an economic or political theory'. To this could be added that ideology aims to influence the attitudes and beliefs of a population with the intention of maintaining or changing the political or economic orientation of the social system. Ideology communicates belief in the relative legitimacy, justice, or effectiveness of a theoretical or empirical system of means to ends, such as could be applied to state policy. My understanding of 'ideology' is close to Mannheim's definition of utopia, although Mannheim (1960: 184) understood utopianism as the opposite of ideology: 'Ideas which later turned out to have been only distorted representations of a past or potential social order were ideological, while those which were adequately realized in the succeeding social order were relative utopias'. I understand ideologies to be cognitive rationalizations of concrete reality for ideal purposes. In contrast, Elster (1983: 141) describes ideology as 'a set of beliefs or values that can be explained through the position or (non-cognitive) interest of some social group'. It is easy to agree that ideology is a biased belief, a disposition towards one opinion or interest rather than another. Yet ideology can be a true expression of social-science data, founded on fact and logic. It can also be detached from the values or interests of the group or the individual. As a cognitive innovation rational ideology may be hostile to capitalism, or a carrier for the stock of knowledge favouring capitalist transition.

'Rationality' as it relates to policy is the effort to calculate optimum means to the end. One thinks rationally by applying a scientific style of reasoning to the decision. Weber said that 'rational technique' is 'a choice of means which is consciously and systematically oriented to the experience and reflection of the actor, which consists, at the highest level of rationality, in scientific knowledge' (Weber 1978: 65). Rationalism aims for precision in the estimation of the outcomes of an action, in order, as far as is reasonably possible, to control experience.

> Rationalism ... means one thing if we think of the kind of rationalization the systematic thinker performs on the image of the world: an increasing theoretical mastery of reality by means of increasingly precise and abstract concepts. Rationalism means another thing if we think of the methodical attainment of a definitely given and practical end by means of an increasingly precise calculation of adequate means.
>
> (Weber 1947: 293)

Rationality is never perfect. But even imperfect rationality is indispensable for development policy. We can keep in mind Popper's observation that 'true rationalism [is] the awareness of one's limitations, the intellectual modesty of those who know how often they err, and how much they depend on others even for this knowledge'. On the other hand, rationality 'is the only means for learning – not to see clearly, but to see more clearly than before' (Popper 1962: vol. 2, 227). The 'qualified' rationality discussed later in this chapter is sufficiently effective to enable policymakers to act scientifically when emulating known institutions. Rationality is not diminished by being bounded. I suggest how a variety of factors often thought to elude rationality – behavioural values, substantive interests, and objective facts – can be incorporated in the everyday means-end calculation of effective policy. Policymakers reckon the cost–benefit of an action, the procedural rules, and the objective facts that inform the action. They are able routinely to calculate as much as they *need* to know about the material, ideal, status, and procedural interests of all persons who are likely to be involved in the action or be affected by it. Finally, policymakers are also able to make informed choices about the social values and behavioural standards that can be applied to the action to ensure its success. As long as they are adequately motivated, policymakers can act fairly rationally in constructing capitalism.

'Interest' motivations can fall conceptually within both rationality and ideology. There is a tendency in some areas of the social sciences to exaggerate the strength of group interests while neglecting the influence of ideology. Two commonplace observations about the prospects for institutional or economic transition are that (1) various aspects of it will be resisted by some interest groups and embraced by others, and (2) it will be in the interest of some groups but not of others. We can see immediately that ideology enters the picture and might precede interest. In the case of (1), an individual or group interest may be revealed, rejected, or modified by ideologies. In the case of (2), it may be the analyst who decides, because of their sympathy or antipathy towards one group, their ideological view of capitalism, or their knowledge of the concrete circumstances, that these interests are 'true' or 'false'. Indeed, the assumption that not every person knows their true interest serves to justify the existence of the social scientist who will often claim to be able to identify it on their behalf.

The conceptual separation of ideologies and interests can be quite artificial. Ideologies often have a group-interest dimension. Group interests are frequently articulated in ideological form. It is usually true to say that the attitudes, beliefs, and actions of interest groups are decisive in the prevention or facilitation of every economic or institutional reform. On the other hand, policymakers and citizens frequently justify, pursue, or conceal their interest by adopting an ideology, and it is often also the case that an ideology influences the direction of interests. In political action, interest groups use ideology as a means of self-identification, or they may use ideologies as a means to change other people's perceptions of self-interest, group interest, or public interest.

Just as ideology can be a true belief formulated, correctly or in error, through an interpretation of the facts, so interests can also be expressible wants or needs, including awareness of the means for satisfying those wants. The argument in this chapter is not that contra-capitalist interests can be easily defeated by pro-capitalist ideology. Rather, since the interests that resist capitalist transition often justify themselves ideologically, and since anti-capitalist ideologies often appeal to a broad range of interests, it can equally be true that a change in the ideology may cause people to perceive their interests differently. *Rational ideology*, which is the product of efforts to acquire mastery over social-scientific facts, and which aims at methodical attainment of practical ends with appropriate means, requires a calculation of how the confluence of diverse interests, values, and ideas either facilitate or obstruct a policy action. Good ideologues, like good policymakers, take account of complex *sets* of interests. They calculate their own action motives as well as the motives of the intended receptors of policy and ideology.

'Culture' as an explanation of development, sometimes called 'culturalism', views social values or norms as variables that substantially influence economic and institutional action. In so doing, culturalism tends to downplay the agency roles of ideas and interests. In fact, culturalism may go to the extreme of including almost all institutions and political, legal, or economic patterning within culture. The Tocqueville's (2002: 275) description of 'the whole moral and intellectual state of a people' is, for present purposes, a helpful way of defining the amorphous 'culture'. Culture is a slowly evolving complex of learnt values, attitudes, and symbols that guide human interactions within societies. It is shared knowledge passed from one generation to another by imitation or learning about manners, morals, customs, habits, and beliefs that allow people to understand their social surroundings and that help them to adjust their behaviour to others. As such, culture also has a role in shaping the responses of entire peoples to external stimuli.

In this book, the juxtaposition of culture with ideology is a way of emphasizing the latter's transformational function. If ideology is seen as a subcategory of culture, then in effect ideology is eliminated as a counterweight to culture. Like culture, ideology can be imitated, learnt, and seeks to be shared. Like ideology, culture can be a cognitive cement that reduces the adaptive efficiency of societies. Unlike culture, however, ideology is selected. It is rarely taken for granted. Unlike culture, ideology can undergo rapid and possibly revolutionary change. Ideology is not a system of norms that regulates social behaviour in a style or pattern. It is not the whole intellectual or moral condition of a people. Unlike culture, ideology can be a design or innovation in content or transmission. Ideology implies opposition and analysis. It exists to be questioned. It is invented, used, abused, adapted, reconstituted, and superseded. Ideology can change culture when new ideas generate new norms, new ways of doing things, and new ways of life. Ideologies are naturally and legitimately subject to scientific scrutiny. Among a people there are always at least two ideologies competing for influence. Substantial numbers of people resist being permanently dominated by either one.

Free to choose?

Throughout the book I have referred to 'the policymaker' as the agent of institutional change. At the centre of the present analysis of contemporary capitalist transitions is a senior individual in any of the peak organizations that provide leadership in state institutional domains of law, administration, and political representation. Policymakers are defined as persons who are empowered to collect data, make plans, and implement plans with the authority of the state and within a framework of state rules. They design or select policy, or they adjust policy at the implementation stage. We might imagine them as benign, modest, intelligent, and subject to the frailties and passions of human nature. Yet psychological personality is of little importance in the present context. Nor is it absolutely necessary to establish whether a policymaker merits their position by any criteria. Here, our interest lies in the social personality of policymakers; how they articulate individual or group interests, internalize values, form ideological preferences, and calculate optimum means to the end. We expect much of the policymaker in cognitive and volitional terms.

The first step in the analysis is to consider the structural parameters of policy agency. How much choice does the policymaker really have? When speaking of the structural complex of restraints on policy agency during capitalist transition I mean external limitations on a policymaker's capacity to utilize their authority strategically and exercise their will when responding to and shaping their environment. Even if they were in possession of complete knowledge, political power, and technical and financial resources, policymakers would still be prevented in various ways from exercising their free will by the institutional environment and system of domination, and by the dominant mode of economic organization, each of which are fairly impervious to short-run policy change. In their own area of operation policymakers are also constrained. Regardless of what they feel they do or wish to do, policy elites are placed in roles and positions that already define their functions and power resources. The practical question of 'freedom for choice' in policy making can be broadly addressed by examining the potential misfit between policy agency and socioeconomic structure. Some uniform requirements of system reproduction precede policy choices and impose constraints that policymakers must incorporate in their calculations.

In this context, 'structures' are needs and imperatives relating to the mode of material provisioning, the prevailing value system of society, and the physical environment. If it is to reproduce itself every society must cope, at the simplest level, with the imperative for persons to eat, sleep, and have shelter. As Talcott Parsons explained, there are 'biological prerequisites of individual life, like nutrition and physical safety', as well as 'affectional support and security', which are 'minimum needs' and 'conditions to which the social system must be adapted' (Parsons 1991: 28). Such needs remain constant even during higher-level transformations in social and economic organization, such as industrialization. Indeed, 'industrialism' itself also becomes a 'structural characteristic' of society, whose needs relate to increasing productivity, competition, profit making, private consumption, private property, government, rule of law, and so on (Parsons 1999: 272). Schumpeter similarly wrote about the imperatives of capitalist development, which structure or even predetermine the range of human choices along a given path:

> whether favourable or unfavourable, value judgements about capitalist performance are of little interest. *For mankind is not free to choose.* This is not only because the mass of people are not in a position to compare alternatives rationally and always accept what they are being told. There is a much deeper reason for it. Things economic and social move by their own momentum and the ensuing situations compel individuals and groups to behave in certain ways whatever they may wish to do – not indeed by destroying their freedom of choice but by shaping the choosing mentalities and by narrowing the list of possibilities from which to choose.
>
> (Schumpeter 1947:129–30)

Schumpeter was sympathetic to a central argument in Karl Marx's materialist economic history. Marx believed that all modes of production, in spite of their distinctive social relations and methods for creating and distributing resources, have a way of operating 'behind men's backs'. The 'economic structure of society is the real foundation on which rise legal and political superstructures and to which correspond definite forms of social consciousness' (Marx 1962: 5–6). Marx argued that 'mankind always sets itself only such tasks as it can solve ... [and] it will always be found that the task itself arises only when the material conditions for its solution already exist or are at least in the process of formation'. On the other hand, as Cohen (1978: 134–79) tells us, in stressing the primacy of productive forces Marx did not intend to 'demean humanity'. Marx had faith in 'human rationality and intelligence', and he assigned to people the agency roles of acquiring knowledge to deal with material scarcity and to improve life situations. Whatever his true intention, Marx succeeded in illuminating an everyday structural force that impinges both on public policy and private production. He did this in a single evocative phrase – the '*dull compulsion of economic affairs*' (Abercrombie *et al.* 1980). On this point, Schumpeter substantially concurred:

> the rational attitude presumably forced itself on the human mind primarily from economic necessity ... I have no hesitation in saying that all logic is derived from the pattern of the economic decision.... This is due to ... the unemotional drabness of the underlying rhythm of economic wants and satisfactions. Once hammered in, the rational habit spreads under the pedagogic influence of favourable experiences to the other spheres....
>
> (Schumpeter 1947: 123)

The apparently straightforward observation that policy action is structurally conditioned is, in reality, hard to conceptualize in the study of historical processes. Max Weber had a uniquely pluralistic view of the overlapping determinants of human action. Ideas, values, and culture influence patterns of material-want satisfaction, the formation of interest groups, and relations of power. Feelings such as 'duty' or 'fear' can shape individual choices, as do the institutional orders or structures of domination, and what Weber (1978: 947) called behaviour oriented towards '*dull custom*'. Weber also said, 'the forms of social action follow laws of their own ... they may in a given case always be co-determined by other than economic causes' (ibid.: 341). Yet, there is no doubt about the importance that Weber accorded to economic causality in institutional history. His own approach (which he called 'social economics' or 'sociological economics') 'considers actual human activities as they are conditioned by the necessity to take into account the facts of economic life' (ibid.: 312). In most situations the economy is not 'merely a dependent variable', since 'adaptation to the conditions of the economy ... is the principal continually operating force in everyday life' (ibid.: 254). Social 'groups that are not somehow economically determined are extremely rare' (ibid.: 341). The same in politics, where 'every rational course of political action is economically oriented with respect to provision for the necessary means' (ibid.: 65). 'In the vast majority of cases' political domination relies on 'economic power for its foundation and maintenance', and the 'mode of applying economic means ... exercises a determining influence on the structure of domination' (ibid.: 942). Weber was keenly aware of how most action is 'structured' in multiple ways, but he gave special emphasis to economic structuring.

Whereas Weber's even-handed multicausality corrected the excesses of Marx's economic primacy, Parsons defied both Marx and Weber by moving the locus of structural causality towards social values as the 'imperative' of social system maintenance (Parsons 1991). Value systems are shared conceptions of the type of society that is deemed moral and desirable, which are institutionalized in organizations and internalized by individuals. Individuals are susceptible to such influence because their social interactions make them aware of the attitudes and likely reactions of others. Institutionalized value patterns are, according to Parsons, the backbone of the social system. They mediate the motivations of policy actors and define social standards for the solution of problems. A 'structural core' of institutions performs the vital functions of social system maintenance by organizing and transmitting values. 'Regulative institutions' structure individual motivations by defining 'acceptable activity in pursuit of private interests', and the 'acceptable choice of means in pursuit of the realization of goals and values' (ibid.: 52–3). Continuous evolution of societies is not possible without a structural core of institutions that regulate social values. For a social system to reproduce itself during disruptive processes of social and economic change, primary actors must be committed to the dominant value pattern. In these cases, self-interested goal orientations are weighed against value judgements about the impact of the 'flow of gratifications' upon the social order. For example, immediate gratification may be deferred in the expectation of longer-run gains (ibid.: 48–50).

Parsons aimed for a theoretical synthesis of human agency and social structure. Values mediate between the requisites of system reproduction and the indeterminate actions of individuals. Concepts like 'instrumental activism' and 'institutionalized individualism' describe value-controlled patterns in societies where individuals pursue self-fulfilment by internalizing a commitment to shared conceptions of the good society (Parsons 1999: 272–8). In capitalist society these assist 'active adaptation' that maximizes 'autonomy and responsibility' while achieving personal gratification and improving society for others. Parsons's theory can be applied to our understanding of the policies for implementing the *procedural* norms of capitalist society. He distinguished 'values', which define the desired ends of society, from 'norms' which are value-legitimate means for achieving those ends. Normative orders 'implement' value systems in specific action agencies such as government, courts of law, and education (ibid.: 261). Policy agents with independent personalities, constrained by values, interact with citizens in a plurality of roles, acquiring knowledge and performing tasks of goal-selection attainment, adaptation, social integration, and pattern maintenance. Internalization of values *precedes* concrete human agency in the process of system maintenance. There can emerge a new 'instrumental consensus ... at various levels of the organization of society, to undertake whatever activities may be deemed most important to the welfare of that society' (ibid.: 257).

> The values legitimize a *direction* of change ... with respect to such famous formulae as liberty, democracy, general welfare, and distributive justice. The individual is left with a great deal of responsibility, not only for achieving *within* the institutionalized normative order, but for his own interpretation of its meaning and of his obligations in and to it.
>
> (Parsons 1999: 275)

The limitation of Parsons's theory, as noted in the previous chapter, is that it applies positively to advanced society but not to precapitalist society. Bryan Turner (1999: 181) describes Parsons's defence of liberal society in the following way: 'Progressive social systems are characterized by their pluralism, their tolerance of value-diversity, their structural differentiation, their capacity to solve problems without recourse to totalitarian violence, and thus their institutionalization of universalism, achievement-orientation and altruism.' Arguably, the 'structuring' of value systems is only desirable in that context. In societies that are in transition to capitalism, in contrast, policy agency must have as one of its instrumental functions the *disintegration* or *bypassing* of any of the structured values that support the precapitalist social order.

Discussion of agency–structure shows why policymakers are not entirely free to choose. Every question asked and every action undertaken is pre-framed by 'dull compulsions' of social-system survival. Every successful calculation of means and ends will be subject to structural laws and structural audits. Isaiah Berlin described the situation as follows:

> while of course we choose as we choose (we can choose between one thing and another, nobody denies that), nevertheless the objects for us to choose between, and the fact that we are likely to choose in the way in which we do, are determined. In other words, when there are alternatives, though it is of course possible to do either one or the other, the fact that we are placed in a situation where these are the alternatives ... means that we do what we will, but our will itself is not free....
>
> (Berlin 2000: 73)

Marx, Weber, and Parsons regarded human agency – including ideology agency – as being in some degree prestructured by economic, political, cultural, or physical environments. Nevertheless, each of them also recognized the relative autonomy of agency and the potential of agency to modify structure. Rational innovation is sometimes able to transform social values, institutions, or economies. Policymakers *weigh up* the elements of every situation. If they push too hard at the structural boundaries a mismatch may arise between their ambitions and the capacity of the system to accommodate their goals. The agents of policy can be blinded – by ideology as well as other factors of cognition – to the structural requisites of system survival. A structure–agency *mismatch* would be the gap between their awareness of environments and, on the other dimension, awareness of their own capacity to conform to, modify, or circumvent environments.

Transcending culture

Social values and norms, which help to structure policy action, are elements of culture. Policy motivations can result, at least in part, from the individual's internalization of cultural norms (Parsons 1991). However, culture is by no means the only factor shaping policy action and outcomes. It may, in fact, be a relatively weak one. Ideology, for example, also matters. The cultural determinist views all ideas and beliefs as ingredients or a subset of culture. In the present context, the key issue is as follows: If the analyst exaggerates the cultural structuring of capitalism, then the autonomous cognitive actions of *knowing* capitalism and *motivating* capitalist transition are likely to be neglected. In the eyes of the cultural determinist, ideological innovation can only emerge and spread in a cultural environment already predisposed to it. The risk of accepting the logic of culturalism is that, *ipso facto*, the analyst assumes that individuals and governments choose their ideologies or policies *through* their culture. Although this may sometimes happen, there are many more cases of ideological diversity within more or less homogenous cultures. Parsons made an important observation about the ideological structuring of culture. Ideology has a role in choosing between cultural values.

> Ideology ... serves as one of the primary bases of the cognitive legitimation of patterns of value orientation.... So far as this is possible in empirically cognitive terms, an ideology 'rationalizes' these value-selections, it gives reasons why one direction of choice rather than its alternative should be selected, why it is right and proper that this should be so.
>
> (Parsons 1991: 351)

The usual perception is that Weber's tract, *The Protestant Ethic and the Spirit of Capitalism* (1992), represents a culturalist explanation of economic change. In reality, Weber was highly critical of unicausal and purely cultural explanations. In the first place, the 'cultural sciences' can 'give us no answer to the question, whether the existence of cultural phenomena have been and are *worthwhile*. And they do not answer the further question, whether it is worth the effort required to know them' (Weber 1947: 145). Culture should not be glorified as some higher cause. Often, it is only a form of group identification that lends itself in mundane ways to appropriations by group interests. Weber (1978: 388) points out that 'any cultural trait, no matter how superficial, can serve as a starting point for the familiar tendency to monopolistic closure'. A more fundamental issue, however, is the fact that cultural analysis cannot be *scientific*: 'There is no absolutely "objective" scientific analysis of culture' (Weber 1949: 72):

> it is one thing to state facts, to determine mathematical or logical relations or the internal structure of cultural values, while it is another thing to answer questions of the *value* of culture and its individual contents and the question of how one should act in the cultural community.... 'Scientific' pleading is meaningless in principle because the various value spheres of the world stand in irreconcilable conflict with each other ... I do not know how one might decide 'scientifically' the value of French and German culture; for here, too, different gods struggle with one another, now and for all times to come.
>
> (Weber 1947: 146–8)

What passes for 'culture' may hinder or encourage the progress of society. However, there are problems specific to cultural analysis that put obstacles in the path of useful speculation about the comparative prospects for transition to capitalism in different countries. In his introduction to *The Protestant Ethic*, Weber wrote:

> The question of the relative value of the cultures which are compared here will not receive a single word. It is true that the path of human destiny cannot but appal him who surveys a section of it. But he will do well to keep his small personal commentaries to himself, as one does at the sight of the sea or of majestic mountains, unless he knows himself to be called and gifted to give them expression in artistic or prophetic form.
>
> (Weber 1992: 29)

One problem is that 'cultural science' generally does not acknowledge that it exercises a subjective value judgement when it decides what variable will be deemed 'culturally' significant to an issue or event. Culture, after all, is 'a finite segment of the meaningless infinity of the world process, a segment on which human beings confer meaning and significance' (Weber 1949: 81). When choosing 'subject matter', the cultural analyst is often 'unaware ... that he has selected from an absolute infinity a tiny portion with the study of which he *concerns* himself' (ibid.: 82). Because culture is itself a 'value-concept', all analysis of culture will necessarily be 'one-sided'. The analyst can only study the cultural meanings of, for example, commerce and industry in a given period and location from the perspective of their *own* worldview. Thus, 'knowledge of cultural reality is always knowledge from particular points of view' (ibid.: 81). It would be more fruitful for the analyst to attempt instead to identify 'universal values' in the 'real world', because it is only by applying universally valid concepts to the study of each 'fragment of reality' that one can 'distinguish the important from the trivial' (ibid.: 81–2).

Smelser (1992: 21–2) offers a helpful explanation of problems that arise between social science and cultural analysis. Culture presents methodological problems of 'vagueness' ('the multiplicity of meanings makes it an entity difficult to treat as a variable'), 'inclusiveness' (it can be made to encompass almost anything that is incorporeal or material), and 'circularity' ('to say that some institution or item of behaviour is "explained" by culture often amounts to little more than renaming it according to its cultural location or identity'). Culture is not an object with distinctive characteristics. Hence it cannot be tested empirically, and it is impossible to state categorically that it is 'coherent'. Smelser does not suggest abandoning all scientific investigation of culture; only that culture must be regarded as a hypothesis subject to verification.

> Because the notion of culture is often conceptualized as a global, unitary characteristic of the society or a group, to link it causally with phenomena in individual, group, or institutional behaviour poses difficulties in explaining variations in such behaviour ... [The] appropriate question is how useful or powerful is it – from the standpoint of generating scientific explanations – to portray a culture as relatively coherent or incoherent. In short, a cultural description should be assessed primarily on its explanatory adequacy ... rather than on its significance as an empirical description.
>
> (ibid.: 22–3)

Social science challenges the explanatory adequacy of 'culture' by asking whether it is inclusive, tautological, coherent, and empirical. The issues of causality and verification can be addressed in the present context by examining the popular opinion that culture is a form of social *programming*, and then by interrogating that view in the light of empirical observations about causal variables such as markets or law. Clifford Geertz (1973: 44) defined culture as 'a set of control mechanisms – plans, recipes, rules, instructions (what computer engineers call "programs") – for the governing of behaviour'. Variables such as religion or language, he said, have 'ineffable, and at times overpowering, coerciveness in and of themselves' (ibid.: 259).

The idea of culture as behavioural programming has even entered fields where empirical verification is possible. In his influential study of cross-cultural work values, Hofstede (1980: 21) defined culture as 'collective programming of the mind [that] determines the identity of a human group in the same way as personality determines the identity of an individual'. He later claimed – surprisingly in light of actual political and economic changes in the region – that the 'mental programming' of Eastern European countries 'does not allow' market capitalism and democracy to develop there (Hofstede 1996: 162–3). In fact, successive surveys in the field of management psychology by, among others, Hofstede, Trompenaars, and Triandis, find that only one cultural variable – individualism – can be correlated with economic development. 'Individualistic' Western European and North American societies are wealthier than the 'collectivist' societies of Asia, Africa, and Latin America. Yet there is no evidence to suggest that individualism is the *cause* of wealth creation. Only the reverse is true; increases in wealth lead to more individualism. In their survey of the empirical literature, Smith and Bond (1993: 216) conclude that 'values are free to vary in a number of ways independent of a country's level of modernization'. If these findings are correct, Hofstede's claim that some cultural units may be predisposed to resist capitalism or democracy looks wholly unconvincing.

The economic historian, David Landes, has attempted the delicate task that Weber forsook and counselled against, namely the analysis of the 'relative value of cultures'. In *The Wealth and Poverty of Nations* (1998), Landes asserts: 'if we learn anything from the history of economic development, it is that culture makes all the difference' (ibid.: 516). Distinctive social values facilitated economic progress in northern Europe for five centuries, and in North America since European settlement. Some of these values may be present in the East Asian societies that achieved rapid economic growth in the second half of the twentieth century. However, they are largely absent in the rest of the world. Cultural strengths identified and gracefully described by Landes include: technical and organizational inventiveness; curiosity and open-mindedness about other societies and about science; tolerance of religious and ideological difference; work ethics, timekeeping, thrift, honesty, patience, and tenacity; preparedness to make and obey laws; a spirit for breaking inefficient rules; disdain for conspicuous consumption and unearned wealth; a passion for trade and entrepreneurial enterprise; tolerance of political and economic pluralism, and tolerance of status and class mobility; meritocracy in the recruitment of leaders; judicious foresight and secular reasoning; willingness to travel in search of new economic opportunities; a minimum of cultural nostalgia; and responsiveness to external stimuli. Developed countries display these characteristics. Claudio Véliz (1994) advanced very similar arguments to explain the economic and political underdevelopment of Spanish-speaking as compared with English-speaking societies.

Many economists take the view that market expansion and economic incentives largely account for wealth creation and poverty reduction. Culture changes slowly, whereas economic performance can improve or decline rapidly. Landes implies that the two viewpoints – markets on one hand, and culture on the other – may be reconciled. When explaining the surge of invention in medieval Europe as compared with early China, he seems to moderate the culturalist thesis: 'In the last analysis ... I would stress the market. Enterprise was free in Europe. Innovation worked and paid, and rulers and vested interests were limited in their ability to prevent or discourage innovation' (Landes 1998: 59). Landes then says, however, that 'just because markets give signals does not mean that people will respond timely or well' (ibid.: 522). His argument is that society's culture shapes the response to markets.

Eric Jones (2006), also an economic historian, argues that markets, technology, and global movements of people are modifying culture more rapidly than in the past. That culture is no longer as 'sticky' as it used to be can in large part be explained by the fact that global media and cultural industries, by reducing communication costs and increasing the flow of information, create new opportunities to exchange viewpoints and to critically scrutinize culture. Traditional values become 'slippery'. Higher incomes, open markets, weaker community sanctions, and the increasing commercialization of life bring about an increase in cultural exchange and experimentation (ibid.: 195). Jones warns, however, that cultural change may take 'decades or generations', and is unlikely to transform markets and institutions in the short term. He concludes: 'The forces at work lie outside culture itself' (ibid.: 270). In an earlier book, Jones (2000) argued persuasively that political and sociological factors explain the hindrances to market expansion in developing societies better than culture. Rather than search for the elusive cultural values that push economic growth, development theorists should instead focus on dysfunctional governance that inhibits growth (ibid.: 189–90). In many developing countries, private markets are strangled at birth, and administrative resources are squandered on defence, ceremony, and patronage. When economies do change, cultural explanations tend to conceal the underlying – and by implication universal – cause.

> The point about pre-modern values is that they were more likely adaptations to the institutions or politics of the day than mind-sets intrinsically and unchangeably averse to attempts at economic betterment. Once growth begins, such things tend to be exposed as paper tigers. Cultural distinctiveness may persist, but behind the labels celebrating the uniqueness of each society a silent accommodation will have been reached with values common to competitive markets. The old values may still be proclaimed loudly by individuals with a stake in the previous economic order, but modal behaviour will change, sometimes very fast.
>
> (ibid.: xxvii)

The cautionary lesson is that it is difficult to generalize about the relationship between culture and economic development. Jones (ibid.: 45) appears to identify the correct order of things when he says, 'culture is vital for form, but does not replace substance'. However, that begs the question: What exactly is the 'substance'? Hernando de Soto's studies of legal-bureaucratic structures that constrain small-scale business in poor countries with regard to asset titles and enforceable contract rights may provide some insights and answers relating to the *institutional* substance (de Soto 1989; 2000). If people have legally recognized property rights over their assets they can 'draw out' capital from those assets as collateral for production, and connect their assets and labour to the broader economy. The sources of capital, argues de Soto, are legal or political infrastructures that allow transferable assets to be deployed as capital in production. Many development theorists argued in the past that creation of capital related to cultural factors, such as the 'work ethic'. Yet today we clearly see that informal sectors of developing countries are teeming with hard-working, inventive entrepreneurs who display 'capitalist' work ethics. The constraint they experience is the formal institutional structure, which makes it difficult for them to enter the formal economy or to obtain legal titles to housing. Because the problem is found in countries as diverse as Egypt and Peru, it is nonsensical to employ a 'cultural' explanation:

> a great part of the research agenda needed to explain why capitalism fails outside the West remains mired in a mass of unexamined and largely untestable assumptions labelled 'culture'.... One day these cultural arguments will peel away as the hard evidence of the effects of good political institutions and property law sink in.
>
> (de Soto 2000: 225)

Statements about culture can also be tautological. We see this in Claudio Veliz's (1994) claim that the potential for 'cultural change' is reduced if 'dislike of change' is built into the cultural makeup of society. Furthermore, if the breadth of culture is so great that any social phenomenon can be studied from the perspective of the 'cultural sciences', i.e. from the perspective of conferring cultural significance upon social phenomena, then the analyst may be discouraged from disentangling the concrete elements that are more or less susceptible to deliberate change. In the purest most extreme forms of culturalism, all manner of informal or formal institutions and pseudo-institutions are captured by the single concept 'culture' without separating the immutable or given elements from those that are, or can be, designed or constructed. If, however, the analyst loosens the assumption of inclusive culture and looks at every one of its components, the presumed bonds that unite them may begin to unravel.

In one of the most perceptive contributions to debates on culture, Ernest Gellner wrote:

> Cultures freeze associations, and endow them with a feel of necessity. They turn mere worlds into homes, where men can feel comfortable, where they belong rather than explore, where things have their allocated places and form a system. That is what a culture is. By contrast, atomistic philosophy loosens and corrodes these linkages. Atomistic individualism is custom-corrosive and culture-corrosive. It facilitates the growth of knowledge, and of productive effectiveness, but it weakens the authority of cultures and makes the world less habitable, more cold and alien.
>
> (Gellner 1998: 5)

Gellner goes on to say that: 'Cultures are not terminal. The possibility of transcendence of cultural limits is a fact; it is the single most important fact about human life' (ibid.: 187). The fundamental truth, apparently also demonstrated by the surveys of management 'culture' mentioned earlier, is that individualism is the first point of escape from culture. If individualism weakens dysfunctional elements of culture that have influenced the procedural norms of institutions and economies then we must welcome it. Perhaps Weber had this in mind when he wrote: 'One of the most important aspects of the process of "rationalization" of action is the substitution for the unthinking acceptance of ancient custom, of deliberate adaptation to situations in terms of self-interest' (Weber 1978: 30). It is in any case certain that Weber would agree with Gellner's observation that: 'Cultures are socially transmitted, but the converse argument – societies are perpetuated by cultures – should not be accepted lightly' (Gellner 1988: 14–15).

Gellner, in turn, could agree that an ideology, which appeals to a diverse set of individual and group interests, presents a more promising and practical line of enquiry than culturalism if one's objective is to understand transitions to impersonal capitalism. When harnessed to scientific knowledge and human rationality, ideology is the obvious counterweight or alternative to culture. Gellner points out that the communitarian 'cult of *Gemeinschaft*' among 'those who hated the disenchanting vision and naively thought they could escape it' was in the end 'deeply misguided in denying the universal diffusion, authority, and applicability of one particular cognitive style, namely culture-transcending science' (Gellner 1998: 185). An individualistic '*Gesellschaft*' ideology of procedurally impersonal institutions takes quite the opposite cognitive approach to science and culture, without making the world look at all 'cold and alien'.

The basic opposition, it would seem, is between scientific ideology that can transform the worldviews of a population (for example, people's views about markets) and speed up society's selection of institutional practices, and, on the other hand, tectonic culture that moves glacially and is regarded as an obstacle to development. It is possible even that cultural symbols may be appropriated and transformed into valuable instruments by ideologists in their effort to explain and persuade. Yet there can also be countertendencies. Just as the individual is able to turn their back on culture, so ideology may also seep into 'a people's' consciousness of the world without deliberation. Fukuyama (1995: 38–9) describes the North American preference for democracy and markets as an ideology based on experience and persuasive opinions rather than culture in the sense of an 'ethical habit'. Yet from the ideology there did gradually evolve that easygoing 'egalitarian culture' that prizes individualism.

The power of ideology

Theorizations of ideology are often frustrating attempts to explain the unfathomable complexity of deforming, delusional, or distorting ideology. Ideology is sometimes viewed as a deception that conceals social reality from the receiver of ideology or that hides the intention of the ideologist. The notion that those who create or consume ideologies are not aware of what they are doing, but that they do so to justify their interest or to legitimize their situation by methods of which they may be completely unaware, in the grip of social conditioning that fools them about the real nature and purpose of their ideology, is, at best, too psychological and abstract for the present purpose. At worst it underrates the intelligence of the ordinary person. There is usually nothing mysterious, unconscious, or distorted about the ideological influences on policy making in societies that are transiting to capitalism.

On the other hand, it is true that there is frequently an element of *conscious disbelief* in ideologies. The technical factors underlying 'left–right' and 'state–market' policy pendulums in the twentieth century frequently translated into effective ideology, but were just as often wilfully disbelieved by the ideologues. Criticizing anti-capitalist ideologies in Latin America, David Landes (1998: 493) observes that 'just because something is obvious does not mean that people will see it or that they will sacrifice belief to reality'. Dissonance between belief and reality can be a characteristic of ideology. Nevertheless, the reverse may be true when ideology is an innovation or construction of new ideas based on reasonably accurate knowledge of reality. Just because something is difficult to perceive does not mean that people will not eventually recognize it or be persuaded to see it, or that they will always sacrifice reality to belief.

The relationship between ideology and social-science knowledge raises similar issues. Ideology interprets facts through opinions and beliefs. Our knowledge of capitalism is transmitted ideologically. Ideology shapes the supply of knowledge and the demand for knowledge in the social sciences. Most people, scholars included, select their knowledge of capitalism ideologically. How social science interprets capitalism, and how the intellectual carriers of ideologies transmit that knowledge, are questions of special interest in the present study. The recounting of capitalism's positive record, and advocacy of capitalist transition, have long been tasks reserved only for dissenters in the field of development studies. In other areas of social science too, anti-capitalist ideology is strong and inconvenient facts are ignored.

Since the 'battle for men's minds' is ideological, we should examine what Parsons (1999: 253, 265–9) calls the 'positive function of ideology'. In some situations, ideology will simply be a defence mechanism to protect cherished symbols or norms of society. But ideology can be an 'educational mechanism'. Parsons gives the example of ideology functioning to reconcile a social value system with practical evaluations of how best to promote '*procedural mechanisms*' and '*procedural innovations*' that generate consensus about the acceptable means to achieve common ends. A society is motivated ideologically to change the meaning given to a procedural orientation or to justify alternative means to policy ends. It is through ideology that social actors perceive, intuit, legitimize, or give 'cognitive validity' to a value system (Parsons 1991: 349–59). Parsons points out that, as a society modernizes, the ideological system becomes systematically integrated with science. The role of the social scientist is to uncover and challenge the cognitive distortions in ideologies. Parsons says, 'the ultimate authority for the validity of any ideological tenet as a cognitive proposition must be scientific authority' (ibid.: 354). The fact that 'cognitive distortions' in ideologies 'tend to be uncovered and challenged by the social scientist' helps to explain 'a tendency for the guardians of ideological purity in a social system to be highly suspicious of what social scientists are doing' (ibid.: 358).

Science's *potential* role in eliminating errors of ideology is also emphasized by Schumpeter (1994: 33–47). The history of economics, he says, is a history of ideologies. Economic science – and social science more generally – typically starts off with an ideological insight or 'vision'. The vision might turn out to be true and supported by the facts. Nevertheless, argues Schumpeter, it began as an emotional or interested reaction to the particular issue we propose to study. The economist will formulate 'ideas about what is to be considered as fair or desirable in the management of economic affairs' (ibid.: 41). That vision is 'a preanalytic cognitive act that supplies the raw material for the analytical effort' (ibid.: 43). At every stage of the analysis there is a risk that ideology will distort the rules, methods, and findings of the research. However, Schumpeter trusts in the ability of science to arrive at a truer picture. The post-vision scientific method of assembling facts, comparing new facts with old facts, theorizing the relations between facts, and creating concepts to organize the facts, tests the vision's 'consistency and adequacy' and generates demand for more facts to be gathered. Schumpeter says that by proceeding along this path the analyst encounters 'a large number of phenomena that fail to affect [the] emotions one way or another' (ibid.). As a result, the analyst will increasingly focus on methods and concepts that are 'neutral' or 'exempt from ideological influence'. In this way social science should 'crush out ideologically conditioned error from the visions from which we start' (ibid.: 43–4).

Ideologies, it may be argued, differ according to their scientific foundation. They are concerned with preserving a system, improving it, or removing and replacing it. Good science does not, of itself, produce good ideology. Given the obvious weaknesses of most contemporary capitalist ideology, it is easier to conceptualize ideology as the source of resistance to capitalism than as its handmaiden. Schumpeter (1947: 161) bemoaned the fact that capitalist interests compromise when under attack: 'they never put up a fight under the flag of their own ideals and interests'. Douglass North (1981: 53) observes that with the exception of Hayek's writings, capitalist ideology 'has not developed within a comprehensive framework of social political, and philosophical (not to mention metaphysical) theory', and it 'has faced serious difficulties in holding and capturing the loyalties of groups'. Yet Hayek (1982: vol. 2, 112, 116) well understood the reasons for this ideological deficit. In a capitalist society, 'each is made by the visible gain to himself to serve needs which to him are invisible'. Capitalist society provisions itself materially by means of impersonal profit calculation, the price struggle, and market freedom. It is hardly surprising, Hayek argued, that there will be 'emotional resistance' to the idea that the significant ties in capitalist society are 'means-connected' and 'purely economic'.

> Many people regard it as revolting that the Great Society has no common concrete purposes or, as we may say, that it is merely means-connected and not ends-connected. It is indeed true that the chief common purpose of all its members is the purely instrumental one of securing the formation of an abstract order which has no specific purposes but will enhance for all the prospects of achieving their respective purposes. The prevailing moral tradition, much of which still derives from the end-connected tribal society,

makes people often regard this circumstance as a moral defect of the Great Society which ought to be remedied.

(Hayek 1982: vol. 2, 110)

Schumpeter (1947) similarly lamented that logical value judgements do not necessarily follow from the historical facts. Though we have capitalism to thank for the personal freedoms, ever-rising living standards, institutionalized pacifism and altruism in politics, a welfare state, modern medicine, mass education, and consumer products such as the 'airplane, refrigerator, and television' that enable happier and healthier lives, it cannot be taken for granted that people will *feel* 'happier' or better off in capitalism. Likely as not, they 'hate its utilitarianism and the wholesale destruction of meanings'. They resent a system that leaves them 'to their own devices, free to make a mess of their lives' (ibid.: 129). And since the free-enterprise system 'tends to automatize progress', it is easy, from one generation to the next, to forget the reasons for that progress. An understanding of the long-term benefits of capitalism could never be made simple enough to communicate to people who look only at the short-run picture of 'profits and inefficiencies', and at the continual instability of the economy. Capitalism produces almost everything, but not the human feeling that could guarantee its survival:

> emotional attachment to the social order [is] the very thing that capitalism is unable to produce.... Secular improvement that is taken for granted and coupled with individual insecurity that is acutely resented is of course the best recipe for breeding social unrest.
>
> (ibid.: 145)

Emotions and reason do not sit easily together and tend to reject each other. Socialism's advantage was that it appeared, at least rhetorically, to reconcile emotion with reason. In contrast to the means-oriented order of capitalism, socialism's virtue was its orientation to the ends of want satisfaction and equality. In retrospect, want satisfaction was a failed ideal of socialism. Yet socialism remained blessed with the 'myth-generating potency' of egalitarianism, solidarity, and unselfish morality (Berger 1987). Its vision survived economic and political failure because 'real socialism' was always just around the corner and so could not be validated empirically. The sociologist Dennis Wrong (1998: 8) writes that capitalism has the 'ideological disadvantage of actually existing, warts and all', whereas socialism is 'a project, a shared ideal, something to be built'. Socialism could survive on propaganda. 'Wicked' capitalism suffers 'ideological derogation' because it was born of free enterprise and was shaped by Western imperialism (Parsons 1999: 250).

Although the former socialist countries of Eastern Europe now elect governments that proclaim the virtues of capitalism, it still cannot be said that capitalism has won the ideological battle. Ideologists of capitalism might have more success in developing countries today if they adopted the approach recommended by Parsons immediately after the Allied victory over Germany (Parsons 1954: 273). Capitalist ideology should keep silent about self-interested economic ends and means and the virtues of Anglo-American society. It should convey only a vision of the universal legitimacy and efficiency of the institutional *procedures* of modern capitalism. German postwar reconstruction was complicated by deep-seated anti-capitalist conservatism, by a heritage of romanticism, and by the nationalist prestige of an interventionist bureaucratic state. Although German 'culture' might be an obstacle to institutional change, argued Parsons, it would be futile to attempt to change the 'German character'. Occupying powers should give priority to institutional changes that would create conditions favourable to cultural change. Ideological propaganda would be an essential tool in the process, but it should not push for a German 'conversion' to democracy and the values of profit making. To couch reform in those terms would create the perception that foreign values had been imposed, and would intensify Germany's noble idealism and sense of its own uniqueness. Such a strategy would lead to anti-Americanism and a reaction against Anglo-Saxon business culture. Parsons argued that propaganda must appeal instead to impersonal norms, secular values, science, pluralism, personal freedom, and equal opportunity. Although in practice these are synonymous with effective democracy and markets, they are relatively *neutral* qualities of political and economic change. They could appear to have developed spontaneously rather than by force or external intervention.

The conclusion that can be drawn in the light of debates on 'nation building' and the vaunted wish of some Western powers to convert 'failed states' to democracy and free markets is that an ideological method is more likely to succeed if the explicit goal is to change institutional *procedural norms*, which, although they do typify liberal-capitalist societies, can at least claim universal validity for the performance of essential roles in modern social systems. Once they take root, those procedural norms can be maintained in a capitalist society that has institutionalized value-diversity, altruism, and freedom by means of socialization, or what Parsons (ibid.: 173) old-fashionedly called the 'propaganda of reinforcement as an agency of control' to forestall 'deviance'.

Arguably all of these problems of ideology should be understood as examples of a fundamental dilemma of social science, which Weber identified as the relationship between means and ends. In an essay called 'Science as a Vocation' (1947: 129–56) Weber said that the work of the good social scientist and of the good artist are similar in one respect. Both require inspiration and an 'inner devotion' to the task. However, fulfilment of the self can never be a sufficient objective for the scientist. A social scientist should not set out merely to satisfy and sustain a personal value judgement. Every product of science asks to be surpassed by another. Science has no 'meaning' aside from intellectual integrity, unromantic disenchantment with the world, unending progress through experiment, and a commitment to 'inconvenient facts'. Good scientists never subordinate their work to their experience of life, to sensation, sympathy, sacred values, natural orders, or charismatic leaders. Their 'passion' is simply for clarity, and intuitions founded in fact and rules of logic. According to Weber, the fundamental rule of logic in social science relates to judgements made about means and ends, which are also vital for understanding choice making in policy.

> The sciences, both normative and empirical, are capable of rendering an inestimable service to persons engaged in political activity by telling them that (1) these and these 'ultimate' positions are conceivable with reference to this practical problem; (2) such and such are the facts which you must take into account in making your choice between these positions.
>
> (Weber 1949: 10)

> If you take such and such a stand, then, according to scientific experience, you have to use such and such a means in order to carry out your conviction practically. Now, these means are perhaps such that you believe you must reject them. Then you simply must choose between the end and the inevitable means. Does the end 'justify' the means? Or does it not?
>
> (Weber 1947: 151)

Weber strongly attacked the sort of intellectual position that ignores such rules of logic. If this principle were applied to the design of ideologies, the implication would be that only a calculation of means to ends gives clarity, integrity, and consistency to ideological choices. If we incorporate the argument of the present book, and paraphrase Weber, we could then say that if a society desires lasting peace and prosperity, it 'simply must' pursue that end by building the *impersonal* and *formal* institutions needed for market freedom, rule of law, meritocratic state administration, and free political representation. If these means are unacceptable or unattainable, society 'simply must' modify the ends to fit the means. You may be proved wrong, but you have not pursued your goal on a flimsy or romantic whim. As an educational mechanism, ideology presents this choice.

> The teacher can confront you with the necessity of this choice. He cannot do more, so long as he wishes to remain a teacher and not to become a demagogue. He can, of course, also tell you that if you want such and such an end, then you must take into the bargain the subsidiary consequences which according to all experience will occur.
>
> (ibid.)

Any application or reception of ideology in policy making involves technical decisions. It is then the 'technician' (rather than the teacher) who 'has to make decisions according to the principle of the lesser evil or of the relatively best' (ibid.: 151). It was clear to Weber that the policy work of the social scientist involves choices between ideologies that deal, hopefully better than worse, with technical choices about means to ends. As he put it:

> In terms of its meaning, such and such a practical stand can be derived with inner consistency, and hence integrity, from this or that ultimate ideological

position ... but it cannot be derived from ... other positions. Figuratively speaking, you serve this god or you offend the other god when you decide to adhere to this position.

(ibid.: 151)

In other words, by attending to the means-end conundrum social scientists are forced to delve into the practical ideological meaning of their findings and of their policy proposals. It is not a foregone conclusion, however, that they will perform this means-end analysis. In the next section I explain why Weber did not believe the intellectual – as a sociological category – was usually able or willing to rationally confront the means-end conundrum.

Intellectual resistance

In their analyses of capitalism, both Weber and Schumpeter incorporated socio-logical analyses that identify 'intellectuals' as the principal source of ideological resistance to capitalism. When Weber spoke of the 'social carriers' of ideologies he had two types in mind, one that was positive for capitalism and another that was negative. The positive carriers of ideology were the bearers of Protestant ideas who laid the ethical foundations for capitalism in early modern Europe. Theirs was not a conscious delivery of capitalist ideology. Rather it was that Puritan texts and sermons spread an ethos of methodical labour, honesty, prudence, thrift, and deferred gratification, which coincided with the economic ethos of the rising bourgeoisie. Calvinism unintentionally performed the ideological function of legitimizing the acquisition of wealth through property and profit making at a critical juncture in the European capitalist transition. *Social* premiums on personal self-control that regulated the conditions for religious salvation complemented the *economic* premiums that motivated entrepreneurs who seized the opportunity to become competitive on the eve of the industrial revolution. Equivalent 'premiums' would soon spread to modern administration, law, and political representation. For Weber, the key development in this new situation was that: 'Life is focused not on persons but on impersonal rational goals' (Weber 1978: 1200). Religion reconciles its piety and anti-commercial instincts with the material interest of an emerging commercial stratum. Religious valuations, on the other hand, gave the entrepreneur a clear conscience.

Weber did not say so, but it can be argued that the Protestant case study of ideological persuasion suggests the possibility of an unintended *secular* capitalist ideology. In theory, widespread pursuit of 'personal' interests by impersonal methods in a modernizing society could produce an ideological effect equivalent to the complementarity of religious ethics and profit incentives during the first capitalist transitions. Conceivably, the general perception that institutions uphold everyone's right to pursue their self-interest within boundaries that do not prevent others from doing the same might offer foundations for a modern ideology that would help to legitimize a new wave of capitalist transitions. The problem with any such formulation is that a secular ideology of capitalism requires its own intellectual carriers. About that, Weber was not hopeful. The dominant theme in his theoretical writing on ideology was the intellectual's propensity to seek 'escape' from the realities of capitalist transition.

There are three relevant dimensions in Weber's critical analyses of the intellectual condition. The first identifies the motives of those ideologists who rely on public funds and reject any rule of logic that conflicts with their ideal or material interest. Weber attacked the communitarian littérateurs who campaign for moral economics and state corporatism and who display 'blissful and profound ignorance of the nature of capitalism' (1994: 89–90). In Weber's opinion, their muddled ideas are riddled with contradictions. The littérateurs disparage entrepreneurship and complain about the exploitation of workers while praising state protections for national corporations. They fail to see that the 'robber capitalists' are, in reality, 'tied completely to politics'. Littérateurs themselves also 'live off' government dispensation and subsidy. Theirs are 'the parasitic ideals of a stratum of prebendaries and *rentiers* who have the impertinence to judge the hard daily struggle of their fellow citizens who are engaged in physical and mental work against standards dreamed up at their writing-desks'. As a general rule, the littérateurs are blind to the fact that business, accounting, or the commercial fight for a share of the market is 'intellectual work, as good as, and often better than, that done in any academic's study' (ibid.: 84–5).

In his second line of attack, Weber argued that the intellectual 'aristocracy of education' cannot be blamed for its narrow and frightened outlook in the face of material progress. It is, after all, 'a definite stratum of the population without personal interests in economics; hence it views the triumphal procession of capitalism more sceptically and criticizes more sharply' (Weber 1947: 371). The second intellectual type, like the first, is ignorant about capitalism. Nonetheless, these fearful intellectuals may be well intentioned, responsible, and intelligent. Our schools and universities are full of such critical intellectuals.

The third and most important characteristic of modern intellectualism has its origins in the theologian's role of rationalizing religion for the masses by interpreting a faith or set of beliefs in such a way that both the beliefs *and* the intellectual achieve social relevance. Typically, suffering or good fortune came to be rationalized as something 'deserved' in theodicean terms, i.e. with respect to God's will and the existence of evil. This is how the Calvinist doctrine of predestination produced an asceticism and methodical conduct that encouraged capital accumulation and the productive use of property. The intellectual's function is to relate political, economic, and social realities to a meaningful 'cosmos'. Eventually, by a process of intellectualizing the world, religion itself was 'shifted into the realm of the irrational' (Weber 1947: 281). Economic ethics that were anchored in the ethical doctrines of a religion were cut loose, becoming 'this-worldly' and not 'otherworldly'. Intellectual rationalization has far-reaching consequences for society and for the intellectual. In modern society the intellectual becomes a *victim* of capitalism, reduced, in a world where religion loses all claim to rationality, to the 'quasi-proletarian' assembly of alternative meanings of life (Weber 1978: 506–7). Once 'otherworldly' concerns have been rationalized, the 'world's processes ... simply "are" and "happen" but no longer signify anything'. The intellectual becomes *disenchanted*. Weber describes the process of intellectual disorientation and disillusionment that results from rational science's elimination of enchantment without any irony as 'progress', the dispelling of superstition or magic, and the knowledge 'that one can in principle, master all things by calculation' (1947: 139)

> The fate of our times is characterized ... by the 'disenchantment of the world'. Precisely the ultimate and most sublime values have retreated from public life either into the transcendental realm of mystic life or into the brotherliness of direct and personal human relations.
>
> (Weber 1947: 155)

In some branches of the social sciences today, including the 'new' economic sociology, we encounter a similarly frightened retreat from rational and impersonal modernity, and a reinvigorated search for 'direct and personal human relations' in modern economic and institutional life. The efforts continue apace to sustain the intellectual's historical role as the carrier of worldviews that endow mundane activity with quasi-theological 'meaning'. As Weber pointed out, the intellectual endeavour to give 'pervasive meaning' to practical activity, and the 'demand that the world and the total pattern of life be subject to an order that is significant and meaningful', is very likely to conflict with the 'empirical realities of the world and its institutions'. The difficulties 'of conducting one's life in the empirical world are responsible for the intellectual's characteristic flight from the world' (Weber 1978: 506).

Now, as in Weber's day, the impersonal institutional procedure is viewed as an unappealing, objectifying, and 'rationalistic' method of conduct. Intellectuals find no intrinsic value or brotherhood in it. They look instead for communitarian and fraternal sensations, emotions, and expressiveness. Scientific means-end calculation poses a threat to the intellectual's idealization of life. 'Increased fear of the world', said Weber (Gerth and Mills 1947: 59), 'has led to a flight from occupational pursuits in the private economy'. It is hard for the intellectual 'to measure up to workaday existence'. The 'ubiquitous chase for "experience" stems from this weakness; for it is weakness not to be able to countenance the stern seriousness of our fateful times' (Weber 1947: 149). Weber wrote with evident pathos about the individual who proclaims 'redemption from the intellectualism of science in order to return to one's own nature and therewith to nature in general' (ibid.: 142). But to beat a path back to nature, religion, community, or interpersonal relations seems a pitiful intellectual sacrifice. Weber called it the 'modern intellectualist form of romantic irrationalism', a 'method of emancipation from [scientific] intellectualism' (ibid.: 143). He abhorred the 'evasion of the plain duty of intellectual integrity, which sets in if one lacks the courage to clarify one's own ultimate standpoint and rather facilitates this duty by feeble relative judgements' (ibid.: 155).

When Schumpeter wrote *Capitalism, Socialism and Democracy* (1947) he similarly disparaged the 'type of radical whose adverse verdict about capitalist civilization rests on nothing except stupidity, ignorance or irresponsibility' (ibid.: 129). By this time, however, the problem of ideology and intellectualism in modern society had gone beyond escapist communitarianism or simple ignorance of capitalism. Schumpeter believed the very existence of capitalism was under threat from the intellectual hostility towards it. As he said, critical intellectuals were a product of capitalist civilization, which produced the printing press, the liberty to speak out, and the cheap newspaper. Before capitalism, the intellectuals could survive only on flattery and subservience to patrons. Intellectuals obtained their freedom when the economic process produced a sizable and prosperous middle class and the promise of higher living standards for the working class. Capitalist development generated social legislation, political pluralism, the leisure industries, and the avenues for the expression of public opinion. Thenceforth, the new collective patron of the intellectual was the bourgeois public. Yet, the bourgeoisie has been ineffectual, argues Schumpeter, in defending the legitimacy of the system it lives by. Criticism crushed the moral authority of the pre-capitalist institutions. Capitalism's institutional order requires the free exchange of ideas. Nevertheless, by institutionalizing principles of law, administration, and representation that protect the right to criticize, the bourgeoisie rendered itself defenceless. Criticism turned against its values and property.

Schumpeter provides an unflattering sociological portrayal of groupthink, false consciousness, and wilful obfuscation in a sector that considers itself qualified to deconstruct reality and see through the deceptions of mass society. The hostility to capitalism develops, said Schumpeter, when there are groups 'whose interest it is to work up and organize resentment, to nurse it, to voice it and to lead it' (ibid.: 145). Schumpeter encountered what is now called the postmodern position, namely the rejection of rational refutations of the arguments against a social order on the grounds of a rejection of the very existence of rationality (ibid.: 144). Whether grievances about capitalism are based on fact or fiction, most people are bound to derive their opinions of it from the ideas of intellectuals who exercise 'the power of the spoken and the written word'. Intellectuals themselves understandably regard capitalist social order as their 'raw material', and criticism of it as their *raison d'être*. They 'cannot help nibbling at the foundations of capitalist society' because, as a group, they 'live on criticism' of institutions and other groups (ibid.: 151). Usually, the intellectual's situation is that of 'onlooker'. They have little or no responsibility for, or experience of, the practical affairs of law, government administration, business, production, or the arts on which they pass opinion (ibid.: 147).

The relations of production in higher education explain why capitalism 'educates and subsidizes a vested interest in social unrest' (ibid.: 146). Intellectuals receive their training in universities, and many continue to work there. There is a structural inevitability about the production of knowledge in universities. Government and public opinion drive the expansion of higher education. The market mechanism, which limits employment in private-sector industries to the quantity of necessary labour, has not applied with equal force in higher education. The size of universities and the content of their courses tend to evolve out of all proportion to the demand for white-collar professionals. A preference for the experiential or expressive disciplines over those that provide training for the scientific or technical professions produces a disproportionate supply of courses in the humanities and social sciences. Graduates of these disciplines encounter a limited field of employment and so they often look for work in higher education, for which they are best qualified. Relatively poor wages and working conditions, ill-preparedness for the task of teaching, self-imposed closure from alternative career paths, combined with an ever-increasing ratio of students to teachers, means that intellectuals enter their vocation 'in a thoroughly discontented frame of mind' (ibid.: 152–3). This 'well defined group situation of a proletarian hue', says Schumpeter, explains the intellectual hostility to capitalism far better than any 'logical inference from outrageous facts' about the wrongs of capitalism (ibid.: 153). Scholars stand as judges with the sentence of death against any argument in capitalism's favour. The bourgeoisie allows itself to be educated by its enemies. Of greatest concern is that since intellectuals are employed throughout government and the media, 'public policy grows more and more hostile to capitalist interests, eventually so much as to refuse on principle to take account of the requirements of the capitalist engine' (ibid.: 154).

Indeed, if we accept Hayek's argument, the problem of intellectual detachment may be greater even than Schumpeter supposed:

> an ever increasing part of the population of the Western world grow up as members of large organizations and thus as strangers to those rules of the market which have made the great open society possible. To them the market economy is largely incomprehensible; they have never practised the rules on which it rests, and its results seem to them irrational and immoral. They often see in it merely an arbitrary structure maintained by some sinister power.
>
> (Hayek 1982: vol. 3, 165)

It is debatable whether Schumpeter was correct in supposing that capitalism would self-destruct because of hostility towards it from intellectual groups. Schumpeter's polemic does, however, point to a way of identifying certain forces that may shackle capitalist transition in developing countries. Disenchanted intellectuals in the rich countries – in academe, the media, international organizations, and non-governmental organizations – supply much of the institutional and economic policy advice that developing countries rely on. They do not generally offer a composite and favourable analysis of universal institutional structures and change sequences that have proven effective in advanced societies. Also, in developing societies the intellectual group has tended to view capitalism with disdain, playing on feelings of superiority or resentment, or pandering to populist nationalism. Wilful detachment from the facts of capitalism may disguise a vested interest in the status quo. Intellectuals in poor countries sometimes enjoy higher social status than their counterparts in the wealthier countries, so their motivational situation is not necessarily the one identified by Schumpeter. Whatever their motive, ideologues in developing societies have helped to sway mass opinion against economic and institutional policies that could set in train transitions to capitalism.

Yet it is also necessary, as Weber advises, to keep in mind the genuine predicament of the intellectuals. However one chooses to interpret their motives and the anxieties that capitalism produces within the social sciences, the fact remains that it is not at all easy to offer support for an *impersonal* capitalist social order. That problem has more to do with the nature of capitalism than with the type of intellectual group it produces.

Switching tracks

Having discussed available theory and found both positive and negative indicators of the potential power of ideology in capitalist transitions, it is time to take stock. The first point to emphasize is that ideas, or ideologies, have a decisive role in history. Porter (2000: 13), for example, describes the Enlightenment movement of the eighteenth century as an 'ideology' based on 'big ideas', 'epistemological breakthroughs', and new values. Joel Mokyr (2002) documents the explosive intellectual ideas that subsequently underlay the knowledge revolution of the 'industrial enlightenment' and the advent of sustained economic growth. The counterarguments do not stand up to close scrutiny. In a study of seventeenth- and eighteenth-century European endeavours to tame the barbaric passions of warmongering feudal societies by pursuing a common interest in commerce and stable institutions, Hirschman concludes that the ideology of *doux commerce* – on which he says these efforts were founded – failed in its purpose. The leading intellectual opinion of the day was that regulated commerce would civilize and soften the world. It was an example, says Hirschman, of an ideology giving rise to 'actions and decisions' by 'the intellectual, managerial, and administrative elite' that are 'fully expected to have certain effects that then wholly fail to materialize' (Hirschman 1997: 129–31). The evidence for this claim, which Hirschman sets out elsewhere (1992: 105–41), is that the untrammelled pursuit of self-interest in the industrializing societies of the nineteenth century threatened to destroy the moral values that were necessary for the cohesion of market society. In response there arose *contra*-capitalist ideologies.

In fact, Hirschman seems unintentionally to provide ample evidence that ideological innovations, such as the idea of *doux commerce*, can change political and economic behaviour. Once the nineteenth- and early twentieth-century industrial hothouse conditions moderated, and once government actions had diminished the injustices of early industrialization, the expectations of *doux commerce* proved to be quite correct (McCloskey 2006). There was, after all, an intimate connection between market expansion and the pressure to construct ethics and institutions that would reasonably regulate the market and society. The outcomes, at least in the more advanced countries, show that on balance and in the long run the early ideologists of capitalism were right. Broadly, they succeeded in their mission. There are grounds for optimism that equivalent ideological and institutional breakthroughs, spurred on by a new generation of intellectuals and teachers of social science, could today occur more rapidly in developing countries.

There is another element to this ideology equation that needs to be explored – that of 'interests'. The battle for people's minds has to take account of people's interests. Since ideology and interest are strong agencies of social change, we should at least ask which of the two may be stronger in determining the timing and quality of capitalist transitions. We should also ask how ideology and interest might impact on one another. In a much-quoted summation of the relationship between interests and ideologies, Weber said:

> Not ideas, but material and ideal interests, directly govern men's conduct. Yet very frequently the 'world images' that have been created by 'ideas' have, like switchmen, determined the tracks along which action has been pushed by the dynamic of interest.
>
> (Weber 1947: 280)

Swedberg (2003: 304) interprets Weber as meaning that *interest* is the main motivator of change: 'It is not only people's opinions that matter – that is, their ideals of how the economy should be organized. You primarily have to connect to the interests of people if you want them to change themselves and the world they live in'. A different reading of the passage, which arguably fits better with Weber's commentaries on ideology, would lay stress on 'the ideas as switchmen'. Weber seems to take for granted the influence of the 'interests'. The novelty of the formulation lies in *ideas* that shape how we perceive our interest and that 'determine' what we do in pursuit of interests. The passage appears in an essay where Weber describes the ideological rationalizations of religious intellectuals. The implied order of ideological causality could apply even more strongly to ideological rationalizations of economic action. Weber could be saying that if you want to change the world you must tailor your ideas about policy in such a way that those ideas will expand people's knowledge of where their interest lies. Gerth and Mills (1947: 65) argue that Weber studied the roles of 'many particular ideologies, which he saw as notions that justify and motivate materially interested strata'. In a footnote to his translation of Weber's *Economy and Society*, Parsons similarly said that Weber 'refused to accept the common dilemma that a given act is motivated either by interests or by ideas. The influence of ideas is rather to be found in their function of defining the situations in which interests are pursued' (Parsons in Weber 1978: 211).

The effects of ideology may be transitory, but their magnitude in the short run can be significant if they help to unveil people's motivation and interest, i.e. if they reveal 'interest' to themselves or to others. It can be noted in passing that the concept of interest is inherently problematic. It is unclear whether an interest can ever exist unless it has been disclosed by the *expression* of a want, a preference, an intention, or an ideological belief. A perception of subjective interest does not necessarily coincide with objective interest. Political groups often presume to know what is best for others, and elected governments have a legitimate representational authority to interpret the interests of citizens. In politics, as in academe, we frequently find one person saying that another person's expressed want is not really in their 'best' or 'objective' interest. The first person might try to persuade the second person to change their mind about their subjective want. In fact, the first person might have a subjective interest in holding their supposedly objective opinion about the other's 'true' interest. Stephen Lukes offers a glimpse of the complexity of the issue.

> How do interests, [once] defined and classified, relate to desires and beliefs? ... First, it seems, on the face of it, odd for someone to believe that he or she has an interest in something but not want it. On the other hand ... one can fail to want something that is in one's interest, either because one does not know it is in one's interest(s), or because one does not know it is causally related to what is in one's interest(s), or because one may have other overriding wants, principles, or passions.
>
> (Lukes 1986: 6)

It is as well to acknowledge, in addition, that it may be in the intellectual's *self*-interest to claim that ideas have greater causal weight than interests in determining a political or economic outcome. The power of ideas glorifies the intellectual's role in society. Yet the intellectual is probably right to take this view. It seems apposite to quote Maynard Keynes, whose economic theories enjoy a lasting influence. Keynes himself might not have approved of how they were frequently used to justify *dirigiste* and quasi-socialist policy in the developing world, but there can be no doubt about the immense practical impact of his ideas:

> the ideas of economists and political philosophers, both when they are right and when they are wrong, are more powerful than is commonly understood. Indeed the world is ruled by little else ... I am sure that the power of vested interests is vastly exaggerated compared with the gradual encroachment of ideas ... soon or late, it is ideas, not vested interests, which are dangerous for good or evil.
>
> (Keynes 2007: 383–4)

This is a well-known passage about the relative weights of ideas and interests in public policy, but Keynes was not the first to draw the conclusion. David Hume, for example, wrote, 'though men be much governed by interest; yet even interest itself, and all human affairs, are entirely governed by *opinion*' ([1741] 1987: 1. vii. 14). Such views on the stronger role of opinion could, in part, result from the difficulty of discovering the relative influence of interest. The average person will admit to being regularly conscious of their everyday interests. One reason for the intermittent awareness of self-interest is the *inconstancy* of interest. Interest is a response to a situation, and people's interests may change when the environment or the motivational situation change, or simply when their likes and dislikes change. Furthermore, because they can be aware of the interests of other people, every individual has the option of *choosing* a different interest. Interests also change as a result of new knowledge becoming available. What someone thought was their interest in the past may no longer be so in the present or in the future. Finally, although one's personal interest often equates with the public interest, the latter easily changes when state policy is influenced by sectoral or group interests.

Interests and ideologies are alike in this respect. Ideologies are also transitory. Economic ideas influence state policy once they are distilled, reworked, and diffused widely enough to influence government officials and public opinion. The influence of an idea is variable over time. In response to external factors, experience, and trial and error, ideologies disappear and reappear in modified form. We can always find a residue of dormant or rejected ideologies ready to be rediscovered or revitalized at the appropriate moment. Although the intellectual core of the major modern ideologies is quite constant over time, the ideological momentum might be short-lived. As one writer says, ideologies 'tend to wear themselves out' (Platteau 1994: 773). Yet during the intense periods when they maintain their vigour, ideologies can transform the beliefs of policymakers and segments of a population. For that reason, the study of capitalist transition should be especially attentive to moments in time when new ideologies arise, or when dormant ideologies are revived to resolve immediate problems that become apparent because of crises.

If capitalist transition is to succeed it must do so in spite of all these difficulties. Obviously the rational ideologist must have in mind the goal of satisfying interests. No ideology can effectively transmit knowledge and opinions unless it incorporates a rational calculation of the interests of the persons it seeks to persuade. When their ideas are well adapted to the times, intellectual entrepreneurs can shape understandings of the world as it is and as it could be, and they can influence the nature and pace of institutional change. As ideologists they can legitimize the aspirations of groups that are relatively deprived, or that are victims of injustice. But ideologists must appeal directly to many people's self-interest. They are likely to fail if they want people to accept ideas that appeal only to some conception of *common* interest. Weber based his critique of socialism partly on the irrationality of assuming the existence of common economic interests.

> It is of course true that economic action which is oriented on purely ideological grounds to the interests of others does exist. But it is even more certain that the mass of men do not act in this way, and it is an induction from experience that they cannot do so and never will.
>
> (Weber 1978: 203)

On the assumption that people may act upon a variety of interests simultaneously, we need to *broaden* the concept of interest. For example, a successful ideology cannot rely only on appeals to material interest. Once ideologists and policymakers understand the complex sets of interests, they will be better able to calculate their own action motives as well as the motives of those who respond to their actions in terms of rational assumptions about the diversity of individual and group interests in society. Using broadly Weberian conceptual criteria, four relevant types of interest motive can be classified – *status, ideal, material*, and *procedural*. Although status interests normally fall under the heading of ideal and material interests, their special impact on institutional change means they deserve separate discussion. The category of 'procedural interest', it can be noted, is a new one. I will suggest that the concept of 'procedural interest' can tell us a great deal about the reasons for the importance of impersonal procedural norms in the modern institutional system.

Status interest

Status, which can be a positive or negative motivational factor in state decision making, refers to a person's standing, esteem, or rank within a group or organization. Status can be a means of obtaining or preserving a position of power, privilege, or wealth. Political power status can create opportunities for material advantage. Depending on the existing rules of the game, advantages might include job security, promotion, or bribes. However, status can be a source of gratification in its own right. Weber wrote: 'Man does not strive for power only in order to enrich himself ... [it] may be valued for its own sake' (1978: 926). Aside from power, the rewards of status can include prestige, respect, glory, honour, reputation, or a style of life. All those who have 'vested interests in the political structure tend systematically to cultivate [the] prestige sentiment' (ibid.: 912).

A characteristic of status honour is that it 'always rests upon distance and exclusiveness' (ibid.: 935). As observed previously (Chapter 2), the cultivation of status groups within the state is a frequent cause of dysfunctional governance. Exclusion of outsiders means that the status group is monopolistic. It exists to protect its members from competition or control by outsiders. Entry is controlled according to particularistic criteria of convention, tradition, or vocation rather than universalistic criteria of achievement, merit, or skill. In contrast to commercial classes in the market, a status group arises in an organizational framework. The exclusiveness of status groups in the state is antithetical to market capitalism, since status groups are threatened when groups and persons are able to obtain honour or acquire goods and services through purely economic actions. Bureaucratic status groups of the state maintain their power against the market and are alienated from the market, while economic groups seek power through the market. In defence of their status privileges, public officials characteristically limit market exchange of some goods and services, or create discriminatory entitlements to public monies and services.

More positively, the distance and exclusiveness of status groups in the state can be the source of autonomy, insulation, and *esprit de corps* that facilitates a reform effort. Group closure within the state on the basis of positive status rewards could, for example, be a way to obtain shelter from group interests that oppose capitalist transitions. For this 'detachment' to be beneficial we assume a prior ideological commitment, the existence of countervailing types of interest inside the state that reproduce or reinforce desirable styles of life, and the predominance of meritocratic criteria that define power, reputation, honour, respect, prestige, or glory in terms commensurable with the reform objectives.

Finally, it is also possible for status interest to motivate positive nationalism and the satisfaction of belonging to a rich or otherwise successful society. The sentiment of nationalistic status could legitimize an economic policy which requires for its implementation that all or part of a population postpone some gratification. People might work tirelessly and long for little remuneration if their sacrifice will promote the prestige of the nation. Such is the nature of status, however, that it is rarely the dominant motivation of a group or individual.

Ideal interest

Ideal interest may be defined as value motivation or spiritual motivation by combining the English noun 'ideal' (a moral principle or standard of behaviour) with the German adjective 'ideell' (denoting non-material or spiritual). Ideal interest is, then, motivation based on the intrinsic value of action rather than the instrumental purpose of action. Ideal interests could be otherworldly religious premiums, or they could be educational, moral, and political motivational principles as distinct from material motives. It is also possible for social values to shape economic action. We may select a mode of profit making because, by our chosen standard, it seems ethical. I will show in the next section how an ideal interest in the intrinsic value of a policy differs fundamentally from a rational calculation of how values might instrumentally determine the success of that policy.

The question of greatest importance in the present context is the distinction between 'ideal interest' and 'ideology'. Ideology is inherently instrumental. It is a motivational mechanism for implementing, among many other things, ideal interests. It can aim to legitimize or give cognitive validity to a system of moral values. Ideology is one means, in other words, for expressing or satisfying an ideal interest. But an ideology is much more than belief in the intrinsic value of a mode of life, a behaviour, or a spiritual goal. It is the end result of many calculations of means to ends, not all of which involve ideal interests. With a single ideology it may be possible to pursue ideal interests quite separately from other interests. To give some relevant examples: There may be no conflict whatsoever between maintaining an ideal interest in community or charity and forming a practical interest in competitive market freedom and impersonal institutional order. Capitalist transition can be materially motivated without any compulsion to forsake an ideal interest in honesty or fraternity. No person renounces their ideal interests in ethics, honesty, community, or public peace and generalized prosperity by adopting a capitalist ideology. It is simply a case of being persuaded that other ideological ends, e.g. socialism, could not satisfy all of these interests simultaneously.

Material interest

In common parlance 'interest' often means material interest, and this may indeed reflect the actual weighting of different interests. Weber spoke of 'the "true" or economic interest' (1978: 601). It is not surprising that economic want satisfaction is 'always the result of struggles between different interests', or that 'determination of action in terms of pure self-interest ... is characteristic of modern economic life' (ibid.: 351, 43). It should also be noted, however, that 'economic motives ... operate wherever the satisfaction of even the most *immaterial* need or desire is bound up with the application of scarce material means' (Weber 1949: 65). That motivational principle certainly applies to political action.

Furthermore, in relation to the processes by which groups form, there are circumstances in which 'purely ideological group existence is a less effective lever than economic interest' (Weber 1978: 345). Political parties founded on the propaganda of shared ideals find that their economic interests eventually become vital to survival. Even voluntary associations may compete for membership by offering economic benefits and advantageous economic connections. The modern state first evolved because of the commercial benefits it gave to interest groups. The 'special institutions' that were 'well suited for the emerging modern capitalism ... produced a variety of bodies of law corresponding to the needs of different concrete [economic] interest groups' (ibid.: 688). A legal order of property rights was initially the result of monopolistic interest-group closure (ibid.: 342). On the other hand, money-grabbing self-interest is rarely a sufficient explanation of economic action. The desire for 'utilities' is at the root of all economic action. Utilities are 'concrete, real or imagined, advantages'. The varied sources of utility, according to Weber, include goods and services, as well as social relationships, constellations of interests, customs, or a legal order (ibid.: 63–9). Values or ideologies can influence how people identify and prioritize these disparate utilities.

Procedural interest

Procedural interest can be defined as the interest of individuals and groups in the procedural *practicality* and *ease* of an activity. It is debatable whether 'procedural utility' is most usefully defined as the '*non*-instrumental pleasures and displeasures of processes' (Frey 2008: 107). In fact, the instrumental outcomes of processes may carry more weight with ordinary people. Or, procedural interest could simply be instrumental, intrinsically ideal, and pleasurable in more or less equal measures. The ease or practicality with which action is undertaken may be reason enough for gratification. But, as well as the pleasures so derived in relation to subjective feelings of self-worth or 'innate needs for autonomy, relatedness, and competence' (ibid.: 107–26), gratification might just as likely result from satisfaction of an *ideal interest* in the moral or spiritual principle embodied by the procedure, or from a *status interest* in the honour of being granted a particular procedural privilege.

It is generally found, however, that the sense of process gratification extends to satisfaction in the *outcome* (material or otherwise) that has been *facilitated* by the procedure. In many instances, it is very likely that a means-end action would not be undertaken at all were it not for the likelihood that the procedure is relatively easy (convenient, expeditious, etc.) in practical terms. If it is just too difficult in procedural terms to pursue a status, ideal, or material interest, then a person is unlikely to be able fully to satisfy those interests and may abandon the effort altogether. The satisfaction of conventional interests depends initially on being able to satisfy this 'procedural' interest.

Predictability, calculability, reliability, and impartiality are the typical characteristics of a procedure that *motivates* or *satisfies*. Behavioural norms and known rules of action generate greater certainty about how things should be done in a situation, and about the likely expectations and responses of other people involved in the action situation. Formal procedures exist for passport applications, enrolments in universities, registering with a medical practitioner, and voting in an election. Informal procedures exist for making and keeping friends, serving and eating food, and for celebrating and grieving. All these forms of procedure are routine instruction frameworks for achieving a goal expeditiously and in a socially acceptable manner. They are so common in life that we hardly recognize them as interests. Yet without them life becomes impractical. A procedural interest is an interest in the rule structure that provides some certainty about agency outcomes. The procedural interests of individuals or groups differ according to the nature or objective of an activity.

In the study of capitalist transitions the important procedural interests have to do with the impartiality and calculability of formal state institutional procedural norms, which are not only fair but also efficacious and efficient in a variety of instrumental ways. Relevant examples of areas where state regulation affects the ease and practicality of everyday procedures are listed on the contents page of *Doing Business 2008* (World Bank 2008): 'starting a business', 'dealing with licenses', 'employing workers', 'registering property', 'getting credit', 'protecting investors', 'paying taxes', 'trading across borders', 'enforcing contracts', and 'closing a business'. Arguably, the entire world has a procedural interest in improving the ease of 'doing business' in developing countries. To paraphrase Weber (1978: 1116–17), in their rational determination of means and ends, the broad masses accept or adapt themselves to the technical resultants of bureaucratic orders which are of practical significance for their interests. By changing the bureaucratic orders it is possible to change the people and the conditions and opportunities of that adaptation. As Parsons (1999: 256) similarly observed, 'it is a fundamental proposition of social science' that the institutional 'systems of normative order' have a role in 'structuring interests'.

In conclusion, since each type of interest can be an encouragement or a hindrance to the construction of capitalist institutions, we should study people's attitudes towards institutional reform in terms of their respective *sets* of status, ideal, material, and procedural interests. By breaking up 'interest' into these four categories it is possible to move beyond the broad aggregates of competing interest groups and to include conflicting and compatible interests within and between each group. Capitalist transition is the result of struggles between interests and eventual compromise. Ideology is a key variable in the process of establishing consensus among competing interests, and of expressing those interests in policy terms. It is not inevitable that ideology will play that role, but it is evident that it has played that role in every successful case of capitalist transition.

Rational choices

I have suggested that social-scientific means-end logic should be the raw material of the ideological and policy innovations that set in train capitalist transitions. The question that remains is this – are policymakers and ideologists up to the task? Can they act and think rationally? Rationality, as defined here, *is the effort to calculate optimum means to an end*. I identify the impersonal institutions of capitalism as a conceivable 'end', and a Weberian sequence of reforms (markets to law, law to bureaucracy, bureaucracy to democracy) as the conceivable 'means'.

Since it is futile to devise a detailed blueprint for capitalist transition, the process of emulating advanced-country institutions remains, within the guidelines of the policy sequence, *rationally experimental*. It is undertaken by fallible policymakers who, to the best of their ability, calculate optimum means to the end. Karl Popper (1991: 64–5, 87–8) argued that successful institutional construction is achieved by 'social engineers' who employ the 'scientific method of trial and error' – 'the task of the piecemeal social engineer is to design social institutions, and to reconstruct and run those already in existence'. They 'will look upon them from a "functional" or "instrumental" point of view as means to certain ends, or as convertible to the service of certain ends'. In the context of Weberian transitions, where the *speed* and *sequencing* of institutional change are important, Lindblom's (1988) advocacy of 'intelligently exploratory' policy making offers an additional insight. Lindblom argues that if policymakers tolerate untidiness, incomplete data, and limited competency, 'skilfully sequenced trial and error' can be the feasible method of achieving quite 'fast-moving' change without a requirement for complete 'synoptic' rationality.

If policy-led capitalist transition is to be viewed as a realistic proposition for developing societies, we must be able to identify the *types* of policy rationality and the *instrumental* relationship between rational cognition and policy processes. Before classifying policy rationality, some general explanatory comments are needed. The concepts of rationalism (a belief in the value of systematically applying reason in decision making) and rationalization (the process by which rationality spreads through many spheres of action) should be qualified. What I call 'rationality' will henceforth refer to qualified-rationality as distinct from the ideal but unattainable perfect-rationality.

The straw man of *perfect*-rationality has borne the brunt of criticism in social-science literature. Realistic *qualified*-rationality, in contrast, factors in multiple motivations, information scarcity, limited human capacities to process knowledge, countervailing forces that unexpectedly hinder action sequences, and the variable environmental or structural constraints. The 'qualified' form of rational policy making is an imperfect cognitive process through which decision makers develop a degree of mastery over an environment by accumulating empirical knowledge, interpreting technical constraints, and calculating the relevant social values and political and economic interests. As Popper said: 'human beings hardly ever act quite rationally (i.e. as they would if they could make the optimal use of all available information for the attainment of whatever ends they may have), but they act, none the less, more or less rationally' (Popper 1991: 140). To clarify: Perfect-rationality is an ideal type that helps in 'estimating the deviation of the actual behaviour of people from the model behaviour' (ibid.: 141). Qualified-rationality, on the other hand, represents the inevitable deviation, and the acceptance of good-enough outcomes. You *strive* for perfect-rationality in full knowledge that it may be unattainable. Unless you try for 'first-best' processes you will never obtain 'second-best' outcomes.

Herbert Simon put forward much the same idea. Rationality is an ideal but necessary objective: 'If we are planning an action through conscious rational calculation, and if we are smart enough, we can look ahead through some period of time ... and conceive of the possible consequences of the action over that period' (Simon 1983: 66). Deliberate adjustments of means to ends in task-oriented actions clearly indicate that 'intended rationality' can often be 'efficacious in attaining its goals' (Simon 1997: 88). Similarly, Amartya Sen explains that instrumentally rational outcomes may be pursued by applying knowledge and intelligently calculating the unintended effects.

> The idea that unintended consequences of human action are responsible for many of the big changes in the world is not hard to appreciate.... There is, however, nothing embarrassing in all this to the rationalist approach.... There are plenty of examples of success in social and economic reforms guided by motivated programs.... It is not so much that some consequences are unintended, but that causal analysis can make the unintended effects reasonably predictable.... If this is the way the idea of unintended consequences is understood (in terms of anticipation of important but unintended consequences), it is by no means hostile to the possibility of rationalist reform.... Economic and social reasoning can take note of consequences that may not be intended, but which nevertheless result from institutional arrangements, and the case for particular institutional arrangements can be better evaluated by noting the likelihood of various unintended consequences.
>
> (Sen 1999: 254–7)

Furthermore, by restricting our analysis to the manifestations of policy rationality during capitalist transitions we can eliminate or diminish some of the problems generally associated with perfect rationality. In this book, I discuss particular circumstances and circumscribed policy dilemmas relating only to the opportunities and powers for institutional *emulation*. Emulation, as opposed to *design*, presupposes quite extensive knowledge about what the policymaker sets out to achieve. When the policy goals and constraints upon policy making are already understood, then the dilemma of 'bounded rationality' – i.e. limited knowledge – has to a large degree been overcome.

I propose qualified rationality as a purposive technique or procedure for achieving desired outcomes. As Weber (1978: 65) describes it, a 'purposive-rational technique' has the same function in any type of action, namely the choice between available means to achieve an end. In the course of the following discussion it will become apparent to readers who are acquainted with Weber's original dichotomy of sociological rationality (instrumental as opposed to value rationality) and economic rationality (formal as opposed to substantive rationality) that I borrow his concepts quite freely and use them differently. In contrast to Weber, I focus only on *instrumental* rationality as it might apply to institutional decision making. I subsume the other Weberian types (i.e. value rationality, formal rationality, and substantive rationality) within one 'instrumental' category, which Weber himself defined thus:

> Action is instrumentally rational when the end, the means, and the secondary results are all rationally taken into account and weighed. This involves rational consideration of alternative means to the end, of the relations of the end to the secondary consequences, and finally of the relative importance of different possible ends.
>
> (ibid.: 26)

Rational instrumental policy action, as I describe it in the remainder of this section, should comprise three discrete calculative orientations: (1) *formal*-procedural methods of calculation, (2) the calculation of *substantive* ends, and (3) the calculation of behavioural *values*. By adapting Weber's instrumentality concept in this way, i.e. by integrating several rational-action orientations in one new concept of 'instrumentally rational decision making', it should be possible to expand the practical applications of a theoretical explanation of means-end policy making. The process of calculating means to ends will be viewed as an analytical mode of action incorporating multiple motives, multiple values, in addition to purely technical criteria. The three instrumental rationality orientations – formal, substantive, and behavioural – are explained as follows.

Formal rationality

Instrumental formal rationality in policy action aims to measure with technical precision the cost–benefit of policy. There are three relevant measures of formal rationality – the policy should be *economical*, it should conform to *institutional* rules, and it should employ a *scientific* standard of known facts. In general, the 'standard of rationality' for a 'technical question' about the choice of optimum means to an end will be 'the famous principle of "least effort" ' or 'the attainment of a result with the absolute minimum of means' (Weber 1978: 65–6). When the policy choice has economic implications, the practitioner will choose means that are 'comparatively economical of effort' (ibid.: 66).

Economic action is most suited to accurate calculation because it can be measured quantitatively in money terms. Money, Weber points out, 'is the most "perfect" means of economic calculation' (ibid.: 86). Businesses calculate the difference between the valuation of the total assets before and after a profit venture is undertaken. They also calculate market conditions, the availability and cost of factors of production, costs of complying with law, costs of infrastructure, and so on, from the point of production to final sale. Rational *political* action similarly involves bookkeeping and the impersonal calculation of money costs incurred in attaining a policy goal within government budget constraints. More broadly, government policy often needs to be premised on calculations about the economic environment, including the prospects for profitable enterprises and the taxation receipts that will flow from them. Much of the state's performance can be measured numerically in terms of policy supply, target compliance, constituency needs or demands, and other variables. Thus, functionally equivalent formal rationality can be said to exist both in policy making and profit making.

The second formal orientation of policy making is *procedural* or *institutional*. In modern systems of law, administration, and political representation, policy decisions have to take into account the *formal rules* of organizational processes. Formal constraints imposed by institutional subsystems provide a calculable and potentially predictable framework for guiding the actions of legal professionals, officials, politicians, and the citizens who must transact with state agencies in the conduct of their everyday affairs. Law is formal to the extent that it deals with the concrete facts of a case, and to the extent that legal proceedings involve the formulation of fixed concepts and enforcement of written rules. Public administration is formal to the extent that written codes relating to duties, procedures, qualifications, and hierarchies of authority clearly frame the conduct of official business. Political representation is formal to the extent that parliamentary decision making is subject to rules of the 'political battlefield' and pre-established procedural systems for compromise, monitoring, and accountability. A policymaker might therefore 'measure' the benefit and cost of a means-end calculation that has legal, administrative, or political ramifications by calculating the extent to which it will conform to or deviate from the formal procedural rules. A decision reached purely through the influence of personal connections, for example, would not 'measure up' to these procedural rules.

The third category of formal rationality is qualitative instrumental action that calculates costs and benefits by applying an understanding of *objective facts*. 'Rationally correct action ... uses the objectively correct means in accord with scientific knowledge' (Weber 1949: 34). The scope for technical progress using this type of formal rationality is almost limitless. Rational policy action draws on the stock of knowledge derived from direct experience of the world; knowledge which is deemed unambiguous and reliable at any given moment. In political decision making, a means-end calculation will be more effective if it factors in hard data about incentives and the structures of power and domination in society. For example, it may seem 'rational' to aim at a redistribution of income in society. Yet, the action is only formally or objectively rational if a realistic calculation is made of *known* forces of interest and authority in society that might seek to prevent such an outcome, but also of the potentially unintended and harmful economic and political consequences of such a redistribution.

In each of these three types of 'formal rationality' – *quantitative, procedural,* and *cognitive-scientific* – it is implicit that the action employs impersonal criteria and objective procedures to assess the calculable costs and benefits of an action. Technical calculability relates to formally defined decisional inputs and outputs. To break the 'rules' of institutional procedure or cognitive-scientific procedure will mean having to pay a 'cost' that is *functionally equivalent* to the monetary cost of breaking the rules of rational profit making in the market (even if the 'costs' are not as severe). Finally, the three types of formal rationality are functionally *interrelated*. Action in the legal, administrative, and representational spheres of the state must, if it is to be rational, incorporate technical calculations about what is relatively economical and correct in terms of the procedural rules and the available knowledge.

Substantive rationality

Substantive rationality in policy action aims to estimate the likely motive of a policy in terms of its 'measurable' impact on people's *interests*, which could include status, ideal, material, or procedural interests (as defined in the previous section). This is not exactly the meaning that Weber gave to 'substantive rationality', which he described as 'the degree to which the provisioning of given groups of persons ... is shaped by ... ultimate values regardless of the nature of these ends' (Weber 1978: 85). However, it seems to be implicit in Weber's examples that 'provisioning' of groups could be interpreted as a means to satisfy motive interests. The 'criteria of ultimate ends' of this provisioning can 'measure the results of the economic action' in terms of 'substantive goal rationality', which may, for example, be 'ethical, political, utilitarian, hedonistic', or 'egalitarian' (ibid.: 85–6). The ends might be philosophical, moral, or spiritual, i.e. for their own sake. But they might equally be instrumental in terms of satisfying interests.

In the present context, the importance of substantive instrumental rationality lies in the fact that policymakers cannot very well formulate policies for capitalist transition unless they think instrumentally about the substantive provisioning of persons. As previously noted, capitalist transition cannot succeed unless it is seen to offer specific advantages and opportunities to diverse interests. Although an objective is that policy should not respond *directly* to the demands of interest groups during the contemporary transition process, policymakers must still have knowledge of group interests. The legitimacy of a reform depends on satisfying the largest possible number of groups. By strategically calculating the impact of reforms upon interest groups the policymaker identifies potential resistance to reform and the potential allies. The policymaker 'calculates' the struggle of interests while deciding on the means to the end. Moreover, picking up our earlier theme about the effect of ideology on interests, ideology is likely to have an *ex post* role shaping and communicating interests once the policymaker has 'interpreted' these interests. Policymakers will look at how a market reform is going to impact on lawful economic opportunities for upward mobility by individuals, and its impact on want satisfaction or wealth distribution. Or, they may look at how a legal reform will affect people's response to new economic rights or their perceptions of social justice.

Furthermore, the policymaker's *own* interests cannot be excluded from the calculation. For policy to qualify as rational it must include a self-conscious calculation of a policy's compatibility with the policymaker's self-interest, its impact on all the relevant group interests, and the degree to which it is desirable in the public interest. Public officials who do not allow their self-interest ever to enter into their policy work are extremely rare, which is why it is rational to design institutions on the assumption that self-interest motives do exist in state decision making. More generally, it is necessary to analyse state organizations from the point of view of the individuals within them and their interactions (Weber 1978: 13–15). Policymakers rationalize their own status, ideal, material, and procedural interests when calculating the rewards that flow from the adoption and implementation of a policy. It is advisable to factor policymakers' interests into the study of development processes, and to analyse their probable competence and incentive to calculate their own self-interest in the light of countervailing social or political interests and obligations.

Value rationality

By value rationality I mean the purely instrumental (i.e. outcome-oriented) action that policymakers perform when they calculate the *behavioural* norms that should be embodied in the policy or the policy process *in order to ensure the success and legitimacy of the policy*. Norms, as explained earlier, are an 'implementation' of values. The value-rational element of policy action is a means-end reckoning that relates to the desirable or necessary normative standard of the means or the end. This could include, to take one example, the values inherent in a demand to conform to the impersonal procedural norm of state policy. Policymakers consider *how* the action is to be performed, and they calculate whether the *content* of the action and its practical consequences will be compatible with values and norms in society. The action may be procedurally oriented to the norms of the state organizations that undertake policy design and implementation. Or, the policy may be intended to conform to the values of those in society who will be affected by the policy. In the light of my earlier criticism of Parsonsian theory, it is important to note that during large-scale institutional change it may be instrumentally rational for a policy to be *dispro-portional* in value terms. The policy has to go 'against the grain' of the dominant value system if the latter impedes capitalist transition. In many cases, therefore, policymakers must incorporate the value system in their calculation of the potential conflicts and outcomes of implementation.

This is not the usual way of viewing value rationality. Weber defined it as 'conscious belief in the value for its own sake ... *independently* of its prospects of success' (1978: 25). It is difficult to see how Weber's concept of value rationality can be relevant to most policy making. Policy, by definition, is tailored to outcomes. Weber recognized the problem. If seen from the vantage point of 'instrumentally rational action', he said, value for its own sake would always look 'irrational' (ibid.: 26). Indeed, the more 'value' is embodied in an action the more irrational it is likely to become: 'For the more unconditionally the actor devotes himself to this value for its own sake [e.g. devotion to duty for its own sake] the less is he influenced by considerations of the consequences of his action' (ibid.). There is, however, a way of getting around this conceptual problem. I suggest, in contrast to Weber, that if policy action is 'valued' for its own sake it is better to conceptualize it as a substantively rational calculation of the *ideal interest* of the policymaker or groups affected by the policy. Ideal interest is a motivation based on the intrinsic rather than instrumental value of action. The concept of 'value rationality' can then be reserved only for explaining instrumental, i.e. outcome-oriented, actions.

Value rationality in policy making is ideally a rational choice among alternative values. For the sake of the success of a policy, it tailors policy to existing social values or it substitutes alternative value standards reckoned to better satisfy a concrete interest or to better achieve a technical goal. As in all processes that search for efficient means-end solutions, policymakers calculate the scale of urgency of alternative policies as well as the alternative value-behavioural standards most likely to be commensurable with those policies. They may calculate how much deviation from the conventional value standard will be *tolerated* by society. Value rationality involves choice, the acceptance of some values and the rejection of others. During transitions to capitalism policymakers try to estimate the form and severity of the clash between precapitalist and modern values when introducing impersonal procedural norms, and whether the costs of pursuing a particular value path will outweigh the benefits. The rational determination of values is part of the story of capitalist transition. Values help to structure policy agency, and it is necessary for the policymaker to try to calculate the likely behavioural impact of a policy in terms of society's values.

In practice, of course, it is complicated to identify social values. Much of what I describe as value rational calculation may be highly speculative. As Weber (1978: 5) said, values 'often cannot be understood completely, though sometimes we are able to grasp them intellectually. The more radically they differ from our own ultimate values, the more difficult it is for us to understand them.' A policymaker's intuition about what constitutes 'national character' may, for example, be an unreliable measure of actual values. Within a society there are numerous value systems, and 'values' are even more difficult to define than 'interests'. Empirical comparative *value surveys* could facilitate the factoring of a society's value system into calculations of the means and ends of policy. Yet, as Weber points out, rational analysis of means to ends has inherent limitations when it is applied to the value sphere.

> To apply the results of this analysis in the making of a decision is not a task which science can undertake; it is rather the task of the acting, willing person: he weighs and chooses from among the values involved according to his own conscience and his personal view of the world. Science can make him realize that all action and inaction imply in their consequences the espousal of certain values and the rejection of certain others.
>
> (Weber 1949: 53)

I have argued that *qualified* means-end rationality, which incorporates formal, substantive, and value-behavioural calculations, is a feasible technique for facilitating effective policy during capitalist transitions. Indeed, a focus on rationality can include all the structure–agency dimensions of policy causation discussed in this chapter – economic structure, value structure, ideologies, and relevant 'sets' of individual, group, and public interests. Although it is no simple matter to combine these elements in a single decision, there is no fundamental contradiction between them. So, we return to the key individual acting unit, a senior policymaker who wields state power in a developing country during transitional policy sequences. The tasks involve more than marshalling technological, managerial, institutional, and economic knowledge and resources, and more than calculating the functional relationships between market enterprise, law, administration, and political representation. All of these are certainly everyday requisites of policy action during transitions. But the cognitive task is of an even higher magnitude. In every decision, the policymaker should endeavour to attend to a range of causality factors. In order to achieve these things the policymaker must act and think rationally. They must attempt to calculate the optimum means to the end. This means trying to achieve the greatest benefit with the least 'cost' in the formal, substantive, and value terms described above.

Anyone who is psychologically prepared to do so can accept second-best results in the last resort. You do not set out with the intention of delivering a second-best or good-enough outcome. When you act rationally you know in advance that your knowledge, your means of selecting appropriate knowledge, and your application of that knowledge to problem solving will be imperfect. *Within* these cognitive constraints you set out to achieve the best possible result. Knowledge of uncertainty helps you arrive at more certain deductions. And it is clear that second best is far better than third or fourth best. You still advance a long way and arrive at a satisfactory 'qualified' proportionality of means and ends. You have not given up the ends. You struggle to achieve them. But given the facts that emerge through trial and error, you eventually accept less than perfect means and less than perfect ends. Sufficiently rational policy is in reach of practitioners who define an end and the relative urgency of attaining it, and who adjust the end in the light of their calculation of scarce means for achieving the end. Decisions are shaped by estimations of how the action sequence will be absorbed in the economic and institutional environment, of how policymakers *and* citizens will behave and react. In deciding effective means to the end the practitioner calculates the tolerable behavioural norms of policy. Rational policy includes deliberate plans to keep friction or resistance within bounds. It aims to generate greater certainty about outcomes.

Finally, the schema of rational policy action outlined in this section contributes to understanding instrumental knowledge-driven *ideology*. In cognitive terms, rationalism suggests the accumulation and organization of a stock of knowledge. Rationalism is not only a heuristic process for rendering an understanding of the workings of society or facilitating the calculation of effective action. By explaining a mode of life or a type of social system rationally, an ideology may also gain ascendancy and influence. Ideology resembles any other theoretically formulated ideal type that aims to make sense of phenomena in terms of their cause and purpose. As Weber observed:

> the rationality, in the sense of logical or teleological consistency, of an intellectual-theoretical or practical-ethical attitude has and always has had power over man, however limited and unstable this power is and always has been in the face of other forces of historical life.
>
> (Weber 1947: 324)

The deliberate application of rational techniques when formulating an ideology will increase ideology's potential power to influence developments.

Ideology should be rationally designed and constructed, and must remain adaptive to changes in the environment. The likelihood of its success can be calculated in terms of the accuracy of the facts and the attractiveness of the ideas that it conveys. It supplies motivational knowledge about means and ends of capitalist transition. A rational ideology can make people aware that capitalism's advantages in terms of its costs and benefits, procedural standards, and substantive provisioning outweigh its disadvantages in the same terms. As far as possible, the procedures by which a policy ideology is designed and transmitted should – like all rational policy action – employ measures of formal efficiency, satisfaction of wants, and value legitimacy. Ideology can be calibrated by combining calculations of utilitarian and normative criteria. Its design takes into account the compatibility of the ideology with the interests and values of the policymaker and receptor groups in society. Practitioners show leadership skills by translating desirable procedures, interests, and values into persuasive ideological idiom. They acquire scarce information, evaluate the urgencies of want satisfaction among social groups, calculate the constraints and opportunities of policy agency, and then adopt or build ideologies that foster citizen support. The factoring of variables of cognition (learning to achieve) and volition (the will to achieve) requires 'managerial' competency in ideological action.

This discussion relates back neatly to the theme of structure–agency examined earlier in the chapter. Unrealistic expectations create the conditions for human agency to try to escape structure. Development practitioners driven by their passions to achieve mastery over nature frequently allow utopian impulses to influence their thinking about economy and institutions. Such emotions can mesh easily with ideologies that resist capitalism. There is often a difference between what policymakers want to do and what they should do. When policymakers act romantically, agency is unrestrained. When policymakers act rationally, agency is constrained by a recognition that structural imperatives exist and that cognition and technical resources are limited in practical ways. Policymakers desire to achieve certain ends, but they have limited means for doing so. Nonetheless, we do find policymakers daily resolving instrumental conflicts of formal, substantive, and value rationality more or less effectively. Despite the constraints, the blended outcomes which power holders and opinion formers seek to achieve may be reconciled with available means or technical methods for attaining these goals.

Constructive ideology

I conclude this chapter with a positive analysis of Hayek's writing on ideology, using it to draw together the themes of rationality and ideology more fully. Good reasons for disagreement with Hayek's critique of constructivist rationalism have already been outlined. As Rothschild (2001: 141) rightly says, Hayek displayed an unjustified 'disregard of intentions' and 'reverence for the all-seeing theorist'. Fear of the unintended effects of conscious design can make the theorist unreasonably 'reluctant to provide advice on how to set the rules of economic institutions' (ibid.: 152). Nevertheless, criticism of Hayek's attitude towards institutional design can be balanced, I argue, by full agreement with his rather more elusive *constructivist* thesis on ideology. The irony is that Hayek offers a more persuasive analysis of ideology, and particularly of ideological design, than the most avowedly 'constructivist' scholars.

Hayek (1960: 112–16) had a positive view of 'the rule of ideas' and 'opinion' in history. He approved, for example, of John Stuart Mill's dictum that 'speculative philosophy, which to the superficial appears a thing so remote from the business of life and the outward interest of men, is in reality the thing on earth which most influences them'. As I noted at the start of this chapter, Hayek also considered ideology to be the 'vital' foundation of public policy (Hayek 1982: vol. 1, 58). Hayek focused on ideologies that promote the *procedural principles* of institutional policy rather than the built *architecture* of institutions. His preference for 'principles' reflected his acute scepticism about the practical worth of built organizations. In so far as he focused on procedural policy, Hayek's position resembles Parsons. Both believed that a successful capitalist ideology must appeal to *neutral* procedural concepts, such as impersonal norms, secular values, scientism, pluralism, freedom, and equality of opportunity. Counterintuitively, an ideological focus on profit making or democracy could be much less revealing of the inherent efficiency and fairness of advanced social systems, and will often be viewed with suspicion and hostility.

Hayek was a great ideologist. His practical ideas were espoused by some of the most successful political leaders of the Western world in the 1980s, and helped shape a new global consensus favouring economic liberalization. Hayek advised limiting government's role to the defence of rule of law, the provision or financing of some services that markets cannot adequately supply, measures that afford 'security against severe deprivation', and the enforcement of rules that protect the private sphere of economic activity but do not discourage market competition. He was also specific about the policies that might unintentionally beat a path to socialism (Hayek 1960: 220–33; 1982: vol. 3, 41–97).

However, Hayek's analysis of procedural policy proved of little help to development practitioners who grapple daily with tasks of institutional construction in underdeveloped polities. It is concerned, instead, with maintaining or improving institutional rules of 'just conduct' that are *already* practised in the more advanced societies and that first evolved incrementally. Hayek's central message is that it is too risky to interfere with the spontaneous order, and very difficult to draw a halt to such interference once it gets underway.

But what if the spontaneous order does not yet exist in a society? Would interference of a particular kind then be justified for the purpose of creating spontaneous order more quickly than by natural evolution? A Hayekian theme that can now be introduced into the theory and practice of development policy deals with the type of relationship of policy to ideology that encourages consistent adherence to a definite set of *procedures* of conduct (Hayek 1982: vol. 1, 60). Hayek explained why effective rules of political and economic conduct are based on the 'negative principles' that provide guidance about what *not* to do and what to *reject*. These principles first emerged from 'unconsciously held ideas about what is right and proper, and not particular purposes or concrete desires' (ibid.: 69). At the beginning these principles did not reflect confident 'knowledge of cause and effect'. They were not rules laid down and enforced by state authority. The foundations of these principles lay in 'knowledge of the *manner* in which one must act in order to achieve any result' (ibid.: 80). The relevant issue is as follows: 'It is not so much what men aim at, as their opinions about permissible methods which determine not only what will be done but also whether anyone will have the power of doing it' (ibid.: 69). Agreement about permissible methods is the kernel of an emerging institution. It has a direct counterpart in the ideological agreements that Hayek believed are ultimately the truly 'dominant power' in institutional evolution.

> There are few things which must impress themselves more strongly on the student of the evolution of social institutions than the fact that what decisively determines them are not good or bad intentions concerning their immediate consequences, but the general preconceptions in terms of which particular issues are decided.
>
> (ibid.: vol. 1, 70)

Hayek's thesis is relevant to our effort to explain impersonal procedural norms in terms of agreements about the *methods* for deciding a course of government action. These norms foster positive preconceptions about the parameters within which government can most usefully and durably contribute to development. When they have been analysed scientifically and transmitted ideologically, procedural principles become vital for the 'determination of policy'. Hayek's key statements in support of ideological policy merit frequent revisiting:

> ... it is only by constantly holding up the guiding conception of an internally consistent model which could be realized by the consistent application of the same principles, that anything like an effective framework for a functioning spontaneous order will be achieved.... Utopia, like ideology, is a bad word today; and it is true that most utopias aim at radically redesigning society and suffer from internal contradictions which make their realization impossible. But an ideal picture of a society which may not be wholly achievable, or a guiding conception of an overall order to be aimed at, is nevertheless not only the indispensable precondition of any rational policy, but also the chief contribution that science can make to the solution of the problems of practical policy.
>
> (ibid.: vol. 1, 64–5)

This passage takes us to the heart of a potential compromise between constructivist and incrementalist views of institutional change. Although Hayek remains intransigent about organized institution building, underlying his theory of evolution we find a strong and practical argument about the need for policies that aim to spread knowledge of capitalist institutions *ideologically*. Arguably, such a policy is itself a form of constructivism. This ideology contains two interrelated elements. The first, as just stated, are principles of just conduct, which for present purposes we must interpret as the principles that justify an impersonal and formal state procedural norm. The second element is that 'the present order of society has largely arisen, not by design, but by the prevailing of the more effective institutions in a process of competition' (Hayek 1982: vol. 3, 155).

The challenge is to reconcile these two declarations. Hayek's theory of spontaneous order rests on the idea that freedom and competition in the economy and in the ideological sphere produce a more rational cast of mind. The motive forces of competition compel all persons to emulate principles of conduct that evolved through time because they proved to be the most 'competitive' principles. Ideological freedom permits the trials and experiments through which knowledge about successful institutions emerge, and ideological freedom disperses that knowledge among millions of individuals (Hayek 1982: vol. 3, 75–7). In capitalist society, the essential role of the state is to enforce general rules in order that principled economic and ideological competition will continue to grease the wheels of a spontaneously evolving order. The purpose of 'state activity', Hayek (1944: 29) wrote, must be to '*create* conditions in which competition will be as effective as possible' and 'to supplement it where it cannot be made effective'.

I previously quoted Hayek as saying: 'All we can do is to create conditions favourable to [progress] and then hope for the best' (1982: vol. 3, 169). He did not intend this remark to be interpreted as a constructivist statement. Arguably, however, the policy task of capitalist transition is to build institutional conditions in which such competition will be as effective as possible and then 'hope for the best'. Once the institutional conditions that support 'just competition' are adequately understood there is much less reason to argue against the speedy construction of institutions that first set in train, and then maintain, the processes of spontaneous evolution. Borrowing words immortalized in another context, we could say that the 'unknown unknowns' of eighteenth-, nineteenth-, and early twentieth-century *evolving* capitalism have increasingly given way to 'known knowns' and 'known unknowns' of the contemporary *constructed* capitalism.

Although Hayek is convincing when he discusses the damage inflicted by the 'intentionalist fallacy of constructivism' that gave rise to twentieth-century socialism, corporatism, and *dirigisme*, he is wrong to conclude that the fault lay with 'constructivism' itself. More can be done by using the levers of state policy to build capitalism where it does not yet exist; more, at least, than Hayek was willing to admit. Reformers in developing countries have no choice – they must undertake institutional engineering. Indeed, Hayek's argument can be turned back on itself. The evolutionary precondition for the competitive discovery and selection of successful policy strategy in less advanced societies is a resoluteness to seize recurrent opportunities for building the institutional conditions of the evolved capitalist order, i.e. the order which is uniquely able to engender and sustain such competition. In order to obtain spontaneous orders more rapidly in the contemporary world, developing societies first need the formal institutions which alone can guarantee the regulated freedom and procedural impersonality that a spontaneous order requires to work its magic. Even if this statement were not quite true, it would still be reasonable to say that since the advanced societies evolved because their more effective institutions prevailed in competition, that is reason enough to encourage the emulation of those institutions in countries that need not wait for experimental evolution to take its long and winding course.

6 Models of crisis

Crises in developing countries provide an opportunity for the ideological determination of capitalist transition policy. The objective in this chapter is to identify the main forms of crisis, their causes, and the policy options arising during crises. I focus on two dynamic crisis-prone models of political economy – 'activism' and 'neoliberalism'. A characteristic of activist and neoliberal models is that they do not transit successfully between the Weberian sequences of institutional reform – markets to law, law to bureaucracy, and bureaucracy to democracy – which this book depicts as the ideal path for emerging capitalism in the developing countries. Nevertheless, activist and neoliberal models – and their corresponding crises – will be described here as 'developmental'. They are not the best methods of transition, but do have potential to generate change in a capitalist direction. Each can be an intermediate mechanism in so far as, for a period of time, an activist or neoliberal model increases the scope or quality of market activity, promotes economic growth, and achieves goals of social development.

Three preliminary observations can be made. First, activist and neoliberal 'developmental' crises, unlike the Schumpeterian 'long-wave' crises discussed in Chapter 4, are in principle more likely to be *avoidable*. They are similarly 'structural', however, in the sense that they reveal an incompatibility between existing institutional forms and the pattern of economic change. Second, each of the progressive policy models – activist, neoliberal, and capitalist – are *ideological* in Hayekian terms. By viewing them as 'transition ideologies' we can compare the relative soundness of their scientific foundations and prescriptive utility. Third, crises in the developing countries, like Schumpeterian crises in the capitalist countries, tend to be *recurrent*. Crises that repeat at intervals provide recursive opportunities for sequenced institutional change. Development crises are 'revolving doors' of opportunity rather than merely 'windows' of opportunity for institutional reform. Crises that can help to transform societies are not rare events.

The plan for the chapter is as follows. The first section proposes a typology of crises. Its purpose is to classify the kinds of crises that dysfunctional institutions cause, and their comparative transitional prospects. Once the variations in development crises have been identified, it should be easier to assess the knowledge that policy leaders require in order to exploit periodic volatility and propel capitalist transitions forward. The following four sections substantiate the theoretical claims and present an overview of activism and neoliberalism in East Asia and Latin America. The extended analysis of Latin America's twentieth-century economic-policy trajectory serves to illustrate several theoretical themes from earlier chapters, including state dysfunctions, government–business relations, and the role of leadership and ideology during policy transitions.

Development crises

Crises signal an internal or external threat to the sustainability of the social system. The short-term destructive effects of crisis can be undesirable, above all because the poorest members of society may be the most severely impacted. If social systems were more adaptively efficient to begin with, and if better knowledge were available to decision makers in the lead-up to crisis, many crises could be anticipated and avoided. It needs to be recognized, on the other hand, that a crisis is the propitious moment to radically reform a dysfunctional social system. By forcing a re-examination of institutions and policies, crises can compel societies to adapt to the external world. Most major turning points in social, cultural, political, and economic history involved a crisis in some form. If many people learn from crisis, and if its causes can be eliminated, a social system may be changed in crucial ways. The crisis and the society might then be viewed as evolutionary. If crises repeat regularly for the same or similar reasons, it would be reasonable to say that the crises are cyclical and that the society is stationary.

In a comparative analysis of structural reforms in Africa, Asia, and Latin America, Grindle and Thomas (1991) explore differences between policy reforms during crises and politics-as-usual. Absent a crisis, the stakes will be low, the consequences of failing to implement reforms will not be severe, and policymakers lean towards incremental or marginal change. During politics-as-usual decisions typically revolve on organizational issues, bureaucratic manoeuvring, and the slow process of building supporting coalitions. Policy elites may be preoccupied with maintaining patronage networks and satisfying interest groups. State agencies with a stake in the reforms often fight over goals relating to power, prestige, budgetary resources, careers, and personal rewards. During a crisis, policy elites come under pressure to reform with urgency. They are more innovative and take bigger risks. Major issues of legitimacy and social stability come to the fore. Reformers are more likely to undertake radical change. In fact, during politics-as-usual reformers sometimes manufacture a perception of crisis in order to get their policies onto the political agenda. In crisis situations policy elites can be expected to have more autonomy to set agendas. A sense of urgency means politicians and citizens are willing to grant policymakers quite wide-ranging powers and to insulate them from political pressure. In addition, crises may disorganize and weaken interest groups that would otherwise resist reforms (Williamson and Haggard 1994).

The more general point is that social systems adapt to the sensation of strain, and policy making is conditioned by awareness of strain. Actual or perceived crises generate the atmosphere and conditions for progressive policy innovations.

> Behaviour in human societies differs from behaviour in animal societies or in physical systems, in that it not simply reacts to 'disturbances' but to inter-pretative and anticipative – correct or false – diagnoses of them. Real or supposed drifts and trends may count as much as or more than facts, threats as much as actions, indefinite threats more than specific ones, in creating the psychic environment in which the nation's work has to be done.
>
> (Schumpeter 1964: 418–19)

I suggest a binary typology of *development* crises: (1) regressive cyclical crises will be called *underdevelopment* crises; (2) evolutionary crises will be called *developmental* crises. Both types of crisis were typical outcomes of the policy trajectories followed for much of the twentieth century in developing countries. A developmental crisis is potentially a progressive event in the trans-ition to capitalism. An underdevelopment crisis is unproductive because it main-tains the precapitalist equilibrium. This is not intended to be an exhaustive typology. The conceptual distinctions are not necessarily clear-cut. Elements of both types of crisis can combine in individual countries, and they sometimes alternate in very quick succession. Underdevelopment and developmental crises may also combine with other types of crisis. For example, the *capitalist* crises of the more advanced societies (see Chapter 4) may act as an external environ-mental influence on the nature and timing of underdevelopment and develop-mental crises in precapitalist societies.

Development crises are the result of one or a combination of three policy ori-entations commonly adopted by developing countries that could be in transition to capitalism – *populism, activism,* or *neoliberalism* – (1) Economic populism is redistributive economic policy, with the purpose of winning short-run political support from substantial sectors of the population; (2) Economic activism is *diri-gible* state intervention to directly promote particular firms, industries, sectors, or activities, with nationalist objectives to the fore; (3) Economic neoliberalism is remedial macroeconomic stabilization and correction of public finances forced upon policy regimes in the wake of populist or activist crises, and often has the further objective – with variable motives – of restoring or expanding market forces by means of privatization and liberalization. These three types are distin-guished from the *capitalist* model, which can combine neoliberal-style economic policy with parametric market regulation as one element of a logical succession of interlocking institutional policies designed to deepen and sustain the market-oriented economic pattern of an emerging open society.

These are simple concepts that help to identify the economic-policy thrust of a political regime. Distinct tendencies separate the broad-brush categories from one another, although they may overlap in practice. Populism can incorporate features of activism, neoliberalism, and sometimes both. Similarly, other sub-types of political economy such as corporatism or socialism can be hard to differentiate from populism or activism. The populist-activist-neoliberal classification of the causes of development crises does not purport to capture all possible scenarios. For instance, highly insulated *predatory* types of political regime can maintain aberrant and violent precapitalist equilibrium routines for long periods of time in seemingly perpetual low-intensity 'crisis' with little if any 'development'. Arguably, Burma and some of the most impoverished African countries currently fall into this category. Three further – purely *speculative* – examples will help to illustrate the range of potential deviations from the ideal populist-activist-neoliberal types.

First, some forms of development crisis might not be determined primarily by the model of political economy. Although recurrent crises in many African countries may seem to be conditioned by populism, activism, or neoliberalism in some measure, they often stem at root from tribal or communal infighting that infuses failed state-building projects, which in turn reflects problems of geography or social structure that long predate colonial rule. This makes them different from crises arising in political units where the formal authority over territory has been more or less consolidated for an extended period of time (Herbst 2000). On the other hand, tribal politics may be viewed as a proxy for interest-group politics, in which case there may be less reason to create a separate conceptual category to explain the resulting crisis.

Second, the present analysis excludes *non*-crisis situations of *non*-transitional closed societies that long exist in a stable, often highly sophisticated and elaborately structured traditional-authority equilibrium. These societies endlessly weather the external shocks and grinding stasis of long-run underdevelopment characterized by primordial forms of impoverishment and low-level uncertainty and insecurity, without experiencing the dramatic oscillations occasioned by a structural disproportionality between economic and institutional change. Examples might include the neopatrimonial societies of Southeast Asia. The so-called 'bureaucratic polities' – such as Thailand (Riggs 1966) or Indonesia (Crouch 1986) – only experienced recurrent development crises after they had begun to pursue reformist paths of populism, activism, or neoliberalism under the banner of modernization. An implication is that capitalist transition, and rapid development in general, is, at least in the early stages, an intensely disequilibriating process.

A third – hybrid – scenario is a slow-moving equilibrium of capitalist evolution maintained by a judicious mix of populist, activist, neoliberal, and Weberian institutional policies. The legitimacy of the model depends on steady economic growth, with some populist policies to placate key groups. Activist policy is selectively applied by one or two relatively efficient enclaves of the state, either in commanding heights of the economy or in politically important commodity markets. Neoliberal trade opening, privatization, and deregulation may at the same time be applied to less strategic swathes of the economy, exposing substantial populations to vigorous market competition in commerce and production. Meanwhile, institutional reforms may incrementally ratchet up improvements in the legal, administrative, and political subsystems through a creeping depersonalization of state procedural norms. The model is moderate, but requires a high level of political control or political consensus, as well as management expertise at the centre and knowledgeable commitments to best-practice development strategy. There are signs of this *balanced* approach in some countries. Present-day Indonesia or Uruguay come to mind. If the hybrid model can be sustained, crises may be minimized or at least be confined to the respective sectors where populist, activist, and neoliberal policy are applied. These countries stay out of the headline development news. Progress is not dramatic. The model may be stable, but is no more developmental than any other.

The next step in the modelling is to disaggregate the ideal type populist-activist-neoliberal crises and policy models. Because they are regressive and not transitional to capitalism, *underdevelopment* or *populist* crises are not directly relevant to the present study. They need to be briefly described in order to distinguish them conceptually from developmental crises. Characteristically underdevelopment crises occur in the downswing of a boom–bust economic cycle. The crisis is destructive without being creative. The cycle, which in policy terms is a recurrent alternating adjustment between populist and conservative regimes, is typically found in societies without institutionalized checks and balances where governments routinely manipulate policies to favour some interest groups over others. The unsustainable expansionary economic policy of a populist regime creates this crisis, which is commonly followed by a drastic stabilization programme that can worsen the effects of the crisis. Over several decades a country might swing uncontrollably between the extremes of populism > crisis > correction > populism.

Populism derives its political legitimacy from the emotions and rhetoric of nationalism, communitarian values, anti-capitalist ideologies, and extravagant promises of public spending targeted at citizen groups that see themselves as marginalized from the modernization process and from the centres of political power. No populist government ever formulates a coherent program for long-run economic development. Instead, economic policies are geared to the exigencies of political survival. An economic boom can be engineered through two or three years of expansionary, interventionist, and distributive policy. To pay for populist pump priming, income redistribution, and nationalist projects, government can spend its budget reserves, obtain foreign loans, siphon the surplus from resource sectors, and manipulate tariffs and exchange rates. Price controls, wage controls, and protections from competition contribute to worsening productivity in industry and agriculture. Loose monetary policy leads to high inflation. Populist regimes are characteristically profligate and beholden to vested interests. Discretionary economic policy, politicized bureaucracies, undisciplined budgetary management, and the lack of effective rule of law make these regimes especially prone to corruption.

In the wake of populist crisis, an orthodox and often repressive regime applies a stabilization programme, including controls on foreign borrowing, measures to restructure the economic system, strict credit and fiscal policies, retrenchment of the public sector, deregulation, and the emasculation of labour groups.

Eventually, austerity and repression run up against resistance from the intended beneficiaries of the previous populist regime. The effects of crisis and post-crisis adjustments, which may include a sharp increase in unemployment, hurt the poor and the middle classes most. The corrective regime initially enjoys quite broad public support, despite austerity measures and despite the suspension of political liberties. However, the initial thrust of reform evaporates as resurgent conflict and political de-legitimization weaken the authoritarian government and divide it *internally*. Policy incoherence allows pressure to build for a return to expansionary policies. The gains of stabilization are undone. Public expenditure returns to unsustainable levels, and the cycle repeats.

Capitalist transition cannot occur in societies where cyclical underdevelopment crises are the norm. Boom–bust crises were common in Latin America throughout the twentieth century. Archetypal populisms included socialist, clientelist, or corporatist regimes in Argentina (1946–55, 1973–6), Brazil (1946–64), Chile (1970–3), Mexico (1970–82), and Peru (1985–90). In most cases, populism overlapped with activism. Sometimes, as in Peru in the 1990s, a 'new populism' overlapped with neoliberalism. In much of Latin America, the populist crisis-correction pattern is almost as common as changes in government. Whereas every generation views the crises of their time as uniquely disturbing, in reality the boom–bust pattern has been quite constant over time.

The nineteenth-century liberal statesman, Juan Bautista Alberdi, observed that the causes of Argentina's economic crisis in 1876 were essentially the same as those of the crises of 1840, 1852, 1860, 1865, and 1870 (Alberdi 1996: 427). Although all were manifested as bank crises, they were 'not economic but rather political and social'. According to Alberdi, citizens and governments did not understand that – as evidenced in the United States – wealth creation entails sacrifice, thrift, discipline, work, production, and commerce. Instead, borrowed money was used recklessly. Foreign loans were spent on luxuries or political patronage rather than on productive investment. Alberdi had a modern-sounding institutional explanation for these crises. Profligacy, corruption, and the dysfunctions of the credit system all 'arise from the disorder of the *institutions* and from vested interests' (ibid.).

> It is well known that all crises explode at the end of a period of great prosperity. That is not the reality, but rather the way it appears to be.... What was taken for prosperity was profligacy, the squandering of capital investments in bad businesses and vain possessions.... The sickness of crises is very difficult to cure ... because it has its roots in the basic laws of the nation, in institutions that have been sacred for many years and, finally, in the beliefs or prejudices of the country itself. These laws, institutions, and traditions are what organize public and private debts in the dangerous forms that they now take.
>
> (this author's translation of Alberdi 1996: 56, 381)

Activist and *neoliberal developmental crises*, in contrast, need not be lost opportunities. They occur in the aftermath of a coherent economic programme, when further progress in achieving economic objectives is prevented by institutional dysfunction. The cause of the crisis is a disproportionality, lag, or mismatch between economic policy and governance capacity. The economic policies begin to fail because the institutional mechanisms that would be required for them to succeed do not *yet* exist. In the case of *socialist* activist policies it is clear that the proportionally effective institutions could *never* exist. Crisis creates the pressure for a change in economic policy. Projects may be undertaken to construct better institutions. The problems that give rise to a developmental crisis are remediable, and the destructiveness of the crisis can be creative.

Activist and neoliberal policies can be effective in achieving medium-term objectives. Each is unsustainable because the focus on economic reforms crowds out attention that should be given to commensurate reforms of the regulatory institutions. The state either manipulates economic activity (activism) or it loosens its control over economic activity (neoliberalism). Yet the state lacks legal, administrative, and political machinery either to control the economy or to prevent abuses occurring as an immediate consequence of the relaxation of economic controls. '*Activist decay*' is the term I will use to describe the decline of state capacity as a result of the prolongation of statist economic policy, while '*neoliberal myopia*' describes the institutional short-sightedness of liberalizing economic regimes. Examples of each type will be examined in the following sections.

To sum up: In contrast to varieties of precapitalist non-transitional equilibrium routines, and in contrast to populist underdevelopment cycles, activist and neoliberal policies can be developmental and can promote capitalist transition. The conclusion that will be drawn, however, is that economic activism and neoliberalism are at best temporary solutions to the problems of development. The most favourable thing that can be said is that they are starting points or middle points in an unnecessarily long transition process. This issue will be clarified in the next chapter, where I outline a Weberian crisis-induced policy sequence for emulating advanced institutions more rapidly and smoothly. The important lessons for the majority of developing countries lie in knowledge of the costs of not implementing change in a Weberian sequence. By definition, countries pursuing activist or neoliberal strategies have missed an opportunity for capitalist transition. On the other hand, I will argue that if a country had to choose between them, neoliberal policy has more affinity with capitalist institutional transformation than does activist policy.

Activist transition

This section criticizes activist transitions on logical and empirical grounds. Activist economic policy is founded on a belief that strengthening state bureaucracies in order that they may fine-tune discretionary economic policy should generally take precedence over measures to build market freedom based on rule of law. Typically, activist intervention involves state directives or subsidies and other incentives to guide firms and economic sectors towards specified targets while monitoring their performance. Activist ideology can take different forms. Where activism was successfully applied to industrial policy in East Asia it is sometimes explained as a pragmatic rationalist-technocratic approach with roots in recent colonial rule, in the threat of Communism and related national-security issues, or in a Confucian value system of collectivism, personal ties, conformity, egalitarianism, and consensual decision making. Whatever the reasons for it, the beginnings of economic activism in East Asia had something to do with a high social valuation of technical education and the prestige, meritocracy, authority, and discipline of state bureaucratic positions. In Latin America and parts of South Asia, activism has tended to be associated with *dirigiste* economics, or socialism and anti-imperialism. I will discuss activism in East Asia and Latin America, before turning to more general issues.

State programmes to shelter some firms from domestic or international competition have promoted advanced industrialization in some countries when state administrative capacity was high, and when the cost of needed 'knowledge-based assets' far outweighed the price of labour or capital in sectors where national elites were unwilling to encourage or permit foreign direct investment (Amsden 2001). Moderate, selective, and flexible industrial policy can foster rapid economic growth for limited periods of time, for so long as – (1) honest and competent officials pursue a coherent export strategy concurrently with complementary social and educational policies; (2) domestic institutions, national values, and political attitudes facilitate effective state economic interventionism; (3) patterns of world trade and economic regulation provide opportunities for newcomers to enter international markets. These conditions combined for a few fortunate and deserving East Asian countries in the 1970s and 1980s. By building up resources, capacity, and entrepreneurship in sectors that were exposed to global competition, activist policies gave a boost to capitalist transition.

Over time, however, it became evident that the well-documented successes of industrial policy in East Asia could not endure. I have argued elsewhere (Heller 2000) that the underlying cause of Asia's economic meltdown of 1997–8 was a prolonged emphasis on activist policy and the failure to create the institutions to regulate modernizing economies. Despite differences among the affected countries in terms of the intentionality, motive, method, and intensity of activist policy, and differences in levels of economic or political development and the composition of economic activity, all the Asian crises of the late 1990s related in one way or another to the decay of state activism. Systematic discretionary intervention combined with the neglect of non-discretionary regulatory policy were eventually responsible for business inefficiency and government inflexibility, and produced economic structures that were vulnerable to sudden growth collapse. Industrial and financial policies encouraged a concentration of economic power in large often family-owned conglomerates that relied on privileged relationships with politicians and special treatment by state bureaucracies.

The most important instruments of state activism were credit and subsidy allocations that socialized the risks of leading private firms. State agencies assumed they could maintain discretionary efficiency while setting targets, monitoring performance, and penalizing misallocations of credit. As economies grew larger and more complex, however, state subsidies created problems of moral hazard; standards of evaluation and compliance declined; and planning tasks multiplied exponentially. A purely technical aspect of the problem was the one identified by Karl Popper (1991: 69) as 'unplanned planning'. The unintended consequence of pervasive state planning is an endless spiral of new solutions that must be improvised to cope with unforeseen outcomes of state plans. In addition, interventions that were intended to impose discipline on private firms relied on an unreasonable expectation of perpetual probity and discipline on the part of officials. Repeated personalistic interactions between firms and officials create 'embeddedness' between them. As a result, states become gradually less autonomous and less catalytic.

Moreover, national firms were increasingly less compliant. Rapid economic expansion combined with state efforts to set performance standards created an enormous private demand for cheap credit that could escape government control. When Asian governments finally liberalized financial sectors in the late 1980s and early 1990s, it was evident that the focus on guiding firms and sectors had been pursued at the expense of stronger market regulatory policy. Toxic debt was tolerated for years before and after financial deregulation. Private enterprises had little experience of credit-risk evaluation. Liberalization occurred in an opaque business environment that denied officials and investors accurate information about the credit worthiness of firms or the exposure of banks. Poorly regulated markets were a blessing for uncompetitive firms, but created the incentives for negative speculation and crime. In the past, high-performing soft-authoritarian Asian states had sheltered from interest-group pressures while using public monies and organizations to achieve industrialization targets. By the 1990s, however, state activism had entered a period of decay. A combination of weak political institutions, personalized and discriminatory styles of policy making, and reluctance to enforce the law in private transactions, made it difficult to change course. State autonomy had become the source of market uncertainty, and lack of transparency in state decisions made it easier for private business groups to both influence and resist policy.

A general problem is that the more direct economic functions a government takes on, the more likely it is that dysfunctional collusion will develop among and between state agencies and private firms. Consultation about agreements for the allocation of subsidies, licences, and other assistance requires intimate contact between enterprises and officials. During activist policy's second-round effort to monitor the performance of firms that had received subsidies and permissions, officials could not avoid entanglement in their commitments to enterprises. Effective assessment of credit risk requires an impersonal approach and formal rules of negotiation. Two categories of institutional reforms had not been undertaken in the 'miracle' economies prior to the point at which activist decay began. At the macrolevel, Asian countries lacked: a universalistic legal system to reduce reliance on networks of informal trust; enforceable rules to lend transparency and predictability to economic activity; state procedural rules to eliminate particularism in government–business processes, and to increase the calculability of policy processes; and systems of free political representation to enable adequate parliamentary supervision of the agencies of public administration. At the microlevel, these countries lacked formal arm's-length regulation and credible enforcement procedures in financial accounting and audits, corporate disclosure, competition policy, and regulations dealing with credit and stock markets. A recent book on the 'nexus' of law and economic development argues:

> A surprisingly strong case can be made that the trigger for the Asian financial crisis was a series of institutional failings. These failings were particularly striking in the financial sector – poor corporate governance, directed and related lending, and absence of effective bankruptcy laws, as well as a perceived implicit government guarantee to banks and poor banking supervision facilitating 'crony capitalism' ... [One] view of the Asian Tigers' rapid growth followed by crisis is precisely that those countries achieved very rapid growth despite weak institutions so long as they were still at a relatively low level of economic development, but that they failed to invest their growing incomes in improvement of institutions and eventually the failure to do so led to the Asian financial crisis.
>
> (Dam 2006: 241, 277)

Without regulatory safeguards, and with access to easy credit, there were insufficient incentives for private firms to be honest, prudent, or competitive. Government–business relations may not have been corrupt or illegal, but concessions, contracts, and licences fostered the conditions for rent seeking and cronyism. There is ample evidence that Asian policymakers were aware of the risks posed by their pervasive and discriminatory style of economic governance. At times during the 1980s technocrats in Indonesia, Thailand, Malaysia, South Korea, and Japan timidly tried more orthodox measures to prise open the networks of civil servants, banks, and industrial monopolies, including limited trade and foreign-investment liberalization, privatization, and the restructuring of conglomerates. Already, however, the interest groupings of state activism were deeply embedded.

Partly because of preexisting bureaucratic competencies, a number of East Asian countries could exploit their comparative advantages and favourable international conditions prior to 1997 while using activist policy to promote industrialization and economic growth. Post-crisis – and post-decay – developmental state strengths were reinvigorated and combined with a surge of investment and imports in the United States at the turn of the century to facilitate East Asia's timely adaptation and recovery. Ten years on from the Asian financial crisis, it is obvious that the region remains adaptively efficient relative to other parts of the developing world. The dynamism and discipline of East Asian state activism was again evident after 1998 as governments retreated from industrial policies that had involved heavy public subsidies, relaxed some restrictions on foreign investment, and improved accounting standards as well as bankruptcy and corporate governance procedures. The countries that were hardest hit by the Asian financial crisis rapidly accumulated foreign-exchange reserves, reduced public debt, and achieved current-account surpluses.

On the other hand, it has proved very difficult to reverse the patterns of economic governance established during decades of activism. Consensual business and politics continues to be a cover for monopoly privileges and insulation against reform. Measured against Weberian normative-procedural yardsticks of impersonal law, administration, and political representation, East Asian countries remain 'precapitalist' in institutional terms. The equilibrium of political profit making and regulatory closure has proved to be highly resilient. The international financial press regularly criticizes the pace of structural and institutional reform in South Korea, Malaysia, Thailand, Indonesia, the Philippines, and Japan. Export performance has been impressive in some countries, but many East Asian economic sectors remain state-dominated or protected from competition and foreign investment. Government regulation and taxation often continue to be unpredictable; capital markets are relatively undeveloped; privatization programmes have generally stalled; corporate and public debts are still problematic; and many institutional reforms failed to materialize. A report by the Asian Development Bank (2007: 16) finds that indicators of economic governance – accountability, political stability, government effectiveness, regulatory quality, the rule of law and control of corruption – show little improvement in East Asian countries since the crisis, and 'on balance, suggest deterioration'.

Discussion of the causes and consequences of activist crises in East Asia necessarily involves balancing evident failures against enormous successes. As I have defined it, an activist crisis is avoidable but can be developmental. Unlike cyclical underdevelopment crises, developmental crises in a few countries with preexisting institutional advantages – most notably, historically endowed state administrative discipline and competence – can be evolutionary by avoiding regressive boom-and-bust cycles. Notwithstanding that their institutional development is lagging, high-performing Asian economies are pursuing premeditated, responsive, selective, and disciplined paths of convergence with advanced economies. There is reason to be confident that Asian tigers will work their way towards completing the indispensable institutional reforms.

However, it would be unrealistic to expect similar levels of *activist* state performance elsewhere. Most governments do not display equivalent organizational capacity, attitudes, or expertise. In the majority of societies, economic interventions of the kind undertaken in East Asia place unreasonable demands on the know-how and probity of public officials. Even in autonomous states with a highly disciplined bureaucracy, *dirigiste* policy eventually decays. Policy making in developing societies is especially susceptible to capture by self-serving economic groups. Yet few if any governments anywhere in the world have the competence, foresight, discretion, and nimbleness to discriminate systematically between competing claims for state economic protection, or the strength and discipline to sustain their relative autonomy from vested interests while doing so.

The point that must be emphasized again is that activist crises in East Asia were developmental and recovery was sustainable. These societies are not necessarily caught up in an underdevelopment cycle of crises that repeat for the same or similar reasons. By comparison with developing countries in other parts of the world, the more advanced East Asian countries have shown that they can often be appropriately cautious and strategic about the kinds of long-run policies that this book identifies as necessary for a transition to capitalism. Overt and fixed ideological preferences on a left–right political spectrum have not played a strong role in policy decision making. Some East Asian elites seem willing to rebuild state institutions. The political conditions for quite effective state autonomy during institutional transitions have been maintained in this region for unusually long periods of time.

For most developing countries the much less impressive Latin American experience of state activism will be more instructive. The underlying dynamic of prolongation and decay of activist economic policy was broadly similar in both regions. Compared with East Asia, however, Latin America's devastating debt crises during the 1980s showed that the region was more vulnerable to serious crisis and less flexible in the aftermath.

The term 'inward-looking development' describes the general thrust of statism in Latin America from the twilight of 'liberal' export-led growth in the 1930s until the post-crisis market reforms of the 1980s and 1990s. Although many factors contributed to the growth of activist ideology in Latin America during the first half of the twentieth century, the spread and adoption of key ideas can be dated to the founding of the United Nations Economic Commission for Latin America (ECLA) in 1948, and ECLA's policy papers dealing with technical strategies for nurturing infant industry. Whereas classical theorists such as John Stuart Mill and Friedrich List had concurred in the opinion that *temporary* taxes on industrial imports could be justified but ran the risk of creating vested interests in inefficient policy, ECLA's ideologists regarded industrial 'protection as necessary during a rather *long* transition period' (Prebisch 1984: 179). This was a fundamental error. State activism in Latin America was prolonged, and created vested interests in its own perpetuation. Raul Prebisch, the main intellectual author of the approach, conceded only a decade after its inception that the administration of industrial policy by governments in Latin America had rapidly lost any semblance of discipline.

> An industrial structure virtually isolated from the outside world thus grew up in our countries.... The criterion by which the choice was determined was based not on considerations of economic expediency, but on immediate feasibility, whatever the cost of production ... tariffs have been carried to such a pitch that they are undoubtedly – on an average – the highest in the world. It is not uncommon to find tariff duties of over 500%. As is well known, the proliferation of industries of every kind in a closed market has deprived the Latin American countries of the advantages of specialization

and economies of scale, and owing to the protection afforded by tariff duties and restrictions, a healthy form of internal competition has failed to develop, to the detriment of efficient production.

(Prebisch 1963: 71)

The results of implementing ECLA ideas should have provided sharp lessons for future development practitioners about the unintended consequences of state activism, but also about the ideological potential for international organizations to shape policy outcomes in the developing world. Despite the early warnings of impending difficulties, between 1950 and 1970 *Import-Substitution Industriali-zation* (ISI) policies did broadly achieve their targets and did not derail the region's trajectory of steady economic growth. State-managed and subsidized industrialization built upon an earlier period of nineteenth- and early twentieth-century *natural* industrialization based on non-durable consumer goods and the processing of agricultural products (Bulmer-Thomas 1994). By 1980, industry accounted for nearly a quarter of gross domestic product in the more advanced economies of Latin America – Argentina, Brazil, Chile, Colombia, and Mexico. The huge transfer of capital and labour resources out of agriculture and into urban industry in the space of only two decades had far-reaching social, polit-ical, and economic consequences, both positive and negative.

Of interest in the present context is the relationship between economic decisions, ideologies, and interests. The 'easy' phase of ISI, roughly until 1960, encouraged production of labour-intensive consumer goods. Once domestic markets for these goods reached their limits, policymakers faced three options (Kaufman 1990: 120). They could return to maximizing comparative advantages in mineral and agricultural products, increasing rural incomes and widening the market for domestic industry. Or, they could 'deepen' ISI by moving into inter-mediate or capital goods and consumer durables, with all that implied in terms of capital investment and the upgrading of technology and skills. Or, they could adopt the approach that South Korea and Taiwan would promptly pursue in the 1960s after the exhaustion of their own short-lived phase of 'easy ISI', namely to aggressively establish competitive positions for low-skill labour-intensive manufactures in world markets through a planning mix of selective market opening and manipulation of tariffs and financial credit, close coordination with business groups to manage labour and investment strategy, stable macroeco-nomic policy, and infrastructure development.

In Latin America, the ideological crusade – initially encouraged by ECLA – against trade, export dependency, and landowning elites ruled out the first and third options. Industrialization was largely financed by the state siphoning the surplus from traditional exports. As a result, the competitiveness of primary and particularly agricultural sectors had declined. Protected industries operated at very high cost, having never faced a level of competition in domestic markets that could prepare them for entry into world markets. Governments were unlikely to create conditions that would expose domestic industries to competi-tion. They were not sufficiently autonomous from strong interest groups that by now depended on protected markets. Industrialization coalitions were complex and finely balanced. They comprised domestic businesses, labour groups, professionals, public employees, military industrialists, political-technocratic elites, and foreign investors attracted by incentives to operate behind tariff walls. State-led industrialization was, by the 1960s, a pragmatic but inflexible alliance against market liberalization. Moreover, a broader 'structuralist' agenda dominated political thinking. It aimed for redistribution of income and a squeeze on upper-class consumption. Populist-socialist policies to expand public-sector employment, food subsidies and social services dovetailed with the state's growing bureaucratic promotion of industries and well-paid urban-industrial labour.

The big Latin American economies pursued the second option, turning further inwards. The plan was that vertically integrated production lines in new industries would source intermediate inputs and machinery locally. States would orchestrate the quantum leap in skills, technology, and capital investment. Policymakers apparently did not anticipate that a deepening of ISI would aggravate structural problems and balance-of-payments difficulties. The goal was self-sufficiency, but the second round of ISI relied on ever-larger doses of external capital to finance investments in foreign equipment, licences, royalties, and expertise. Ironically, the new nationalist industrial policy forced a relaxation of foreign-investment codes in order that multinational companies could substitute for domestic capital and technology. The extension of ISI into upstream industries should have broadened supporting coalitions. In practice, capital-intensive industries did not generate enough jobs for a rapidly expanding urban population, and excluded groups became a source of political unrest. Excessive public spending and inflation only compounded existing problems of social inequality, rural–urban migration, labour-market distortions, and the neglect of agricultural sectors.

The most favoured solution to problems encountered in the 'hard' phase of ISI was to expand the number and size of state-owned enterprises (SOEs). Public ownership was intended to supply investment and output in upstream industries and infrastructure, and to subsidize private industry. SOEs enabled labour absorption, state capital accumulation, and social projects to solve political problems. Thus, SOEs became essential for propping up ISI economic and political coalitions. For the most part, however, SOEs were inefficient and corrupt. In addition, they came to rely heavily on foreign loans. The fact that international banks often sought a government loan guarantee helps to explain why SOEs were the chief recipients of loans to Latin America in the 1970s. In effect, foreign private banks helped finance a further nationalization of peak economic sectors in Latin American economies.

The immediate causes of the catastrophic Latin American *activist crises* related to levels of public debt. In the 1970s international economic events furnished developing countries with opportunities to borrow on an unprecedented scale. Private banks pressed almost unlimited credit on to capital-hungry countries with little if any conditionality. Latin America responded eagerly. The region's historical pattern had always been one of low domestic saving and accumulation, and heavy dependence on external sources of capital. Faced with the burgeoning costs of a failing industrialization strategy, foreign loans allowed Latin American countries to postpone restructuring. Easy credit substituted for the reforms that had long been advocated by the 'monetarist' critics of ISI. Monetarists would have raised tax revenue, improved corporate management, reduced public expenditure, and tackled root institutional causes of domestic market failure.

A large proportion of the borrowed money went into consumption or the financing of balance-of-payments deficits, or flowed back into private overseas bank accounts. Capital flight, both legal and illegal, became a major problem. Compared with East Asia in the same period, Latin America used foreign loans less productively for long-run growth (Fishlow 1991). Poor export performance would in any case have made it difficult to keep up debt servicing. In addition, external financing channelled into state projects met the expenditure demands of social interest groups and represented a way of sustaining activist political coalitions (Thorp 1998). Mexico was the first country to threaten default in 1982.

To borrow the phrase of a distinguished economic historian, the experience of state activism in Latin America was one of 'development without efficiency constraints' (Landes 1998: 494). An exception was Colombia, the only major country not to reschedule its foreign debt. Another exception was Chile, whose public debt barely increased in the decade preceding the debt crisis. Chile's own crisis of *private*-sector debt in 1982 was a hiccup in an otherwise dynamic reorientation of economic policy away from socialism and towards the expansion of markets. In most of Latin America, non-conditional state subsidies to non-competitive firms in captive markets was a strategy that fuelled modest growth at the expense of stunting private-sector development. The protectionist strategy delayed institutional reforms that should have created much-needed incentives for entrepreneurship. Indeed, the most inefficient industries often received the greatest protection. Activist ideology and interest groupings blocked a timely move away from failing ISI policies.

Activism in Latin America seemed actually to worsen the performance of government institutions. Compared with the model of liberal export-led economic growth, which between 1880–1930 had evolved hand in hand with impressive institutional development (Whitehead 1998), state activism only accentuated a personalist style of intra-state and government–business relations (Purcell and Purcell 1977; Heller 1990; 1993). As had always been the case previously, to get something done, to exercise a right or to obtain a privilege, in Latin America one had to know people – family, friends, patrons, or clients – or to pay people in the right places. In principle, everyone is formally equal before the law. But behind the legal-administrative façade, in business, public administration, the judiciary, and political life, successful transactions depend on informal connections. It seemed to be implicit in the activist model that state support to industry could not function adequately alongside personalistic influence peddling, sinecures, patronage and clientelism, monopolistic entitlements, or rent seeking. Yet, this was how 'intereses' had historically held sway in Latin American polities (Wiarda 1973).

It was predictable, therefore, that additional state economic controls would only create extra incentives for such behaviour. Complex administrative systems for allocating industry-related licences, permits, cheap credit, import quotas, wage and price controls, as well as government contracts in a personalist institutional order expanded the distributive networks operating among public officials, industrialists, and trade unions. Government controls became the object of lobbying for concessions, and decisions about income transfers to industry fell prey to privilege and corruption. Industrialists and some of the political and bureaucratic elite clearly profited from activist policies, but the costs to societies were productive inefficiency, the further politicization of economic life, and debilitating debt crises.

A critique of neoactivism

What can we learn about state activism as a model for capitalist transition? The key lesson seems to be that effective state activism demands extremely high pre-existing levels of state administrative capacity. But even in countries that displayed that capacity, the mismatch between institutional forms and economic change was the eventual cause of activist crisis. The experiences of East Asia and Latin America suggest that crises resulted from inevitable declines in state bureaucratic capacity to manage inevitable increases in economic complexity. Moreover the effort governments invested in designing administrative mechanisms for the direct control of economic sectors crowded out energy and resources that could have gone into constructing the institutions for a competitive market economy. Crises revealed that state agencies in charge of industrial policy had become inflexible and were resistant to market liberalization. Non-state groups that benefited from opaque regulations and entitlements to subsidies became politically powerful and resisted reform. A focus on 'engineering' the growth of firms that will be globally competitive in terms of cost and quality of their products and processes tends to produce a corresponding neglect of tasks aimed at creating a level playing field for all firms. Sooner or later, the business sector must stand on its own feet. Yet, activist crises can seriously damage an economy long before that point is reached. It is a characteristic of activist regimes that having reached the stage when it becomes extremely urgent to abandon the intrusive planning approach in favour of market deepening and parametric regulation, political and administrative agencies have lost the political autonomy and policy flexibility needed to make that change easily.

The situation in many developing countries today, even in those where state activism seemed to produce some spectacular successes, is not unlike the one described by Schumpeter 70 years ago:

> what we know from experience is not the working of capitalism as such, but of a distorted capitalism which is covered with the scars of past injuries

inflicted on its organism.... The very fundamentals of the industrial organisms of all nations have been politically shaped. Everywhere we find industries which would not exist at all but for protection, subsidies, and other political stimuli, and others which are overgrown or otherwise in an unhealthy state because of them.... Such industries are assets of doubtful value, in any case a source of weakness and often the immediate cause of breakdowns or depressive symptoms. This type of economic waste and maladjustment may well be more important than any other.

(Schumpeter 1964: 7)

Most of the developing countries that pursued an activist path in the last century have made slow progress towards impersonally regulated capitalism. The nature of activist tasks can impose impossible demands on state agencies from the outset. Or, after an initial period of successful intervention, agencies are less able to perform increasingly difficult and costly tasks. Either way, the institutional bottlenecks that produce crisis are manifested in a decline in the quality of state decision making. Regardless of the initial quality of policy leadership, or 'conducive' cultural and external environments, within a decade or two *dirigiste* policy becomes counterproductive. The state becomes overconfident of its market-control capacity and protective of its discretionary powers, and is slow to build up skills and resources that would prepare the ground for parametric economic regulation. Business comes to rely too heavily on government-backed guarantees, which itself creates a political constraint on change. There is little evidence anywhere of a successful unravelling of personalistic intra-state, inter-business, or state–business relationships after a long phase of activist intervention.

Although activist ideology has moderated noticeably in the wake of the Asian financial crisis, it is still common to hear foundational principles of activism enunciated by scholars and by international organizations that wield considerable influence in developing countries. Well-intentioned experts might today advise a South Asian or Latin American technocrat to attempt to replicate what technocrats once did in South Korea and Taiwan or what they now do in China, but with many caveats. 'Do get a move on', they might say, 'but be careful how you go about it, and pay attention to our long list of dos and don'ts'. The experts run the strong risk that the people who receive their advice will not read between the lines and will not examine the fine detail. The eager technocrat who listens to the expert is likely to focus on the central message, 'you can do it too'.

In the remainder of this section I will evaluate how the Weberian policy sequence compares with newer and more tempered support for activism. An insightful report of the World Bank-sponsored Commission on Growth and Development (2008) – chaired by the Nobel Laureate economist Michael Spence – points out various institutional and economic reasons for activist success or failure. Its determined effort to find a balance among the pros and cons of activist policy is worth quoting in full.

Some sceptics might concede that markets do not always work, but they argue that industrial policies don't either. This is either because governments do not know what they are doing – they lack the expertise to identify successful targets for investment, and will waste resources on plausible failures – or because they knowingly subvert the process to their own ends, dispensing favours to their industrial allies. There is, of course, considerable variation across countries in the competence of government and in the undue influence of special interests. But those who worry about government competence or capture would prefer to rule out promotional activities altogether. The risk of failure or subversion is too great, they say; better not to try. But there are also risks to doing nothing. A flourishing export sector is a critical ingredient of high growth, especially in the early stages. If an economy is failing to diversify its exports and failing to generate productive jobs in new industries, governments do look for ways to try to jump-start the process, and they should. These efforts should bow to certain disciplines, however. First, they should be temporary, because the problems they are designed to overcome are not permanent. Second, they should be evaluated critically and abandoned quickly if they are not producing the desired results. Subsidies may be justified if an export industry cannot get started without them. But if it cannot keep going without them, the original policy was a mistake and the subsidies should be abandoned. Third, although such policies will discriminate in favour of exports, they should remain as neutral as possible about which exports. As far as possible, they should be agnostic about particular industries, leaving the remainder of the choice to private investors. Finally and importantly, export promotion is not a good substitute for other key supportive ingredients: education, infrastructure, responsive regulation, and the like.

(Commission on Growth and Development 2008: 49)

It is evident even in the Commission's report that the tasks of 'jump-starting' an industrial export sector while remaining *disciplined*, *neutral*, and *agnostic*, and then withdrawing support at precisely the right moment, place very onerous demands upon state institutional capacity. How confident can the experts be that those who listen to this advice really have enough motive, cognitive disposition, and structural leeway to pick up the nuances and act on these fine-tuned policy disciplines, and how sure can they be that the approach will be kept within strict limits? Going back at least as far as the Economic Commission for Latin America's not dissimilar advice for disciplined interventions in the 1950s, many countries have attempted the activist approach. Few have succeeded in doing it well.

The Commission on Growth and Development also conjures up a familiar straw man. It criticizes the idea that government's only role is to 'stabilize, privatize, and liberalize', and follows that with the observation that 'active, pragmatic governments have crucial roles to play'. It then says, 'bad policies are often good policies applied for too long' (ibid.: 5). I present a somewhat different argument in this book: bad policies, i.e. activist policies in most developing countries that lack certain preexisting institutional advantages, sometimes do produce good outcomes for a short time. But that is insufficient reason for international organizations and experts not to advise *all* developing countries to pursue the *eventually* good policies, i.e. market expansion and rule of law, as a priority from the outset. In context-specific terms, economic policies are *only* as good as the government that implements them, and the institutions that maintain them. In more general terms, an economic policy is *only* as good as its logical and scientific feasibility with respect to the kinds of cognitive, volitional, and structural imperatives of rational technocratic action that were examined in Chapter 5.

It may be better, in other words, to apply existing state capacity to the arguably less demanding but in the long run indispensable task of jump-starting market-expansive and regulatory sequences while remaining temporarily insulated from political competition and interest-group counter-pressure. If what has been said about capitalist transition thus far in this book can be believed, expansive but impersonally regulated markets that encourage autonomous entrepreneurial risk taking by domestic *and* foreign businesses may be the priority means to the end. The transitional non-discriminatory state has enough on its hands enforcing laws, making monetary and fiscal policy, and helping to finance and improve the various service infrastructures that will support external trade and internal commerce. Both the activist and capitalist approaches are idealistic in some degree, but it is important that the final choice should favour the more pragmatic of the two. Even assuming that it might attain some of its initial aims, the danger of unleashing an activist regime is that it rapidly builds around itself an iron cage for incubating a living organism of state and business relationships, doctrines, organizations, and procedures that will be difficult and costly to wrench apart when it is no longer functional. The consequences of attempting to unshackle the iron cage of activism in a country like China might well be explosive beyond the country's borders.

The choice between activist policy or market regulatory policy probably boils down to a means-end decision about the best utilization of scarce state administrative resources, and perhaps also a philosophical quasi-spiritual choice about how much 'faith' to have in government. In the past two or three decades scholars have marshalled piecemeal empirical evidence for and against activist industrial policy. For every success one can find a failure. It might therefore be time to return to classic social-scientific logic. A recent book by Rodrik (2007) offers a comprehensive and perhaps definitive assessment – from an activist viewpoint – of the feasibility of activist industrial policy, which relies in the final analysis on a refreshing dose of logical thought. It will be interesting to see how Weberian arguments stand up to the counter-logic. Rodrik's conclusions in defence of new activism are summarized in three main thoughts on government competence and the utilization of scarce bureaucratic resources. Let us examine each of them in turn.

Yes, the government cannot pick winners, but effective industrial policy is predicated less on the ability to pick winners than on the ability to cut losses short once mistakes have been made. In fact, making mistakes (picking wrong industries) is part and parcel of good industrial policy when cost discovery is at issue.

(Rodrik 2007: 150)

From a Weberian perspective there are at least four critical responses to this statement. First, there is evidently still a wasteful effort to identify a winner, without which the state would not need to be involved in correcting the error. If you know the goal of the task is impossible to achieve, why try at all? Liberal philosophy does tell us that learning is by doing, i.e. by trial and error. But there should be prior analysis to decide on worthwhile action in the light of available knowledge of cause and effect. There is no point in making further errors deliberately for the sake of learning more. A better way to learn, as Sen (1999: 257) recommends, is to start with an intentionally rational 'causal analysis' that will make 'the unintended effects reasonably predictable'.

Second, economic success depends on the *economic actor* knowing that the consequence of failure could be the loss of market power or extinction. Private enterprises sensibly seek research and development advice, information, and services from many sources, including government. But if the enterprise or industry is to stand on its own feet, the onus of 'cost discovery' lies, from the beginning, with the winning firm rather than with the government. Weber called this a 'special kind of coercive situation which, as a general principle, applies without any discrimination to workers, enterprisers, producers and consumers ... in the impersonal form of the inevitability of adaptation to the purely economic "laws" of the market' (Weber 1978: 731). That helps to explain why bankruptcy laws are a vital dimension of transitional state-regulatory reform.

Third, the most basic argument against activist policy is the state's limited knowledge of markets, which is not just a problem of 'picking winners'. Having chosen a firm or industry to 'nurture', the activist state must monitor its performance and the surrounding market much as a parent monitors a child and the child's environment. These are knowledge-intensive functions – if applied across extended families of industries – that the state is unlikely to perform well or dispassionately. Moreover, classic dilemmas of state planning rationality and opportunity costs of public investment are still present when the state tries to establish benchmark criteria for identifying 'mistakes' and the effective responses to them. It is worth repeating Weber's remark that when officials intervene in economic life their actions tend to 'take an unforeseen and unintended course or are made illusory by the superior expert knowledge of the interested [business] groups' (ibid.: 994).

Finally, when the state acts discretionally by identifying potential winners and eventual *losers*, incentives exist for public officials to pursue their own interests or to fall in with private interests. The more functions a state takes on, the more incentives will exist for the misuse of power. Any systematic promotional relationship between state and business – whether it is face to face or quasi-corporatist and coordinated by a 'council' – is prone to conflicts of private and public interest.

'Once mistakes have been made', state officials may feel committed and will be reluctant to see the 'loser' fail. Moreover, a 'mistake' lies in the eye of the beholder. Interest-group coalitions can form expressly to perpetuate *profitable* 'mistakes'. Furthermore, effective monitoring for mistakes requires an army of proactive officials, and the dangers of state overload will be magnified. In a market-regulatory framework, the state's more important function is to investigate wrongdoing or threats to public safety, and to enforce laws at the behest of plaintiffs.

> Competent bureaucracies are a scarce resource in most developing countries, but most countries do have (or can build) pockets of bureaucratic competence. In any case, it is not clear what the counterfactual is. The standard market-oriented package hardly economizes on bureaucratic competence. As we have discovered during the last decade, and as the expansion of the Washington Consensus agenda into governance and institutional areas indicates, running a market economy put a significant premium on regulatory capacity. Industrial policy is no different.
>
> (Rodrik 2007: 150–1)

This statement implies that more or less equivalent 'bureaucratic competence' would be needed for successful activist and market-regulatory actions. Weberian theory suggests instead that more or less optimal parametric regulatory capacity is less demanding of state resources, less risky, and far less costly in the long run than intrusive, administration-intensive, and knowledge-intensive state activism. Logically, then, it is desirable to perform the essential tasks of regulation from the outset, which might mean having to leave non-essential tasks until the capacity to perform them well has been built up. Regulatory competence has to be built eventually, whereas activist competence is at best a temporary need for as long as it takes to get infant industries onto their feet.

Regulatory competence can also be acquired in 'pockets' of the state's legal-administrative apparatus, whose primary goal is to enforce a small number of tightly focused procedural rules. 'Regulatory capacity' is a circumscribed and manageable engineering task, which, by comparison with industrial policy, requires less human capital, is less dispersed, and has fewer unforeseeable consequences. If state competence is a scarce resource, it would be better not to use it up in hazardous efforts to outsmart market forces or to mould the decisions of entrepreneurs who, in practice, have superior knowledge about the exigencies of economic survival. Institutional weakness is to be expected in the early stages of development, which is why economic policies that place unrealistic demands on institutions should be avoided.

> Industrial policies can be captured by the interests whose behaviour they aim to alter. But once again, this is little different from any other area of policy. In many countries, privatization has turned out to be a boon for insiders and government cronies.
>
> (Rodrik 2007: 151)

There is an obvious weakness in this argument. Developing states should from the outset be aiming for policies whose *primary means*-oriented objective is to eliminate the possibility of capture, i.e. to prevent political profit making and regulatory closure. Capitalist regulation operates at the boundary of an economy to maintain market freedoms in line with public safety, rather than through direct and discriminatory interventions. Its designable purpose is to prevent opportunities and incentives for sectional interests to seek influence within the state. Activist policy is intrinsically prone to capture since it depends on state procedural discretion to select the firms, sectors, or activities that it intends to promote. The implicit counterfactual is neoliberal policy. Privatization is prone to capture only if the *method* by which it is conducted has *already* been 'captured'. In practice, it is easier to establish a transparent competitive bidding process for a few large privatizations – discrete events open to all contenders, supervised by independent monitors, and decided only on merit – than it is to sustain (inevitably interpersonal) activist transactions with multiple firms for the extended time it takes to nurture each of them to 'adulthood'.

The three key theses in defence of new industrial policy convey exactly the kind of memorable and empowering 'expert lesson' that a *dirigiste*-minded technocrat in the developing world will seize on enthusiastically. To the criticism I have offered, the expert might reasonably reply that their message is actually much more complex and subtle. But will the technocrats read between the lines and look at the small print? Even if they do, does the state really have the capacity to implement activist policy without falling prey to pressures of political profit making and regulatory closure?

The intention of new activism seems to be to distance itself from the cruder *dirigiste* policies of the past. For example, it argues that 'public support must target *activities, not sectors*', i.e. activities that can assist market expansion, such as language and technical training, feasibility studies, infrastructure, technology adaptation, or venture-capital funds (Rodrik 2007: 114–15). Not many orthodox economists would object to that. Yet it is difficult to reconcile such reassuring statements with more conventional activist advocacy in the preceding pages on behalf, for example, of government promotion of fishing, motor vehicle, or computer sectors (ibid.: 109).

New activism's intricate 'design principles' and elaborately layered 'incentive programmes' for industrial policy are peppered with recommendations that ring alarm bells (Rodrik 2007: 114–19). When promoting and subsidizing industry, *the state* must be 'discriminating' and 'experimental'; set 'clear benchmarks for success and failure'; use 'criteria of productivity' that are 'notoriously difficult to measure' and therefore require 'project audits by business and technical consultants'; create 'automatic sunset clauses' that 'phase out support by default'; undertake 'analysis' of the 'spillovers and demonstration effects'; give authority only to 'agencies with demonstrated competence'; select a 'cabinet-level politician' to 'monitor' state agencies engaged in the promotion of industries and to 'protect the agencies against capture by private interests'; 'build safeguards' and engage in 'productive discovery'; establish government–business 'coordination and deliberation councils ... at the national level as well as the regional and sectoral levels'. In countries struggling to implement so-called 'second-stage' institutional reforms, being encouraged to implement third-, fourth-, or fifth-stage reforms will seem premature. The difficulties that still plague political decision making, state planning projects, and state–business relations in even the most advanced developing countries – South Korea, Chile, *et al.* – give cause to question the wisdom of these general neoactivist design principles for the developing world.

Alternatives to state-engineered protections for national champions do exist, and developing countries ignore them at their peril. If the 'missing factors' of industrialization capacity are the assets of knowledge and human, physical, or financial capital, then global economic changes have opened up a vast panorama of opportunities. Proprietary or leasing rights over many core technologies and technical skills can be acquired relatively cheaply off the shelf in international marketplaces. In the majority of developing countries, these technologies are sufficiently advanced to meet the needs of infant industries that are still learning the arts of entrepreneurship. State-subsidized incubation of leading-edge innovation by indigenous 'champions' can be a very costly and hazardous undertaking in developing countries. A recent report by *The Economist* on technology development in Asia suggests a better strategy.

India and China's precocious economies have done more piggybacking than leapfrogging. They have made clever use of foreign technology – assembling it, copying it, servicing it and customizing it – but their firms have yet to create very much to rival it. The nationalists may fret about this, but an economist instead finds much to applaud. A country should face the risks and frustrations of invention only when it has no easier route to economic progress. Besides, firms enjoy great scope for innovation, even if they do not march across the technological frontier. Indian and Chinese firms have a comparative advantage in finding new uses for existing technologies, and combining them in novel ways.... If [the state] is ready to mix and match, and to learn from foreigners and from its own consumers, it will thrive. But the state should not fancy that technology can be owned from bottom to top, or that innovation can be accomplished by decree.

(*The Economist*, 10–16 November 2007)

Finally, it is obvious that the national origin of enterprises is increasingly less important as a determinant of national economic growth and performance, employment conditions, wage levels, productivity, investment, or technology transfer. In a new world of highly mobile firms and mobile finance it matters less whether the executive directors and shareholders of an economic enterprise hold national citizenship, as long as a *net* benefit is generated for the country where the enterprise or its subsidiary locates. The challenge is to maximize the advantages by building institutions that attract beneficial investments, and then to regulate them adaptively in ways that will ensure the continuity of those advantages. Worldwide surveys by the World Bank indicate that 'various dimensions of governance, such as the quality of the regulatory regime, rule of law, and control of corruption, matter very significantly' to a country's level of foreign direct investment; more indeed than 'macroeconomic stability' (Kaufmann 2004: 139–40).

The presence of many competitive foreign firms in a market generates unparalleled pressure for the construction of better institutions, and also enables emerging national firms in the expanding economy to learn directly from their more advanced counterparts. Keeping foreign investors out of an economy is often only a strategy to protect narrow group interests. Giving foreign firms similar shelters against competition in order to entice them into a national market only replicates the mistake. In the short term it is possible that local elites give foreign firms special institutional concessions without modernizing the regulation of the domestic economy. Yet it is implausible that such a situation could be sustained without in the end driving away foreign investors or producing a serious crisis of domestic legitimacy for the governing elite.

The familiar critique of activism equates the superior efficiency of open-market economies with competition, property and contract rights, the role of prices and moderate taxes, fiscal discipline and limited public expenditure, and liberal finance, investment, and trade policy. Economists have added supplementary factors to this list in the light of difficulties encountered during market reforms in recent decades (Krueger 2000; Kuczynski and Williamson 2003). There clearly are strong economic alternatives to activism. My criticism has focused on neglected 'institutional' reasons for the failures of activism. In earlier chapters I have pointed out the variability of institutional incentives under alternative economic governance regimes.

I have argued, first, that the intrinsic cognitive constraint upon the administrative rationality of activist regimes means that in most situations public officials know less about the markets they 'guide' than do the firms they subsidize. A valid generalization is that state officials are usually unable to rationally discriminate for any meaningful length of time between industries that really are or are not worthy of subsidy or protection. They are not endowed with sufficient foresight to do so. The eventual decay of activist regimes is largely a result of the ineluctable detachment of state officials from information that is generated in the private economy. Second, there are political constraints. If democratic checks and balances are weak or non-existent there is little chance that public agencies will be properly supervised. State officials are increasingly likely to prioritize their own interests or non-state group interests rather than impersonal goals and genuinely 'public' interests. It has been a characteristic of overconfident activist states that their institutions of law, administration, and political representation do not adapt quickly to changing economic patterns. Third, close guidance and monitoring of firms inevitably requires a high level of personal interaction between officials and private individuals, which increases the susceptibility of state agencies to the most pernicious kinds of business influence. Despite some of its keenest proponents being political scientists, activist ideology fails to recognize the threat that discriminatory state economic interventions pose to the probity and adaptive efficiency of polities and officialdom.

Neoliberal transition

The second broad type of *developmental* crisis is *neoliberal*. I use the term 'neo-liberalism' here to refer to proto-capitalist policies that cope with failed state activism by restructuring economies along market lines, but without prompt and corresponding reforms to the institutional framework of economic regulation. Neoliberal policies typically focus on urgent macroeconomic stabilization, lower public borrowing, withdrawal of public subsidies, retrenching of public-sector workforces, privatization of state-owned enterprises, and market deregulation. There is an empirical *sequence* from activism to neoliberalism. Research on major development crises in Latin America, Asia, Africa, and Eastern Europe since the early 1980s indicates that the combination of activist or populist policy failures and international shocks produced macroeconomic chaos, recession, hyperinflation, and debt crises. 'The response' was usually 'a profound shift in development strategy, away from state-led, inward-oriented models of growth toward emphasis on the market, private ownership, and greater openness to trade and foreign investment' (Haggard and Kaufman 1995: 3). In a comparative study of 21 developing countries, Lal and Myint (1996) argue that neoliberal economic reforms attempt to restore order to economies and political systems that were made unmanageable by populist or activist economic policies, when 'only a crisis' can resolve the 'resulting paralysis of the polity and economy' (ibid.: 296). General reasons for economic-policy reversals in the 1980s included changes in the ideological climate, an increase in the power of interest groups that stood to benefit from market reforms, global technological trends that favoured and facilitated radical policy changes, as well as the self-destruction, through crisis, of statist economic models (Hood 1994).

These crises of the 1980s and 1990s offered opportunities for a major overhaul of institutions in many developing countries, because they increased 'the probability that opposition will be directed not just at the government but at the fundamental rules of the game' (Haggard and Kaufman 1995: 7). I will argue in this section that neoliberal reforms were *myopic* in institutional terms. The neoliberal emphasis on market-oriented policies could have been commensurate with a Weberian policy sequence of capitalist transition. That it was not can be explained largely by the fact that even the best-motivated and most knowledgeable reformers were unable to escape the institutional overhang of populism and activism, and they possessed neither the ideological force nor the political power to push forward the appropriate institutional adjustments. Whereas activist crisis principally takes an economic form, neoliberalism is more likely to suffer a *political* crisis of legitimacy. The immediate reasons for the eventual political backlash against neoliberalism include short-sighted expectations, democratic processes, failure to design a sequence of reforms or to implement reforms in full, ideological uncertainty, and corruption during privatization and deregulation. The deeper roots of neoliberal crisis stem from the preceding activist crises and pre-existing institutional problems, especially the personalistic nature of government policy networks and insufficient rule of law.

Many economic reforms that East and Southeast Asian countries introduced in the wake of activist crises could also be called 'neoliberal'. That this or any equivalent descriptor for market-friendly policies is not used so much in an East Asian context may perhaps be explained by the fact that policy swings have been less accentuated and ideological debate about economic policy comparatively more pragmatic and muted in that region. Whatever the reasons, political and intellectual discourse about neoliberalism has not captured the public imagination in East Asia as explosively as it often has in Latin America. Furthermore, the *institutional* emphasis of post-crisis reform has been considerably stronger in East Asia. For this reason alone, it may not be quite appropriate to call East Asian post-crisis reforms 'neoliberal'. On the present definition, neoliberalism is institutionally 'myopic'. Nor, despite strong protests against it in one or two countries, has post-crisis deregulation and re-regulation in East Asia yet resulted in full-scale 'neoliberal crises'. Again, this may reflect greater moderation, conformity, and discipline in policy approaches, or a different pattern and atmosphere of political discourse. It is clear that Latin American neoliberalism has been more prone to crises of legitimacy than the corresponding post-activist reforms in Asia.

The Latin American experience of reform in the 1980s and 1990s reveals the limitations of neoliberal economic policies, but also the enduring effects of the damage wrought by activist policies. Many Latin American economists and politicians initially responded to the region's debt crises by laying the blame on foreign banks and the world economy. There were influential calls for a new round of protectionism and the deepening of activist policy. However, the eventual consensus in response to conditionality attached to new external financing, and as a consequence of the election of new governments and an apparent ideological reorientation in the top echelons of Latin American states, was favourable to market-oriented stabilization and structural adjustment. By the early 1990s in countries such as Argentina, Mexico, Brazil, and Peru, highly qualified state managers who announced credible proposals for market reform and had few pre-existing commitments to traditional political establishments were in control of economic policy. Their public proclamations on economic as well as judicial, administrative, and electoral reform led many outside observers to conclude that Latin America had discovered a new vocation for modernization, globalization, and probity.

It is noteworthy that all the Latin American neoliberal governments of the 1990s were democratically elected. In several countries, economic crisis had brought about the collapse of authoritarian regimes. No electorate in the region was ready to vote for a political party that promised a permanent change in ideological orientation or a 'shock' programme of economic reform. In fact, most political leaders who spearheaded neoliberal reforms came to power on a platform of broadly populist promises and made a policy U-turn on taking office.

State technocrats who were appointed by elected politicians were granted strong powers. In the early stages of reform they often circumvented legislative approval processes. Presidential decrees were frequently employed to pass controversial legislation, and peak state agencies were insulated from political infighting.

Technocrats found allies in internationalized business sectors and academic think-tanks. But to a large extent they also enjoyed public support. Latin America was already accustomed to acquiescing in painful recoveries from recurrent inflationary spirals, and there was general recognition of the trade-off between temporary austerity and recovery. Midway through the 1990s, electorates signalled their acceptance of the short-run technical logic of belt tightening, public sector retrenchment, liberalization of prices and wages, relaxation of foreign-investment rules, and elimination of industrial subsidies as part of packages to stabilize economies made volatile by previous fiscal indiscipline. Several neoliberal governments were returned to office after the first stage of reform. In elections in Mexico in 1994, as in Argentina and Peru in 1995, there could be no doubt in anyone's mind that a vote for the ruling party should mean another round of neoliberal adjustment. The momentum of reform was further encouraged by the demonstrable success of Chile and Mexico, countries which had pioneered the first wave of neoliberal restructuring in the mid-1980s.

Differences among Latin American countries in terms of the intensity, scope, and duration of neoliberal reforms make it difficult to generalize about the outcomes. Aside from privatization and some sporadic attempts at labour-market reform, neoliberal reforms in the region broadly achieved the following goals: restructuring, rescheduling, and reduction of foreign debt; tax reforms that increased fiscal revenues; cutbacks in public expenditure; more market-responsive exchange-rate policies; reforms to reduce the state's discretionary control of credit; some central-bank independence in setting interest rates; measures to increase domestic saving and investment and to improve the business and regulatory environment; trade and foreign-investment liberalization with the aims of reducing biases against exports and promoting economic growth, employment, and productivity in the export sector. As noted, such reforms were politically acceptable. The removal of price and exchange controls or public-sector layoffs could to some extent be compensated by renewed job creation in the private sector, easier access to personal credit, and – often for the first time – affordable and high-quality imported consumer goods and services. Sound monetary and fiscal policies and greater market freedom did have immediate and positive impacts on stability and economic growth. When push came to shove, it was clear in the 1980s that Latin American governments could turn macroeconomic imbalances around at considerable speed (Edwards 1995).

Other policies of longer gestation were required, however, in order to consolidate these reforms. Reformers and observers commonly distinguished between 'easy' first-stage reforms for stabilization and growth recovery in the immediate aftermath of crisis, and 'hard' second-stage reforms needed to achieve gains in efficiency and relative equity for long-term growth. Macroeconomic stabilization is easier to deal with in the aftermath of crisis than structural reforms – such as the creation of agencies to regulate newly privatized firms – which require complex but perhaps seemingly less urgent institutional designs. Second-stage reforms should include two major components: policies for social services and poverty reduction, and broader institutional reform. Finessing market regulation, assisting marginalized groups, and restructuring public-sector organizations to make them more effective, transparent, and accountable is harder for technical and political reasons. Although targeted social-welfare policies during neoliberal reforms were sometimes surprisingly successful, it was also apparent to more perceptive analysts that the long-term solution for poverty would lie in thoroughgoing macrolevel deregulation and reregulation of economies (de Soto 1986; Castañeda 1992).

In a milestone book published at the highpoint of neoliberalism, the World Bank's chief economist for Latin America explained the objectives of deregulation and reregulation (Edwards 1995). *Deregulation* reduces unnecessary and arbitrarily administered state controls that constrain flexibility in the business sector. *Reregulation* strengthens property rights and judicial systems, and improves the operation of markets through measures such as anti-monopoly legislation or consumer and environmental safeguards. Reregulation should also create regulatory agencies independent of government and business influence, adequately financed, and staffed by technical experts. Even after a decade of reform Latin American economies were overregulated. State regulatory mechanisms were not well coordinated; legal systems were defective; property rights were not always properly enforced; and economic-policy processes lacked transparency. Excessive regulation prevented efficiency improvements in business and state sectors, and perpetuated institutional incentives for corruption. Two decades after the initiation of neoliberal reforms, further studies (World Bank 2004a) refined the analysis of what constitutes a 'good business climate'. Latin America lagged internationally on key indicators, such as the relative ease with which a business can be started, workers hired and fired, contracts enforced, credit provided with good legal safeguards for both borrowers and creditors, and a business closed. On several of these scores the region had, in 2004, the lowest or second to lowest ranking in the world.

In a timely reminder to Latin American technocrats coinciding with a reversal in the discipline and momentum of neoliberal reform, a 1996 report on the region's 'unfinished revolution' identified numerous problems, including uncontrolled state expenditures, high unemployment, low domestic savings, weak banking sectors, poor health and education services, antiquated civil services, and a climate of crime and insecurity aggravated by the neglect of legal reforms (Burki and Edwards 1996). Incomplete removal of trade and industry controls and the relaxation of budget discipline contributed to the problems. The toughest reforms to implement in the second phase of reform were labour-market deregulation, pension privatization, and constraints on subnational government spending and endemic tax evasion. Arguably, a third phase – health, education, environment, the civil service, police, and the judiciary – had barely begun even in those countries that had gone furthest with neoliberal reform, Mexico and Chile.

Above all, Latin America's antiquated and corrupt legal systems considerably constrained effective neoliberal or capitalist reforms. Closely related to the regulatory issues identified by World Bank studies of the business climate in Latin America are the lack of an effective, independent, and impartial judiciary in most countries. A growing literature on this topic highlights the poor administration of justice in the region, which greatly increases the transaction costs of economic activity. Hindrances to market reform, economic efficiency, and international integration are evident in the operative regulatory framework for business and investment, in laws relating to contracts, settlement of commercial disputes and bankruptcy, and recognition of property rights. As identified by the Americas Society and Council of the Americas (2007: 2), 'the substance of a country's laws matter little if the institutions set up to interpret and enforce those laws are inefficient, arbitrary or corrupt'. Plaintiffs who bring issues before the courts face chronic delays, high costs and onerous bureaucratic requirements, poor quality procedures, unpredictable outcomes, lack of accountability, and routine bribery and personal influence. Rents in the judicial system create strong incentives for bias and privilege. In Latin America, notes one observer, the 'dysfunctional legal-judicial framework' encourages 'political opportunism and personal enrichment' (Buscaglia 1998: 22). Judiciaries are not independent. Appointment and removal of judges is subject to presidential whims and populist patronage (Dam 2006: 114–15). Constraints on economic and political reform are also mirrored in the legal systems. The 'greatest impediments to reform of the [legal] system are to be found in clientelistic practices, corruption, and existence of dispute resolution systems exercised by certain groups that benefit from an inefficient system' (Jarquín and Carrillo 1998: ix). Inadequate legal enforcement exacerbates problems of inequality and personalism.

> There are many deficiencies in [Latin American] legal systems ... But an even greater problem is inadequate enforcement of existing laws. The Brazilian saying – 'To my enemies I wish the law' – is apt for most Latin American countries. The contracting environment is poor; dispute resolution mechanisms are ineffective; court procedures are so slow as to be considered useless by many in the business community; and the extrajudicial mechanisms for settling disagreements work poorly or not at all. The already strong tendencies for wealth to be concentrated are exacerbated because impersonal, long-term, and spatially separated contracts involve added risk; making it prudent for entrepreneurs to deal only with people they know.
>
> (Holden and Rajapatirana 1995: 103)

The weakness of the rule of law in Latin America did not bode well for the success of privatization programmes in the 1980s and 1990s. Although other neoliberal reforms were important, the policy approach taken towards privatization was especially revealing of the actual *motives* and *procedures* of Latin American policy making, particularly the obvious lack of real commitment to competition policy and modern government–business ethics. Analyses of policies towards newly privatized enterprises also provide a good impression of the regulatory environment during the period of neoliberal reforms. Finally, the corruption of privatizations was perhaps the greatest single reason for the political backlash against neoliberalism.

On the positive side, several studies document remarkable progress in Latin American privatization. In the region as a whole 'major privatizations of infrastructure have generally increased access to power, telephone services, and water, particularly for the poor, who, before privatization, often had no services or paid higher prices' (Nellis and Birdsall 2005: 26). Broadly, it is clear that privatizations have benefited the countries that undertook them (Chong and López-de-Silanes 2005). Most state-owned enterprises operated at a loss and were heavily subsidized. Selling them to domestic or overseas investors offered governments one-off proceeds and more efficient streams of tax revenue. In areas such as telecommunications, divestiture brought new investment and improved productivity, output, quality, and profitability, with positive multiplier effects throughout national economies. The creation of large new private enterprises boosted capital markets and demand for financial services. In many cases welfare gains were also achieved by expanding consumer access to goods and services at lower prices. Finally, the evidence is that privatizations directly encourage a range of state regulatory reforms that improve competitiveness and facilitate market expansion, such as new laws to deal with bankruptcy, creditor rights, shareholder rights, and information disclosure.

Nevertheless, deficiencies in the planning and implementation of privatizations meant that the economic and political gains were fewer and smaller than they might have been. Three main problems were evident. First, policymakers were generally motivated by short-term considerations. After the debt crises, many privatizations were hastily undertaken in order to resolve immediate balance-of-payment problems, to attract foreign finance and investment, or to placate international financial organizations. Second, the methods of privatization were not ideal (ibid.). Competent, centralized, and accountable state agencies should have drawn up plans of the types of enterprise to be sold, mechanisms for obtaining the highest sale price, and methods and requirements of sale. Evaluation of purchase bids and the terms of contracts and disclosure should have been transparent and predictable in order to discourage rent seeking and collusion. The task of restructuring an enterprise should have been left to the new owners, since state attempts to restructure prior to sale often reduced performance and created opportunities for corruption. The contracts should have established clear arm's-length post-privatization relations between the enterprise and government so as to reduce the risk of continuing market distortions. A balancing of deregulation and reregulation should have occurred at the same time as the divestiture, exposing new owners to genuine competition on a level playing field, forcing efficiency upon firms and shielding consumers from monopolistic market power, and establishing other guidelines in law for corporate governance and consumer protection.

The third problem, which largely explains the inadequacies of privatization policy, related to the systemic *personalism* of state decision-making procedures. In-depth studies of policy processes document the close personal relationships that shaped economic policy making, particularly with respect to privatization, in countries such as Argentina and Mexico (Heller 1990, 1993; Manzetti 1999; Teichman 2001). Business personalities enjoyed access to executive-level government policy networks. In the early stages of neoliberal reform, informal close-knit groupings and discretionary face-to-face contact gave state technocrats and private entrepreneurs an advantage by insulating them from intra-state factional conflicts over policy turf and societal resistance to neoliberal reform. Post-activist personal networks enabled the new elites to circumvent lobbying by clientelist, corporatist, and industrial-bureaucratic networks opposed to market reforms. The most charitable view of the problem would be to say that the closed personalistic nature of decision making about privatization policy simply reflected the efficiency 'law of small numbers' and the political sensitivity of neoliberal policy. However, personalist policy making, which was customary in Latin America long before neoliberalism, undermined the objectives of market reform. The 'honey pot' around which personalist networks swarmed in the neoliberal era was divestiture of public assets. Business allies of political leaders obtained preferential treatment in rigged bidding procedures for the sale of state-owned enterprises. Ad hoc secretive terms of sale were arranged privately with investors. The speed of privatization in the wake of crises probably also facilitated illegality.

The personalist style of policy process and closure against outside scrutiny help to explain the failure to construct formal and impartial institutional frameworks for the oversight of privatization agreements. In the rush to entice investors, privatization contracts contained extraordinary concessions (such as price and profit guarantees), and clauses that offered incentives for further monopolization and future rent seeking. Post-divestiture renegotiations of contracts were similarly undertaken through unaccountable networks. Regulatory agencies, if they existed at all, were underfinanced, understaffed, and headed by political appointees who lacked independence.

In many countries, 'the divestiture process did not lead to greater competition, but merely reassigned rents to the private sector without any regulatory structure for the supervision of the new monopolies' (Manzetti 1999: 329). An emasculated judiciary in Argentina quashed legal challenges to privatization and stalled investigations of irregularity and collusion. A study of telecommunications privatization noted that: 'Argentina's institutional heritage offers few tools for credibly committing government to refrain from arbitrary behaviour' (Hill and Abdala 1996: 209). Mexico only undertook serious institutional reforms to limit government–business collusion in privatization after 1994, following its entry into the North American Free Trade Agreement. Exceptions to the regional pattern, however, include Brazil and Chile. In Brazil, parliamentary, judicial, and media scrutiny of privatization prevented flagrant abuse of state discretionary power. In Chile, under both military and civilian governments, relations with business have been less clientelist, legal property and contract rights are more secure, and economic-policy networks are fairly disciplined and ideologically rational.

Widespread popular cynicism about corruption in privatization processes was a major reason for the discrediting of neoliberal reform in Latin America. As one observer noted, 'market reform in general, and privatization in particular has become associated with a corrupt process that created costly monopolies, concentrated wealth, and lined the pockets of corrupt political leaders and their cronies' (Teichman 2001: 213). Privatization and market deregulation are by far the most politically controversial elements of neoliberal reform. Selling off state enterprises and freeing markets has always had the greatest symbolic impact on public consciousness of neoliberal reforms. When governments that initially undertook coherent macroeconomic reforms finished up being thoroughly corrupted by privatization, this effectively sealed the political fate of neoliberal reform in general. Privatization debacles became the obvious target for criticism by neoliberalism's opponents.

Political backlash against neoliberalism was largely due to failure to implement the second-round reforms, which were to have focused not only on institutional reforms affecting privatization and market liberalization, but also other solutions to long-standing problems of poverty and extreme inequality. In the time it took for these 'hard' reforms to be planned and implemented, political resistance gained momentum. Anne Krueger (2000: 588–9) writes that the 'limited political capital' for market regulatory reform explains why 'failures at the early stages of reform can lead to the reversal of the entire process'. Resistance to neoliberalism was based on an incorrect perception that neoliberal reforms had been fully tested but had not worked as intended over five to ten years.

On the other hand, the first raft of post-crisis corrective reforms for medium-term reactivation of economies were hardly 'easy' for societies to absorb. When fully implemented, the reversal of activist and populist policies, including the freeing of labour markets, would, in the short term, bring bankruptcies and job losses, lower real wages, upward movements of prices, cuts to welfare and public services, general austerity, and the related social dislocation. Lower living standards were the costs of the failure of the previous models. By some estimates per capita consumption in Latin America declined by 20 to 30 per cent in the 1980s. The more extreme the preceding populist or activist model, the deeper was the crisis, the more extreme were the remedies, and the more severe was the impact on vulnerable groups.

There is a limit to what democratic governments can rapidly achieve in post-crises situations. Policies implemented by presidential decree eliminated some vestiges of economic activism. But even in presidential systems it was difficult for dominant parties to obtain majority support in legislatures for policies to

increase the level of economic competition, or to reverse excessive labour protections and over-generous state pensions. To maximize their chances of survival
in office, reformers were forced to compromise with pressure groups inside and
outside the political parties. Every advance in the reforms required some compensation to the losers. Limited state autonomy required political concessions in
return. This impeded reforms in key areas such as the management of local government finances and civil-service recruitment. Democratic constraints help to
explain why neoliberal reforms were often half-hearted, and why technocrats
were slow to design the institutions needed for economic modernization.

> Market reforms were the result of a political negotiation between audacious
> reformers and risk-averse politicians.... Orthodox sectors were quite insist-
> ent about the areas that were off-limits to technocrats: labour issues, the
> internal workings of the bureaucracy, the management of social services....
> The reforms of the 1990s granted reform-resistant sectors substantial polit-
> ical protection, that is, assured positions within parties and bureaucracies,
> access to and control of state resources, participation in policymaking,
> freedom to build clientelist-electoral machines, and monopolistic control of
> markets.
>
> (Corrales 2003: 98–9)

It proved difficult for neoliberal technocrats to explain the essential complemen-
tarities between reform components to their political constituencies. A macroeconomic reform in Argentina, called the 'convertibility law', fixed the peso to
the US dollar and prevented government from emitting more money than it held
in foreign-currency reserves. Almost overnight *convertabilidad* eradicated
Argentina's habitual inflation and fiscal deficits by making it impossible for
political power brokers to spend more than the state already held in public
coffers. But since the currency board confiscated the exchange-rate policy tool,
the technocrats understood that other measures, notably labour-market reform,
were needed to create a competitive export regime and to encourage new technologies. Existing labour laws restricted the adjustment capacity of business and
the public sector, and made it impossible to regenerate formal-sector employment growth after the first-round reforms. The Argentine parliament rejected the
reform proposals put forward by the technocrats. Blejer (2000) argues that when
Argentina was hit by a credit crunch following Mexico's financial crisis of
1994–5, the public misread the reasons for the resulting bankruptcies and layoffs. To a degree, this episode explains the political retreat from reform and
Argentina's return to populist-activist policy after 1995:

> it proved difficult to convince a sceptical public that reducing labour secur-
> ity and facilitating the firing process is bound to improve labour market con-
> ditions.... While in fact most of the bankruptcies took place in firms and
> sectors that were not fit to compete in the new, liberal environment created
> by the overall reform process and therefore reflected a delayed consequence

of the modernization strategy initiated a few years before, in the public's mind the increase in unemployment was rooted in macroeconomic factors and not in the structure of the labour market. This created demand for expansionary macroeconomic policies rather than support for reforms in labour relations.

(ibid.: 334)

A common pattern in Latin America was that redistributive and expansionary political pressures built up in the absence of second-stage reforms that, among other objectives, could have quarantined corrupt politicians. Technocrats were sidelined, and the resulting return to fiscal indiscipline and poor governance simply added to the popular perception – resulting from the privatization debacles – that the entire neoliberal exercise was motivated by malfeasant cronyism. However, neither the hijacking of reforms by political and business mafias, nor the concessions made to the vestiges of populist or activist political constituencies, can fully account for the failure to create pro-competitive regulatory frameworks for private enterprise or to reform judiciaries in Latin America.

The problems I have described fed into long-standing ideological ambivalence about capitalism in Latin America. In the immediate aftermath of the debt crises in the 1980s, dominant ideologies in Latin America remained statist and deterred market reforms. By the late 1980s and early 1990s, activist coalitions had fragmented. Much of the region experienced an ideological transformation by default, as some countries converged towards the open-economy model that Chile had doggedly pursued under an authoritarian regime since the previous decade. Even so, the motives of leading policymakers were complex. Neoliberal ideologies and interests were strong enough to change the overall direction of economic policy, but were not strong enough to prevent the capture of privatization by private interests. As one observer of the reforms has written: 'Presidents who privatized did not do so out of ideology. They took from the privatization philosophy what was convenient to them' (Manzetti 1999: 329). By the late 1990s, some countries had returned almost full circle to old habits and beliefs.

The preceding activist regimes had an ideological advantage. In the absence of well-articulated counterarguments, the protection of domestic economic enterprises appealed to nationalists, communitarians, and to the large urban coalitions of labour, middle-class, and business interests that benefited from import-substitution industrialization subsidies. It was more difficult for neoliberal democracies to maintain the momentum of reform and overcome long-held suspicions about market liberalization and foreign investment. Although liberalization of trade and investment reduces poverty, this cause–effect relationship is not easy for electorates to comprehend (Bhagwati 2004). Societies lose patience with structural changes that do not show quick and tangible gains.

Arguably activism had another perceptual advantage over the form of neoliberalism that thrived in Latin America. Corruption had always been present in the region. Even under ideologically activist regimes, it was widely known that powerful individuals were spectacularly enriched by corruption. Low-level routine and decentralized corruption was also an essential transmission belt for clientelist patronage in the public sector. But when undisciplined and personalistic styles of privatization and deregulation were grafted on to the dysfunctional system of political economy without impersonal rule of law, corruption underwent a modal change. It suddenly appeared to become more concentrated and unequal. Added to that, the process of democratization during the era of neoliberalism exposed state officials to public scrutiny as never before. As fewer people benefited from the old corruption, the new corruption was revealed and became an easy target of political opposition to neoliberalism.

Neoliberalism in Latin America generated dramatic spurts of economic growth and a temporary return to stability. Import and credit bonanzas produced neoliberal boomlets. In principle, neoliberal policy should have ruled out politically motivated injections of government money in the economy. However, a long history of pump priming under populist and activist regimes bequeathed unrealistic expectations of immediate gains in economic fortune. For much the same reasons identified by Juan Bautista Alberdi in the late nineteenth century, the region had become accustomed to artificial short-lived prosperity built on unsustainable foundations without ever seeming to learn the lessons of crisis. The way that privatization was implemented in most of Latin America simply reinforced capitalism's bad image in a region characterized by extreme income inequality. The region was long familiar with the systematic abuse of monopolistic political and economic power, yet completely unfamiliar with capitalism itself. Privatization was suspected with some justification of eliminating a source of state revenue – a milking cow – to pay for social services and political patronage, and as a policy that further enriched members of the elite. Brave leaders who proclaimed a market-reform agenda were bound to fail, as the novelist and liberal politician Mario Vargas Llosa found in 1990 when he lost to Alberto Fujimori in Peru's presidential elections (on winning, Fujimori wasted no time in implementing the 'shock' programme that Vargas Llosa had promised).

Yet even the limited ideological progress in Latin America during the decade of neoliberal reform demonstrates that vested interests are not insurmountable obstacles to economic reform. A quite broad coalition of economic interests aligned with neoliberalism. When political and economic crises coincide with coherent technocratic and political leadership and a new intellectual orientation, the ideological brew can be a powerful one. Well-designed and skilfully implemented capitalist-leaning reforms can produce rapid and tangible benefits for large populations. By and large, ministerial cabinets in Latin America during the 1990s were economically literate. A substantial number of the region's leading public officials were graduates of management and economics faculties in North American universities, and felt at home with theories of the 'free market' and 'lean government'. It was not inevitable that technocrats who conscientiously pursued orthodox market policies for a few years would subsequently succumb to the pressures and temptations of personalist political networks. In Argentina, it was rather a case of some effective technocrats being pushed aside by a corrupt political class.

Given the real possibilities of reform within constrained political timetables, the remaining questions – aside from availability of relevant knowledge and the quality of ideology – relate to best-practice sequencing. Krueger (2000) offers useful examples of 'nuts and bolts' trade-offs during second-stage reforms. It is clear that many of the needed reforms are closely interrelated in functional terms. But is there a higher payoff from removing minimum-wage requirements or reducing job protection? Payoffs from labour-market reform may be similar to those of tax reform. If both are contentious, does one choose one or pursue both together? To give another example, privatization may be more successful when a well-developed financial sector already exists. Decision makers may operate better when faced with such choices if they can judge when to tolerate second-best solutions rather than pursue unattainable goals. Arguably the decisions relating to trade-offs between privatization and market regulation are of special importance because of their potential political significance for broad swathes of the population in Latin American societies where – by comparison with most of East Asia – there is considerable and long-standing political and press freedom. In Brazil, for example, democratic oversight delayed the divestiture process for some years. As a consequence of this public scrutiny, subsequent approval of privatization remained comparatively high. Yet in Brazil it was touch and go whether privatization would occur at all.

In theory, governments that sell loss-making public enterprises should aim to construct regulatory frameworks that provide incentives for new owners to create modern private enterprises. In this sense, each privatization experience can be thought of as a microcosm of the challenges faced by a developing society in transition to capitalism. Privatization is a relatively new post-activist or post-socialist phenomenon. In the 1980s and 1990s there were few if any privatization 'templates' available to policymakers anywhere in the world. Fine-tuning continues to this day. During neoliberal reforms, appropriate choices about the methods of privatization, and public confidence that the chosen methods are correct and will be properly applied, is largely determined by the available knowledge about best practice but also by the quality and flexibility of the political leadership and the decision-making processes. Those qualities reflect modes of governance and the nature of institutions in society. Yet, it is also important to consider the specific *techniques* of privatization. Technical methods of privatization have the potential to generate their own significant institutional effects. Could privatization have contributed more generally to institutional modernization?

Decisions about effective regulation inevitably involve issues of policy sequencing. Should regulation precede privatization? It may be difficult to build up political momentum behind radical regulatory reform before a society has experienced the harsh reality of *imperfect* privatization. On the other hand, investors may be more likely to show an interest in state divestitures (and to pay a higher price) if they see that institutions act predictably; that property rights and contracts are fairly secure; and that government has already legislated for sustainable and transparent post-privatization commitments to markets and

private enterprise. Meaningful regulatory reform after privatization can be difficult if state officials are reluctant to admit that errors were caused by inadequate
regulation. Post-privatization regulatory reform is also complicated by the fact
that privatized entities and their shareholders and employees will be in a better
position to bargain to maintain existing privileges; to renegotiate rents on advantageous terms; or to threaten non-compliance with regulations. It may be hard to
bring about changes in regulation after privatization.

Chong and López-de-Silanes (2005: 54–5) make these arguments forcefully.
But they conclude that the risks are *greater* if policymakers do *not* proceed with
privatization in the absence of good regulations. Perfecting the regulatory framework may take time, and this must not be an excuse for postponing privatization.
Even without the preexisting institutional deficiencies in countries such as
Mexico, Argentina, and Peru, it would not have been easy for modernizing technocrats to obtain and maintain political support for a policy sequence that constructed regulatory frameworks prior to privatization. Technocrats had enough to
do just securing passage for first-stage macroeconomic and deregulatory projects.
Post-crises opportunities for privatization were of short duration, and needed to
be capitalized on quickly. A simultaneous raft of institutional reforms would have
required motivations, power, resources, skills, and expertise that almost certainly
were not available at the time. Governments that were not averse to displeasing
nationalistic elements might have obtained technical support for reregulation from
international agencies and consultants. However, institutional change takes longer
than divestiture and market liberalization, and regulatory reforms would have
faced opposition in hostile parliaments. Technocrats also had to overcome resistance to privatization within their own political parties.

All these factors help to explain why privatization in Latin America was often
rushed, and why the bulk of the relevant regulation logically followed privatization rather than preceded it. Milton Friedman, whose ideas helped to shape Latin
America's earliest neoliberal reforms in Chile, later commented that: 'Privatization is meaningless if you don't have the rule of law' (Friedman 2002: xviii). He
was referring to privatizations in Russia, which created huge private monopolies
with enough power to recentralize market planning in private hands. It is clearly
true that privatization will not promote long-run growth unless there is 'rule of
law'. Yet three counterarguments, which Friedman might well have endorsed,
are relevant in the short run. First, there are strong theoretical and historical
reasons for supporting the view that market expansion is itself the critical vector
and pressure mechanism for the evolution of modern institutions (see Chapter 2).
Second, when a country has a post-crisis political opportunity to privatize rapidly
it would be unwise to delay until such time as a legal-regulatory system can be
established. This, in essence, was the advice that some noted economists offered
to Eastern European countries in the 1990s. In their discussion of the Russian
privatization experience, Hay *et al.* (1996) make the point forcefully.

Several writers on transition have argued for the introduction of legal and
regulatory institutions before privatization, so that privatized firms can from

the start operate in a market environment. Unfortunately, before privatiza-tion, when all property is state-owned, no private parties are interested in institutional reform, and hence such reforms are unlikely to take place. The effective political pressure for legal reform appears only after privatization. Surely, some of the laws that the property owners lobby for serve their private, rather than social, interest (protection from imports and from entry are good examples). Still, property owners would typically oppose the bad laws that prevent them from using the legal system, and support laws that conform to the standard business practice. Both of these positions are part of a good reform.... The politically feasible order of institutional reform, then, is privatization first, introduction of legal rules second, and bureaucratic reform only in the very long run.

(ibid.: 565)

A third argument is relevant to the discussions of Latin American and East Asian market reforms. Countries in both these regions did not face the very high risk of criminality that former socialist countries ran in the 1990s. Premodern procedural norms in the Asian and Latin American state institutions were clearly far from being perfectly compatible with market reforms. Yet arguably the exist-ing basic framework of state legal-administrative structures was sufficiently evolved to sustain a market-reform program. In sharp contrast, the formal insti-tutions of socialist countries were already re-engineered to perform socialist functions. Fear, propaganda, secrecy, and totalitarianism had institutionalized doctrines, habits, and organizations that were diametrically opposed to market freedom. In that context, a loosening of socialist structures caused the disinteg-ration of political and economic order. In the resulting vacuum, new alliances were forged that permitted 'robber capitalists' to operate with impunity. The functionally equivalent political transitions in both Latin America and East Asia were different. Even during periods of authoritarian rule in the 1990s, economic reforms still had to be justified and legitimized politically. Although checks and balances were not as sophisticated as in capitalist societies, quite intense legal, media, and parliamentary scrutiny of market-reform processes in Latin America did at least demonstrate that existing institutions offered a reasonable degree of protection against the severest abuses of economic privilege.

Lessons of neoliberalism

Neoliberalism can simply grind to a halt because economic reforms have not worked as they should in theory and could in practice. However, the underlying difficulties in Latin America related to continuing entanglements with the pre-ceding mode of economic governance, poor leadership, lack of imagination and foresight, errors of implementation, inadequate economic regulation, the weak-ening of a regime's resolve to reform, and, in some countries, an eventual return to old ways. Neoliberal crisis results not from economic policies, which are usually designed to remedy the ills of activism, but rather from their implementation in environments characterized by economic and political turmoil, forced retrenchment and painful restructuring, ingrained personalistic and discretionary procedural norms of policy making, deeply embedded political profit making and regulatory closure, and the lack of credible institutions to enforce market competition. After too little market competition there was suddenly much more, but often of the wrong kind. New markets created by deregulation and privatization lacked transparency and incubated new forms of rent seeking.

Despite all the debate about neoliberalism's *impact* in the 1980s and 1990s, it is worth noting that few countries implemented a comprehensive neoliberal project (as defined by neoliberals). The reforms tended to be hesitant, limited to a few sectors, and were prone to reversal. Most reforms were short-run pragmatic solutions to short-run pressures. Although some reformers aspired to full-scale modernization, the overriding policy rationale of neoliberal policy was to urgently restore economic health after catastrophic populist or activist crises. Strategies to improve the long-run flexibility of economies were not uppermost in the minds of policymakers in the aftermath of crises.

From the perspective of this book, the broad lesson is that neoliberalism was a lost opportunity to undertake the sequenced Weberian capitalist transition – market to law, law to bureaucracy, bureaucracy to democracy. The intention here is not to dismiss the utility of neoliberal reforms that were undertaken, nor to disparage the ideas and motives behind them. It is easy to understand that they were undertaken under extreme pressure and faced many constraints. Even if it failed to respond to structural pressures for regulated market competition, there is no doubt at all that neoliberalism raised the scope and quality of market transactions to new levels in Latin America.

It was justifiable to proceed with privatization when appropriate judicial and regulatory frameworks were not yet in place. Especially in Chile, Mexico, and Brazil, the market-oriented economic approach did, in fact, complement genuine efforts to strengthen the rule of law and to make state administrations more accountable, impersonal, and effective. It is apparent with hindsight that these efforts and experiences raised the skills of policymakers, and spread knowledge about the functional interdependence of modern economies and institutions (Santiso and Whitehead 2006). However, it cannot be said that neoliberal reformers in most countries genuinely expanded markets in a rational sequence, or that they undertook capitalist reforms with integrated economic and institutional components. Too often it was apparent that the professed commitment to neoliberal reform was not a commitment to transparency, predictability, genuine competition, and impartial justice.

Neoliberalism self-destructs because of the institutional lag of legal-regulatory development, which in Latin America was largely a consequence of continued and sometimes heightened personalism linked to policy processes. In part, therefore, the inability to progress towards second-stage institutional reforms represented a general failure of leadership. On the other hand, we have seen that neoliberalism did not have the stage to itself. In return for some autonomy, technocrats were forced to compensate numerous political interests.

Neoliberalism traverses a dangerous political period between painful post-crisis adjustments and the eventual outcome of economic restructuring. Even when neoliberal reforms begin to show positive results in some areas, further trade and price liberalization can quickly alter the power balance and motivate interest groups to engage in political action against neoliberal reform. For these reasons, the political causes of neoliberal crises have ultimately been more important than the technical and economic causes.

No single factor can adequately account for Latin America's failure to construct better regulatory institutions. Analysts and practitioners who want to draw valuable lessons from neoliberal crises in Latin America should consider the following points. The intensity or harshness of neoliberal reform reflects the severity of the preceding crisis, which in turn reflects the extremeness and longevity of the activist model. Neoliberal reforms, even by their own limited criteria, were not fully implemented. Democratic processes and political bargaining limited the power of neoliberal reformers. The fate of neoliberal reform was sealed by the fact that reforms were mainly economic in nature and neglected essential institutional components. In addition, future reformers might consider whether it was right to rely on personalist policy networks as the procedural means for achieving reform outcomes, even when the 'law of small numbers' counsels in its favour. They should also assess the optimal speed of sequencing between stages of reform, in order not to lose momentum and legitimacy. Perhaps the most important lesson is to be aware that avoidable failures of neoliberal policy – in particular with respect to the markets–law nexus – can discredit capitalist solutions and strengthen anti-capitalist prejudices. The resurgence of populist socialism in some Latin American countries is testament to that.

If the institutional reforms advocated in this book had been undertaken during a 'second stage' of neoliberal reform but had ended in crisis, the analysis would need to refocus on crises resulting from attempted *capitalist* transitions. That did not occur. The country that went furthest with second-stage reforms, Chile, did not experience such a crisis. This points to a more general conclusion. Despite the disappointing results in Latin America, neoliberalism is generally preferable to activism. Both are 'developmental' in the sense that they can lay foundations for capitalist transition and may evolve in a capitalist direction. But whereas 'neoliberal myopia' can be cured with good institutions, the sources of 'activist decay' probably cannot be eliminated without a major change in economic-policy orientation. Statist regimes have no equivalent option of institutional upgrading to prevent crisis. Institutions that could indefinitely perform the technical tasks of economic activism have not been invented. Given what is known about the limits of human rationality, they probably never will be. Compared with relatively parametric neoliberal policies, discretionary state activism is far more knowledge-intensive and exerts greater demands on dispersed and everyday human rationality.

These arguments are not intended to repudiate activism altogether. In moderation, some selective activism might be justified if institutional capacity is sufficient to bear its weight safely. But countries can and should learn from the dismal sequence that follows prolonged and wholesale activism. Although the efficiency time-span of state activism is inherently very limited, its decay time-span can be indefinite. If activist decay results in activist crisis, it is also possible that the neoliberal effort to cope with the effects of that crisis will itself result in neoliberal crisis. That is because neoliberalism, which almost by definition is a corrective to activism, inherits a dysfunctional yet deeply embedded institutional structure that is difficult to reform. A Weberian sequence, on the other hand, aims to establish good policies and effective institutions at the outset, without too many unnecessary evolutionary detours, and without veering from one extreme to another.

7   The transition sequence

Previous chapters have examined the institutional nature of capitalism and of precapitalism, general dynamics of institutional change, factors of human agency that drive change, and reasons why societies do not make the transition to capitalism. What are the relevant policy lessons? How might motivated and rational technocrats put transition theory into practice? How does the Weberian model translate into workable guidelines for reform? The plan of the chapter is as follows. The first section explores a policy priority sequence. The second section suggests a crisis-induced sequence of opportunities for initiating and sustaining capitalist transition. In the remaining two sections I look in more detail at how reforms might be implemented in the legal and administrative subsystems, and examine the insights that can be gleaned from literature on legal and administrative reform.

For capitalist theory to be practically applied by policymakers it is necessary to bring to light and systematize the procedural principles that give shape and consistency to a 'causal chain' of market-led and law-led transformations, which lead, in turn, to the modernization of public administration and political representation. I propose a succession of discrete policy regimes of fairly short duration that overcome obstacles to the construction of institutions. The sequence is a *mechanism for building state strength*. Its key procedural goal is the depersonalization of the state.

Policy priorities

In ideal but unrealistic circumstances, all the reforms needed to unleash capitalist transition could be undertaken simultaneously. The state would be strong, flexible, and autonomous from anti-reform interests. Policymakers would be knowledgeable, honest, competent, prudent, and powerful. Economic and political conditions would allow policymakers sufficient time and resources to plan and implement reforms. All the needed expertise, technology, and financing would be on hand. This is a utopia. It is unreasonable to expect that institutional reforms of law, administration, and political representation could be undertaken together during a single policy regime. It may be impractical to undertake complex and possibly unpopular economic reforms at the same time as institutional changes that are poorly understood by citizens and whose purpose is to overturn long-standing customs and privileges. In addition, policymakers face formidable cognitive and motivational constraints.

If only for reasons of expediency, therefore, the social scientist and the reformer must find a way of achieving capitalist ends in manageable stages. They need to evaluate theory and evidence and to form a reasoned view of the ends and means of capitalism. The present chapter tries to identify more precisely the *priorities* among the *means*. Should policy priorities always be decided by judging the apparent suitability of their implementation in a particular national context, as proponents of many development recipes argue? Or, should some precedence be given to logical priorities, like the ones we find in Weber's extrapolations from history? Is it not useful to try objectively to specify social-scientific 'laws' applying to the calculation of means to ends in almost all situations? Weber said the following about sociological method.

> Sociological generalizations ... as 'laws' [are] typical probabilities confirmed by observation to the effect that under certain given conditions an expected course of social action will occur, which is understandable in terms of the typical motives and typical subjective intentions of the actors. These generalizations are both understandable and definite in the highest degree insofar as the typically observed course of action can be understood in terms of the purely rational pursuit of an end, or where for reasons of methodological convenience such a theoretical type can be heuristically employed.... In such cases it is legitimate to assert that insofar as the action was rigorously rational it could not have taken any other course because for technical reasons, given their clearly defined ends, no other means were available to the actors.
>
> (Weber 1978: 18–19)

If this line of reasoning is applied to the study of capitalist transitions, it could justifiably be said that in *most* developing societies only *some* rational-functional means are actually available to policymakers (i.e. the procedural means identified in this book). On the other hand, we have seen that 'typical motives' or 'subjective intentions' of political and economic actors do not guarantee a good correspondence between the actions they actually choose to pursue and the 'law' of means to ends. Historical experiences of calculating means to ends might well suggest a contrary 'law', one that says policymakers *do* routinely set themselves goals that they are simply unable to achieve. Because their actions are heavily influenced by their emotions, ideologies, values, and interests, policymakers are frequently unable or unwilling to fully evaluate whether the chosen or available technical means will really be adequate for attaining their ideal ends.

So, what are the relevant 'generalizations' about means and ends of capitalist transition? From Weber's writings I have extracted a realistic hypothesis about workable phases of economic and institutional reform. Elements of a development priority schema are revealed by weighing up the relative importance of causal-functional relationships that logically and empirically exist between market expansion, impersonal third-party regulation, the depersonalization of state administration, and free political representation. The schema is a synthesis of institutional changes during capitalism's emergence, and a conceptual apparatus for revealing how the original evolutionary patterns of the transition can be compressed into shorter, focused, and more manageable *policy* processes. The following summary of the main findings outlined in Chapters 2 and 3 describes the raw material for such a schema:

1   The transitional state establishes formal-legal parameters and impersonal procedures for regulating the state's internal and external relationships. This is the basis of the predictability and continuity of modern state action. The procedural norms are non-discriminatory and meritocratic, and they presume a formal separation of public authority from personal authority.

2   The enforcement of impersonal procedural norms has the effect of delimiting the scope of state economic action (and state economic activism is minimized as a means of facilitating the implementation of state impersonality). The state's primary economic functions are legal-regulatory, namely the diminishment of particularistic privileges and protection of general privileges or rights. Its secondary functions are the natural state monopolies, mainly monetary and fiscal policy. The impersonal state largely abstains from activist tasks, which by definition are discretionary.

3   A major cause of state dysfunction is the transitional state's continuing natural impulse to control economic action pervasively rather than parametrically by creating opportunities for economic advantage that arise from political decisions. By increasing its functions the state creates incentives for discretionary and exclusionary behaviour by officials, and diminishes the chances of depersonalizing the state.

4   The state can dominate business because it has unrivalled authority to impose its will. It has the incentive to exercise economic controls in order to maintain its authority. However, since the state's knowledge of markets is limited, its regulatory authority is more efficiently employed at arm's-length. Further, if the state is not itself regulated impersonally public officials are likely to pursue their own interests or to fall in with non-state interests. Officials are naturally hostile to impersonal market freedom, which they find threatening, hard to control, and hard to understand.

5   Rule of law in the economy is the first institutional condition of capitalist transition. The evolving relationship of law and economy begins with the expansion of markets and emergence of market ethics. If they prove to be efficient, informal market norms evolve into socially sanctioned convention or directly into state regulation. If a formal infrastructure of enforcement exists, market ethics can transmute rapidly into law. Market interests create the demand for formal guarantees of continuous public peace and protection of rights. Property rights may begin as negative privilege, but become general guarantees of legitimate market freedom.

6   Law becomes the instrument for achieving outcomes of economic regula-
     tion. But legal development that occurs in the absence of market expansion
     can have objectives that are unrelated to capitalist transition and may
     impede the transition. On balance, market liberalization remains the source
     of the requisite pressures for economically effective legal reforms.
7   Motivated technocratic leadership facilitates and speeds up capitalist trans-
     ition. In early stages of capitalist transition, organized interest representation
     in the political process can overload the state and diminish demands for
     market liberalization, impartial law, and impersonal administration. Soon,
     however, democracy and capitalism 'belong together'.

Weber's theory of the origins of capitalism guides a rational contemporary
sequence for the construction of capitalism. First, the expansion and liberalization of markets makes almost *everybody* acutely aware of the legal imperative
for regulation of markets. Second, the parametric function of the state reduces
the scope for discretionary intervention in the economy. In consequence, the
impersonal mode of legal regulation restricts or eliminates what may hitherto
have been large-scale economic roles of public administration. An underdeveloped state cannot realize its comparative advantages through discretionary economic administration. Instead, reformers strengthen the state by focusing on its
parametric roles. Third, out of the consolidating legal-administrative order
emerge new and more productive roles for state bureaucracy, and the foundations are laid for genuinely competitive forms of modern political representation.
Once the legally enforceable impersonal order is established, new and feasible
roles for the state *might* include a variety of interventionist actions that could not
have been successfully carried out by a precapitalist or transitional 'activist'
regime. When the state has largely been depersonalized, thorough democratization of all levels of the polity can also be more safely undertaken without
risking the continuity of the transition.

    All of this amounts to (1) a set of warnings about the risks of overextending
the transitional state with non-priority functions, and (2) compelling arguments
for giving overriding priority to measures that will depersonalize state procedural processes. Translating these insights into policy proposals is no simple
matter. The concepts we are utilizing at this stage of the discussion are already
highly distilled ideal types. Some factors that prospective critics of a Weberian
model of rapid transition might identify as impurities or defects in the ideal type
– such as doubtful logic, or an empirical exception to the rule – have been considered, evaluated, and left behind in the historical data. Inevitably, there is a
trade-off between gains to be had from presenting the lessons in pure conceptual
format, and the loss of explanatory detail that results from abstracting from the
messy reality of economic and institutional processes. Such problems can never
be fully overcome. However, policy practitioners are legitimately entitled to
access distilled ideas that capture key lessons in order to safely guide early
reform efforts. The schema is formulated here as a set of questions and answers
to consider when an opportunity for reform arises. It can be noted that the

following 'objectives' relate to the sequence itself rather than to the implied rewards – such as economic growth – that come from following the sequence.

1   What policy designs are needed even if construction of the corresponding formal institutions is not immediately feasible? Answer: *Market liberalization*. Objective: The cognitive and ethical experience of impersonal market exchange.
2   What institutional constructions are most difficult and most perilous to delay? Answer: Impersonal *legal regulation* and the enforcement of market freedom and formally equal economic rights. Objective: Beneficial market competition.
3   What institutional constructions are needed soon, but can be delayed and are relatively easily achieved? Answer: Impersonal *public administration* and limits on the scope of state action. Objective: Strongly adaptive parametric state rule.
4   What institutional construction is needed soon, but might be better to delay? Answer: Impersonal *free political representation*. Objective: Ongoing selections of good leaders and good policies, and the maintenance of state procedural norms.

An assumption underlying this sequence is that the dynamic of *market* expansion is autonomous from law, administration, and political representation, while market and legal reforms generate systemic pressures for administrative and political reforms. As well as being the cause of long-run prosperity and technological progress, the expansion of private enterprise in the internal and external economies reveals the desirability of social norms and property and contract obligations that improve the environment of economic as well as political transactions. A proto-institutional market ethic is therefore the initial source of the political pressure for the creation of a legal-regulatory order that formally enforces norms of market behaviour, and which benefits producer and consumer interests alike. Since most developing countries already possess at least a rudimentary formal infrastructure of law, this political pressure can, in the sorts of empirical circumstances examined in Chapter 6, show some instantaneous results.

Based on the analysis thus far, I conclude that if countries were to be faced with a stark choice between activist industrial policy and the market policies advocated by the 'Washington Consensus' (Kuczynsky and Williamson 2003; Williamson 2006), the latter are preferable because they fit better with a transition sequence – beginning with market expansions – that is likely to encourage the creation of impersonal institutions. Pursuing the logic of economic and institutional proportionality found in Weberian economic sociology, I draw the conclusion that economic activism will in the end be dysfunctional but is at best a temporary solution to development problems, while economic neoliberalism will have more affinity with capitalist transformational goals. The basic point is that market expansion first breaks down the social barriers to the construction of the modern state.

The ethical transition, being 'informal', is perhaps the least tangible link in the sequence, and merits further discussion. Ethical change could be left out of the sequence altogether if legal transition were *certain* to quickly follow market transition; a leap that would require very motivated and resourceful policy leadership. On the other hand, even institutionally myopic market liberalization can be a positive force for creative destruction, irrespective of whether it instantaneously stimulates economic growth and institutional reform. A sudden market opening jolts society, induces useful kinds of learning and adaptation, and creates the *atmosphere* of entrepreneurship and innovation. It is better that populations become accustomed to operating markets sooner rather than later.

It can be justifiably asserted that the experience of markets induces ethical development. On that point, Weber's explanation of history is persuasive. Commerce breaks down communitarian norms of hostility towards outsiders, creating impersonal communities in which economic action is oriented to calculation of profits, exchange of commodities, and competitive survival. In Weber's words: 'The market is a relationship which transcends the boundaries of neighbourhood, kinship, group, or tribe. Originally, it is indeed the only *peaceful* relationship of such kind' (Weber 1978: 637). Subsequently, the ethic of fair dealing carries over from the old community to the new community of market exchange simply because almost *everybody* knows that in markets, exactly as in every other social relationship, 'honesty is the best policy'.

There is no developing country in the world where most people do not *already* know in principle, and were not reared to know, that 'honesty is the best policy'. When markets become open and when competition becomes extensive a learning process commences that consists of finessing the market ethic and adapting it to a more complex economic environment. The process of learning the ethic can happen almost overnight. A peasant farmer in Peru who begins to make the weekly trip to the local marketplace to sell a bundle of produce quickly learns to truck and barter, to remonstrate and haggle, and to cheat little if at all. In time, the same individual may move to the city and there rapidly *relearns* the ethic of fair dealing as befits a more sophisticated urban informal market. If government incentives encourage it, the next stage could be this person's graduation to formally regulated markets where the risks and burdens of premodern ethical regulation are alleviated. However, and this is the central issue, whenever the state *suppresses* markets the old norms of hostile zero-sum dealing will again begin to permeate social, political, and economic transactions.

The opposing argument, of course, is that 'free markets' know no ethical bounds at all. Looking at the mafias of politicians and robber capitalists who became dominant through market liberalization in Russia or Argentina in the 1990s, it is difficult to accept the claim that market expansion will of itself produce desirable market ethics in the *short* run; indeed, it is hard to believe this proposition even if one does have historical knowledge of the *longer*-run evolution of ethics and law. It is easier to give credence to this apparently controversial claim if it is kept in mind that Russian and Argentine political and economic mafias created narrow monopolistic markets by capturing state agencies responsible for deregulation, and hijacking the bidding process for the privatization of public enterprises. The model of policy sequences proposed in this chapter requires the dominant group of policy technocrats to be more appropriately *motivated* and to have *knowledge* of the sequence; they are not blindly muddling through, and they are not hostage to interest groups. Robber capitalists are really no different from the peasant farmer. They also know that 'honesty is the best policy'. The problem in Russia and Argentina was that existing incentives worked to neutralize that principle. The essential market competition was missing. The unravelling of socialist structures in Russia and of statist-corporatist structures in Argentina in the 1990s created institutional vacuums where fresh alliances of regulatory closure and political profit making were forged, allowing robber capitalists to control new markets with impunity.

Notwithstanding such problems, we can be sure that ethical transition will occur subsequent to privatization, albeit more slowly. As long as the ruling elite permits political dissent and institutional checks and balances, and as long as the relevant information flows to citizens, the corruption of privatization is certain to generate widespread ethical awareness that the resulting *market* failure was in this instance caused by *government* failure to control corruption. Ethical viewpoints will be heard and political pressure for regulatory reforms will grow (so far that has happened to a greater extent in Argentina than in Russia). As I argued in Chapter 3, market ethics are not determined solely by national culture. Rather like the market itself, ethics are autonomous and spread by selection. An ideology that promotes the market ethic can be the instrument for prising open a closed economy.

There is a further issue to consider. Although it applies well to most developing countries, there are possible deviations from the ideal-type sequence of reform. An obvious exception is the rare circumstance of a developed meritocratic state administration existing prior to market freedom and rule of law. This was the case when East Asian countries with strong Confucian and/or British late-colonial bureaucratic traditions – in particular Japan, South Korea, Taiwan, China, Singapore, Hong Kong, and Malaysia – fomented rapid economic growth that depended on state-guided forms of market expansion. There are good reasons for supposing, however, that the imperatives of the Weberian sequence will prevail regardless of cultural or bureaucratic exceptionalism. Without countervailing institutions of impersonal law and free political representation, effective state administration is only ever a temporary phenomenon. Furthermore, no argument to the effect that the Weberian developmental sequence can be circumvented has yet been validated empirically, since none of the 'bureaucracy-first' transitions have yet produced a capitalist institutional system.

A very different type of exception to the sequence is not wholly unrelated to the first. It may seem logical to suggest a four-part sequence for the simple reason that a capitalist social system consists of four discrete institutional subsystems. However, it is not the 'separateness' of the subsystems that dictates their phased construction. It would be better and faster if they were built all at once. The fact that dominant ideologies and vested interests are hostile to capitalist transition is the primary reason why this does not happen. By comparison with the ideological obstacles, the technical and resource difficulties of institutional construction are considerably less important. Were it not for ideological and interest-group resistance, a rapid two- or three-stage transformation would be constrained only by cultural, cognitive, and economic structures, which are certainly not insurmountable.

In any event, a four-stage construction schema does have the advantage of building in safety measures that typify the 'steady and sure' incremental path of institutional change. In the words of Charles Lindblom (1988: 245), a 'fast-moving sequence of small changes can more speedily accomplish a drastic alteration of the status quo'. Unlike proposals for once-only holistic change, rapid small steps 'do not stir up great antagonisms and paralyzing schisms'. That lesson applies especially well to policy change achieved through 'partisan mutual adjustment' in an advanced democracy. Similarly in a developing country, however, a revolutionary depersonalization of the entire state apparatus from one year to the next would be ill advised. Instead, fast-moving sphere-by-sphere reform of markets, law, administration, and representation permits policymakers to focus energies on one subsystem at a time while better restraining the forces that would prevent reform.

A crisis-induced sequence

Having identified the primary *direction* of causation in capitalist transitions, we can turn our attention to the usual catalyst or propelling *mechanism* of change. The relevant institutional and economic changes can be viewed as punctuated knock-on or multiplier effects of crises. In one form or another, crises pattern and motivate the sequence of reforms. The periodic transformational incidents of capitalist transition normally reflect predictable behavioural characteristics of social systems under strain. Crises have a disturbing way of disclosing the functioning of a system. When something goes wrong this may permit the first glimpse of a better way of doing things.

Let us begin by recalling the various types of crisis. *Development* crises expose the malfunctioning of precapitalist societies, the process by which economies try to adapt to institutional conditions, and the institutional requisites of the transition to capitalism. *Capitalist* crises that regularly occur because of wave-like movements of alternating prosperity and downturn in the advanced economies, lay bare the workings of capitalism itself. A structural crisis of either type signals that institutional adjustment is urgently required or is already underway to correct a mismatch between institutional forms and the nature or pace of economic change. Since capitalism's *continuing* development is related to the society's capacity for discontinuous adaptation in response to theoretically foreseeable but in practice unexpected turbulence of global or local origin, and since this capacity is both rare and difficult to maintain, the social scientist can learn more about capitalism by studying the maladaptations. Having recognized crisis as the signal for reform, it is then possible to examine how policymakers react, and the interests and ideologies that seem to work for and against recovery and transformation. It may be possible to suggest better adaptations in preparation for subsequent crises.

I have identified three major classes of crisis. The first are retrogressive *cyclical* crises that reproduce underdevelopment in societies where, in the absence of real ideological alternatives, populist promises of rapid economic gratification interact with political clientelism, patronage systems, and discretionary modes of policy making. The second are potentially evolutionary *developmental* crises produced by a regime's persistence with coherent but ultimately unsustainable models of political economy (typically activist or neoliberal), giving rise to disproportionality between institutional capacity and the economic policies. The third are evolutionary *capitalist* crises resulting from intense market competition for diminishing profits from clusters of technological and managerial innovations in the dynamic heartlands of advanced economies, which hold out the promise of a future wave of prosperity founded on even more technological and economic innovations and institutional adaptations.

The second and third forms of crises are compatible with capitalist development in disequilibrium. The appropriate policy response is rapid institutional innovation designed to create or restore proportional regulatory architecture. Recovery from crisis and commencement of new growth is achieved by simply correcting the institutional lag, or by entirely changing the economic model. It can also be observed in each class of crisis that the opportunity for change is *recurrent*. Furthermore, I have drawn a distinction between largely unavoidable *functional* crises of an evolving capitalist system and the relatively more avoidable *dysfunctional* crises of precapitalist systems. Recovery in either case depends on creative destruction, the quality of political leadership, and the incentives a population has to overcome strains without externalizing their causes or adopting escapist doctrines that offer illusory protection against needed change. Leaders and populations may be unwilling to recognize the underlying institutional causes of crisis. The effects are more catastrophic and long-lasting if state organizations are not equipped to adapt to turbulence. An acute dilemma for developing societies is that the ability to cope with strain reflects preexisting institutional strengths. The purpose of the Weberian policy sequence, then, is to build up that strength and break the vicious cycle.

At every opportunity skilful policy leaders can implement their plans for subsystem reform in relatively quick succession while adjusting for earlier errors. The policy imperatives correspond closely, though not perfectly, with the historical sequences of the original development of capitalism. Jumping forwards to 'administrative' or 'democratic' economic interventions while delaying construction of an impersonal legal order for market governance is likely only to result in regressive crisis. On the other hand, some crises, while avoidable in theory, are probably inevitable. Either way, crises can structure the Weberian sequence.

The *crisis-induced policy sequence* outlined in this section identifies precapitalist beginnings, basic reform priorities for emulating advanced institutions, and recurrent reform opportunities. It provides an alternative route for countries that regularly miss opportunities to initiate or deepen capitalist transition. For convenience, our starting point will be the stylized condition of a twentieth-century country in South Asia, Southeast Asia, or Latin America with a quasi-modern formal institutional façade, whose governments have in the past – for prolonged periods of time and with a variety of genuine or deceptive motives – pursued nationalist or quasi-socialist central planning models, often with endorsement from Western development economists. Inter alia, these countries nationalized enterprises or protected them from competition, and otherwise repressed markets by restricting trade and suppressing the price mechanism. Eventually, however, a turning point is reached. The state is overextended. Markets have not flourished because they have not become impersonal. Neither the state nor markets adequately provision society. The legitimacy of rulers is in decline. Economic and political crisis looms on the horizon.

The following list represents an effort to distil the aetiology of crisis-induced policy sequences down to its most basic elements. It identifies the underlying cause in each of a succession of crises.

1   The first crisis – of the model of state economic intervention – signals the urgency of market expansion. Stabilization and market reforms, especially privatization and market liberalization, encourage growth, competition, and innovation. The population experiences a surge in market delivery of goods, services, and employment. But there is a mismatch between the pace of economic and institutional change. Market reform occurs without complementary reform of the regulatory framework. The resulting abuses of market power delegitimize the reforms and dampen competition.

2   The second crisis – of the legal system – signals the urgency of improving regulatory capacity with respect to property and contract rights, competition policy, and aspects of corporate governance. Once rule of law is applied in the economy, the legal system interprets and enforces government legislation and court rulings. It investigates malfeasance and responds to plaintiffs against monopolistic and fraudulent practices. Limited, clear, and realistic priority rules of market action are enacted. Nevertheless, rule of law is hindered by parts of the state that remain unaccountable, unresponsive, or discriminatory.

3   The third crisis – of state administration – signals the urgency of enforcing impersonal procedural norms in state organizations and of limiting state economic functions to those that are really feasible and essential as priority mechanisms of modernization. The public sector, still a law unto itself, is characterized by intra-state and inter-agency competition for discretionary functions and resources. Reforms redefine the regulatory roles of public administration, eliminate or restructure agencies, subject officials to public scrutiny, and prosecute malfeasance. As yet, however, there is no real guarantee that public administration will remain impersonal.

4   A fourth crisis – of the representational system – signals the urgency of making parliament the effective instrument for supervising the depersonalized state. Politicians are reluctant to surrender their powers to discriminate

in favour of narrow interests. Reforms open up the political process to public scrutiny and implement the separation of legal, administrative, and political powers. Democratic assemblies must themselves operate impersonally in the competitive selection of leaders and policies. Reforms improve the functioning of the state, and they legitimize both the polity and the economic model.

As can be observed, the ideal type crisis-induced policy sequence arranges the Weberian factors of capitalist institutional development – markets, law, public administration, and political representation – and suggests the economic and political patterning that might occur in practice. Each sequence on the list comprises an immediate *determinant* of crisis, a policy *solution* designed to eliminate the cause of crisis, and an *effect* that reveals the origins of the next crisis and of the next solution. This is not a proposal that countries have to follow exactly, mechanically, and rigidly. Indeed, in the past no country ever has. The purpose of the schema is to identify *emphases* of action that should guide policy decisions in a defined direction. For reasons that will be further explained, development will be faster and better if the initial thrust of attention is given to law. This is not the same as saying that at any point in time countries must focus exclusively on law and ignore administrative or political reforms.

Present-day capitalist transition is deliberately compressed in time. Yet for historical or conjunctural reasons there can be variations on the sequence. A few societies have developed 'out of sequence' for a decade or two with definite benefit, or at least without preventing a timely return to the capitalist sequence when crisis reveals the underlying error. Variations might occur if it is difficult to determine which are the primary and non-primary causes of a crisis. The crisis of an *economic* model could manifest bureaucratically or politically in ways that disguise the underlying problem. If it is hard to distinguish between subsystem dynamics that are specific to economic regulation, law, administration, or representation, it might also be complicated to identify the 'stage' of development at the moment of crisis. Reforms to public administration, for example, are likely simultaneously to be 'legal' and 'economic' reforms. Notwithstanding such caveats, the crisis-induced policy sequence is useful as a means of pulling together or simplifying lessons of successful transitions to capitalism, and as a method of illustrating the theoretical issues.

The reasons for democratizing in the final sequence were outlined in previous chapters, and may be worth reiterating. There are well-meant moral and practical arguments for political participation as a priority over market expansion and legal reform. The priority of rapid democratization has been a dominant assumption in the study of developing countries (witness the deluge of books on democratic transitions as compared with the trickle on law and legal reform). The tendency is to ignore predictable unintended consequences, such as distributive demands placed upon political structures that will outrun the economic potential to satisfy those demands, or the diminishment of autonomous state leadership capacity. Far from being the initial force of modernization, democratization in

The transition sequence 251

many precapitalist polities during the twentieth century reproduced and expanded patronage politics, reinforced clientelist and corporatist interest-group representation, and strengthened resistance to needed economic and institutional reforms. Although there were exceptions to this pattern, populist democracy has often been the effective mechanism for maintaining rather than breaking precapitalist equilibriums.

The static equilibrium of extra-legal personalism in politics and administration would usually be the justification for giving economic liberalization precedence over political liberalization in order to generate the pressures that will rupture the equilibrium. Much depends, of course, on how 'democracy' is defined. I have argued that genuine 'free political representation' is, in historical terms, the final sequence of capitalist transition. Without it the power of the bureaucracy would be overtowering and would itself be the recruiting and reward mechanism for particularistic constituencies. Free representation is, in the end, the mechanism for selecting good leaders and good policies, for passing universalistic laws, for enforcing impersonal procedures throughout the state, and for legitimizing economic policies. The Weberian sequence proposes that post-crisis political reform eventually results in the modernization of parliamentary processes, but that effective free representation is *conditional* on a preexisting level of rule of law. The way of getting around this sequence would be for the social sciences to design a capitalist ideology that is sufficiently persuasive to win successive elections. This is not a wholly unreasonable expectation, and there are signs of movement in that direction, but it presupposes a paradigm shift in academe and the intellectual professions.

Finally, delay in starting the difficult process of capitalist transition is a common reason for cyclical, destructive, and *non*-evolutionary development crises. On the other hand, the correlation between a four-stage crises sequence and a four-stage policy sequence does not rule out the possibility of fairly rapid economic and institutional modernization in the absence of development crises. Consistent with the Schumpeterian theorization of discontinuous change in Chapter 4, it could be feasible for endogenous institutional modernization to be driven forward by exceptional technocrats who intentionally emulate the institutions of advanced societies and reform state procedural norms during politics-as-usual. Autonomous, skilled, and motivated leaders who have the appropriate sort of knowledge and are supported by key interest groups could bring about a departure from the precapitalist equilibrium without the stimulus of crisis. Again, however, this would require unusually strong ideological commitment to capitalist institutional change. As a rule, significant and rapid change in the absence of a crisis trigger is unlikely.

Putting law first

Once conditions have been created for a capitalist sequence to begin, policymakers are faced with numerous challenges. How, in practical terms, should they proceed with reforms? We can now look at ideas relating to the optimal short-run implementation of changes in law. The discussion in Chapter 3 emphasized that law and the market economy have evolved hand in hand since the commencement of capitalism. Similarly, in today's developing countries a commitment to appropriate legal reforms has to involve a corresponding commitment to market reform.

The argument about law and capitalism can be briefly restated. Formal legal regulation is the primary task of modernizing states. Legal systems favourable to capitalist transition were originally created in response to the demands of market interests for pacification and further extension of the market order on the basis of the protection of rights. Although contract and property rights first served the interests of existing owners of property, formal legal equality eventually empowered all market enterprises. But the legal standing of the state was also a precondition for revolutionary change in the procedural norms of public administration and political representation. The structural imperative of rule of law in capitalist society enables the enforcement of impersonal rules in politics as much as in the economy. Reform of legal systems precedes other institutional reforms.

The risk of an *autonomous* legal construction in the absence of established market interests that can shape and defend it is that legal reforms may be reversed or could be designed in a manner that would fetter the progress of capitalism. Economically relevant law, as we have seen, is ideally *parametric*. The parametric state operates predictably and continuously as an impartial procedural boundary mechanism that establishes rules, adapts rules to the changing environment, and responds to plaintiffs by enforcing rules. From a Weberian perspective, law's first function is to create safe conditions of market freedom, with all that implies, by natural extension, for other institutional subsystems of social order in terms of the corresponding market ethics, administrative impersonality, and political freedom.

Law is described here as 'instrumental', but only in the practical sense of being a rational instrument for *constructing* capitalism. This is the reverse of the meaning found when law is defined as 'instrumental' for the furtherance of particularistic individual or group interests and ends (Tamanaha 2006). In theory, an application of 'instrumental law' using the second meaning of the term would be antithetical to the non-discriminatory parametric state. These concepts are, however, just a guide to the relative *emphasis* of legal action. In reality, some instrumentality on behalf of interests could be necessary, even if only as a means of persuading interest coalitions to support capitalist reforms.

We thereby arrive, through a series of logical means-end deductions informed by Weber's theories and historical scholarship, at strong conclusions about the 'causal primacy' of markets and legal institutions in transitions to capitalism. A body of empirical economic literature dealing with the contemporary interactions of institutions, policy, and economic outcomes largely confirms the validity of the argument. In particular, Robert Barro (1997; 2000) calculates available data to show that 'better maintenance of the rule of law' is the main determinant of economic growth. Lower government consumption and lower inflation are also decisive determinants of economic growth, while health, education, fertility, and terms of trade are slightly less important – or less clear-cut – causes (Barro 1996a; 1996b). Some of Barro's most important work has aimed to measure the relationship between democracy and economic growth. He finds not only that democracy is not a determinant of economic growth, and is unlikely to survive in the absence of economic growth, but also that growth-functional expansions of rule of law are relatively independent of the movement towards democracy.

> For a country that starts with weak institutions – low levels of democracy and rule of law – an increase in democracy is less important than an expansion of the rule of law as a stimulus for economic growth and investment. In addition, democracy does not seem to have a strong role in fostering the rule of law. Thus, one cannot argue that democracy is critical for growth because democracy is a prerequisite for the rule of law.... If a poor country has a limited amount of resources to accomplish institutional reforms, then they are much better spent in attempting to implement the rule of law – or, more generally, property rights and free markets. These institutional features are the ones that matter most for economic growth.... Moreover, in the long run, the rule of law tends to generate sustainable democracy by first promoting economic development. Thus, even if democracy is the principal objective in the long run, the best way to accomplish it may be to encourage the rule of law in the short run.
>
> (Barro 2000: 230)

Barro's findings are confirmed in empirical research by Glaeser *et al.* (2004), though with slightly different emphases. The authors note that many influential writings dealing with the linkages between economic growth and institutional development do not adequately distinguish between institutional outcomes that place constraints on government – such as democracy or judicial independence – and policy choices that helped create those outcomes, such as the initial enforcement of rules. Property rights that promote investment are often considered elements of the institutional constraints on government, which might lead one to suppose that legal systems or democratic polities should *produce* such constraints. However, since property rights can also be enforced by dictators who are unconstrained, there may be little causal correlation between institutions, as defined by Glaeser *et al.*, and the factors promoting economic growth.

Institutions do matter as durable constraints on government in the long term, and may explain durable economic growth. But shorter-run economic growth can depend on more *immediate* regulatory actions that are less deeply institutionalized, in particular the enforcement of basic rules. Institutional effectiveness – as measured, for example, by the quality of public administration or the independence of the judiciary – is broadly an *outcome* of economic development. Glaeser *et al.* (2004) emphasize three complex findings from the data. First, economic growth leads to better institutions and democracy, not the other way around. Second, although the initial direction of causality is not absolutely clear, higher education levels and human capital formation are good prognosticators of future economic growth. Security of property rights, on the other hand, is the fundamental predictor of growth. Third, an authoritarian government can provide secure property rights. The authors conclude as follows.

> If the experience of poor countries in the last 50 years is a guide, politically constrained government may *not* be a viable strategy for them to secure property rights. Rather, these countries need to emphasize economic policies and choices that ensure such security, even by dictators. Growth in these countries may be feasible without immediate institutional improvement, and is likely in turn to lead to institutional improvement. At least this is what the data show.... Our results suggest that research in institutional economics, and in particular on the consequences of alternative institutional arrangements, must focus on actual rules.... Countries that emerge from poverty accumulate human and physical capital under dictatorships, and then, once they become richer, are increasingly likely to improve their institutions.
>
> (ibid.: 274–5, 298)

Glaeser *et al.* say their evidence confirms Barro's view of the world. The Weberian policy sequence also supports their emphasis on 'actual laws, rules, and compliance procedures that could be manipulated by a policy maker to assess what works' (ibid.: 298). Arguably this is the purpose of 'rule of law' in the short run; i.e. enforcement of priority rules without immediate need for the whole sophisticated infrastructure of a modern legal system. Furthermore, although 'economic growth' is not necessarily the same as 'market expansion', there is scope for agreement about giving priority to the interconnection between market expansion and laws to maintain market freedom, with rather less urgency for administrative upgrading and democratization.

Most importantly in the present context, the findings of Barro and Glaeser *et al.* lend strong support to what is known as a *'rules first'* approach to legal reform in developing countries. In respect of legal reforms that are intended to improve the operation of markets, this can be taken to mean a focus on enforcing simple and consistent 'bright line' rules that will ensure a level economic playing field for competition and entrepreneurship within well-defined legal boundaries for the protection of property and contract compliance. Parametric bright line rules can be designed to prevent regulatory closure and political profit making, and to discourage fraud and crime. Once market enterprise coexists with a rudimentary legal and administrative machinery able to enforce these rules, societies could be in a position to *skip stages* in the long evolution of legal systems.

The advantages of 'rules first' can only be appreciated by understanding the failings of legal systems in developing countries. The populations of more advanced countries take for granted a highly evolved, interconnected, and relatively accessible legal system. Rules, standards, and procedures have been carefully designed and thoroughly tested. An extensive infrastructure of courts, judges, lawyers, and other legal professionals interacts quite reliably with other jurisdictions of public administration, machinery for enforcing laws, and organizations that supply official and scientific data. By and large, the system is efficient, predictable, accurate, honest, and impartial. These comfortable conditions stand in complete contrast to the legal environment in most of the world. Even in countries that already have a solid body of substantive law, reasonable enforcement infrastructure, and a well-populated legal profession with a steady supply of law graduates, the non-enforcement of existing laws can still make a mockery of 'rule of law'. A supplementary priority for extending the benefits of economic growth in developing countries is to integrate the many people who are excluded from 'rule of law' because they work in the informal economy and because their property rights are not recognized in law.

Hay *et al.* (1996) identify 'bad courts' and 'bad laws' as reasons why people may not use the legal system in developing countries. Legal fees are high; judges and police are uninformed, corrupt, or incompetent; and the courts are politicized, inefficient, and unpredictable. Laws often 'contradict standard business practice and common sense' (ibid.: 560), or are incomplete and provide inadequate guidance to courts. It is difficult to verify the information required to make a decision, and decisions and enforcement are equally unpredictable. Measures to improve the situation could seem quite *unrealistic* in the short term. The needed investments, skills, technocratic manpower, technology, and knowledge appear to place rule of law beyond the reach of developing countries. Well-intentioned reformers would, in any case, face resistance from interests that are better served by the existing power equilibrium.

Daniel Kaufmann (2003), a World Bank analyst, argues that because 'misrule of law' is such a serious problem in developing countries, solutions may only be found *indirectly* by *non*-legal means. The habitual problems – judges who are not appointed on merit and who are prone to corruption and political influence, the 'privatization' of law because of bribery, etc. – make it unlikely that a conventional reform programme of technical assistance, skills training, and new technology could make much difference.

> Thus, bolder approaches ... will be required, including the choice of reform entry points in institutions *outside* of the judiciary or legal arena. This could include budgetary institutions, regulation within the administration, competitive enterprise and financial sector development, international courts, and specialized non-governmental organizations. These may be expected to apply pressure for a revamp of dysfunctional legal or judiciary institutions.
>
> (Kaufmann 2003: 25)

These countervailing forces can bolster the impetus for reform. Yet faster solutions could surely be achieved if technocrats were to act *directly* on the legal arena during a crisis-induced reform sequence. In such circumstances, 'rules first' could be effective alongside market liberalization. Hay *et al.* (1996) suggest reforms should focus initially on eliminating bad rules and creating new rules rather than on overhauling the legal system. If the priority is to ensure that markets function, courts and enforcement agencies can be made to operate better with the introduction of bright-line rules for formulating, verifying, and enforcing contracts. Such rules lack completeness, but can be clearly specified. They leave less room for discretion and interpretation by the courts, and reduce opportunities for abuse. Rules can be designed to deal with pressing anomalies and uncertainties, and to make the existing system more consistent and objective. Elimination of inappropriate or vague rules will encourage people to *utilize* the legal system. Furthermore, since pressure from business groups has been the usual force for eliminating resistance to legal reform, *priority* must be given to economic liberalization and privatization (ibid.: 565).

> In the short run, a reforming country needs a system of rules ... that enables judges to make decisions and thus begin developing precedents. In this situation, simple bright line rules have the major advantage that they can immediately begin to be used by courts and hence by the private parties. Unlike the more elaborate rules, they [can be made to] fit the existing legal institutions and business practice.... As laws are used more, courts will begin to gain credibility and places to resolve disputes. They will also become more predictable as a body of precedents develops, and private parties begin to anticipate more clearly how courts make decisions. In this way, laws will converge to those of developed market economies even if the initial system is more primitive. The basic point, then, is that to get to the rule of law in the intermediate term, it is best to begin with rules that are suitable for both private agents and the courts, and then to allow this system to develop as the needs of private agents and the capabilities of the courts develop over time.
>
> (ibid.: 566–7)

The legal theorist, Richard Posner (1998), commends these proposals – 'it is more costly and time-consuming to create efficient legal institutions than to enact efficient rules for the existing inefficient institutions to administer' (ibid.: 4). Economic reforms create the demand for thoroughgoing legal reform, but in the meantime a modest rules-first strategy can be effective and inexpensive. Where human and financial resources are scarce, the 'fundamental trade-off is between making a rather modest investment in better rules and making a big investment in the judiciary' (ibid.: 7). Legal reform can be simplified by importing sections of a tried and tested legal code from another country. The code can be adapted to local conditions without incurring the expense of bringing in foreign technical expertise or drafting new codes. *Re*-codification can produce rapid improvements in rule of law.

Posner makes the case for giving priority to rules as opposed to 'standards'. Standards, such as guidelines about 'negligence, bad faith, [or] unreasonable restraint of trade', give courts great discretion in the administration of justice, and presume a preexisting level of competence and honesty (ibid.: 5). Standards can be hard to understand, and are more likely to be subject to political interpretation. Simple rules, in contrast, deter undesirable behaviour by clearly defining unwanted conduct. Although they are rigid, their advantage is that 'determining whether they have been violated is a relatively mechanical, cut-and-dried process' (ibid.: 4). Rules do not require as much processing of information, and it is easier to monitor their enforcement. Drawing on research relating to how law is applied in advanced capital markets, Kenneth Dam similarly concludes that 'standards are likely to be difficult for developing country judiciaries to apply effectively' (Dam 2006: 177).

The 'rules-first' method is consistent with Weberian theory, especially with regard to the desirability of improving *procedures* and minimizing *discretion* while state capacity remains weak. As Posner (1998: 4) says, 'a rule is procedurally efficient if it is designed to reduce the cost or increase the accuracy of using the legal system'. Examples include a requirement for legal contracts to be written, or establishing time limits for reporting alleged infringements of rights. Efficient rule procedures also reduce the potential for abuse of legal discretion: 'The less discretion a judge has in making decisions, the easier it will be to determine whether a case has been decided contrary to law or whether there is a pattern favouring one class or group of litigants over another' (ibid.: 5).

Weberian and 'rules-first' approaches can look for additional support in Kenneth Dam's book, *The Law-Growth Nexus* (2006). The most relevant findings in this expert analysis of issues relating to rule of law in developing countries can be summarized in four key points. First, it is clear that legal institutions are a vital determinant of every country's economic progress. Dam suggests this has now been recognized even by policymakers in China, which is not, as some Western scholars insist, immune from the imperative to create a modern legal order for market regulation. Second, although he argues that 'on balance' the 'causation runs from institutions to growth rather than vice versa', Dam emphasizes that economic crises and expansion of markets create the appropriate and strong pressures for legal reform (ibid.: 274, 276, *passim*). Third, the overwhelming weight of legal theory and historical evidence suggest that neither common law nor civil law will be superior in the encouragement it gives to economic development. A country's 'legal origin cannot be changed', and the difficulties and costs of changing a legal system or legal culture make conversion from one to another impracticable (ibid.: 36, 100, 226).

Dam's fourth argument – the one most relevant to a 'rules-first' approach – is that *enforcement* of law is the critical variable. The quality of enforcement matters more than substantive content of law in developing countries. Good or good-enough law dealing with even sophisticated financial, corporate, or bankruptcy regulation is often already on the books. What is frequently absent is a credible expectation that law works. Effective enforcement depends in the first instance on the judiciary. Economic development is held back by weak judiciaries that are unable promptly, honestly, predictably, impartially, or transparently to perform key functions of protecting property and contract rights. The strength of the judiciary depends on operational factors, such as their remuneration and the physical, technical, and human resources at their disposal; but also, most importantly, on their independence from political and economic interests (Jarquín and Carrillo 1998; Buscaglia and Ratliff 2000).

Judicial effectiveness reflects the quality of procedural rules, which should be designed to increase the accuracy, fairness, and predictability of results without being so formal that they inhibit flexibility and speed of outcomes (Dam 2006: 96–100). A key measure of judicial efficiency is the time taken to dispose of a case. Inefficiencies are not due only to problems of technical resources, budgets, or the quantity of judges (ibid.: 103). The important issues are the relative independence, impartiality, and honesty of the judiciary, which have 'structural' and 'behavioural' origins (ibid.: 106–22). Structural independence is a function of formal mechanisms by which government and the judiciary supervise each other, and relates closely to the separation of powers. Behavioural independence is influenced by factors such as the 'education, values, and prestige' of the judiciary, and whether tenure of judges is fixed or arbitrary and politically determined.

The seductive reasoning of those who question the indispensability of rule of law entirely on the grounds that some countries experienced rapid economic growth for a decade or two without genuine rule of law should be resisted. China is now the most talked-about country whose future economic prosperity will depend on whether impartial legal institutions can replace personal and particularistic network-based mechanisms for ensuring compliance in exchange contracts (Root 1995). Although Glaeser *et al.* (2004) offer China as an example of a dictatorship that achieves economic growth by prioritizing good-enough security for property rights, other observers question whether China will improve economic governance fast enough to avoid disaster (Root 2006: 187–217).

Dam (2006: 233–77), on the other hand, detects a promising 'guided evolutionary approach' to rule of law that could allow China to avoid serious economic crises. Political leaders seem to be coming around to an awareness of the need to enforce market rules. The momentum of reform is halting. Since there is no effective separation of powers in the Chinese state, the quality of the judiciary and law enforcement is very poor. But if one considers that China 'had essentially no legal system when the economic reforms began in 1978', progress since that date would appear to be 'adaptive' and 'intelligent' (ibid.: 248, 269). Dam views the expressed interest of China's leaders in the lessons of new institutional economics as possible evidence that 'they know their institutions are not sufficiently strong for sustained growth' (ibid.: 275).

If one believes – whether on logical or empirical grounds – that rule of law in developing countries must receive priority over other institutional improvements, then clearly there are viable strategies for achieving it. Of course, all the usual caveats about cognition and volition apply. Bueno de Mesquita and Root (2000: 7) point out that although 'it is easy to erect institutions with the gloss of the rule of law ... the key is to ensure that politicians are given institutional incentives to enforce the rules'. No one can be certain this will happen. Uncertainty is heightened by the fact that critics interpret the available evidence on rule-of-law reform in contradictory ways (Carothers 2003). If it can be achieved, however, enforcement of rules is a priority goal that accords with the theoretical conditions for capitalist transition that I have sought to identify in this book.

By way of conclusion, it can be noted that 'rules first' is compatible with Hayek's view of institutional change, since it implies only limited constructivism. It entails no requirement to 'redesign completely the legal system as a whole, or to remake it out of the whole cloth according to a coherent design' (Hayek 1982: vol. 1, 65). Regular interventions ensure that existing law can perform its minimum purpose of undergirding the market ethic and preventing dishonesty in economic action. Whether it is simple or complex, enforced or not enforced, instrumental or non-instrumental, law may become useless or unjust only because it 'has lain in the hands of a particular class or group' (Hayek 1982: vol. 1, 89). Even the spontaneous order 'may lead into an impasse from which it cannot extricate itself by its own forces', so that measures will be required to deal with laws and legal systems that have developed in 'undesirable directions' (ibid.: 88).

> In no system that could be rationally defended would the state just do nothing. An effective competitive system needs an intelligently designed and continuously adjusted legal framework as much as any other. Even the most essential prerequisite of its proper functioning, the prevention of fraud and deception (including exploitation of ignorance), provides a great and by no means yet fully accomplished object of legislative activity.
>
> (Hayek 1944: 29)

Hayek goes one step further. In the special circumstances of late-developing countries, 'enforcement of the law' may be the only truly essential requirement of the state, if for no other reason than that it represents the best use of scarce resources and capacity.

> It may be true that in certain conditions, where an underdeveloped government apparatus is scarcely yet adequate to perform this prime function [of enforcing law], it would be wise to confine it to it, since an additional burden would exceed its weak powers and the effect of attempting more would be that it did not even provide the indispensable conditions for the functioning of a free society.
>
> (Hayek 1982: vol. 3, 41)

Finally, 'rules first' also fits well with Popper's view that the overriding priority of institutional engineering in transitions to the open society is a 'legal framework' that can be 'known and understood by the individual citizen ... [It] should be designed to be understandable' (Popper 1962: vol. 2, 132). A focus on clarifying and enforcing the rules and minimizing judicial discretion would lessen the likelihood of capture of the legal system by political or economic interest groups. More broadly, a reformed subsystem of economic regulation can become a force behind reforms that depersonalize other subsystems of the state.

Building the service state

After law, the priority in a sequenced capitalist transition is to enforce the *procedural rules* of public administration. In one sense, the task is to extend rule of law from the economy into the state itself. Whereas the rules of contract and property in the market economy are rights enforced in private law, rules governing procedures of state are subject to *administrative law*. The distinction is explained by Weber, who defined 'public law' as 'norms which regulate state-oriented action, that is, those activities which serve the maintenance, development, and the direct pursuit of the objectives of the state'. 'Private law', in contrast, comprises the 'norms which, while issuing from the state, regulate conduct other than state-oriented conduct' (Weber 1978: 641). Public law establishes the 'duties' of state officials, whereas the regulation of 'relations between those who exercise authority and those who are subject to it' falls within both public and private law (ibid.: 642–3). As I noted in Chapter 2, Weber argued that the separation of 'public law, which regulates the relationships of the public agencies among each other and with the subjects, and private law which regulates the relationships of the governed individuals among themselves' can be fully achieved only with the '*complete depersonalization*' of the state (ibid.: 998).

To begin with, some general comments are needed on the significance of the state administrative sphere during capitalist transition. A guiding Weberian maxim – 'honesty is the best policy' – may be said to have identical purpose in both the spheres of economy and public administration, namely to prevent fraud and crime. Another Weberian maxim relevant to both regulated markets and regulated bureaucracies is 'without regard to persons'. Markets and government operate best when the decision making of the actors is impersonal. Rules of economy are designed to encourage competition and discourage discrimination and fraud. Rules of bureaucracy are designed to ensure equal treatment of citizens and to discourage political profit making and regulatory closure. The two spheres are, in the end, mutually reinforcing. Effective market freedom is not possible without state impartiality, and vice versa.

It is a sociological 'law' that the depersonalization of the state will minimize the *quantity* of state administrative functions. Once the area of personal discretion for public officials is reduced, there is less the state *can* do. When public bureaucracy undertakes fewer permissions and authorizations – and fewer follow-up inspections to verify compliance with conditional assistance given to firms, activities, or sectors – the need for personal discretion is inevitably diminished by a similar margin. More pervasive functions means more incentives for particularism and more incentives for monopolistic closure by officials. State strength is generally greater when the *quality* of administration is maximized 'at the boundary' only by extending and improving the key parametric functions of the state (which can include regulation of services contracted out to private enterprise by public bureaucracy). A classic problem of development is that the administrative apparatus attempts highly complex and detailed tasks that require many decisions and interactions, but is too weak to perform them well. Advanced-country administrations tend to move in the opposite direction, performing fewer functions with more effective powers of enforcement.

Although it is fairly clear how transitional and modern states should operate in theory, the practical application of these principles is not easy. Common pathologies of states, often called 'bureaucratic politics', include fragmentation, duplication, competition, and monopolization among agencies of the state. The goal of bureaucratic politics is to maximize the resources, functions and bureaucratic territory that officials can appropriate in order to increase their relative powers, and also to satisfy the many vested interests inside and outside the state that can be served by those powers. More functions mean more incentives and opportunities for dysfunctional state action. Once this vicious circle ensues within the state, it can be hard to stop.

An objective of the reform of state administrations is to replace *negative* competition among state agencies with *positive* or surrogate competition that improves state behaviour. Another objective is to replace, as far as is reasonable and technically feasible, the *production* functions of the state as a provider of services with *regulatory* functions where the state acts as the contractor and monitor of services. These are general principles for the transitional states. Highly evolved states are more competent to take on additional functions with less loss of institutional efficiency. For example, even when introduction of new methods of public administration involving greater discretion and informality might be realistic in advanced societies, they are likely to be idealistic and corrosive of state capacity in developing societies. This is because the initial priority of depersonalizing the state requires the bypassing or weakening of traditional norms and interests, which means less discretion and less informality rather than more.

In general terms, therefore, effective state action depends on formal institutional constraints that minimize incentives and opportunities for public officials to exercise personal discretion as their means of pursuing individual or group interests outside or within the state. The main problems of the underdeveloped state stem from the insufficiency of commitments to predictable impersonality on the part of state agencies. The depersonalization of the state reduces the scope for discretion and *enforces* the impartiality of officials. In economic policy, pervasive state activism will be reduced as parametric regulatory intervention is increased. In broader terms, rules about impartiality will be applied to internal state recruitment, to the state's internal and external conduct, and to decisions about the delimitation of administrative jurisdictions. This process takes in the fusion of legal and administrative functions of the state, the separation of the public and private interests of officials, and universal rules governing decision making and operational routines. In short, the problems of administrative modernization during capitalist transition are reduced to three key variables – *formal discipline*, *control mechanisms*, and *discretionary powers*.

The objective in this section is to revisit the Weberian priorities of administrative reform in the context of current academic debates and policy proposals.

The fusion of non-discretionary law and public administration is essential if the state is to perform its core monetary and fiscal functions while promoting market freedom and ensuring adequate provision and regulation of public and private infrastructures in areas such as communications, health, and education. Adaptive societies continually renegotiate the boundaries between public and private provision of infrastructures, and redefine the optimal role of government vis-à-vis service providers in fulfilment of agreed development functions. There is a distinction between first-order priorities of *expanding markets* and *building institutions*, and the second-order benefits that flow in terms of capacity and resources made available for *improving services*. The following discussion will focus on basic principles that guide the building of state capacities for good decision making and implementation in these areas.

The relevant Weberian assumption is that administrative institutions of the state are purposeful, designable, and constructible organizations. In his book *State-Building: Governance and World Order in the Twenty-first Century* (2004), Francis Fukuyama points out that organizational or public administration theory, as compared with political, legal, and cultural theory, is the field of social science where knowledge about institutional design should be most plentiful.

> It is fairly clear that the bulk of transferable knowledge [about institutional design] lies ... in public administration and the design and management of individual organizations. At this micro-level, organizations can be revamped, destroyed, created anew, or managed for better or worse in ways that draw on the historical experience of a wide range of countries.
>
> (Fukuyama 2004: 31)

> Of the different components of institutional capacity, public administration is the one that is the most susceptible to systematization and transfer. The existence of public administration schools all over the world is testimony to this fact. The kinds of institutional reforms and changes in formal incentive structures that have brought about more professional and less corrupt government in the United States, Great Britain, and other developed countries can also be applied quite successfully in developing countries as well.
>
> (Fukuyama 2004: 83–4)

These passages might seem to prepare the ground for a constructivist view of public-administration reform. In fact, however, Fukuyama's purpose is to explain three areas of 'organizational ambiguity' – *goal-setting*, *control*, and *discretion* – where the performance and reform of public administration is heavily constrained. Although organizations of the state have formal characteristics that facilitate the rational manipulation of incentive structures as means to ends, Fukuyama argues that the effectiveness of state organizations is principally a function of informal, i.e. cultural, norms. Informal norms limit the means-end optimality of formal institutional organizations, whereas more appropriate informal norms might conceivably lead to better organizational outcomes.

Although disagreeing with this argument, I find that it provides a useful starting point for the discussion of alternative ways of resolving the problems of public administration in developing countries.

Fukuyama (ibid.: 77–9) first says that *goal-setting* cannot be 'rational' because organizations 'are pervaded by norms and other a-rational sources of behaviour', which act as 'substitutes for formal monitoring-and-accountability'. Behaviour in organizations is shaped by a 'social process that colours, distorts, and changes the cognitive process', by 'myths, histories, and traditions', and also by 'norms of loyalty, reciprocity, professional pride, or the desire to maintain tradition' (ibid.: 52, 77). All of these influences might be positive if traditional authority has already inculcated the desirable norms. East Asian countries, for example, progressed rapidly because they 'had highly developed norms of professionalism in public service *before* they modernized' (ibid.: 66). However, if the informal norms in a society are familial or clientelist, those norms will take precedence over the formal norms, preventing impersonal laws and rational bureaucracies from overcoming patronage and corruption (ibid.: 67, 82).

Second, Fukuyama claims that informal norms account for whether there can be adequate *control* – i.e. monitoring and accountability – over administrative activity. A literature on institutional 'specificity' indicates that dispersed activities in which policymakers make many small decisions are not easy to specify in terms of objectives, methods, rewards, time frames, or outcomes. The operation of a central bank or an army is highly specific, involving relatively few decisions and interactions. It is more easily controlled in terms of success and failure criteria. However, social services such as education or health lack high-specificity measures, and so are control-averse. They are oriented imprecisely to dispersed human behaviour rather than to numerical or technical targets, and they require a higher volume of decisions and interactions to achieve their targets. Legal systems also involve many decisions and interactions, many agents and clients, and extensive areas of enforcement. Fukuyama argues that control over low-specificity sectors is only achieved by internalizing appropriate informal norms through 'education, training, and a socialization process' (ibid.: 66). Organizations 'get optimal performance out of low-specificity activities not by setting up elaborate systems of monitoring and accountability and use of complex individual incentives but rather by relying on [informal] norms' (ibid.: 62). Thus, 'social capital substitutes for elaborate formal incentive systems', and 'organizational culture' will matter more than 'fixing formal lines of authority' (ibid.: 63).

Third, Fukuyama argues that informal norms account for whether organizational *discretion* can be successful. In private organizations, complex activity can often be better performed by delegating discretion down the hierarchy. Doing away with centralized and standardized procedures can improve the creativity, quality, speed, and efficiency of decision making. However, agency discretion in public administration only works if officials are honest, professional, and immune from rent-seeking influences. Delegation of discretion may be desirable, but it is the most complex and difficult task faced by organizations.

Delegated authority is resistant to formal Weberian monitoring, and is prone to capture by corrupt or clientelist networks. Fukuyama believes that discretion will be 'safer' when 'agents share the same value framework as the principals, even in the absence of a formal monitoring and incentive structure' (ibid.: 80). He claims that East Asian social norms neutralized the risks of state discretion. Growth-inducing industrial policies delegated 'a huge degree of discretion to the economic planning agencies' (ibid.: 74). The 'mandarin bureaucratic tradition specific to each country' can explain the East Asian state's 'relative competence, professionalism, and independence from rent seeking societal interest groups' (ibid.: 30, 75).

As can be seen, Fukuyama is sceptical about the feasibility of using state organizational hierarchies to enforce formal procedural norms. It should be noted that he also rejects 'market-based solutions to public sector dysfunction', but only on spurious grounds that they are 'very controversial and not politically possible in most jurisdictions' (ibid.: 59). Instead, Fukuyama views informal norms as the source of administrative problems and solutions. It seems to be implicit in this approach that since attempts to build or rebuild public administration are always and everywhere conditioned by culture, institutional-reform *priorities* or *sequences* could be decided by whether a sector is susceptible to informal controls rather than on the basis of instrumental evaluations of the relative *functional* importance of particular activities or institutions. It may be impossible or too costly to manipulate low-specificity sectors by formal means. High-specificity sectors, on the other hand, are 'most susceptible to technocratic reform' (ibid.: 84). Law is inherently a 'medium- to low-specificity' activity. Whereas ' "ten bright technocrats" can be air-dropped into a developing country and bring about massive changes for the better' in high-specificity activities like central banking or telecommunications, 'there is no legal system in the world that can be "fixed" by ten technocrats, no matter how bright' (ibid.).

Fukuyama does not discuss the possibility of adjusting reform priorities within existing formal parameters of law. Transitional law, as described by advocates of 'rules first', has as its explicit purpose the design of legal reform that would increase the *specificity* of law in developing countries. 'Rules first' is more mechanical than sophisticated systems of law in wealthy countries; it simplifies decision making and monitoring, defines conduct, reduces the scope for interpretative behaviour oriented to ambiguous standards, reduces discretion, minimizes costs and increases accuracy, and requires less processing of information. Legal reform looks more manageable when viewed from a 'rules-first' perspective. In Fukuyama's analysis, the complexities of legal reform are largely reduced to problems of societal norms. Rule of law is, in any case, less of a priority because good informal norms can *substitute* for law. Again, examples of such substitution seem only to be found in a handful of high-performing East Asian states. Fukuyama's general argument, which is set out in more detail elsewhere (Fukuyama 1995), is that 'economic trust' is founded on cultural or moral consensus that diminishes the need for recourse to law by economic actors.

Arguments like these do carry a lot of influence in the development field. If they appear to be faulty, it is important to debate them. In earlier chapters I identified a complex of structural, cognitive, and volitional factors that influence the capacity of state actors to shape outcomes, among which 'culture' is a comparatively minor element. I have argued that rationality, leadership, knowledge, ideas, and interests can be harnessed to the design and construction of formal institutions, and that law is a precondition of developmental progress in other fields. Similarly, in the context of public-administration reform it is important to consider the relative weightings of various *volitional* factors. In developing countries, in fact, the resistance of vested interests is usually more significant than cultural constraints. Often rulers lack the motivational incentive to alter the power equilibrium. Hilton Root (2006) observes, for example, that fairly straightforward improvements to public administration in the developing world may be prevented mainly because it is not in the perceived interest of rulers to undertake the reforms.

> Public-sector weaknesses exist because they deliberately and strategically offer private benefit to leadership. Gaps in public accountability, weak internal financial and performance management systems, public procurement procedures, public-sector accounts and management information, regulation of corporate accounting, external public audits of government accounts, inadequate legislative scrutiny of audits, and inadequate public access to information are all readily correctable with fewer resources than it would take to build a highway or a dam. Such deliberate evasions of accountability are enmeshed in domestic political institutions....
>
> (Root 2006: 44)

Given that a variety of cognitive and volitional factors do constrain reforms, how might the constraints be overcome? If social-science knowledge does offer sufficient reason for believing that state actors *can* be more or less rational in setting goals, that the formal norms and authority mechanisms of the state *are* adequate for controlling service activities, and that states *can* perform developmentally while avoiding the problems of discretion, then there are solid grounds for guarded optimism. Even if claims about the functionality of informal norms for goal setting, control, and discretion were true for a limited time in a small number of countries with very rare preexisting institutional advantage, they do not offer *general* solutions for other developing countries. Great caution should be exercised, since the impression could be given that traditional bureaucratic forms of authority should be cultivated in preference to neutral or general laws of rational administrative authority. In the absence of clear statements to the contrary, enthusiasm for the claimed functional relationship between effective informality and traditional authority in parts of East Asia suggests the value of (re)creating versions of that nexus elsewhere. Emulating premodern authority mechanisms – Confucian or otherwise – as a contemporary method of strengthening developing states would be foolish and dangerous. It reverses the world forces of progress.

The alternatives that I discuss in the remainder of this chapter relate to the three problems of public management that Fukuyama has identified – organizational goals, control, and discretion. I will focus mainly on some recent World Bank studies and reform proposals for public administration in developing countries, which seem to offer practical refutations of 'culturalist' and 'informality' approaches. These World Bank reports, it can be observed, propose Weberian-style solutions from the hands-on perspective of development practitioners.

The first issue to deal with is the *formality* of effective procedures of administrative goal attainment. When the criteria for decision making in underdeveloped polities are interpersonal and informal, state performance will usually be weakened. Evidence-based support for this argument can be found in the World Bank's *World Development Report 2004*, which emphasizes the reform priority of 'formality in public sector institutions'.

> Many aspects of government performance rest on an ingrained institutional discipline or formality. Actual behaviour follows written rules, or actual budget outcomes bear a close resemblance to the legislatively agreed budget. Informality emerges in weak institutional settings where incentives and procedures do not match formal rules, rewards, and procedures.
>
> (World Bank 2004b: 194)

Formality clearly does not mean façade formalism, i.e. rules for rules' sake, legalism, and red tape. Rather, the aim is to create disciplined structures for the implementation of means to ends that cannot easily be circumvented or undermined by the playing out of interest-group pressures. Public policy is meaningless unless it can be reliably calculated that administrative instructions will be carried out. In the management of state administrative staff, for instance, formality will mean 'explicit rules on recruitment, promotion, pay determination, and monitoring'. In developing countries, 'personal connections' often determine who is employed in the public sector, their level of pay, and 'even whether [employees] have to show up at all' (ibid.). In budget management, informality will mean that a 'budget is made and remade constantly during execution' (ibid.: 195). The World Bank recommends 'strengthening discipline and formality so that recruitment, promotion and pay determination are based on explicit rules, the significance of personal connections reduced, and the credibility of the budget process restored', all of which requires the 'entrenchment of common rules and principles' (World Bank 2002: 40). When formality is not yet the norm, the priority is to depoliticize public bureaucracy by establishing 'checks and balances' that 'legally define' the rules of decision making and operational procedure (World Bank 2004b: 195).

A *sequenced* strategy to formalize state administration is advisable. The 'first-stage reforms provide incentives to achieve or strengthen formality [in] a weak institutional setting'. Once this has been achieved, 'second-stage reforms build on a foundation of formality in stronger institutional environments' (ibid.). Thus, 'formality represents a necessary base on which other public management reforms can be built' (World Bank 2002: 19). Once discipline has been ingrained and a *'threshold of formality'* is reached, more ambitious reforms are possible (ibid.: 25). Second-stage reforms can break the mould, for example by contracting services to the private sector or introducing performance-related conditions of pay and employment. If complex reforms like these are undertaken 'in an informal institutional environment', they might attract support for the 'wrong reasons', i.e. in anticipation of 'private gain' (World Bank 2004b: 199). The message from the World Bank practitioners is that formalism is the priority for improving the capacity of administration to manage its planning, delivery, monitoring, and contracting of services such as infrastructure, health, and education.

Social scientists understand that informal norms have a role in improving cooperation and work values in organizations that have undergone depersonalization and formalization. Informality will, to some extent, substitute for formal discipline. Modern organizational leaders routinely try to construct an organizational culture of positive norms and group identities designed to motivate employees to work harder for common goals. The crucial issue, however, is that formal norms will *set the boundaries* of informality. Herbert Simon, a psychologist and Nobel Laureate in economics, offered this vital insight.

> The term 'informal organization' refers to interpersonal relations in the organization that affect decisions within it but either are omitted from the formal scheme or are not consistent with that scheme. It would probably be fair to say that no formal organization will operate effectively without an accompanying informal organization ... and each new organization member must establish informal relations with his colleagues before he becomes a significant part of the working organization.... On the other hand, the formal structure performs no function unless it actually sets limits to the informal relations that are permitted to develop within it. In particular, it is an important function of the formal organization to prevent the development of organizational politics – struggle for influence and authority – to a point that would be deleterious to the functioning of the organization; and a further function to detect and eliminate unnecessary duplication and overlapping in the work of the parts of the organization. Perhaps a more positive function of the formal, in relation to the informal, structure is to encourage the development of the latter along constructive lines. That is, a proper allocation of duties and the maintenance of adequate channels of communication may ... relieve the need for the growth of informal channels....
>
> (Simon 1997: 198–9)

Finally, observations on the respective values of formality and informality return us full circle to Weber's writings. A recent state-of-the-art evaluation of 'bureaucracy in the twenty-first century' argues that Weber's views have been fully vindicated. Formality and hierarchy matter more than informality.

> Fixed and official jurisdictional areas ordered by rules, laws, or regulations, the first characteristic of bureaucracy, is so ingrained in modern governance

that realistic alternatives do not present themselves.... While Weber may have oversold the need for bureaucracies to have regularized processes and procedures at the time he was writing, since then it has become even more a part of bureaucracy and will likely continue through this century.... The persistence of bureaucracy and hierarchy clearly demonstrates that hierarchy must provide some vital function.

(Meier and Hill 2005: 65)

We can now consider how *control* of public administration activities might be achieved by combining the use of 'specificity' indicators with competition counter-measures. When Arturo Israel (1987) devised the 'specificity' index as a way of measuring the feasibility of organizational control, he also identified *competition* as the mechanism to improve control in *low*-specificity activities. Some public-service outputs are difficult to measure and evaluate. The greater the specificity of activity in terms of objectives, methods, control systems, and timing, 'the more intense, immediate, identifiable, and focused will be the effects of a good or a bad perform-ance' (ibid.: 48–9). If an activity is not easily monitored the provider is less likely to be accountable for its performance. When an institutional activity is not transparent in monitoring terms it will also be difficult to design or reform it. Although meas-ures such as training and managerial techniques can be adopted to improve control in low-specificity activities, specificity itself is determined by the activity rather than by the techniques of organization. Specificity, in this respect, is beyond the control of policymakers (ibid.: 150–64). In these conditions, competition becomes a tool for improving performance within the public sector: 'The challenge is to create competitive, market-like conditions that will increase the output and improve the performance of an institution' (ibid.: 165). Competition positively influences insti-tutional performance *regardless* of the specificity of the activity. There is even a suggestion that competitive pressure may *create* specificity by forcing organizations to find ways of monitoring their own performance (ibid.: 92–3).

Not all forms of competition will be equally useful (ibid.: 96–101). There are four feasible types, only one of which occurs in the marketplace. The others 'simulate' competition by creating 'competition surrogates', which are market-equivalent incentive systems in areas where direct economic competition may not be technically or politically feasible (ibid.: 90–2, 166–76). Their purpose is to exert performance pressures on public agencies.

1   Public entities compete with private entities that produce similar goods and services, or they subcontract parts of their operations, or public entities are privatized and exert competitive pressure on remaining public entities.
2   Public agencies become accountable to pressures from 'clients, beneficiar-ies, or suppliers' who 'voice' their demands for improvements in performance.
3   Public agencies are subject to countervailing pressure from politicians and regulators who act as 'clients or shareholders', principally through the budget process.

4   Competition is induced inside the public sector by means of semi-independent divisions, decentralized functions, delegated responsibility, and performance rewards.

The World Bank (1997; 2000) takes a favourable view of competition in the provision *and* regulation of health, education, and infrastructure services. Competition is useful as a way of revealing failure and punishing poor performance. However, the World Bank is now more cautious than Israel about inducing competition mechanisms *inside the state* through decentralization or performance incentives. The latter step, if desirable at all, should only be undertaken as a 'second-stage' reform, once the necessary threshold of formality has been passed (World Bank 2004b: 195–9). That is sensible. For reasons that were discussed earlier, negative competition inside the precapitalist state fetters depersonalization and formalization, and leads to administrative dysfunction. Inserting new layers of competition within an undisciplined state would only cause conditions to deteriorate. When introducing competition to offset problems of goal setting, discretion, and control it is important also to discourage self-serving budget maximization and duplication of functions.

In its *World Development Report 2004*, the World Bank supports the first three of Israel's competition proposals (markets, voice accountability, and countervailing institutional monitoring). These can be effective even in transaction-intensive and low-specificity services that are prone to corruption or abuse and are hard to monitor. First, 'competition *in* the market' by private service providers is easier now that 'technological advances have made it possible to open services formerly believed to be natural monopolies to competition' (ibid.: 102). In addition, 'if natural monopolies exist, there can be competition *for* the market'; i.e. the state organizes competitive bids for concessions to operate. Furthermore, 'benchmark competition' can be used when states allocate funds for public works, i.e. sourcing market data from competing contractors about prices, costs of production, and consumer preferences.

With formal safeguards in place, contracting or selling concessions to the private sector, or transferring responsibility to local government, can often be viable alternatives to traditional public-service delivery. The World Bank points out that most state services in advanced countries were originally provided by the private sector. Historically, the state's *first* role was regulation: 'The state began as an independent outside monitor and regulator of private activities. It largely retained that independence as a monitor after the same activities became public' (ibid.: 99). Whichever sequence they choose – first the market or first the state – developing countries need to build regulatory capacity. When services are 'contracted out' it is important that the provider remains accountable to the state (ibid.: 95–108). Arm's-length relations between policymakers and providers insulate the providers from the play of politics and facilitate the enforcement of rules by the state. Clear contracts must have built-in performance rewards and penalties. Effective monitoring and accountability also depends on accountability to 'clients'. The World Bank suggests giving consumers a choice among service providers, creating localized oversight mechanisms, and producing and disseminating government-generated information that is designed to empower consumers in the market. Once a separation is established between providers and the state bureaucracy, new channels can be created for consumers and citizens to exert pressure on providers directly or through the state agencies.

It can also be argued – although the World Bank does not do so explicitly – that the state should provide more incentives and leeway for private firms to set up and compete legally with the public sector in regulated markets irrespective of state subcontracting arrangements. This would replicate the historical pattern, i.e. markets and regulation first, and could to some extent diminish the problem of distinguishing between first- and second-stage feasibility criteria. In other words, what little discipline and formality does exist in public administration can initially be focused on monitoring and enforcing universal rule criteria for the private sector relating to public safety, security against generalized risks, competition, honesty, and prevention of fraud. The state can do this in parallel with the tasks of improving its own operations rather than *first* improving internal governance and *then* moving on to the perilous and possibly unnecessary stage of micromanaging an extensive range of individual contracts with private suppliers. An effect of this kind of market-first strategy would be to 'formalize' – i.e. bring into the formal sector of the economy, and thereby regulate and improve – many private services that are already dynamically supplied, though sometimes dangerously and badly, through informal markets (everything from transport to schooling, and dentistry to money lending). Governments should, in any event, resist the temptation to replace informal markets with planned markets.

Finally, reform of public administration in developing countries must deal with the problem of *discretion*. During the 1980s and 1990s governments in several industrialized countries sought to correct the excesses of administrative depersonalization. The initial goals of so-called New Public Management (NPM) were to reduce rigidities in state procedures, decentralize the state and make it more responsive to stakeholders, encourage managerial discretion and organizational subsidiarity, and de-bureaucratize public-service delivery (Hood 1991). Delegation and discretion within modern public administrations was viewed as an antidote to red tape, a method for increasing responsibility and creativity, providing incentives for better performance, and improving organizations by bringing decision makers closer to the task and to the client. The results were mixed. Attempts to balance the risks of discretion against hoped-for improvements in efficiency often had unintended consequences, and scholars continue to debate the merits of NPM (Pollitt and Bouckaert 2004).

Giving the civil service a more personal face might be safe and desirable where institutions are highly developed, where formal rule compliance and enforcement is a routine, and where norms of procedural impersonality have been internalized by civil servants. But a drive to decentralize aspects of administration in developing societies that have not yet gone through the formative phases of depersonalization could simply further institutionalize interpersonal relations and related patterns of clientelism, patronage, and rent seeking. It stands to reason that the perennial problems of political profit making and regulatory closure might then be magnified and extended on an even larger scale.

Development scholars influenced by New Public Management recommend that local government officials in poor countries be given more discretion to deal directly with citizens (Tendler 1997). The World Bank's response to this fashion for personalizing the bureaucracy–bureaucracy and bureaucracy–citizen interface has been to underscore the need for formal rules, discipline, and procedural standards in public administration before broadening the scope for discretion and decentralization: 'When institutions are weak or dysfunctional, simple policies that limit administrative demands and public discretion work best' (World Bank 2000: 7). The 2004 *World Development Report* evaluates the evidence and concludes that delegation of administrative discretion in societies with poorly developed rule of law and undisciplined bureaucracies weakens meritocratic principles in licensing, monitoring, public employment, and the allocation of resources. In a report published in 2000, the World Bank voiced its concerns about New Public Management.

> [The NPM strategy] may open the door to corruption and abuse if basic public institutions are not sufficiently developed.... It took generations for most developed countries to embed these capabilities; the process can be accelerated but cannot be bypassed altogether.... When [formal] norms and practices are internalized, governments can safely improve managerial performance and the quality of public services by eliminating many procedural rules and empowering managers.... Where the rules are not internalized, however, and public management is highly informal ... broadening managerial discretion may encourage 'anything goes' behaviour.
>
> (World Bank 2000: 36–7)

Weber would have approved, since he systematically linked the underdevelopment of institutions in precapitalist societies with an excess of bureaucratic discretion and the dearth of formality, impersonality, impartiality, predictability, unambiguity, and continuity. Even in the modern societies, 'creative administration (and possibly judicature) would not constitute a realm of *free*, arbitrary action and discretion' (Weber 1978: 979). Before the ideal of 'creative discretion' can be attained, 'general norms' for regulating administrative activity are needed to prevent 'personally motivated favour and valuation'. It is *always* the case that, 'equality before the law and the demand for legal guarantees against arbitrariness demand a formal and rational objectivity of administration, as opposed to personal discretion' (ibid.: 979). The following comment by Weber on the findings of early twentieth-century 'public administration theory' is especially interesting in the light of these recurring themes in recent debates.

> The reduction of modern office management to rules is deeply embedded in its very nature. The theory of modern public administration ... assumes that

the authority to order certain matters by decree – which has been legally granted to an agency – does not entitle the agency to regulate the matter by individual commands given for each case, but only to regulate the matter abstractly. This stands in extreme contrast to the regulation of all relationships through individual privileges and bestowals of favour.

(ibid.: 958)

The work of Nobel Laureate James Buchanan can offer additional theoretical support for the view that discretionary state action should be limited. Constitutions may be used to remove incentives that encourage public officials to exercise a level of discretion that is dysfunctional or unnecessary. Constitutions are designable institutional instruments for improving state effectiveness. They establish the procedural rules for political and legal action. Ideally, the smallest number of formal rules can manageably guarantee a desired outcome without running the risks of government overload. An obstacle to this goal, however, is the widespread '*intellectual* failure to distinguish procedural and substantive norms' of government action (Buchanan 2000: 127). Decisions relating to government goods and services tend to be influenced by substantive norms that reflect the 'personal preferences' of bureaucrats and politicians about claimed 'social goals' and 'national priorities'. Instead, processes of government decision making should 'be interpreted as a surrogate for a complex of exchange among all citizens in the community ... [in which] all outcomes that are reached through agreed-on and efficient *procedures* for decision-making become equally acceptable' (ibid.: 127–8). In other words, the decision reached will be 'desirable provided only that the procedural norms are followed'.

Government decisions are too frequently an outcome of the 'grubby, quasi-corrupt, day-to-day settling of intergroup, interpersonal claims'. The enforceable constitutional 'choice of rules' on how policy decisions should be made represents a 'higher-stage' of 'rule-making politics' (Buchanan 1999: 237–8). Rather than discretion, 'the proper principle' for politics and administration 'is that of generalization or generality' (Buchanan and Congleton 2003: xix). Procedural rules of administration, which could be written into constitutions, should, as far as is practicably possible, discourage discriminatory decisions about public expenditure and public services. The discriminatory mode of governance is always based, in the final analysis, on a 'personalized identification' with some groups over others employing criteria of interest, culture, or ideology.

Hayek similarly advised against allowing the coercive authority of government to become the arena of 'constant clashes between the demands of sectional justice' and 'the requirements of a universal justice equally applicable to the stranger and to the member of the group' (Hayek 1982: vol. 2, 143). These classical insights into the utility of universalistic procedural norms remain relevant to public-administration reform. Weber's outlook on goal setting, control, and discretion, which combines enlightenment about procedural principles with a pragmatic emphasis on rationality and the formal machinery of state for implementing procedural norms, has held up especially well.

The Weberian–Schumpeterian crisis-induced policy sequence described earlier in this chapter is intended to suggest a new institutional design for the faster construction of basic legal and service competencies in developing societies. I have tried, in the latter half of the chapter, to show that evidence and practice demonstrate the soundness of the theoretical vision that underlies the design. Reforms of the institutional subsystems of law and administration can give priority to relatively simple functions of formal rule implementation as solutions to the most *pressing* problems of development. The basic institutional change during a capitalist transition is the creation and systematic enforcement of rules and procedures in institutional spheres that are or could be subject to adequate levels of control by state organizations. The goal is to minimize the complexity of state activity in these areas, and to perform the most important activities more effectively by focusing on manageable tasks. Special emphasis should be given to procedural rules that improve the state's capacity to undertake parametric tasks of economic governance following market liberalization.

Rules about how rules are made are ultimately of greater importance in determining the quality of economic policy than the technical content of the policy itself, because the rules tend to shape the content. Rules that limit the scope for state discretion will discourage the most dysfunctional forms of economic intervention by the state. Rules that strengthen state powers of impartial rule enforcement will enable the policies that expand markets and sustain economic growth. One specific policy lesson relates back to the discussion in Chapter 6 about the decay phase of economic activism. Since discriminatory actions in pursuit of sectoral rather than general objectives is the greatest source of inefficiency, the transitional parametric state is defined in practical ways by its limited powers to shape particularistic outcomes. The safest general advice is to avoid broad-based activist economic policy. Keeping state activity within bounds diminishes the need for bureaucratic discretion in economic life. Conversely, discretion is limited in order to avoid creating the incentives for state activism. These observations take Weber's arguments to their logical conclusion.

8   Making the change

In 2007 the World Bank published its worldwide governance indicators for the preceding ten years based on surveys conducted in 212 countries (Kaufmann *et al.* 2007). The indices are an effort to measure relative political freedom and political stability, the effectiveness of public administration and rule of law, the quality of economic regulations promoting private enterprise, control of corruption, and state impartiality. The results show progress overall in much of the developing world. 'In less than a decade', the authors write, 'a substantial number of countries exhibit statistically significant improvements', indicating that 'governance can and does change even over relatively short periods' (ibid.: 1–2). Although these are highly imperfect 'perception-based' evaluations, they may be the best available data on the pace of institutional progress in developing countries. They offer reasons to question the commonly held view that such change only occurs over many generations.

New institutional economics presents a disheartening vision of the possibilities for institutional development. It has tended to focus on constraints and what is not known rather than on what can be known and achieved (North 2005). In current institutional theory it is usual to find expressions of regret that there is no certain knowledge of effective formal institutions, of the interrelated macroproperties of institutions, or of the co-evolution of institutions and economies. Thus: 'The making of comprehensive institutional policy is usually a walk in the dark or at least in poor visibility: modern social science is far from having a reliable theory of social change' (Eggertsson 2005: 140). Similarly: 'There is no body of theory [comparable to theories of economic development] that can serve as a guide in the design of a program to strengthen the institutions of governance or to achieve a liberal political order' (Ruttan 2003: 267). Many theorists of institutions are so firmly set on critiques of perfectly rational neoclassical man and models of completely accurate cognition that they effectively dismiss the possibility of more or less rational selections among relatively optimal macro-institutional systems. There is a widespread view that social scientists and policymakers cannot possibly arrive at reasonably precise conclusions about desirable and effective *universal* types of formal institution for developing countries, or the means of obtaining them.

The social sciences can never supply complete knowledge of institutions and institutional change. The argument I have put forward in this book, however, is that the best available knowledge is not always the knowledge that is selected. Furthermore, the best knowledge that is available could be sufficient to enable much faster institutional progress. The confidence encountered in new institutional economics and some areas of political science about the insufficiency of institutional 'know-how' seems often to be contradicted in the same writings by surprising firmness of conviction about culture and informality as perennial determinants of institutional outcomes (or even as real alternatives to institutional formality), about the tenacity of social and political equilibria, about the relative unimportance of new ideas in overcoming resistance to change, about the limited capacity of policy leaders to intentionally fashion breakthroughs, and about the infrequency of opportunities to undertake change. Such certainties about the uncertainties bedevilling institutional change look unreasonably pessimistic alongside the more upbeat clarity and commitment to policy by Weber, Schumpeter, Parsons, Popper, and sometimes even by Hayek. Nor can it really be argued that there is now greater *evidence* for such assertions. The leading theorist of new institutional economics himself concedes that lessons of history tend to lie in the eye of the beholder.

> If, as historians state, history is rewritten every generation, it is not typically because subsequent evidence has developed clearly refutable tests of previous hypotheses but because different weights are assigned to the existing evidential material to provide different explanations consistent with current ideology ... [Even] in the present world, replete with immense quantities of information, the ability of scholars to develop unambiguous tests of complex, large-scale hypotheses that are involved in explaining secular change is very limited. Therefore, competing explanations tend to have a heavy ideological cast.
>
> (North 1981: 52)

An objective of this book has been to identify connections between motives and methods for generating social-scientific knowledge about institutional designs, the content of that knowledge as it applies to institutional architecture and reform sequences, the potential for voluntarist transfers of knowledge, and the forces that convert knowledge into ideology and policy, i.e. that join cognition to volition. In this concluding chapter I sum up some of the arguments from earlier chapters by addressing basic questions about the feasibility of comprehensive institutional change, and by noting other opinions that can support the logical and empirical case for constructivist institutional policy. There is no doubt whatsoever that the challenges of institutional reform are enormous. Achieving the desired outcomes will require a combination of intelligence, leadership, opportunity, motive, and knowledge. Success will depend on the willingness, competency, power, legitimacy, and credibility of technocrats who pursue institutional goals. Yet feats like these do lie within the bounds of human rationality.

Can institutions be built? Karl Popper was in no doubt that they could. He argued that policy leaders – and social scientists who advise them – must not be overly precious about the tasks that will confront them when they set out on this path. They should boldly adopt the kinds of 'activist' and 'technological' principles that guide physical engineering (Popper 1991). For, in the end, institutions are not so different from mechanical 'levers' that allow us to 'multiply our power' and achieve particular aims that are 'beyond the power of our muscles' (Popper 1962: vol. 1, 67). Like machines, institutions cannot operate 'entirely automatically'. In order to supervise them intelligently we need adequate knowledge of their purposes, of the regularities of their functions, and of their inherent limitations. Above all, the social engineer must understand that institutions, like machines, always operate in accordance with rules. The vital element of any institutional design is the specific 'norm' that will transform the physical and human structure into a functioning unit for regulating human behaviour in pursuit of given purposes. Popper could be saying, in words more familiar to our own study, that the primary tasks of institutional construction are to ensure that particular procedural norms are implemented:

> fundamentally, institutions are always made by establishing the observance of certain norms, designed with a certain aim in mind. This holds especially for institutions which are consciously created; but even those – the vast majority – which arise as the undesigned results of human action are the indirect results of purposive actions of some kind or other; and their functioning depends, largely, on the observance of norms. Even mechanical engines are made, as it were, not only of iron, but by combining iron and norms; i.e. by transforming physical things, but according to certain normative rules, namely their plan or design.
>
> (ibid.: 67–8)

James Coleman advanced a similarly 'constructivist' argument when discussing the challenges of social policy during transitions from the primordial or interpersonal society to the impersonal society 'populated by large corporate actors' (Coleman 1990a: 614, 651). In his 1992 presidential address to the American Sociological Association, Coleman (1993) issued a clarion call to the social sciences – 'our task is not merely to describe and analyse the functioning of society ... but is a task of institutional design'. The relevance of social research will be increasingly judged by the ability to imitate the concerns of disciplines like architecture or economics, and to utilize concepts such as 'maximization' and 'optimization'. Its purpose will be 'the explicit design of institutions', or the 'optimal design of the constructed social organization' (ibid.: 10–14).

Incomplete knowledge, unexpected outcomes, and the near impossibility of meaningful optimality, design, and rationality have been constant themes in Hayekian incrementalist theories of institutional change. The more positive viewpoint presented in this book is closer to Popper than to Hayek. Knowledge of capitalism and of its institutions does increase through time, and it could now be time for social scientists to have more confidence in the knowledge that exists. Cognitive rationalization, by expanding the body of technical knowledge, reduces uncertainty. Popper reminded us that in the *closed* society 'the conscious design of institutions is a most exceptional event, if it happens at all', whereas 'today, things may begin to be different, owing to our slowly increasing knowledge of society, i.e. owing to the study of the unintended repercussions of our plans and actions' (Popper 1962: vol. 2, 94). Popper says what Hayek dared not say. Because of the knowledge that is made available, it is possible that *'one day, men may even become the conscious creators of an open society'* (ibid.). In that new situation, which is most relevant to today's developing societies, unintended consequences could be made more predictable, and optimality could become what Weber took it to mean – consistent with Popperian qualified rationality – namely the 'relatively greatest result with the least expenditure of means' (Weber 1978: 339).

What are the forces of change? Can knowledge of how institutions function in capitalist society be transferred to precapitalist societies and thereby enable them to use such knowledge in constructing better institutions? Will policy leadership be, in this sense, 'external'? It is clear that in the past colonialism sometimes played a progressive role by transferring production, communication, and administration capacities to the world's periphery. By comparison with Spanish and Portuguese rulership in Latin America, which generally was fearful of commerce, industry, and political debate, European colonization of Asia was in some places favourable to development. Trocki (1992: 79) describes the remaking of Southeast Asian public administrations as accelerating with *'blinding rapidity'* in the late nineteenth century. Bureaucracies grew in size and function, much economic activity was recorded by government, and formal machineries of state substituted for traditional forms of governance. The imposition of legal order, censuses, and cadastral surveys went alongside the construction of transportation networks, offices for a professional civil service, police services, irrigation works, and so on. The 'discipline of clocks, railroads, timetables, and of the civil engineer swept out from colonial urban centres across paddy fields, hill farms, forests and seas of the region' (ibid.: 108). Despite colonial controls, political discourse managed to flourish. Not all of these effects were durable, but colonial institutions did leave a legacy of formal rules that might subsequently have been engaged to promote dynamic commerce, law, and administration.

Today, even though colonialism is ruled out of order, there is a widespread belief that where domestic demand for institutional reform is weak, some direct external force will be needed to clear the logjams. During emergencies or extreme threats to security, external political, humanitarian, or military intervention is certainly justified. However, the more advanced societies are rarely prepared formally or for long periods to commit to governing another political territory. Reforms imposed by an outside power are unlikely in any case to be sustainable, since in the end they are illegitimate and generate dependency. Reform conditionality attached to massive foreign aid or international credit is, in general terms, not an ideal solution. Sometimes it works to change behaviour, but the record of actual compliance is poor and in many cases atrocious (Easterly

2006). In addition, it must be recognized that reforms introduced in developing countries by international organizations will, in practice, face the very same cognitive and volitional constraints that local technocrats encounter (knowledge, rationality, interests, ideology, etc.).

One possible way around these constraints might be to internationalize the 'rules-first' approach discussed in Chapter 7. International laws and charters, and conditions attached to sought-after membership of international bodies or regional economic zones, such as the World Trade Organization (WTO) and the North American Free Trade Agreement (NAFTA), can be designed and used forcefully to exert pressure on countries to apply the rule criteria of impartiality and transparency in national economic regulation, law enforcement, government administration, and public services (Kaufmann 2003; Collier 2007). It is apparent that Mexico's entry into NAFTA and China's accession to the WTO helped significantly to improve laws and regulatory standards in those countries. A related and incontrovertible though still largely unheeded argument is that more advanced societies can best assist developing countries (and themselves) by lowering barriers to trade and creating international mechanisms to enforce 'bright-line' parametric regulatory standards for impersonal economic exchange in global markets.

The emphasis in this book, however, is firmly on creating the *internal* demand for institutional change and the *internal* capacity to supply the reforms, which in the short term are the most likely to be the effective, legitimate, and therefore durable means of national development. The only systematic external force for change in developing countries discussed in this book is the Schumpeterian long wave and its 'gale of creative destruction'. In the capitalist societies, technologies and economic conditions of production and consumption are continually revolutionized, usually for the common good. The resulting pressures for institutional adaptation are felt systematically in all territories of the world that maintain more or less open borders. Regardless of how powerful that external force can be, however, the norm in many developing societies today is non-evolutionary precapitalist equilibrium. Societies become locked into avoidable local economic and institutional disproportionalities, which seem to reproduce their underdevelopment indefinitely even while the world around them changes rapidly. In practice, therefore, the opportunities that regularly arise for radical reform stem from *localized* disproportionality within individual territorial political units and their structures of formal institutions.

The recurrent internal force for change is a *crisis* that arises because of the prolongation of an unsustainable model of political economy. In the more dynamic developing societies, we find in operation the Schumpeterian mode of adaptive 'internal disequilibrium change' led by exceptional motivated policymakers in the wake of crises. Discontinuity offers the possibility for institutional innovation. Although autonomous leaders should in theory be able to undertake comprehensive reforms without the stimulus of crises, it seems that policymakers learn best in hothouse conditions of turbulence, uncertainty, and forced experimentation to ensure survival. Crises remove some political obstacles and provide both the opportunity to reform and a pressured cognitive environment conducive to developing better understanding of problems and solutions. Whichever more or less effective post-crisis strategy for economic growth is chosen (e.g. activist, neoliberal, or capitalist), strong and enlightened leadership is essential. If durable colonialism and imperialism are now ruled out of order, local technocrats can substitute for the missing external force. Hopefully they do so with encouragement from foreign powers and from at least some of the more prestigious opinion shapers in capitalist societies.

A crisis can make all the difference between incremental politics-as-usual and radical discontinuous reforms. Arnold Harberger, a Chicago economist who advised several Latin American governments during the debt crises of the 1980s, became aware of the catalytic role played by 'a handful of heroes', an educated and energetic technocratic team with the will, vision, and decision-making power to break the historical mould. In most cases, a positive 'policy would in all likelihood have failed (or never got started) but for the efforts of a key group of individuals, and within that group, one or two outstanding leaders' (Harberger 1993: 343). A crisis was often the decisive factor determining the contribution of these leaders and the risks they were prepared to run.

> It [was] no accident that waves of modernization and liberalization in Argentina, Bolivia, Brazil, Chile, Peru and many other countries were concentrated in periods of crisis. Later, when the crisis was past, additional steps in the reform process came slower and with more difficulty, in the face of popular indifference, bureaucratic inertia and political resistance and manoeuvring.
>
> (Harberger 1998: 3)

What are the political conditions of change? Even without the crisis catalyst, change will not occur in vital governance areas if there is insufficient commitment to universalistic reforms in the peak agencies of state. In public administration, where the priority is to build discipline and formality, leaders must 'exploit or create opportunities' for reform, generate 'leverage' and 'traction', and 'lessen opposition' to change (World Bank 2002: 43). The challenges are the same in the case of legal reform, though the impediments may be even greater, among other reasons because politicians can be reluctant to promote legal reforms that would make the judiciary a rival power, and the most skilled lawyers often represent wealthy vested interests opposed to change. Hernando de Soto points out that strong centralized leadership in promotion of 'meta-rights' is especially important in the developing societies, which cannot afford the *luxury* of incremental and microscopic change.

> Only at the highest political level can [legal] reform command overwhelming support and wipe out the wilful inertia of the status quo. Only the top level of government can prevent bureaucratic infighting and political conflicts from paralyzing the progress of reform.... Politicians are needed

because existing institutions are inclined to favour and protect the status quo. It is a political task to persuade technocracy to make itself over and support change. Political intervention is also necessary because government organizations ... are generally not designed to undertake swift, broad reform programs. They are usually organized as special departments, a structure that makes more sense in developed nations, where only gradual change is necessary because the law and formal property are already functioning for all.

(de Soto 2000: 188, 205)

It is not that specialized government departments, civil society, nongovernmental organizations, and external assistance have no role in the process of change. Indeed, the attention of development practitioners often seems to be taken up with little else *but* facilitating microlevel government discretion, the struggle for direct political participation by extra-state actors, and maximizing piecemeal foreign aid and external expertise. Rather, the issue is that without a macroscopic vision of priority 'system' changes, knowledgeable ideological commitment to capitalist transition, a solid and compact infrastructure of disciplined government organizations, a 'handful of heroes' in executive and ministerial positions, and political backing in the vital power structures of the state, no amount of decentralized and dispersed state activity or extra-state participative engagement could ever bring about a fast-enough and lasting transformation of the core institutions. This is usually not such a strange idea to the populations of the developing countries, who know better than any foreign academic or technical advisor that the priority lies in strong leadership 'getting things done'.

As Weber described it, the 'power of the state' is the 'technical instrument' whose main function is to 'eliminate the obstacles' to achieving goals and values. Although the long-run objective is to build a polity that will be both consensual and coercive, this depends first on the coercive capacity of a polity that can generate and enforce the 'rules of the game'. The immediate problem lies with the interests that will resist change. It is a straightforward 'sociological law' that 'you cannot introduce political reform without strengthening the opposing forces to a degree roughly in ratio to the scope of the reform' (Popper 1991: 62). The overall conclusion of the most persuasive theorizing about political development is that radical structural reforms in the developing countries will not succeed unless governments first aggregate and then distribute political power (Ruttan 2003: 100–34). Thus growth-promoting institutional reforms will almost always require a concentration of authority to achieve their original goals, yet they will need in due course to be legitimized and improved by the democratic distribution of power.

In the Weberian priority sequence, democracy is the final stage in the transition to capitalism and basic rule of law is the prerequisite for genuine democracy. No system is perfect. Systemic and perhaps unavoidable flaws, which occasionally give rise to capitalist crises, clearly show that policy demand-and-supply mechanisms of even the most advanced and procedurally impersonal parliamentary system can have non-optimal effects on the evolution of a rational proportionality between institutional regulation and market dynamism. Even so, free representation alongside free competition of ideas is indispensable in maintaining and continually improving capitalism within increasingly complex market societies. Quite aside from its moral and pleasure utility, the technical functions of democracy are the efficient transmission of preferences and data from citizens to state and from state to citizens, the competitive and peaceful selection and elimination of policies and leaders through trial and error, the legitimization of policies and policy leaders, the supervision of public administration, and the monitoring and system-wide enforcement of impersonal procedural norms.

During the compressed periods of rapid capitalist transition, premature levels of democratization and dysfunctional interest-group representation in parliament might hold back national development. Hayek's comments, which on this subject echo the arguments of Weber and Schumpeter, are especially relevant to the interim between premodern and modern representation. 'Unlimited democracy', he said, 'may well be worse than limited governments of a different kind', if it means that through the mechanisms of 'bribes' and 'booty' in return for votes the 'holders of discretionary powers are forced to use them, whether they wish to or not, to favour particular groups' (Hayek 1982: vol. 3, 138–9).

As I have argued, the *transitional* political situation in developing countries is accurately described in Schumpeterian terms as analogous to 'imperfect competition' in the market. Temporary shelter from political competition is an incentive mechanism that buys time for leaders to *innovate* policy reforms in the general interest. Deliberate restraint on the idealistic participatory dimension of politics is most commonly a response to development crisis, with the intention of facilitating recovery through modernization, rationalization, and reconstruction. It has been common in the past during severe structural crises for insulated technocrats to be appointed by elected politicians or for a corrective regime to break the political stalemate and circumvent the parties. *Only* if the benefits outweigh the costs, a society might tolerate those conditions for years. The most impressive advances during the last half century in developing countries are owed to leaders who were somehow freed from many of the irrational allegiances to sectional interests in order to undertake sequenced institutional transitions. The enormous political risks of a temporary concentration of public power among initially well-motivated technocrats can, in the circumstances carefully described, pay social and economic dividends.

How willing are societies to change? Another challenge to management of change is that some societies cope better than others with crises depending on the types of institutions that already exist. Advanced societies have a comparative advantage during crises. Unwillingness to face up to the root causes of crisis is a special characteristic of precapitalist countries that regularly experience regressive crisis cycles. Wishful thinking and the readiness to find scapegoats make it hard to learn from mistakes. Extreme responses to the strains of social change are not uncommon. Talcott Parsons observed that the psychological reactions to economic crises in the 1930s were idealistic in Germany, but more realistic in the United States.

> One of the most important reactions to elements of strain ... is the formation of patterns of wishes or idealized hopes which ... the established institutional patterns ... do not permit to be fully realized. They hence tend to be projected outside the immediate social situation into some form of idealized life or existence. Since they are the results of certain emotional tensions which develop only in so far as people are imperfectly integrated in an institutionalized situation, they tend to involve a conspicuous element of irrealism. They are associated with a negative valuation of the existing situation and ... involve an element of escape. This phenomenon [as in *Germany*] may be called 'romanticism' – its essence is the dissociation of the strongest emotional values from established life situations in the past or the future.
>
> (Parsons 1954: 120)

> [Societies cannot] undergo major structural changes without the likelihood of producing ... 'irrational' behaviour ... [There] will tend to be high levels of anxiety and aggression, focused on what rightly or wrongly are felt to be the sources of strain and difficulty ... [as well as] patterns of belief with a strong regressive flavour, whose chief function is to wish away the disturbing situation.... But under favourable circumstances [as in the *United States*] these reactions are superseded by an increasingly realistic facing of the situation by institutionalized means ... [The] need to mobilize ... society to cope with a dangerous and threatening situation which is also intrinsically difficult ... can clearly only be coped with at the government level; and hence the problem is in essence a matter of political action, involving both the question of leadership ... and of the commitment of the many heterogeneous elements of our population to the national interest.... Consequently there has come to be an enormous increase in pressure to subordinate private interests to the public interest....
>
> (Parsons 1999: 212–13)

The reasons Parsons offers for these contrasting responses to crises relate to the respective levels of institutional development and the decisions and quality of national leaders. Some countries are adapted institutionally to limiting the duration and intensity of strain, and their populations are also mentally better adapted to coping with such situations. In contrast, escapist responses to crises explain why many countries (Argentina comes to mind) were unable to break free from cycles of underdevelopment crises in the twentieth century. Irrational responses to crises are also evident when policy elites, unconstrained by society's institutions, give free rein to their emotional impulses to achieve mastery over nature in economic life. In the past, the left's preference for holistic state intervention – planning for market and distributional symmetries – informed much of the unrealistic external advice routinely offered to policymakers in developing countries.

Policies that today prematurely give priority to expanding the realm of state discretion or to devolving state power, although perhaps less extreme in their consequences, are no less romantic responses to recurrent crises in developing countries. As well as unwillingness to change, another problem is unwillingness to be realistic about the optimal kinds of change at a given level of development.

What is the knowledge role of ideology? Key differences in the quality of policy outcomes are due to the ideas that guide policymakers when they seize the opportunities for reform, and, more broadly, how effectively those ideas are communicated to citizens. There is no point in having strong leaders who implement bad policies that will remain forever unpopular or ineffective. It should be clear by now that I favour an approach advocated in different ways by Weber, Parsons, and Hayek, which is to focus on forms of ideological persuasion relating not to 'Western' slogans of 'democracy' or 'free markets' but rather to underlying *impersonal procedural mechanisms* governing political processes and decision making about market expansion and economic regulation. The important issue is that an ideological position focused on procedural rather than substantive norms cannot easily be motivated by substantive interests, and is value-neutral about the performance of essential roles in all modern social systems; hence it may be more likely to circumvent the opposition to reform. It fits a broader argument that economic policy making in capitalist society is mainly oriented to enforcement of agreed formal means for achieving impersonal ends (leaving people free to pursue their chosen ends subject to property and contractual rights) rather than to prescribed ends and substantive rules about distributional outcomes.

An ideology will have a less positive role in the construction of capitalist institutions if it gives more of its attention to ultimate ends than to procedural means. Though it may be scientifically true that capitalism has greater success in producing a given universal set of socioeconomic ends than any other institutional system, capitalism does not evolve as a direct consequence of the pursuit of those ends (and many people are disinclined to believe the relationship exists even when it stares them in the face). If intellectuals and practitioners who are sympathetic to the historical logic of capitalism have been unable to legitimize capitalism ideologically it might be because they neglect that means-end relationship. A capitalist ideology does in one sense have a rational end, but its aim, as Hayek said, is an 'overall order' of permissible procedural principles for market and political freedom. Its system *end*, in other words, is to create rational *means* for governing capitalist society. *Only* the means permit the realization of prosperity and public peace. The intellectual challenge for the twenty-first century is to communicate the idea that the structural source of capitalism is the impersonal procedural norm, which is formally institutionalized within the state, i.e. to point out the procedural bridge between the means and the desired ends.

How is knowledge applied? To paraphrase Weber, 'if you want such and such an end you must understand the methods of achieving it in practical terms, and must take into the bargain the subsidiary consequences which according to all experience will occur'. I have argued that the minimum but feasible condition of twenty-first-century market-led capitalist transition is that functional subsystems of legal regulation, public administration, and political representation are *made* to be formally impersonal and are *induced* to be procedurally and dynamically interactive. What can be understood with confidence about the means to the end? First, quite a lot is known about components of successfully evolving institutional systems in capitalist societies. Predictable errors and unexpected outcomes of modernization policies in developing countries result from not systematizing, transmitting, and utilizing available knowledge about mutually reinforcing macroproperties of markets, law, administration, and political representation. Following Weber, we *do* know in broad outline the interlocking elements of the modern institutional system, and the unambiguously universal character of the procedural mechanisms underpinning it.

The commensurability of institutional subsystems is something that can be constructed. The nuts and bolts of institutional development must be tackled at the level of organizations. The problem is, however, that the organizations are not all of equal significance or urgency in the context of a capitalist transition. Although it would be foolish not to exploit any existing institutional strengths – such as public administration that is already meritocratic, and disciplined – reformers should also recognize that a single subsystem institutional strength cannot be sustained in a modernizing society unless other core subsystems for regulated market freedom, calculable rule of law, and competitive representation will soon reinforce it, i.e. unless there will be proportional interactivity between the domains. Resources invested in predictable and impersonal administration of law are compensated in the short run by greater ease of goal setting and control in other institutional spheres.

Once the Weberian architecture of capitalist institutions has been identified, the next step is to make a policy distinction between ongoing 'design' in capitalist countries and the short-run *sufficiency* of 'emulation' in developing countries. Scholars have explained the *sui generis* construction of institutions over periods of a few decades or centuries, and their continual redesign in the more advanced societies. The late Vernon Ruttan (2003: 19) pointed out with justifiable optimism that 'with the institutionalization of research in the social sciences and related professions, the process of institutional innovation has begun to proceed much more deliberately'. Yet developing countries need not and should not be concerned with expensive design by experimentation. Their alternative, and their comparative advantage, lies in the replication and adaptation of institutional 'products and processes' that advanced societies have tested and invested in.

Emulative strategy is important as a solution to institutional dysfunction in developing societies. Dismissive criticism of idealistic and naively rationalist constructivism can be side-stepped by shifting the focus to practical strategies for reproduction rather than original design. It is obvious that not all of the successful macro-institutions of the modern state emerged by 'invention'. Knowledge for the deliberate design of institutions is fragmented and costly to acquire. The designers cannot accurately predict exactly how things will work out. In contrast, to reproduce an exemplary institutional structure requires far less knowledge in spite of complex variations in the nature of host environments where the reproductive process occurs. Imitation is more certain to succeed, and sooner. The demand for institutions might also be different when a society emulates rather than designs. Routine redesign is a response to the slowly accumulating pressure of ideas and interests, in contrast to highly pressured emulations in reaction to periodic development crises.

But there is yet another useful difference. The demand for institutional emulation acquires momentum more rapidly as competing units (individuals, groups, or societies) observe, through their experiences of the world, that other units are performing comparatively better. Hayek's insight about the effect of market competition on rationality and emulation could just as well apply to *institutional* competition between nations.

> Competition is not merely the only method which we know for utilizing the knowledge and skills that other people may possess, but it is also the method by which we all have been led to acquire much of the knowledge and skills we do possess.... The basic contention ... [is] that competition will make it necessary for people to act rationally in order to maintain themselves. It is based not on the assumption that most or all the participants in the market process are rational, but, on the contrary, on the assumption that it will in general be through competition that a few relatively more rational individuals will make it necessary for the rest to *emulate* them in order to prevail.
>
> (Hayek 1982: vol. 3, 75)

Wanting or needing to perform as well as or better than more rational societies is a legitimate and strong endogenous motivational force for policy leaders – with support from citizens – to emulate institutions. Of course, in order to do so they need to make plans and sacrifices, gather knowledge, marshal resources, and decide the sequence of implementation. They need to rationally strategize how the formal institutions that 'magically' facilitate the spontaneous order in advanced societies can be brewed up in their own society. Contrary to conventional Hayekian thinking, and within reason, there is really no contradiction in *planning* for a spontaneous order. Knowledge of institutional evolution needs somehow to be joined to knowledge of how institutions can emerge in societies where evolution has not triumphed, but without repeating the grinding evolutionary process.

In a world of competing institutions, can a preexisting formal institutional structure provide competitive advantage? A common refrain is that replicating formal institutional designs in backward societies is a recipe for disaster if the host environment is not yet equipped culturally or socially to receive them. To take one example, the present dysfunctions of institutions in Latin American countries are sometimes offered as evidence that it was naive and misguided of them to 'import' North American constitutions and laws in the nineteenth century. This is a disingenuous argument, since the reason for the weakness of formal institutions in many developing countries is that they are not, in practice, operating formally. Instead, there is the organizational façade of a modern state, behind which lies the reality of systematic informality. Despite the surface architecture of modernity, the impersonal procedural norm is not operative. It is a moot point whether it would be easier to begin capitalist transition with an institutional *tabula rasa*. Arguably not, since there will always be a dominant socio-political order and enforcement mechanism – formal or informal – that is embedded and hard to dismantle. It might, for instance, be tribal, patrimonial, theocratic, or state socialist. All of these equilibria are hard to breach, yet presumably countries that earlier 'imported' North American or Western European systems of law and government at least have a head start.

Continuing this line of argument: If the transitional formal institutional order is to consist in large part of 'bright-line' rules and compact disciplined administration, the argument might be made that there will be benefits in not having to wrestle with burdensome disincentives of sunken costs and vested interests in an overblown, unwieldy, aging, and habit-formed state apparatus. Latecomer countries have some advantages in this respect. But there must surely be comparative utility for countries where the preexisting formal façade at least resembles the more advanced structure. Their task is simpler – to *enforce* procedural norms in the state's organizational machinery rather than build the entire system from scratch. Compare that with China, where regulatory institutions are either nonexistent or lack any semblance of independence from a monolithic Communist Party. In both China and Latin America, nevertheless, once development has reached a threshold beyond which state authority is capable of implementing the formal rule procedures, then ill-defined informal norms – which are so often random, formless, and ambiguous in society – are less of an obstacle. With sufficient political will and enforcement machinery, formal institutions are powerful enough to supply behavioural incentives or to coerce officials into following rule procedures. So, a government faced with choices about reform sequencing must consider which institutional *segments* have superstructures that disguise very deeply embedded precapitalist relationships, and which, on the other hand, are to some extent already modern and worth building on. This kind of consideration should be uppermost in the minds of policymakers.

Can ideas about 'capitalism' as a constructible formal and impersonal institutional system be the basis for a compelling ideology? There might seem little appeal in an ideology of procedural means rather than substantive ends. Yet the issues I have discussed from a procedural perspective – expansion of market opportunities, rule of law, impartial public administration, and free political representation – are of direct concern to most people in developing countries. It is with good reason, for example, that political parties in transitional countries 'campaign against corruption' in their competitive struggle for votes. Run-of-the-mill governance problems relating to pervasive red tape and corruption, perceived capture of state agencies by private interests, and chronic closure and unpredictability in the instrumental social and economic relations of daily life, all of which affect people's relative opportunities in mass society, are, as defined in this book, problems of unremitting precapitalism during the modernization process. The advantage of parametric impersonal governance – which is the capitalist method – is that it not only removes impediments to economic growth, technological progress, and sustained prosperity, but also achieves other practical but not merely economic ends such as effective service delivery, public peace, calculable justice, and easy procedures. The procedural means are simple enforceable principles relating to the permissible and expeditious methods of conduct in an open society. Because their purpose is to eliminate routine governance malfunctions that everyone encounters in everyday transactions, they can be the content of a persuasive ideology.

Of course, a rational meshing of science with ideology cannot always be relied on. Failed visions are also defended with pseudo-science. The claims of the dominant paradigms may no longer be tested. When defective policy models decay it is easy to blame their failure on externalities, such as the aggressiveness of another nation, the actions of racketeers and robbers, or the seepage of alien ideas into the body politic. A decaying model can be made impregnable to falsification. If the facts do not fit the ideas, the facts must be deficient, and so ideology conquers science. Persistent ideological errors about the real causes and outcomes of capitalist progress help to explain why aspiring emulators of capitalism take so many wrong turns.

Nevertheless, the systems of ideas that form the foundations of political and economic theories have been the force for change in the modern world. The ideas of ideologists such as Marx and Hayek ruled the twentieth century. Their rise and demise was the product of the action of vision upon science, and of science upon vision. Ideologies will continue to have this role in the future. New ideas about the functions of an ideal state and optimal relationships between state and market can change people's perceptions of their own interests. Culture matters up to a point, but there are times when more tractable variables, like leadership and ideology, push culture into the background. Good policy ideas, I have argued, can be rationally calculated using knowledge of objective facts, procedural rules, means-end logic, behavioural values, and substantive interests.

Reformers can do all this with ideas for the sake, if nothing else, of the success of a policy. An ideology is an instrument for persuading people of the value of a set of ideas and for simplifying the understanding and enactment of complex policies. It may be especially important at moments of crisis when disequilibrating forces create strong incentives for initiating institutional change. Whether 'underdevelopment' crises can be avoided, and whether 'developmental' crises can be exploited to facilitate change, will depend ultimately on available knowledge and policy ideas. On the eve of the explosion of Latin America's crisis of economic activism, Milton Friedman offered a timely emphatic observation on the interplay of crisis, ideas, and change:

> There is enormous inertia – a tyranny of the status quo – in private and especially governmental arrangements. Only a crisis – actual or perceived – produces real change. When that crisis occurs, the actions that are taken depend

on the ideas that are lying around. That, I believe, is our basic function: to develop alternatives to existing policies, to keep them alive and available until the politically impossible becomes politically inevitable.

(Friedman 1982: xiv)

Crisis provides the opportunity to be decisive in the short run, and ideology supplies motives to be resolute in the longer run. It should be apparent from everything that has been said that the most revolutionary innovation for progress in contemporary developing societies would be the design of a capitalist ideology so persuasive that it could win elections. It is important to recognize that ideas, and the knowledge they convey, will be a powerful 'external' force for change. Big new ideas about institutional construction could be on the agendas of governments in the developing countries. The useful 'resource' that more advanced countries can transfer to the rest of the world is knowledge of the impersonal institutions that enable durable development and knowledge of policy means for obtaining those institutions. The aim of this book has been to suggest that Weberian and Schumpeterian theories can be the sources of that knowledge.

Bibliography

Abercrombie, N., Hill, S., and Turner, B. S. (1980) *The Dominant Ideology Thesis*, London: George Allen & Unwin.

Alberdi, J. B. (1996) [1895] *Escritos Póstumos de J. B. Alberdi: Estudios Económicos, Tomo 1*, Buenos Aires: Universidad Nacional de Quilmes.

Alexander, J. C. (1995) *Fin de Siècle Social Theory: Relativism, Reduction, and the Problem of Reason*, London: Verso.

Americas Society and Council of the Americas (2007) *Rule of Law, Economic Growth and Prosperity: Report of the Rule of Law Working Group*, New York: Americas Society and Council of the Americas.

Amsden, A. H. (2001) *The Rise of the Rest: Challenges to the West from Late-Industrializing Economies*, Oxford: Oxford University Press.

Arndt, H. W. (1987) *Economic Development: The History of an Idea*, Chicago: University of Chicago Press.

Asian Development Bank (2007) *Beyond the Crisis: Emerging Trends and Challenges*, Manila: Asian Development Bank.

Barro, R. J. (1996a) *Getting It Right: Markets and Choices in a Free Society*, Cambridge, MA: MIT Press.

—— (1996b) 'Determinants of Economic Growth: A Cross-Country Empirical Study', NBER Working Paper no. 5698, National Bureau of Economic Research, August.

—— (1997) 'Determinants of Democracy', HIID Development Discussion Paper no. 570, Harvard Institute for International Development, January.

—— (2000) 'Democracy and the Rule of Law', in B. Bueno de Mesquita and H. L. Root (eds) *Governing for Prosperity*, New Haven: Yale University Press.

Baumol, W. J. (2002) *The Free-Market Innovation Machine: Analyzing the Growth Miracle of Capitalism*, Princeton: Princeton University Press.

Baumol, W. J., Litan, R. E., and Schramm, C. J. (2007) *Good Capitalism, Bad Capitalism, and the Economics of Growth and Prosperity*, New Haven: Yale University Press.

Bendix, R. (1964) *Nation Building and Citizenship*, New York: John Wiley & Sons.

Berger, P. L. (1987) *The Capitalist Revolution: Fifty Propositions about Prosperity, Equality, and Liberty*, Aldershot: Gower.

Berlin, I. (2000) *The Roots of Romanticism*, London: Pimlico.

Bhagwati, J. (2004) *In Defence of Globalization*, Oxford: Oxford University Press.

Blejer, M. I. (2000) 'Comment: Labour Market Reforms', in A. O. Krueger (ed.) *Economic Policy Reform: The Second Stage*, Chicago: Chicago University Press.

Boyer, R. (1988) 'Technical Change and the Theory of Regulation', in G. Dosi,

C. Freeman, R. Nelson, G. Silverberg, and L. Soete (eds) *Technical Change and Economic Theory*, London: Pinter Publishers.

Brennan, G. and Buchanan, J. M. (2000) [1985] *The Reason of Rules: Constitutional Political Economy* (Collected Works of James Buchanan; vol. 10), Indianapolis: Liberty Fund.

Buchanan, J. M. (1980) 'Rent Seeking and Profit Seeking', in J. M. Buchanan, R. D. Tollison, and G. Tullock (eds) *Toward a Theory of the Rent-Seeking Society*, College Station: Texas A & M University Press.

—— (1999) *The Logical Foundations of Constitutional Liberty* (Collected Works of James Buchanan; vol. 1), Indianapolis: Liberty Fund.

—— (2000) [1975] *The Limits of Liberty: Between Anarchy and Leviathan* (Collected Works of James Buchanan; vol. 7), Indianapolis: Liberty Fund.

—— (2001) *Moral Science and Moral Order* (Collected Works of James Buchanan; vol. 17), Indianapolis: Liberty Fund.

Buchanan, J. M. and Congleton, R. D. (2003) [1998] *Politics by Principle, Not Interest: Towards Nondiscriminatory Democracy* (Collected Works of James Buchanan; vol. 11), Indianapolis: Liberty Fund.

Bueno de Mesquita, B. and Root, H. L. (2000) 'When Bad Economics Is Good Politics', in B. Bueno de Mesquita and H. L. Root (eds) *Governing for Prosperity*, New Haven: Yale University Press.

Bulmer-Thomas, V. (1994) *The Economic History of Latin America since Independence*, Cambridge: Cambridge University Press.

Burki, S. J. and Edwards, S. (1996) *Dismantling the Populist State: The Unfinished Revolution in Latin America and the Caribbean*, Washington, DC: World Bank.

Buscaglia, E. (1998) 'Obstacles to Judicial Reform in Latin America', in E. Jarquín and F. Carrillo (eds) *Justice Delayed: Judicial Reform in Latin America*, Washington, DC: Inter-American Development Bank.

Buscaglia, E. and Ratliff, W. (2000) *Law and Economics in Developing Countries*, Stanford: Hoover Institution Press.

Camic, C., Gorski, P. S., and Trubek, D. M. (2005) *Max Weber's Economy and Society: A Critical Companion*, Stanford: Stanford University Press.

Carothers, T. (2003) 'Promoting the Rule of Law Abroad: The Problem of Knowledge', Carnegie Endowment Working Paper no. 34, Rule of Law Series, Carnegie Endowment for International Peace (January).

Castañeda, T. (1992) *Combating Poverty: Innovative Social Reforms in Chile during the 1980s*, San Francisco: International Centre for Economic Growth.

Chong, A. and López-de-Silanes, F. (2005) 'The Truth about Privatization in Latin America', in A. Chong and F. López-de-Silanes (eds) *Privatization in Latin America: Myths and Reality*, Stanford: Stanford University Press.

Clapham, C. (1990) [1985] *Third World Politics*, London: Routledge.

Cohen, G. A. (1978) *Karl Marx's Theory of History*, Oxford: Oxford University Press.

Coleman, J. S. (1990a) *Foundations of Social Theory*, Cambridge, MA: Harvard University Press.

—— (1990b) 'Commentary: Social Institutions and Social Theory', *American Sociological Review*, 55, 3:333–9.

—— (1993) 'The Rational Reconstruction of Society: 1992 Presidential Address', *American Sociological Review*, 58, 1:1–15.

Collier, P. (2007) *The Bottom Billion: Why the Poorest Countries Are Failing and What Can Be Done about It*, Oxford: Oxford University Press.

Collins, R. (1986) *Weberian Sociological Theory*, Cambridge: Cambridge University Press.

—— (1999) *Macrohistory: Essays in Sociology of the Long Run*, Stanford: Stanford University Press.

Commission on Growth and Development (2008) *The Growth Report: Strategies for Sustained Growth and Inclusive Development, Conference Edition*, Washington, DC: World Bank.

Corrales, J. (2003) 'Market Reforms', in J. I. Dominguez and M. Shifter (eds) *Constructing Democratic Governance in Latin America*, Baltimore: Johns Hopkins University Press.

Cox, G. W. and McCubbins, M. D. (2001) 'The Institutional Determinants of Economic Policy Outcomes', in S. Haggard and M. D. McCubbins (eds) *Presidents, Parliaments, and Policy*, Cambridge: Cambridge University Press.

Crouch, H. (1979) 'Patrimonialism and Military Rule in Indonesia', *World Politics*, 31, 4, July.

—— (1986) 'The Missing Bourgeoisie: Approaches to Indonesia's New Order', in D. Chandler and M. Ricklefs (eds) *Nineteenth and Twentieth Century Indonesia: Essays in Honour of Professor J. D. Legge*, Clayton: Monash University.

Dam, K. W. (2006) *The Law-Growth Nexus: The Rule of Law and Economic Development*, Washington, DC: Brookings Institution Press.

Dasgupta, P. (2005a) 'The Economics of Social Capital', *Economic Record*, 81, S1:S2–S21. Available at: www.econ.cam.ac.uk/faculty/dasgupta/pub07/soccap.pdf (accessed 18 November 2008).

—— (2005b) 'Common Property Resources: Economic Analytics', *Economics & Political Weekly*, 40, 16:16–22. Available at: www.econ.cam.ac.uk/faculty/dasgupta/pub07/commons.pdf (accessed 18 November 2008).

Dogan, M. and Pelassy, D. (1984) *How to Compare Nations: Strategies in Comparative Politics*, Chatham: Chatham House Publishers.

Dominguez, J. I. (1998) 'Market Economics and Political Change: A Historical and Theoretical Examination', in J. D. Cheek and T. Lindau (eds) *Market Economics and Political Change: Comparing China and Mexico*, Lanham: Rowman and Littlefield.

Dosi, G. (1990) 'Economic Change and Its Interpretation', in A. Heertje and M. Perlman (eds) *Evolving Technology and Market Structure: Studies in Schumpeterian Economics*, Ann Arbor: University of Michigan Press.

Durkheim, E. (1984) [1893] *The Division of Labour in Society*, New York: Free Press.

Easterly, W. (2006) *The White Man's Burden: Why the West's Effort to Aid the Rest Have Done So Much Ill and So Little Good*, Oxford: Oxford University Press.

Edwards, S. (1995) *Crisis and Reform in Latin America: From Despair to Hope*, Oxford: Oxford University Press.

Eggertsson, T. (2005) *Imperfect Institutions: Possibilities and Limits of Reform*, Ann Arbor: University of Michigan Press.

Eisenstadt, S. N. (1973) *Tradition, Change and Modernity*, New York: John Wiley.

Elliot, J. E. (1983) 'Introduction', in J. A. Schumpeter, *The Theory of Economic Development*, New Brunswick: Transaction Publishers.

Elster, J. (1983) *Sour Grapes: Studies in the Subversion of Rationality*, Cambridge: Cambridge University Press.

Evans, P. (1995) *Embedded Autonomy: States and Industrial Transformation*, Princeton: Princeton University Press.

Ferguson, A. (1996) [1767] *Ferguson: An Essay on the History of Civil Society*, F. Oz-Salzberger (ed.), Cambridge: Cambridge University Press.

Fishlow, A. (1991) 'Some Reflections on Comparative Latin American Performance', in T. Banuri (ed.) *Economic Liberalization: No Panacea, The Experiences of Latin America and Asia*, Oxford: Clarendon Press.

Freeman, C. (1985) 'Long Waves of Economic Development', in T. Forester (ed.) *The Information Technology Revolution*, Oxford: Basil Blackwell.

Freeman, C. and Louçã, F. (2001) *As Time Goes By: From the Industrial Revolutions to the Information Revolution*, Oxford: Oxford University Press.

Freeman, C. and Perez, C. (1988) 'Structural Crises of Adjustment: Business Cycles and Investment Behaviour', in G. Dosi, C. Freeman, R. Nelson, G. Silverberg, and L. Soete (eds) *Technical Change and Economic Theory*, London: Pinter Publishers.

Frey, B. S. (2008) *Happiness: A Revolution in Economics*, Cambridge, MA: MIT Press.

Friedman, L. M. (2002) *Law in America: A Short History*, New York: Modern Library.

Friedman, M. (1982) [1962] *Capitalism and Freedom*, Chicago: Chicago University Press.

—— (2002) 'Preface', in J. Gwartney and R. Lawson (eds) *Economic Freedom of the World 2002 Annual Report*, Vancouver: Fraser Institute.

Fukuyama, F. (1995) *Trust: The Social Virtues and the Creation of Prosperity*, London: Hamish Hamilton.

—— (2004) *State-Building: Governance and World Order in the Twenty-first Century*, Ithaca: Cornell University Press.

—— (2008) 'Do Defective Institutions Explain the Development Gap between the United States and Latin America?', in F. Fukuyama (ed.) *Falling Behind: Explaining the Development Gap between Latin America and the United States*, Oxford: Oxford University Press.

Geertz, C. (1973) *The Interpretation of Cultures*, New York: Basic Books.

Gellner, E. (1988) *Plough, Sword and Book: The Structure of Human History*, London: Collins Harvill.

—— (1994) *Conditions of Liberty: Civil Society and Its Rivals*, London: Penguin Books.

—— (1998) *Language and Solitude: Wittgenstein, Malinowski, and the Habsburg Dilemma*, Cambridge: Cambridge University Press.

Gerth, H. H. and Wright Mills, C. (1947) 'The Man and His Work', in H. H. Gerth and C. Wright Mills, *From Max Weber: Essays in Sociology*, London: Kegan Paul.

Glaeser, E., Porta, R. L., López-de-Silanes, F., and Shleifer, A. (2004) 'Do Institutions Cause Growth?', *Journal of Economic Growth*, 9, 2:271–303.

Granovetter, M. (1985) 'Economic Action and Social Structure: The Problem of Embeddedness', *American Journal of Sociology*, 91:481–510.

—— (1992) 'Economic Institutions as Social Constructions: A Framework for Analysis', *Acta Sociologica*, 35:3–11.

Grindle, M. and Thomas, J. W. (1991) *Public Choices and Policy Change: The Political Economy of Reform in Developing Countries*, Baltimore: Johns Hopkins University Press.

Haggard, S. and Kaufman, R. R. (1995) *The Political Economy of Democratic Transitions*, Princeton: Princeton University Press.

Harberger, A. (1993) 'Secrets of Success: A Handful of Heroes', *American Economic Review*, 83, 2:343–50.

—— (1998) 'Letter to a Younger Generation', *Journal of Applied Economics*, 1, 1:1–33.

Hay, J. R., Shleifer, A., and Vishny, R. W. (1996) 'Privatization in Transition Economies: Toward a Theory of Legal Reform', *European Economic Review*, 40:559–67.

Hayek, F. A. (1944) *The Road to Serfdom*, London: Routledge.

—— (1960) *The Constitution of Liberty*, Chicago: University of Chicago Press.

—— (1982) [1973, 1976, 1979] *Law, Legislation and Liberty: A New Statement of the Liberal Principles of Justice and Political Economy*, 3 vols, London: Routledge.

Heller, F., Pusić, E., Strauss, G., and Wilpert, B. (1998) *Organizational Participation: Myth and Reality*, Oxford: Oxford University Press.

Heller, M. G. (1990) 'The Politics of Telecommunications in Mexico', unpublished Doctoral Thesis, University of Sussex.

—— (1993) 'Hijacking the Public Interest: The Politics of Telecommunications in Mexico', in N. Harvey (ed.) *Mexico: Dilemmas of Transition*, London: British Academic Press.

—— (2000) 'Financial Reform: The Incomplete Transition', in G. Segal and D. S. G. Goodman (eds) *Towards Recovery in Pacific Asia*, London: Routledge.

Herbst, J. (2000) *States and Power in Africa: Comparative Lessons in Authority and Control*, Princeton: Princeton University Press.

Hill, A. and Abdala, M. A. (1996) 'Argentina: The Sequencing of Privatization and Regulation', in B. Levy and P. T. Spiller (eds) *Regulations, Institutions, and Commitment*, Cambridge: Cambridge University Press.

Hirschman, A. O. (1968) *Journeys towards Progress*, New York: Greenwood Press.

—— (1984) 'A Dissenter's Confession: "The Strategy of Economic Development" Revisited', in G. M. Meier and D. Seers (eds) *Pioneers in Development*, Oxford: Oxford University Press.

—— (1992) [1986] *Rival Views of Market Society and Other Recent Essays*, Cambridge, MA: Harvard University Press.

—— (1997) [1977] *The Passions and the Interests: Political Arguments for Capitalism before Its Triumph*, Princeton: Princeton University Press.

Hofstede, G. (1980) *Culture's Consequences: International Differences in Work-related Values*, Newbury Park: Sage.

—— (1996) 'Images of Europe: Past, Present and Future', in P. Joynt and M. Warner (eds) *Managing across Cultures: Issues and Perspectives*, London: Thomson Business Press.

Holden, P. and Rajapatirana, S. (1995) *Unshackling the Private Sector: A Latin American Story*, Washington, DC: World Bank.

Hood, C. (1991) 'A Public Management for All Seasons?', *Public Administration*, 69: 3–19.

—— (1994) *Explaining Economic Policy Reversals*, Buckingham: Open University Press.

Hume, D. (1987) [1741] *Essays, Moral, Political, and Literary*, Indianapolis: Liberty Classics.

Huntington, S. P. (1968) *Political Order in Changing Societies*, New Haven: Yale University Press.

Huntington, S. P. and Dominguez, J. I. (1975) 'Political Development', in F. Greenstein and N. Polsby (eds) *Handbook of Political Science: Volume 3, Macropolitical Theory*, Reading, MA: Addison-Wesley.

Israel, A. (1987) *Institutional Development: Incentives to Performance*, Baltimore: Johns Hopkins University Press.

Jarquín, F. and Carrillo, F. (1998) 'Introduction', in E. Jarquín and F. Carrillo (eds) *Justice Delayed: Judicial Reform in Latin America*, Washington, DC: Inter-American Development Bank.

Jay, E. and Jay, R. (1986) *Critics of Capitalism: Victorian Reactions to 'Political Economy'*, Cambridge: Cambridge University Press.

Jones, E. L. (2000) [1988] *Growth Recurring: Economic Change in World History*, Ann Arbor: University of Michigan Press.

—— (2006) *Cultures Merging: A Historical and Economic Critique of Culture*, Princeton: Princeton University Press.

Kalberg, S. (1994) *Max Weber's Comparative Historical Sociology*, Cambridge: Polity Press.

Kaufman, R. R. (1990) 'How Societies Change Developmental Models or Keep Them: Reflections on the Latin American Experience in the 1930s and the Postwar World', in G. Gereffi and D. L. Wyman (eds) *Manufacturing Miracles: Paths of Industrialization in Latin America and East Asia*, Princeton: Princeton University Press.

Kaufmann, D. (2003) 'Rethinking Governance: Empirical Lessons Challenge Orthodoxy', Discussion Draft, Washington, DC: World Bank (March).

—— (2004) 'Governance Redux: The Empirical Challenge', in M. E. Porter, K. Schwab, X. Sala-i-Martin, and A. Lopez-Carlos (ed.) *The Global Competitiveness Report*, Oxford: Oxford University Press.

Kaufmann, D., Kray, A., and Mastruzzi, M. (2005) 'Governance Matters IV: Governance Indicators for 1996–2004', Washington, DC: World Bank (May).

—— (2007) 'Governance Matters VI: Aggregate and Individual Governance Indicators 1996–2006', World Bank Policy Research Working Paper 4280, Washington, DC: World Bank (July).

Kay, J. and Vickers, J. (1988) 'Regulatory Reform in Britain', *Economic Policy*, 7:286–343.

Keynes, J. M. (2007) [1936] *The General Theory of Employment, Interest, and Money*, London: Macmillan.

Krueger, A. O. (1980) 'The Political Economy of the Rent-seeking Society', in J. M. Buchanan, R. D. Tollison, and G. Tullock (eds) *Toward a Theory of the Rent-Seeking Society*, College Station: Texas A & M University Press.

—— (2000) 'Agenda for Future Research: What We Need to Know', in A. O. Krueger (ed.) *Economic Policy Reform: The Second Stage*, Chicago: Chicago University Press.

Kuczynski, P. P. and Williamson, J. (2003) *After the Washington Consensus: Restarting Growth and Reform in Latin America*, Washington, DC: Institute for International Economics.

Lal, D. (2006) *Reviving the Invisible Hand: The Case for Classical Liberalism in the Twenty-first Century*, Princeton: Princeton University Press.

Lal, D. and Myint, H. (1996) *The Political Economy of Poverty, Equity, and Growth*, Oxford: Oxford University Press.

Landes, D. S. (1998) *The Wealth and Poverty of Nations: Why Some Are So Rich and Some So Poor*, London: Little, Brown, and Company.

Leftwich, A. (1996) 'Two Cheers for Democracy? Democracy and the Developmental State', in A. Leftwich (ed.) *Democracy and Development*, Cambridge: Polity Press.

Lindblom, C. E. (1988) [1979] 'Still Muddling, Not Yet Through', in C. E. Lindblom, *Democracy and Market System*, Oslo: Norwegian University Press.

Lukes, S. (1986) 'Introduction', in S. Lukes (ed.) *Power*, Oxford: Basil Blackwell.

McCloskey, D. N. (2006) *The Bourgeois Virtues: Ethics for an Age of Commerce*, Chicago: Chicago University Press.

Mannheim, K. (1960) [1936] *Ideology and Utopia: An Introduction to the Sociology of Knowledge*, London: Routledge & Kegan Paul.

Manzetti, L. (1999) *Privatization South American Style*, Oxford: Oxford University Press.

Marglin, S. A. (2008) *The Dismal Science: How Thinking like an Economist Undermines Community*, Cambridge, MA: Harvard University Press.

Marx, K. (1973) *Grundrisse: Foundations of the Critique of Political Economy*, Harmondsworth: Pelican Books.

—— (1962) *Marx on Economics*, R. Freedman (ed.), London: Pelican Books.

Meier, K. J. and Hill, G. C. (2005) 'Bureaucracy in the Twenty-first Century', in E. Ferlie, L. E. Lynn, and C. Pollitt (eds) *The Oxford Handbook of Public Management*, Oxford: Oxford University Press.

Mises, L. von (1998) [1940] *Interventionism: An Economic Analysis*, New York: Foundation for Economic Education.

Mokyr, J. (2002) *The Gifts of Athena: Historical Origins of the Knowledge Economy*, Princeton: Princeton University Press.

Nellis, J. and Birdsall, N. (eds) (2005) *Reality Check: The Distributional Impact of Privatization in Developing Countries*, Washington, DC: Center for Global Development.

Nelson, R. R. (1996) *The Sources of Economic Growth*, Cambridge, MA: Harvard University Press.

—— (2005) *Technology, Institutions, and Economic Growth*, Cambridge, MA: Harvard University Press.

Nelson, R. R. and Winter, S. G. (1982) *An Evolutionary Theory of Economic Change*, Cambridge, MA: Harvard University Press.

North, D. C. (1981) *Structure and Change in Economic History*, New York: W. W. Norton & Company.

—— (1990) *Institutions, Institutional Change and Economic Performance*, Cambridge: Cambridge University Press.

—— (2005) *Understanding the Process of Economic Change*, Princeton: Princeton University Press.

Ortega y Gasset, J. (1958) *Man and Crisis*, New York: W. W. Norton & Company.

Parsons, T. (1949) *The Structure of Social Action*, Volume 2, New York: Free Press.

—— (1954) *Essays in Sociological Theory*, New York: Free Press.

—— (1966) *Societies: Evolutionary and Comparative Perspectives*, New Jersey: Prentice-Hall.

—— (1991) [1951] *The Social System*, London: Routledge.

—— (1999) *The Talcott Parsons Reader*, B. S. Turner (ed.), Oxford: Blackwell Publishers.

Parsons, T. and Smelser, N. J. (1956) *Economy and Society: A Study in the Integration of Economic and Social Theory*, New York: Free Press.

Perez, C. (1985) 'Long Waves and Changes in Socio-economic Organization', *IDS Bulletin*, 16:36–9.

Platteau, J. P. (1994) 'Behind the Market Stage Where Real Societies Exist – Part II: The Role of Moral Norms', *Journal of Development Studies*, 30, 3:753–817.

Pollitt, C. and Bouckaert, G. (2004) *Public Management Reform: A Comparative Analysis*, Oxford: Oxford University Press.

Popper, K. (1962) [1945] *The Open Society and Its Enemies*, 2 vols, London: Routledge.

—— (1991) [1957] *The Poverty of Historicism*, London: Routledge.

Porter, R. (2000) *Enlightenment: Britain and the Creation of the Modern World*, London: Penguin Books.

Posner, R. A. (1998) 'Creating a Legal Framework for Development', *World Bank Research Observer*, 13, 1:1–11.

Prebisch, R. (1963) *Towards a Dynamic Development Policy for Latin America*, New York: United Nations.

—— (1984) 'Five Stages in My Thinking on Development', in G. M. Meier and D. Seers (eds) *Pioneers in Development*, Oxford: Oxford University Press.

Purcell, J. F. H. and Purcell, S. K. (1977) 'Mexican Business and Public Policy', in J. M. Malloy (ed.) *Authoritarianism and Corporatism in Latin America*, Pittsburgh: Pittsburgh University Press.

Purcell, S. K. and Purcell, J. F. H. (1980) 'State and Society in Mexico: Must a Stable Polity Be Institutionalized?', *World Politics*, 32, 2, January.

Reijnders, J. (1990) *Long Waves in Economic Development*, Aldershot: Edward Elgar.

Riggs, F. W. (1966) *Thailand: The Modernization of a Bureaucratic Polity*, Honolulu: East-West Center Press.

Rodrik, D. (2007) *One Economics, Many Recipes: Globalization, Institutions, and Economic Growth*, Princeton: Princeton University Press.

Root, H. L. (1995) 'Has China Lost Its Way? Getting Stuck in Transition', Essays in Public Policy no. 62, Hoover Institution on War, Revolution and Peace, Stanford University.

—— (2006) *Capital and Collusion: The Political Logic of Global Economic Development*, Princeton: Princeton University Press.

Rosenberg, N. (1994) *Exploring the Black Box: Technology, Economics, and History*, Cambridge: Cambridge University Press.

Roth, G. (1978) 'Introduction', in M. Weber, *Economy and Society, 2 vols*, G. Roth and C. Wittich (eds), Berkeley: University of California Press.

Rothschild, E. (2001) *Economic Sentiments: Adam Smith, Condorcet, and the Enlightenment*, Cambridge, MA: Harvard University Press.

Ruttan, V. W. (2003) *Social Science Knowledge and Economic Development: An Institutional Design Perspective*, Ann Arbor: University of Michigan Press.

Sabel, C. F. (1994) 'Learning by Monitoring: The Institutions of Economic Development', in N. J. Smelser and R. Swedberg (eds.) *The Handbook of Economic Sociology*, Princeton: Princeton University Press.

Santiso, J. and Whitehead, L. (2006) 'Ulysses, The Sirens and the Art of Navigation: Political and Technical Rationality in Latin America', OECD Development Centre Working Paper no. 256, Organization of Economic Cooperation and Development, September.

Sayer, D. (1991) *Capitalism and Modernity: An Excursus on Marx and Weber*, London: Routledge.

Schumpeter, J. A. (1947) *Capitalism, Socialism and Democracy*, London: George Allen & Unwin.

—— (1964) [1939] *Business Cycles: A Theoretical, Historical, and Statistical Analysis of the Capitalist Process*, Philadelphia: Porcupine Press.

—— (1983) [1934] *The Theory of Economic Development*, New Brunswick: Transaction Publishers.

—— (1991) [1950] 'American Institutions and Economic Progress', in *The Economics and Sociology of Capitalism*, R. Swedberg (ed.), Princeton: Princeton University Press.

—— (1994) [1954] *History of Economic Analysis*, New York: Oxford University Press.

Sen, A. (1999) *Development as Freedom*, New York: Alfred A. Knopf.

Simon, H. A. (1997) [1945] *Administrative Behavior: A Study of Decision-Making Processes in Administrative Organizations*, New York: Free Press.

—— (1983) *Reason in Human Affairs*, Stanford: Stanford University Press.

Smelser, N. J. (1992) 'Culture: Coherent or Incoherent', in R. Münch and N. J. Smelser (eds) *Theory of Culture*, Berkeley: University of California Press.

Smith, A. (2000) [1776] *The Wealth of Nations: Complete and Unabridged*, New York: Modern Library.

Smith, P. B. and Bond, M. H. (1993) *Social Psychology across Cultures: Analysis and Perspectives*, New York: Harvester Wheatsheaf.

Soto, H. de (1989) *The Other Path: The Invisible Revolution in the Third World*, New York: Harper & Row.

—— (2000) *The Mystery of Capital: Why Capitalism Triumphs in the West and Fails Everywhere Else*, New York: Basic Books.

Swedberg, R. (1998) *Max Weber and the Idea of Economic Sociology*, Princeton: Princeton University Press.

—— (2003) *Principles of Economic Sociology*, Princeton: Princeton University Press.

Tamanaha, B. Z. (2006) *Law as a Means to an End: Threat to the Rule of Law*, Cambridge: Cambridge University Press.

Teichman, J. A. (2001) *The Politics of Freeing Markets in Latin America: Chile, Argentina, and Mexico*, Chapel Hill: University of North Carolina Press.

Tendler, J. (1997) *Good Government in the Tropics*, Baltimore: Johns Hopkins University Press.

Thorp, R. (1998) *Progress, Poverty and Exclusion: An Economic History of Latin America in the 20th Century*, New York: Inter-American Development Bank.

Tocqueville, A de. (2002) [1835] *Democracy in America*, London: Folio Society.

Tönnies, F. (2001) [1887] *Tönnies: Community and Society*, J. Harris (ed.), Cambridge: Cambridge University Press.

Trocki, C. (1992) 'Political Structures in the Nineteenth and Early Twentieth Centuries', in N. Tarling (ed.) *The Cambridge History of Southeast Asia, vol. 2: The Nineteenth and Twentieth Centuries*, Cambridge: Cambridge University Press.

Turner, B. (1999) *Classical Sociology*, London: Sage Publications.

Turner, S. (ed.) (2000) *The Cambridge Companion to Weber*, Cambridge: Cambridge University Press.

Van de Walle, N. (2001) *African Economies and the Politics of Permanent Crisis, 1979–1999*, Cambridge: Cambridge University Press.

Véliz, C. (1994) *The New World of the Gothic Fox: Culture and Economy in English and Spanish America*, Berkeley: University of California Press.

Waterbury, J. (1992) 'The Heart of the Matter? Public Enterprise and the Adjustment Process', in S. Haggard and R. R. Kaufman (eds) *The Politics of Economic Adjustment*, Princeton: Princeton University Press.

Weber, M. (1947) *From Max Weber: Essays in Sociology*, H. H. Gerth and C. Wright Mills (eds), London: Kegan Paul.

—— (1949) *The Methodology of the Social Sciences*, New York: Free Press.

—— (1978) [1922] *Economy and Society*, 2 vols, G. Roth and C. Wittich (eds), Berkeley: University of California Press.

—— (1981) [1927] *General Economic History*, New Brunswick: Transaction Publishers.

—— (1992) [1930] *The Protestant Ethic and the Spirit of Capitalism*, London: Routledge.

—— (1994) *Weber: Political Writings*, Cambridge: Cambridge University Press.

White, G. (1984) 'Developmental States and Socialist Industrialisation in the Third World', *Journal of Development Studies*, 21, 1:97–120.

White, G. and Wade, R. (1984) 'Developmental States in East Asia: Editorial Introduction', *IDS Bulletin*, 15, 2:1–4.

Whitehead, L. (1998) 'State Organization in Latin America since 1930', in L. Bethell (ed.) *Latin America: Economy and Society since 1930*, Cambridge: Cambridge University Press.

Wiarda, H. J. (1973) 'Toward a Framework for the Study of Political Change in the Iberic-Latin Tradition: The Corporative Model', *World Politics*, 25, 2 (January).

Williamson, J. (2006) *After the Washington Consensus: Latin American Growth and Sustainable Development*, Keynote speech given at the Seminar on Latin American Financing and the Role of Development Banks, Belo Horizonte, Brazil, March 30–31. Available at: www.petersoninstitute.org/publications/papers/williamson0306.pdf (accessed 18 November 2008).

Williamson, J. and Haggard, S. (1994) 'The Political Conditions for Economic Reform', in J. Williamson (ed.) *The Political Economy of Policy Reform*, Washington, DC: Institute for International Economics.

World Bank (1997) *World Development Report 1997: The State in a Changing World*, Washington, DC: World Bank.

—— (2000) *Reforming Public Institutions and Strengthening Governance: A World Bank Strategy*, Washington, DC: World Bank.

—— (2002) *Building on Strengths: Lessons from Comparative Public Administration Reforms*, Washington, DC: World Bank.

—— (2004a) *Doing Business in 2004: Understanding Regulation*, Washington, DC: World Bank.

—— (2004b) *World Development Report 2004: Making Services Work for Poor People*, Washington, DC: World Bank.

—— (2008) *Doing Business 2008: Comparing Regulation in 187 Economies*, Washington, DC: World Bank.

Wrong, D. H. (1998) *The Modern Condition: Essays at Century's End*, Stanford: Stanford University Press.

Index

rationality and rationalization *continued*
161, 167, 181, 194–5, 287; imperfect and
perfect forms of 154, 187, 193–4; and
impersonal calculation 189–90; of
impersonality 173, 175; and institutional
construction 16, 186, 195–8, 284–5; and
institutional emulation 188, 285; and
institutional predictability 82;
instrumentality of 188; and intellectuals
174–5, 176, 179; and intended outcomes
187; of monetary and fiscal policy 56; of
monopoly 75; of motivation 118, 155; of
parliament 60; of politicians 109–10; of
public administration 72; 'qualified' form
of 154, 186–7, 193–4, 277; of societies
285; types of 186–95; and Weberian
theory 188; *see also* irrationality
regulation: and capitalism 1, 4, 16, 23, 82,
83, 114, 150; and capitalist transition 12,
100, 108, 178, 201, 217, 218; and
causation 100–1, 105; and closure 66, 96;
and competition 19, 84, 87, 269; and
competition policy 42, 208, 228, 237,
249; delimitation of 54, 126; and
deregulation and reregulation 202, 203,
207, 223–38, 246; design of 42–3, 220;
dysfunctional forms of 57, 64, 67, 68–9,
75–7, 82, 140, 214; and ethics 21, 245–6;
evolution of 12, 15, 16, 18–19, 91–3,
100–2; formality of 14, 15, 19, 27, 29,
31, 48, 198; impersonality of 17–18,
23–4, 29, 149, 260, 283; institutional
function of 14, 21, 159; and interests 41,
44, 67–8; international forms of 6, 206,
278; legal imperative of 34, 51–5, 105,
227, 252–3, 257; and market freedom 84,
100, 106, 284; and market reforms 100,
202, 223–38, 243, 249, 269; and means–
end priorities 54–5, 64; and monetary
policy 56; and monopolies 77; neglected
in developing countries 205–9, 214–15,
223, 286; versus neoactivist approach
214–23; and parametric governance
41–3, 50, 106, 201, 214, 260–1; and
policy choice 217; of political
competition 20, 61, 63; and primary state
functions 5, 31, 34, 47, 52, 55, 77, 101,
269; priorities of 219–20, 269–70; and
privatization 226, 228, 234–6; procedural
nature of 22, 185; and proportionality
130, 248, 281; and public administration
49, 261–2, 268, 272; and public and
private law 47, 260; reform of 108, 113,
130; and self-regulation 29, 54, 147; and

sequencing 109, 217, 234–6, 249, 269;
and standardization 48; and state power
70; and status privilege 73, 74; of
structure and conduct 41–3, 55, 71; and
subsystems 46, 81; *see also* market
liberalization; privatization
regulatory closure 65–6, 68, 71, 76, 82,
108, 209, 220, 237, 246, 254, 260, 271
rent seeking 7–8, 27, 34, 35, 53, 58, 84,
118, 135, 208, 228, 229, 237, 263, 270
rights *see* economic rights; generality
principle; law
Rodrik, D. 3, 217, 218, 219, 220
Root, H.L. 258, 265
Rothschild, E. 9, 195
Russia 45, 235, 245–6
Ruttan, V.W. 274, 280, 284

Schumpeter J.A.: on activism 122, 125–6,
127, 214–5; applied Schumpeterian
theory 111, 113, 114, 130, 137, 138–40,
147, 148–50, 199, 251, 278; on
capitalism 111, 124–9, 148–50, 169–70,
175–7; on crises 122, 126–8, 129–30,
143, 201; on discontinuous change 111;
on disequilibrium 126; on economic
development 120–8; on economic
leaders 124; on economic primacy 158;
on economic process 122; on
equilibrium 123, 136; and Hayek 122,
169–70, 177, 281; on ideology 168–9,
170; on imperfect economic competition
124–5; on imperfect political
competition 144–6; on innovation
124–6, 146, 148–9; on institutional
change 122, 129, 131–3; on institutional
leaders 131–2, 139–40; on intellectuals
143, 175–7; on long waves 128, 199,
278; on macroscopic and microscopic
analysis 121; on monopolies 75, 125–6;
on motives 124, 131–2, 139–40; and
Parsons 135, 136; on rationality 158,
176; on reciprocal conditioning 128–30;
on science and economics 168–9; on
self-destruction of capitalism 148–50,
175–7; on structured choice 157; and
Walgreen Lectures 131–3, 150; and
Weber 36, 75, 122, 136, 150–1
Schumpeterian analysis of change: three-
dimensional economic process 122–3;
three-dimensional institutional process
131–2; three-dimensional analytic
process 132
Sen, A. 6, 187, 218